Stalinism and Soviet Cinema

Soviet Cinema

General editor: Richard Taylor,
University of Swansea

Inside the Film Factory
New approaches to Russian and Soviet Cinema
ed. Richard Taylor and Ian Christie

Eisenstein Rediscovered
ed. Ian Christie and Richard Taylor

Stalinism and Soviet Cinema

Edited by
Richard Taylor and Derek Spring

Routledge
Taylor & Francis Group

LONDON AND NEW YORK

First published 1993
by Routledge
2 Park Square, Milton Park
Abingdon, Oxon, OX14 4RN

Simultaneously published in the USA and Canada
by Routledge Inc.
711 Third Avenue, New York, NY 10017

Routledge is an imprint of the Taylor & Francis Group

First published in paperback 2011

Typeset in 10 on 12 point Times by Florencetype Ltd,
Kewstoke, Avon

British Library Cataloguing in Publication Data
Stalinism and Soviet Cinema
I.   Taylor, Richard   II.   Spring, Derek
791.430947

Library of Congress Cataloging in Publication Data
Stalinism and Soviet cinema/edited by Richard Taylor and
Derek Spring.
p.   c.m. – (Soviet cinema)
Includes bibliographical references and index.
1. Motion pictures – Political aspects – Soviet Union.
2. Communism and motion pictures.   3. Stalin, Joseph,
1879–1953 – Influence.   4. Motion picture industry –
Soviet Union.   I. Taylor, Richard, 1946– .   II. Spring,
D. W.   III. Series.
PN1993.5.R9S73 1993
302.23'43'0947—dc20   92-32301

ISBN13: 978-0-415-07285-4 (hbk)
ISBN13: 978-0-415-51335-7 (pbk)

To the memory of
Masha Enzensberger
1943–1991

Contents

General editor's preface

Cinema has been the predominant popular art form of the first half of the twentieth century, at least in Europe and North America. Nowhere was this more apparent than in the former Soviet Union, where Lenin's remark that 'of all the arts for us cinema is the most important' became a cliché and where cinema attendances were until recently still among the highest in the world. In the age of mass politics Soviet cinema developed from a fragile but effective tool to gain support among the overwhelmingly illiterate peasant masses in the Civil War that followed the October 1917 Revolution, through a welter of experimentation, into a mass weapon of propaganda through entertainment that shaped the public image of the Soviet Union – both at home and abroad and for both élite and mass audiences – and latterly into an instrument to expose the weaknesses of the past and present in the twin processes of glasnost and perestroika. Now the national cinemas of the successor republics to the old USSR are encountering the same bewildering array of problems, from the trivial to the terminal, as are all the other ex-Soviet institutions.

Cinema's central position in Russian and Soviet cultural history and its unique combination of mass medium, art form and entertainment industry, have made it a continuing battleground for conflicts of broader ideological and artistic significance, not only for Russia and the Soviet Union but also for the world outside. The debates that raged in the 1920s about the relative revolutionary merits of documentary as opposed to fiction film, of cinema as opposed to theatre or painting, or of the proper role of cinema in the forging of post-Revolutionary Soviet culture and the shaping of the new Soviet man, have their echoes in current discussions about the role of cinema vis-à-vis other art forms in effecting the cultural and psychological revolution in human consciousness necessitated by the processes of economic and political transformation of the former Soviet Union into modern democratic and industrial societies and states governed by the rule of law. Cinema's central position has also made it a vital instrument for scrutinising the blank pages of Russian and Soviet history and enabling the present generation to come to terms with its own past.

This series of books intends to examine Russian and Soviet films in the context of Russian and Soviet cinema, and Russian and Soviet cinema in the context of the political and cultural history of Russia, the Soviet Union and the world at large. Within that framework the series, drawing its authors from both East and West, aims to cover a wide variety of topics and to employ a broad range of methodological approaches and presentational formats. Inevitably this will involve ploughing once again over old ground in order to re-examine received opinions but it principally means increasing the breadth and depth of our knowledge, finding new answers to old questions and, above all, raising new questions for further enquiry and new areas for further research. The present volume, *Stalinism and Soviet Cinema*, is intended to fulfil all these objectives.

The continuing aim of the series is to situate Russian and Soviet cinema in their proper historical and aesthetic context, both as a major cultural force in Russian history and Soviet politics and as a crucible for experimentation that is of central significance to the development of world cinema culture. Books in the series strive to combine the best of scholarship, past, present and future, with a style of writing that is accessible to a broad readership, whether that readership's primary interest lies in cinema or in Russian and Soviet political history.

Richard Taylor

Illustrations

PHOTO CREDITS

The editors are grateful to the following for permissions to reproduce illustrated material: BFI Stills, Posters and Designs; Central Film Museum, Moscow; Central State Archive of Literature and Art of the Russian Federation [TsGALI], Moscow; Novosti Press Agency; Ian Christie; Richard Taylor. Technical assistance from Roger Davies, University of Swansea, is also gratefully acknowledged.

Notes on contributors

Derek Spring is Senior Lecturer in the Department of History and Chairman of the Institute of Russian, Soviet and East European Studies at the University of Nottingham. He is the author of a film *The Winter War and Its European Context*, has edited and contributed to *Propaganda, Politics and Film, 1918–1945*, with Nicholas Pronay, and to *The Impact of Gorbachev*, and is the author of numerous articles on Russian foreign policy.

Rashit Yangirov has been Senior Consultant and Chief Archivist at the Central Film Museum in Moscow. He has published widely in Russian and French, especially on various aspects of national cinema in the former Soviet Union.

Maya Turovskaya is a Senior Research Fellow of the All-Union Research Institute for the History of Cinema in Moscow and a leading film and theatre critic. She has published countless articles and a number of books in Russian and is probably best known to the English-speaking reader for her *Tarkovsky: Cinema as Poetry*, recently also published in Russia.

Peter Kenez is Professor of History at the University of California, Santa Cruz. His publications include *Civil War in South Russia, 1919–1920*, *The Birth of the Propaganda State: Soviet Methods of Mass Mobilization, 1917–1929* and *Cinema and Soviet Society, 1917–1953*.

Richard Taylor is Reader in Politics and Russian Studies at the University of Swansea. His books include *The Politics of the Soviet Cinema, 1917–1929*, *Film Propaganda: Soviet Russia and Nazi Germany*, *The Poetics of Cinema* (editor and part translator) and, with Ian Christie, *The Film Factory: Russian and Soviet Cinema in Documents 1896–1939*, *Inside the Film Factory: New Approaches to Russian and Soviet Cinema* and *Eisenstein Rediscovered*. He is also General Editor of Eisenstein's *Selected Writings* in English and is currently working on *A Cinema for the Millions: Socialist Realism and Soviet Cinema, 1929–38*.

Ekaterina Khokhlova, the granddaughter of Lev Kuleshov and Alexandra Khokhlova, is a Research Fellow of the All-Union Research Institute for the History of Cinema in Moscow. In addition to a number of articles, she has edited the three-volume Russian edition of Kuleshov's writings in Russian and co-edited *Kouléchov et les siens* for the Locarno Film Festival.

Maria Enzensberger (1943–91) was the daughter of the Russian poet Margarita Aliger and the former wife of the German author Hans Magnus Enzensberger. She left the Soviet Union in 1967 and lived in Britain from 1969. She was a scholar, critic and translator and the author of a number of articles on Soviet cinema and the avant-garde. Her translations of Maya-kovsky have been published as *Listen!* and of Mandelstam as *A Necklace of Bees.*

Leonid Kozlov is a Senior Research Fellow of the All-Union Research Institute for the History of Cinema and also teaches at the All-Union State Cinema Institute [VGIK] in Moscow. He is the author of numerous articles on both Russian and Western cinema and has published several books in Russian, including one on Luchino Visconti.

Ian Christie is Head of Special Projects at the British Film Institute where he has helped to foster a renewed interest in both classic and contemporary Russian cinema. His books include *FEKS, Formalism, Futurism: 'Eccentrism' and Soviet Cinema 1918–36* (co-editor, with John Gillett), *Powell, Pressburger and Others* (editor), *Arrows of Desire: The Films of Michael Powell and Emeric Pressburger* and, with Richard Taylor, *The Film Factory: Russian and Soviet Cinema in Documents 1896–1939, Inside the Film Factory: New Approaches to Russian and Soviet Cinema* and *Eisenstein Rediscovered.*

Valeriya Selunskaya is Professor in the Faculty of History at Moscow University. She has written extensively on the problems of Russian agri-culture both before and after the Revolution and, together with Maria Zezina, has for many years developed the use of film in the teaching of history in the former Soviet Union.

Maria Zezina is docent in the Faculty of History at Moscow University. She has written widely on the Soviet intelligentsia and is the joint author of *A History of Russian Culture* in Russian.

Anna Lawton is Professorial Lecturer at Georgetown University and the author of numerous articles on Russian literature and film. Her books include *From Futurism to Imaginism, Russian Futurism through its Manifestoes, 1912–1928, The Red Screen: Politics, Society, Art in Soviet Cinema* (editor) and *Kinoglasnost: Soviet Cinema in Our Time.*

Svetlana Boym teaches in the Department of Comparative Literature at Harvard University and is a film editor of the *Slavic Review.* She is the author of *Death in Quotation Marks: Cultural Myths of the Modern Poet*, of numerous articles on Soviet literature, cinema and other media, of the play *The Woman Who Shot Lenin* and the short film *Flirting with Liberty*. She is currently completing *Common Places: Kitsch, Art and Everyday Culture in Russia*.

Julian Graffy is Senior Lecturer in Russian Language and Literature at the School of Slavonic and East European Studies, University of London. He is the co-editor, with Geoffrey Hosking, of *Culture and the Media in the USSR Today* and, with Ian Christie, of *Yakov Protazanov: A Career in Russian Cinema*.

Acknowledgements

The contributions to this volume originated with a conference that we organised in London in July 1990 on the theme 'Russian and Soviet Cinema: Continuity and Change'. Some of the papers were gathered together in a special issue of *The Historical Journal of Film, Radio and Television* in June 1991, which bore the title of the conference. However, the conference sub-text, almost inevitably, was Stalinism. The papers that related most directly to this theme are grouped in the present volume, *Stalinism and Soviet Cinema*. They have all been revised since July 1990 and the contributions by Derek Spring, Richard Taylor, Leonid Kozlov, Ian Christie and Svetlana Boym have been revised since the attempted coup in August 1991 and the subsequent disintegration of the Soviet Union. Taken together, therefore, the essays in this book provide a moving picture of changing attitudes towards the phenomenon at the centre of the history of Soviet cinema. We naturally hope that the image that this picture imprints upon the reader's mind will not be too blurred.

The task of translating the Russian contributions has been shared equally between us and we have commented on one another's renderings to the point where our separate efforts have become virtually indistinguishable. We must therefore share the blame for any infelicities.

The conference was one of a series organised on behalf of the Inter-University History Film Consortium by the British Universities Film and Video Council. We should like to thank both organisations, and in particular Jim Ballantyne, for their support. The conference was held at the Imperial War Museum, which rapidly became known to the Russian delegates as 'Bedlam'. That the arrangements for the conference were as far removed from Bedlam as is possible to imagine was entirely due to the staff of the Museum, and especially of the Department of Film. We should like in particular to thank Clive Coultass and Anne Fleming. Clive has presided over the arrangements for many of our conferences and this was his last. His calming influence will be sadly missed and we wish him well in his well-earned retirement.

No film conference should ever be without film and we should like to acknowledge the help we received from the British Film Institute and above all from Ian Christie, the Head of Exhibition and Distribution. We also received a good deal of assistance and advice from the Central Film Museum in Moscow and its director, Naum Kleiman, who was unfortunately unable to attend the conference himself. We should also like to acknowledge the support of the All-Union Research Institute for the History of Cinema [VNIIK] and the All-Union State Cinema Institute [VGIK] in Moscow.

No conference of any kind is possible without funding and we are grateful to the generosity of the British Council, the Soros Foundation, the Ford Foundation (through the auspices of the BASSEES Research Committee) and the then USSR Union of Cinematographers for their financial support, which enabled us to entertain the largest ever delegation of Soviet film scholars to attend a conference in the United Kingdom.

The success of any conference depends upon the chemistry of the participants. Despite all the hard work of preparation, despite the 'excitement' that any dealings with the former Soviet Union involved, we both actually enjoyed the conference. Most important of all, the 'Soviet' delegates also enjoyed it and found it stimulating. That is in large part due to Masha Enzensberger, who tirelessly took them on improving sightseeing walks around London when the rest of us preferred to collapse. The conference would not have been the success it was without the warmth and humour of the participants, and particularly of Masha. We should therefore like to dedicate this volume to her lasting memory. This volume contains her last published work and the study of Russian and Soviet cinema will be considerably less lively without her.

Richard Taylor and Derek Spring
May 1992

Note on transliteration and translation

Transliteration from the Cyrillic to the Latin alphabet is a perennial problem for writers on Russian subjects. We have opted for a dual system: in the text we have transliterated in a way that will, we hope, render Russian names and terms more accessible to the non-specialist, while in the scholarly apparatus we have adhered to a more accurate system for the specialist. Accepted English spellings of Russian names have been used wherever possible and Russian names of German origin have been returned to their roots.

The translation of film titles poses problems as Russian does not have either an indefinite or a definite article. We have preferred to insert an article: hence *The Battleship Potemkin*, *The Arsenal*, etc. The convention by which Soviet films are known by bald titles like *Earth*, *Mother*, *Strike* is itself arbitrary: consider, for example, how Chekhov's plays have become known in English as *The Seagull* and *The Cherry Orchard*, but *Three Sisters*.

Chapter 1

Stalinism – the historical debate

Derek Spring

In the Soviet Union from 1985, and particularly from January 1987, the character and legacy of the Stalinist period began to be debated with developing intensity in conditions of increased openness of information and discussion. The process was for long paced and limited by the attempt to achieve a confined and controlled, though highly significant, political change. It gradually and haphazardly integrated into the open Soviet debate much that was common knowledge in the outside world and underground in the Soviet Union itself. Slowly but inexorably the discussion began to escape the limitations which some wished to set to it and, fuelled by the forces released by the process of reform, it finally threatened the very legitimacy of the Communist régime. It also began to produce new evidence haphazardly in the press – memoirs, reminiscences, isolated documents – and, even before the attempted coup of August 1991, it had begun to produce some serious, documented new assessments that go beyond what has been possible with the limited sources available to outsiders.[1]

Important stages in this process were defined by the publication in the Soviet Union of the writings of Western historians such as Stephen Cohen and Robert Conquest in 1988–9 and of dissidents who had published in the West such as Alexander Solzhenitsyn in 1990. Western historians have been engaged in their own debate about the nature and significance of Stalinism which revolved round the labels of the 'totalitarian school', the 'revisionists' and the 'new cohort' of social historians.[2] This debate has become more passionate as the course of developments unfolded and new material became available from Soviet sources, seeming to confirm or contradict preconceived interpretations. Nevertheless there is still no area of Soviet life in the 1930s and 1940s which it has yet been possible to research adequately in the right conditions to enable a scholarly consensus to develop, and research is still liable to be inhibited by preconceived notions and dogmatic thought. Roy Medvedev has gone so far as to doubt whether outsiders have much to contribute to the writing of Soviet history and he makes the point that a certain empathy and cultural understanding of the distinctive Russian/Soviet historical process can only be achieved from the inside.[3] His view has a certain validity but ignores the fact that the writing of history is a continuous process of debate which never reaches absolute truth, and the view from the outside, with its partial share of the whole truth, is a stimulating and necessary – if perhaps an irritating – one to a nation's writing of its own history.

Stalinism as a system was consolidated in its various features in the course of the late 1920s and 1930s. Like any historical phenomenon it had roots in the past, both pre- and post-Revolutionary, as well as in the specific conditions and decisions of the end of the 1920s and 1930s. From 1929 to 1953 it made a distinctive imprint on Soviet society and aspired to totalitarian control of all aspects of life, leaving little private space for its citizens. Politically Stalinism came to an end in 1953 with the death of the dictator and the end of the Terror. Nevertheless the major features of the authoritarian administrative-command economic and political system set up by Stalin have remained up to the present time as a legacy together with the searing, crippling impact on the generations who lived through it and its aftermath.

Analysis of the role of Soviet cinema in and on the Stalinist period is a contribution to the ongoing debate both in the Soviet Union and the West about the phenomenon of Stalinism. This introductory essay surveys the debate about Stalinism in general to provide a context for the more specialised contributions on cinema in the Stalin period. The concluding chapters return to the contemporary debate by focusing on the reassessment of the Stalin period in film since 1985 and the role of film in its development.

The study of Soviet cinema is a multifaceted theme which can produce insights into many aspects of the origins, character and impact of Stalinism. Cinema was important as a modern accessible means of mass communication, one of those instruments which enabled the authoritarian and controlling impulses traditional in Russian history to reach their extremes in Stalinist forms. The study of cinema is of interest both for what it reveals of the efforts of the régime to manipulate and create a new consciousness in society and for the analysis of what was new in this consciousness and what was in fact retrograde and rooted in the past. It is also important as it raises questions about the creative intelligentsia, the extent and forms of their malleability and manipulation, and the extent of the survival in Stalinist conditions of the individual aspirations, intentions and independence of authors and film directors. Study of cinema is also particularly important for an assessment of the impact of the manipulated media of propaganda on the various levels of the public. Cinema's productions were limited in numbers in the 1930s and 1940s. Practically everyone in the cinema-going public saw every film. Those who controlled cinema had a particular strategy and aims in mind in the creation and messages of films. But cinema was a very crude and imperfect instrument of propaganda, which could not take into account the multiplicity of consciousnesses, knowledge and experience in Soviet society, from the dispossessed rural dweller experiencing urban culture for the first time to the remnants of the 'bourgeois' intelligentsia and the inheritors of their traditions. The examination of Stalinism and Soviet cinema can therefore, on a relatively micro-level, help to provide insights into the macro-questions of Stalinism.

Stalinism as the central question of Soviet history has become a matter of impassioned public debate since 1987 in the Soviet Union. For the citizens of the Soviet Union it is not merely a matter of historical truth. It is a question of 'What Is to Be Done?', of the nature and potential of their society, and of how to avoid the mistakes of the past. And it has been a question of 'repentance' and 'guilt' in a way that it has not been for Western historians. It was also a matter of urgency: as one Soviet commentator has recently noted, there is a danger in 'being ready "to get engaged in the struggle" straight away and then only later (and this already for the umpteenth time in our history) to try and make sense of what happened in the past'.[4] Yet too simplistic an analysis of the Stalinist past can produce the dangerous phenomena of national self-disgust and 'Russophobia' or lead to the localising of Stalinism as a phenomenon both conceptually and geographically, and a failure to set it in its historical and universal context.

The historical debate has been a vital part of the struggle first for reform and then in effect for the abolition of the Communist régime. Historical assessments were therefore necessarily not dispassionate, but much coloured by the writer's views on the solutions to current problems. Soviet cinema has played a prominent role in opening up this debate, as can be seen from the final four essays in this volume. Tengiz Abuladze's film *Repentance* [Pokayanie] acted as an important catalyst and, following its release at the end of 1986, it was the writers, journalists and artists rather than the professional historians who were in the forefront of the discussion. Abuladze's *Repentance* was followed by the release of the films of Alexei Gherman, the plays of Mikhail Shatrov, the novels of Vasili Grossman and Anatoli Rybakov and the writings of dozens of journalists, philosophers, economists and historians mostly made or written before the age of glasnost but only then able to be unshelved. They show the deep roots of the attitudinal underpinnings of the reform pressures inside as well as outside the Communist Party. The titles of significant films have signposted the course of the historical debate and its concerns from *Repentance* through Tofik Shakhverdiev's *Stalin Is with Us?* [Stalin s nami?, 1989] to the exasperation of Stanislav Govorukhin's direct and shocking condemnation of the past seventy years of Soviet history in *We Cannot Live Like This* [Tak zhit' nel'zya, 1990]. To an extent they illustrate the continuing attempt to control history by authority, with an initially limited and cautious expansion of openness in historical debate restricted to the Stalin phenomenon and its consequences. But by 1990 in the cinema as in the debate in the press, the spectrum of views on Soviet history had broadened to include even some total condemnations of the whole Soviet period which undermined the legitimacy of the régime and provided a basis for the sudden and dramatic sweeping away of its key institutions following the attempted coup of August 1991.

An important prerequisite for public debate about the past has been the process of filling in the 'blank spots' in Soviet history. This first of all referred to personalities, particularly 'oppositionist' or purged Party leaders such as Bukharin, Rykov, Kamenev, Zinoviev, even Trotsky. A flood of new material has appeared haphazardly in the Soviet media, from creative reconstructions and comment on the period to specific reminiscences, revealing personal experience and detail. Since 1987 most taboo subjects of Soviet history have been broached: the brutal reality of collectivisation, the artificially induced famine of 1933, the full horror of the purges, the secret articles of the Molotov-Ribbentrop Pact, the Katyń massacre of Polish officers, the deportations from the Baltic states and Poland, the real figures for losses in the Great Patriotic War and for deaths in the purges, and even the fate of POWs returning from Germany. The list is endless.

This process was initially directed towards the exposure of the horrors of the Stalinist régime in order to convince people that administrative-command socialism was totally discredited but that there were other alternatives within the framework of Leninist socialism. It began cautiously. It is astonishing to recall that, while in 1985 Gorbachev was still asserting that Stalinism was a fabrication of Western propagandists, by 1990 he was himself using the term 'totalitarian' to condemn it.[5] In his November speech in 1987, his comments on collectivisation and on the outbreak of the Second World War went little beyond those of Khrushchev. But it was evident already in 1987 that the boundaries of the permissible in history were widening with a more positive attitude to the New Economic Policy (NEP) and its supporters, particularly to Bukharin who was fully rehabilitated in February 1988. In this phase the key themes of the debate were the reassessment of the role of personalities, the importance of the moral factor and the reality of a subjunctive mood – the existence of alternatives in Soviet history.

This process of filling in the blank spots of Soviet history still has a very long way to go. It is no longer a matter of mentioning the unmentionables which have long been known in the uncensored world, but of access to the archival sources necessary for serious historical re-evaluations. Until the August 1991 coup continuing restrictions on archives and bureaucratic obstruction were a severe brake on this process. One has only to recall with what delay and reluctance official recognition of the secret articles of the 1939 Molotov-Ribbentrop Pact or the Katyń massacre was admitted. And the archives of the Politburo, the Party, the Council of People's Commissars and the security forces have until very recently been restricted to a small band of institutional historians. It was noteworthy when an article in *Voprosy istorii* [Problems of History] for April 1990 sought to estimate the victims of Stalinism for the first time on the basis of archival sources, concluding tentatively with a figure of 7.9 million between 1926 and 1939.[6] But radical historians such as Yuri Afanasiev still remained pessimistic about the progress made, at least within the historical profession, in freeing itself from the past. For professional historians, of course, it will require many years of working on the mass of new archival materials which are now becoming available, of digesting 'new' facts and evidence and, not least, of becoming quite different historians. But the question of Stalinism will not wait for such a carefully considered and documented answer. The public must exorcise and understand the roots of Stalinism while it has the opportunity. In terms of the time and effort needed for the development of mature historical interpretations, the debate has been proceeding in an open form for an infinitesimal time. The question still remains open of what kind of consensus will emerge but it will undoubtedly be influenced, if not actually determined, by the turn of political events.

At an early stage in the Soviet debate there was evident an emerging orthodoxy represented by writers such as Roy Medvedev and the editor of the Party journal *Kommunist*, Otto Latsis, that Stalin usurped power, acted contrary to Lenin's instructions and carried through a 'partial counter-revolution'. The blackening of Stalin was used to highlight the principled aims and aspirations of Lenin and Leninism. This was evident also for instance in Mikhail Shatrov's play *Onward, Onward, Onward . . .* where Lenin is made unhistorically to concur with Rosa Luxemburg's criticisms of socialism without democracy. These Communist reformist views have subsequently been overtaken by events. But this should not adversely reflect on their validity as historical interpretations. Medvedev continues to hold to the view that Lenin's ideas were not responsible for Stalinism and that 'the essence of Stalinism was the exchange of embryonic democracy in Russia for total bureaucracy'.[7]

Otto Latsis contends that Stalinism arose from Stalin's voluntaristic usurpation of power which achieved a 'partial counter-revolution', helped by the backwardness of society. In his view also Marxism and Leninism should not be identified with Stalinism. Stalin and his followers went against the course and principles of peaceful evolutionary development and continuation of the NEP outlined by Lenin, particularly in his last writings. This interpretation insists that there *were* alternatives and that the voluntarism of Stalin and his followers was responsible for the horrific consequences in the 1930s. This phase of the debate coincided with the publication of Stephen Cohen's biography of Bukharin presenting him as one of the early Western 'revisionists' of the totalitarian orthodoxy and contending that there was a break in continuity between Lenin and Stalin and that there were other alternatives within Bolshevism, particularly that represented by Bukharin.[8]

To this it can be said that, while there were alternatives in theory, yet in the balance the Bukharinist/late-Leninist alternative was found wanting. The question arises not whether there were alternatives, but why one alternative rather than another was 'chosen'. Some in the current debate would attribute this to the failings and qualities of the personalities in the political élite. There has been much discussion about why Lenin's instruction to 'find some way' to remove Stalin was not carried out as this was a crucial point on Stalin's road to power and hence Stalinism. In the West, Graeme Gill has recently emphasised the support necessary for Stalin's success. Stalin became dominant in 1929 not so much because of his control of a strictly disciplined machine but because he was able to play the rules of the political game and generate support in the political élite more effectively than his opponents.[9] And, as Fitzpatrick has pointed out, while there was a Bukharinist alternative in theory, Bukharin was never a figure who could seriously have challenged Stalin.[10] There were weaknesses in his arguments particularly on the grounds of time, if one takes account of the audience he needed to convince. Bukharin, while he was opposed to rapid and forcible collectivisation, was opposed to the means rather than the end; and he sympathised with the radicalism of the Cultural Revolution which was a necessary accompaniment to the early years of the first Five-Year Plan.

In one of the first articles in the Soviet historical journals to broach the problem, B. G. Mogilnitsky argued that Lenin's aim of preventing collective leadership becoming personal power was not achieved and dictatorship ensued because of the personal weaknesses of the Party leadership. But he does go further: the 'proletarian revolutionary spirit' was predominant in the Party and was opposed to legality and evolutionary development. It was these psychological, as well as personal, factors that were crucial. But the experience of the 1920s, in Mogilnitsky's view, did still show that socialist pluralism was possible if only there was a mature political consciousness in society.[11]

In the early stages of the Soviet debate great interest was displayed in these intra-Party struggles of the 1920s as if the origins of Stalinism were simply a question of why Stalin came to dominance in the Party and the country. This tendency served the needs of the reformist Communists of perestroika. But the critical debate subsequently expanded uncontrollably to embrace the Leninist period and the whole Marxist legacy. By September 1990 even members of the Institute of Marxism–Leninism were writing not only that Stalin was a usurper but that the character of Lenin's Party made possible the dictatorship in which Stalin broadly carried out Lenin's programme.[12]

Some have emphasised the historically determined and contextual roots of Stalinism. For instance, Igor Klyamkin agonisingly concluded in an influential article that Stalinism had deep historical roots in pre-Revolutionary Russia. The legacy of an economically and politically backward society, of authoritarian tradition and personal power, and the failure of a law-governed society to emerge meant that there was no alternative to forcible collectivisation as a foundation for Soviet development, which led to Stalinism. His soul would wish that there had been an alternative; but his reason told him there was no other.[13]

In the West, the exiled historians Nekrich and Heller in *Utopia in Power* had sought the failings of the Soviet experiment in its Utopianism, although they did not explore its historical and ideological roots.[14] In a series of much-quoted articles in 1989 Alexander Tsipko took this theme further, arguing that many of the practices and ideas of Stalinism were present in the Russian and international revolutionary movement before the Revolution and were typical of Marxists at that time. Stalinism was an ideological product of the Utopianism of Marxism and of the Russian intelligentsia. The ideological conviction of the Bolsheviks that the peasantry, who were the vast majority of the population, were an obstacle to the building of socialism was a fundamental ingredient of the tragedy.[15] L. Sedov sees the attraction to utopias and the unwillingness to deal with the mundane problems of life as part of the social psychology both before and after 1917 and argues that it is these mass structures of consciousness and culturally given mental stereotypes which the film-makers of perestroika had been able to refer to intuitively and which require serious work by historians.[16] It is significant that this phase of the Soviet debate was accompanied by the publication of sections of Solzhenitsyn's *The Gulag Archipelago* and of Robert Conquest's works in the Soviet press and the emerging condemnation of the whole Soviet period and régime as totalitarian.

In the West some historians in recent works have viewed these Utopian visions as a necessary and valuable part of building a better society and far from being a prelude to Stalinism: 'The Utopian vision . . . was the best thing that nineteenth-century Russian intellectual and cultural history bequeathed to the twentieth century, and not the disaster some critics have called it.'[17]

General explanations of Stalinism have emphasised either personalistic, contextual or essentialistic factors. But an understanding of the origins and essence of Stalinism needs to take account of the different combinations of factors at work in the various phases of its emergence and the different timetables of the development of facets of mature Stalinism. The economic features of Stalinism emerged with the mass collectivisation of agriculture, the rapid state-command industrialisation of the Five-Year Plans and the rejection of the market in 1929. The social changes emerged from the same period with the elimination of the kulaks and almost all elements of private enterprise, the transformation of the peasantry and destruction of the essential elements in its way of life, the rapid expansion of the urban population at the expense of the rural, rapid educational development, the emergence of a new and inflated class of officialdom with the new responsibilities taken on by authority.

Politically Stalinism only reaches maturity in the second half of the 1930s with the Terror and its consequences, the consolidation in power of the 'new class' catapulted upwards in the turmoil of the first Five-Year Plan. Culturally also, the mature 'system' emerged at a later stage after the flush of enthusiasm of the Cultural Revolution of 1929–31. It was brought to an abrupt end with Stalin's reconciliation with the bourgeois specialists and his letter to *Proletarskaya revolyutsiya* [Proletarian Revolution] in January 1931, followed by the abolition of RAPP [Russian Association of Proletarian Writers] in 1932 and the subsequent formation of the Union of Soviet Writers in 1934. This brought the revolutionary phase of Soviet culture to an end and was followed by the purges and the imposition of more nationalistic and conservative cultural values. The Stalinisms of the wartime and post-war periods also need to be examined as different phases of the phenomenon.[18]

All of these aspects of the emerging system also have their own periodisation and turning points which determined their future development. But their previous history contained the potential for development in various different ways. There was no inevitability in the forms which mature Stalinism took. As Andrle notes, the emergence of the Stalinist system was determined not just by the decisions of 1929, but by thousands of microdecisions which had to be made, and in which the dictator's preferences were cumulatively expressed.[19]

Among recent Soviet writers considerable emphasis has been given to the personality and personal role of Stalin. Roy Medvedev's newly revised *Let History Judge* and General Dmitri Volkogonov's four-volume biography of Stalin *Triumph and Tragedy* show this tendency. Medvedev has modified his views in the new edition of *Let History Judge* but still, as one reviewer observed, 'Stalinism for him is predominantly about the violence perpetrated by an all-powerful state on a passive society.' Emphasis is placed on the personal drive to power of Stalin, on his manipulation of his position after the death of Lenin, on his 'coup d'état' of the 'Great Turn' in 1929 and on his responsibility for the Terror.[20] Indeed much of the literature has been concerned with determining personal *responsibility* rather than with what complex of aims, ambitions, problems and circumstances resulted in Stalin taking the responsibility he undoubtedly bears. The second volume of Robert Tucker's study of Stalinism also gives emphasis to Stalin's overwhelming control and manipulation, to his own personal ambitions, aspirations and psychology. Tucker emphasises Stalin's awareness of the Russian national heritage which was reflected in cinema and elsewhere in the mid and late 1930s. In this connection the history of the close involvement of Stalin with

Eisenstein's film on Tsar Ivan IV provides important evidence about the dictator's outlook in the 1940s.[21]

Assessment of the significance of Stalin as an individual is a crucial difficulty for the historian. A similar question has arisen with Hitler: how should historians relate to the historical demon when their task is to understand the past? Do not historians risk exonerating Stalin from his enormous responsibility for the tragedy if they draw attention to the broader context and origins of the phenomenon of Stalinism? Or, on the other hand, do they not risk creating an image of a superhuman force who manipulated all to his will, unshackled by any other forces and influences? In Andrle's careful analysis of the problem, the basic issue is 'whether the historian should ascribe normal phenomena to the Stalin period in place of emphasising the idiosyncratic and bizarre ones or whether such ascriptions only serve to rationalise Stalinist atrocities'.[22]

It would be crass to deny the importance of Stalin's peculiar personality to the course of Soviet history in this period but, as a recent Soviet commentary expresses it, 'The personality of Stalin was not an accidental superstructure on an imperfect régime, but a mature characteristic of the régime itself.'[23] Others have tried to put Stalin in a broader context of the outlook of those who executed his policies, of the Party and its dominant ideology, of the social classes they sought to lead, of the problems they sought to solve and the tools which they had to solve them with – which all, to one degree or another, militated in favour of, or provided favourable conditions for, not simply the emergence of a dictator but of the system which he operated for twenty-five years.

Western writing on Stalinism has also often tended to give prime importance to the personality and to the leadership as in the totalitarian model – to look from the top down at a passive society only manipulated and terrorised by authority. The significance of Stalin, the extent of control exercised by the political leadership, the pervasiveness of the Terror as determining characteristics of the régime continue to be much debated. Sheila Fitzpatrick drew attention to the emergence of a so-called 'new cohort' of 'social historians' of the Stalin period who are examining the phenomenon 'from below' and finding that political actions were a response to the character of the problems to be solved, that there were appeals to the self-interest of certain social groups and that policies were even modified as a result of 'informal social negotiation'.[24] Andrle has more closely defined the distinctive characteristics of the work of this 'new cohort': first, they tend to focus on positive aspects of the society of the time such as education, social mobility, the struggles with bureaucracy, the support and enthusiasm of certain sections of society for the collectivisation or industrialisation campaigns, the limitations of the Terror and the survival of 'normal' life. Second, they present a multicoloured picture of Stalinist reality tending to show that Terror did not overwhelm social life but coexisted with it. Third, the Terror is presented as understandable and the result of a collective process rather than Stalin's caprice. It is a response to social problems and conflicts over policy issues, and Stalin's personal importance is thus de-emphasised.[25]

As a social historian, Moshe Lewin has for long drawn attention to the chaotic character of Soviet society during the first Five-Year Plan and has sought to understand the relationship between society and politics in the emergence of Stalinism. He has taken the view that the bacchanalia of mature Stalinism and the turnaround on the Cultural Revolution resulted as much from the weakness of the régime's control over society as from its strength. The lack of social controls led to the need to intensify formal controls and sanctions. This was, however, aided by a pessimistic view of the consequences of spontaneity, a view which had deep roots in Soviet Marxist, as well as Russian, tradition. Unlike some of the 'new cohort' of social historians, Lewin explores the social underpinnings and context of Stalinism, while conveying a sense of the full horror of the phenomenon.[26]

Stalin cannot be ignored in all this. But Stalin's complicity is an inadequate explanation of the Terror and why it was allowed to happen. Historians have also asked what interests were involved in the political consolidation of Stalinism; and how far sections of society contributed to it by their committed support and not simply brainwashing, or by their passivity and indifference, for instance to the removal of specialists, or by their receptiveness towards the Stalin cult. Stalinism was totalitarian in its ambitions but probably none of the historians who use the term think that this means there were not 'inefficiencies' in the control actually exercised.[27] Others go further in arguing that much room for manoeuvre in the execution of policy was left, for instance, to local leaders because of poor communications, inadequate legislation and the weak development of the governmental and Party system.

The changes of the 1930s did not result only from coercion. There was also considerable and genuine enthusiasm, particularly in the early phases – for instance from the Komsomol and later from the *vydvizhentsy*, the young working class newly educated for positions of authority in the first Five-Year Plan, the beneficiaries of the purges and, in essence, the Brezhnev generation. Trotsky goes too far in playing down the significance of Stalin as only representing what Djilas was later to call the 'new class'. But particularly in the phase of the first Five-Year Plan the input of Party and class enthusiasm for the building of socialism seems to have been an important ingredient at least among a minority.

Sheila Fitzpatrick and the social historians have reacted against what they saw as an excessive emphasis in the totalitarian model on the political élite and system. They have rightly drawn attention to what was going on at the lower levels of society. They have raised questions about how far various social groups aided and abetted, or benefited from, Stalin's policies, about how far the state's control over society did extend and whether the extreme authoritarianism of the régime was a result of weakness rather than strength, of the difficulty of establishing control in a society where no established social controls existed at a time of flux and chaotic transformation. A central issue is also the question of the pervasiveness of the Terror, whether it affected the whole of society equally or whether it was targeted on certain social groups rather than others and benefited from the attitudes of sections of society indifferent to the fate of those purged.[28]

Arch Getty, in a much criticised book on the origins of the Great Purge, has argued that the purges were a limited phenomenon and have been much exaggerated in Western writing. They resulted as much as anything else from bureaucratic infighting about the strategies for development rather than from any personal commitment and urge by Stalin himself.[29] This view certainly requires modification, although it is a healthy reminder that Stalin and his colleagues – in however crude and bloodthirsty a way – were faced with difficult dilemmas in trying to govern the country and to achieve enormously difficult objectives in very unfavourable conditions and with inadequate means. Some Soviet writers have also emphasised that the purges certainly produced fear but that they also resulted from the fears of Stalin and the élite themselves.[30]

Andrle has pursued the argument that Stalinism resulted from the nature of the tasks that were faced in the 1930s and from the limited tools available to solve them. Stalin, in his view, relied on social support as well as on his dominance of the institutions of power. He suggests that the purges of leading personnel in the latter 1930s were aided and abetted by a working class which had little sympathy for the specialists and managers.[31] In assessing the impact of film, this is an important perspective as the most frequent audience must have been urban working class.

One must be careful not to separate the social history from the politics and reverse the totalitarian school's emphasis on the history of the political élite and its actions. Cohen has argued, 'Terror must be included not because it was more important than anything else but because it was an essential part of everything else.'[32] But this does not exclude the possibility that insights into Stalinism could be obtained by taking a different starting point and that there were areas where the impact of the Terror was greater and more direct and others where it was less. The means of control over society were crude and imperfect. The continuing apprehension of the régime about the difficulties of moulding and harnessing society to its objectives is evident from the constant need for new campaigns to root out enemies even after the Terror of the 1930s. There were undoubtedly elements of paranoia in this, but there were also good grounds for apprehension and the ruthlessness of each campaign provided a basis for new fears of society. Society had reason to fear the régime but the régime's reactions should be seen partly in the context of its own fear of society.[33] Society, by passivity, by mobility, was able to a limited extent to frustrate the aim of the régime to control. As for the mental and spiritual world of the public on which the media acted and which is so important for an assessment of the legacy of Stalinism, we know far too little. Cinema acts both in the sphere of élite politics as well as in the area of social history. It relates to questions of mass beliefs and social psychology. Robert Thurston has questioned whether there were different levels of the impact of the Terror in Soviet society or whether its influence was all- and equally pervasive. His work on the family in the late 1930s concludes that the atomisation of society and the destruction of family ties were not by any means universal phenomena and that they contradicted the new conservative official, though erratic, emphasis on the strengthening of the family.[34]

The debate about the numbers of Stalin's victims continues in an ill-tempered tone, fuelled by the contributions from the Soviet Union which have tended to provide evidence for higher rather than lower figures.[35] This is clearly an important issue but, whether we take the higher or lower figures, the enormity of the human losses is totally condemnatory of the régime and the individuals who directly implemented, initiated or fomented the bloodletting. The precise numbers will not make any difference to the question of whether the régime should be condemned. But the hidden agenda behind the debate concerns attitudes towards Stalinism and towards the Soviet régime in general. In the nature of things the calculation of the human losses of the Stalinist period remains based on fragile evidence and leaves room for reasonable doubt and further reasoned debate while accepting the scholarly integrity of the disputants. In the Soviet Union it has naturally become part of the political struggle to overcome the totalitarian and authoritarian legacy. For some in the West it seems to be the key question which precludes asking other questions about Stalinism. Of more substantial interest would be what now may become possible, a more comprehensive and thorough analysis of the Soviet Union under Stalinism to provide some material for the many matters over which we only have a very superficial or fragmentary knowledge concerning how the system operated, what its relationship was to different sections of society, how it achieved its objectives and what its impact was.

Cinema relates to all aspects of the Stalinist phenomenon – political, economic, social, cultural. As an economic and commercial activity, as an industry, it had to adapt to and be fitted into the new economic conditions after 1929. Politically, its importance was recognised by the Party and already in the 1920s its leading directors had aligned themselves with the ambitions of the Bolshevik Party even if they were not members. Its leading figures were in close contact with the Party élite, whose perception of the importance of cinema meant that it could not be isolated from the political struggles of the 1930s. Stalin's involvement with *The Radiant Path* [Svetlyi put', 1940] and with Eisenstein's *Ivan the Terrible* [Ivan Groznyi, 1943–8] provides only the two clearest examples of the close relationship between cinema and the personal dictatorship (see Chapters 7 and 8). Timothy

Dunmore in his study of Soviet politics in the last years of Stalin concluded that of all areas of policy the totalitarian interpretation applied most directly to the field of culture.[36]

Cinema was also related to the process of social transformation, not so much in the change in the character of its own cadres as in the fact of the change in the composition and experience of the audience to which it was directed. Study of cinema, more than of the other arts, cannot avoid consideration of the impact on and reaction of the audience. Cinema fits most obviously into the cultural context of the period but how does it relate to the different cultural levels and worlds of the time which were not monolithic?

In pursuing an understanding of the impact of Stalinism on film and the role of film in the context of Stalinism, the aesthetic, technical or moral judgements on the products and activity of the industry only form part of an analysis. We should not be concerned merely to rearrange the canon of Soviet film directors and reassess the virtues of forgotten or little-known producers. Rather, analysis should take into account the totality of production of the film world from fiction film to historical reconstruction, documentary to scientific film, from agit-film to newsreel as contributing to our understanding of the period. Even the crudest and aesthetically poorest film makes a contribution to our understanding, as for instance Maya Turovskaya's analysis of some of the Cold War fiction films shows.

In the general debate about Stalinism there has been much dispute about the relative importance of political direction and manipulation as against the role of society as either passive or reactive, even creative and contributory. So in the study of cinema these concerns are relevant. That cinema was manipulated by the political authorities even at the highest level is evident, but the significance of this has not yet been fully defined, nor has the contributive, even supportive, role of the cinema industry been evaluated. The various strains of interpretation of Stalinism form the context of our own examination of cinema and film media. Film was produced by a cultural élite and was influenced by the dominant cultural ideological ethos already in the 1920s, even before the imposition of cultural uniformity. From then on, its direct relationship to political life, policies, ideas and objectives is undeniable. But film was not a direct product of the political élite itself. As a major mass medium, it was used by political authority for its own purposes. But those purposes were not necessarily achieved, because of the film directors' own residual autonomy and because of the impossibility of entirely manipulating the audience, who came to film with their own concerns, varying cultural levels and outlooks which determined their various possible reactions. The film, like other arts, could be read in different ways even at the height of the Stalin cult and for a full assessment in the context of Stalinism we need to know as much about the audience and their conditions as about the film-makers and their world. We are still far from knowing, for instance, how far the optimism and enthusiasm in the literature and arts of the time corresponded to a mood in any part of Soviet society.

Whether Stalinism was totalitarian in any meaningful sense is a matter of particular importance for historians attempting to assess the significance and impact of a mass medium such as cinema. In the period of the consolidation of Stalinism the limitations of the impact of film must be borne in mind. Cinema was more of an urban than a rural phenomenon, although society was becoming distinctly more urbanised in this period. It thus had a greater impact on the substantially disorientated expanding urban section of society than on the still larger rural mass. In 1940 the average weekly audience at the cinema was only 3.7 million for the rural population of 131 million, whereas in the towns the weekly audience was 13.5 million for an urban population of 63 million.

In assessing the impact of cinema, therefore, more significant results are likely to be obtained by focusing on the urban audience. Communist Party archives are now becoming accessible to scholars. The local urban Party offices and their agitprop departments (as some recent initial forays already show) are likely to provide us with a more complex picture of changing moods and attitudes at the grass roots. Of course, like any other historical evidence, account will need to be taken of source provenance and intention in assessing the extent to which such material can help us to come nearer to part of the reality of the public mood. But the study of it may well provide some necessary insights for the assessment of the relationship between the controlled arts and propaganda on the one hand and the audience on the other in the Stalinist state.

The study of Soviet cinema therefore is integrated into the ongoing debate about Stalinism and can inform us about many of the processes at work in Soviet society. It undoubtedly responds to the interests of those historians who emphasise the importance of views and actions from above and the manipulation of Soviet society through the mass media. But it is also relevant to the concerns of the social historians to take account of and penetrate the view from below, both at the intermediary level of the role and aspirations of the film-makers as individuals and artists, and at the lower and dimly penetrable level of the audience, their character and their responses.

In every feature and activity of Soviet society of the period we will find clues to making sense of the origins, impact and significance of Stalinism. Film as a medium produced by an intelligentsia élite, in the context of increasingly heavy political and ideological influence and control, and projected to a mass audience whose values, attitudes and position in society were in turmoil, fully deserves our close attention.

Chapter 2

Onwards and Upwards!: the origins of the Lenin cult in Soviet cinema

Rashit Yangirov

In Soviet cinema limitless opportunities for ideological and economic control over the creative cadres have been concentrated in the hands of its individual leaders, the men who actually ran the industry. The daily and varied activity of these men as 'transmission belts' of Party and state direction has not hitherto attracted really serious attention.[1] Yet the individual tastes and enthusiasms of these 'commanders' of film production through the decades have reflected, albeit in mediated form, the more general trends at the heart of state ideology and practice.

A checklist of the names of the leaders of Soviet cinema arranged in chronological order up to the 1950s defines each stage in its history and reveals the almost complete absence of continuity in its progression. Nikolai Preobrazhensky, Dmitri Leshchenko, Pyotr Voyevodin, Lev Liberman, Erast Kadomtsev, Konstantin Shvedchikov, Mikhail Yefremov, Martemyan Ryutin,[2] Boris Shumyatsky,[3] Semyon Dukelsky,[4] Ivan Bolshakov . . .

From May 1921 to June 1922 Pyotr Ivanovich Voyevodin (1884–1964) was head of the All-Russian Photographic and Cinematographic Department [VFKO], one of the founding organisational structures of the nationalised Russian cinema industry. He is not among the best-known activists in Soviet cinema, but he played a part in its history at one of the most critical stages in its development, and laid a foundation stone for the development of the myth of the leader, even within Lenin's lifetime. For Voyevodin himself – a professional revolutionary and Bolshevik, who since October 1917 had belonged to the highest echelon of the Party and state *nomenklatura* – the new post was merely a routine appointment after eighteen months in charge of the Samara branch of Gosizdat, the state publishing house, and the local Proletkult. This background made him look like a candidate who was sufficiently well qualified in matters of artistic policy and it obviously had a decisive influence on the mystifying decision by the Registration and Distribution Section of the Party Central Committee to appoint him as head of the new Soviet cinema industry. For Voyevodin himself the precise nature of his new job was quite a surprise:

Not only was it something I knew nothing about, I had only been to the cinema very rarely before, and it seemed to be a particularly difficult job because, instead of the previous collegiate board, the Central Committee now decreed one-man management [*edinonachalie*] . . .

Nobody asked me how well qualified I was for that kind of work. They simply summoned me to the Central Committee and told me that they were appointing me to run the whole cinema industry and all film activity in the Republic.[5]

The transition to new 'market' economic relations, with the almost complete termination of government subsidies in the cultural sphere, on the one hand, and the already emerging bureaucratic limitations on any independent activity, on the other, threatened to reduce 'to zero any sign of life, not just in VFKO, but in Russian cinema as a whole'.[6] It is therefore not surprising that Voyevodin made so many direct appeals to Lenin in which we can detect muted reproaches for the neglect of the problems and needs of cinema:

Having received requests from a very wide range of departments for the execution of various urgent tasks, often supported, Vladimir Ilyich, by your own conclusions as to the need for 'urgency' or 'haste' etc., I frequently realise that, despite all my energy and fervent desire to set the machinery in motion, I remain completely powerless. From the very first days I have been convinced, Vladimir Ilyich, that only your exclusive attention, your direct intervention, in this area would help . . . to create the photographic and cinematographic industry and to preserve for film work the essential role . . . that is currently so important to us.[7]

The range of urgent questions that Voyevodin raised with Lenin and the heads of the other subdivisions of supreme authority is fairly well known.[8] But the 'pitiful bureaucratic existence' (Voyevodin's own formulation) of VFKO is more clearly revealed in the fairly sizeable corpus of unpublished materials preserved in archival collections.[9]

In one of his very first reports Voyevodin recounts how

the absence of film stock deprives us of the opportunity to test the capability and suitability of the staff of the newly organised cinema troupe, and the delay in the supply of resources and materials is slowing down even the preparatory work on the agreed programme for the production of new pictures . . .

Nevertheless in his next report Voyevodin was already able to announce the completion of the agitational films *The Countryside in Revolution* [Derevnya na perelome], *Andrei Gudok, Everything is in Our Hands* [Vse v nashikh rukakh] and *Hunger . . . Hunger . . . Hunger* [Golod . . . golod . . . golod], a plan for an 'Auto-Cine-Base' [*Avtokinobaza*] to serve peasant audiences, and measures to restore the ruined Moscow film studios.[10]

The 'film stock' crisis, which had made itself felt for the first time towards the end of 1916 and which was to last for almost twenty years, reached its peak under Voyevodin. By his own admission every possible means was used to try and obtain film stock – 'personal, political and Party connections' and even 'smuggling'.[11] There can be no doubt of the pride that Voyevodin felt when he managed to push through his idea for an exchange with foreign countries of pre-Revolutionary films that had been designated ideologically and aesthetically 'alien' to Soviet audiences in return for raw film stock.[12] But even these modest successes could not dispel Voyevodin's sense of hopelessness about the organisation that he headed: the 'catastrophic' and 'terrible' state of nationalised cinema required different – radical rather than palliative – approaches and solutions. Above all, it required an appeal to Western cinema entrepreneurs. From the autumn of 1921 Voyevodin turned his attention to the German film industry.[13] However, the opportunities in Germany did not come up to expectations and the focus of attention then moved to a proposal from the Italian company, Città-Cinema, which was probably largely facilitated by a guarantee from the Communist, Arturo Caroti, who was personally acquainted with Lenin. These discussions were also in the end unsuccessful.

Yet a full assessment of Voyevodin's activity in Soviet cinema must take account of his personal creative ambitions, which were particularly actively aroused at that time. It is still not widely appreciated that there was a general propensity among the highest echelons of the Bolshevik hierarchy for literary creativity, realised across a broad range of genres, and that it was revered and propagated as one of the highest Party virtues. Literary endeavours (naturally in the context of the 'general cause of the proletariat') were yet another testing ground for every Party member who was concerned to further his or her own personal influence and the career advancement that accompanied it. Voyevodin provides one more, somewhat exotic, example of the penetration of 'Party organisation and Party literature' into the sphere of artistic creativity.[14]

Given that as head of VFKO he had absolutely no professional training or, more to the point, cultural education, Voyevodin completed his probation in the film-making profession fairly quickly. In the autumn of 1921 the VFKO authorities announced an open competition for a script for an agitational fiction film on contemporary Revolutionary themes. It ended with Voyevodin's own screenplay for *In the Heat of the Revolution* [V vikhre revolyutsii] being accepted for production, to be directed by Alexander Chargonin.[15]

But at the same time Voyevodin began work on a more ambitious creative project: the script for a monumental 'agitational-fiction, historical-Revolutionary film *Through Obstacles Onwards and Upwards! Vladimir Ilyich Lenin* [Cherez pregrady – vpered i vyshe! Vladimir Il'ich Lenin].

This was a uniquely courageous project for the time, as before 1917 the depiction of rulers – who were sacred national, state and religious symbols – had been strictly regulated in documentary film and prohibited without further ado in fiction film.[16]

The motivation for Voyevodin's decision involved a fairly complex combination of political and personal calculations. If it were to be successfully completed, a film about the leader would become a spectacular statement of the triumph of ideology in cinema and a convincing confirmation of the serious potential of Party art. Voyevodin's personal ambitions did not exactly take a back seat either: if the film was, as he anticipated, a success, this would guarantee that his name would enter the ranks of the first biographers and interpreters of the 'life and works' of Lenin, with all the profitable consequences that would ensue.[17] We can also say with certainty that the choice of a fairly unusual genre – the 'film play' [kino-p'esa] – was not stimulated by the professional habits of a scriptwriter but was a sort of 'official' reaction to a cinematographic event abroad whose significance must not be underestimated.

The event in question was the British film *The Land of Mystery*, made in 1920 by the American director, Harold Shaw.[18] Judging from descriptions, this film (which has not been preserved) was an unpretentious melodrama with elements of the thriller but, in the words of its makers, it laid claim to providing a screen biography of the leader of the Russian Revolution and a history of the birth of Bolshevism. The film – a mediocre nine-days' wonder made on the crest of anti-Bolshevik campaigns in the Entente countries during the Polish–Soviet War (even in that context objections were raised in the cinema press to the depiction of the private life of contemporary political figures on the screen) – would quite deservedly have been consigned to oblivion had it not been for an unusual turn in its distribution fate.

Leonid Krasin who as head of the first Soviet diplomatic mission in London was involved in various intricate diplomatic games,[19] managed somehow to obtain a copy of *The Land of Mystery* and took it to Moscow with the sole purpose of showing it to Lenin himself. Given the complex relations between these two men, we can hardly believe that Krasin was in this instance moved by a desire merely to amuse Lenin. Krasin's motives were probably more serious – we cannot tell – but he may have wished to indicate his opposition to the political course that had been chosen.

Tapping on a metal box and smiling his subtle smile, Leonid Borisovich [Krasin] said: 'I'm risking my neck, but I'll drag Ilyich along . . .'

And he did! The performance was arranged in the Metropole cinema. Vladimir Ilyich arrived with Nadezhda Konstantinovna [Krupskaya]. He was jovial, but a little watchful. Obviously he sensed that Krasin was up to something.[20]

The only memoir evidence that has come down to us about this, one of the first closed Kremlin screenings, quite faithfully reproduces the content of the original 'stupid film made in England' and, even more important, the substance of Lenin's reaction to it. It was only towards the middle of the film that Lenin finally realised whose fate was unfolding on the screen before his very eyes. The other members of the audience were slower to catch on, of course, but, taking their cue from what must have been Ilyich's stunned chuckle, they all laughed out loud in support. This most piquant situation, set up by Krasin, forced Lenin to sit through what was to him already an unwelcome screen spectacle caricaturing not merely the cause to which he had devoted his entire life but also the intimate details of his personal biography, epitomised by the tragic love triangle between Prince Lenoff, the 'peasant noblewoman' Masikova, and Prince Ivan! The screening ended with a conversation between Lenin and Lunacharsky, the People's Commissar for Enlightenment. We know nothing of its content, apart from a later-recalled and barely overheard last remark: '. . . so that cinema penetrates into every workers' settlement, every village. This is the most important thing . . . No, absolutely the most important . . .' It is logical to assume that these words referred directly to the film that had just been viewed and above all that they completed Lenin's directive and its particularly defensive reaction to cinematic inventions. It is well known that the Soviet leadership always overreacted to any such attacks – they had done so right from the beginning. The woman who wrote the memoir quoted above was a senior official of the Party Central Committee at the time of the event, and it was no accident that she corroborated her memory by referring to a review in the British press that nobody has ever heard of. For her, apparently, the screening ended with her being told to gather comprehensive information on the film.

For Voyevodin, there had to be a routine response to an 'attack' by class enemies. It is appropriate to point out that in practice the whole composite phenomenon of Bolshevism as a type of *Weltanschauung* had always been honed on the rocks of 'criticisms', 'rebukes', 'exposures', etc. But the response would be tinged inevitably with hagiography, because it touched on the most delicate subject matter which categorically rejected any possibility of discussion or debate. It would be wrong to imply that scholars have known nothing about Voyevodin's proposed 'Life of Lenin'. On the contrary, quite a lot is in fact known about it through the repeated publication of Krupskaya's and Lenin's negative comments, which seem to have barred the way to the screen of a crude and clumsy attempt to immortalise the image of the leader on the screen.[21] A paucity of details about the material, derived in any event at 'second hand', has, however, sufficed to ensure that Voyevodin's opus completely disappeared from scholarly attention and has, with the course of time, become just one more cinema myth. Regardless of its limited artistic value, which is very clearly revealed by even a cursory reading,[22] Voyevodin's work does at least deserve analysis. Recent work on Voyevodin's personal archive has not merely resurrected the script but has also shown convincingly that the story of the Lenin film was much more complicated than we have been led to believe. The return of this very remarkable film text to scholarly circulation has introduced new and unexpected emphases into a long-since hopelessly compromised subject. It resurrects in its original form the exaggerated ideological essence that has, in varying concentrations, overflowed into Soviet cinema art in the following decades. The resurrection of this forgotten episode permits us to establish new signposts to the currents in the aesthetic evolution of 'the most important of all the arts' and to evaluate more profoundly its fatal dependence on state ideology.

One undoubtedly valuable aspect of Voyevodin's concept of the script in its first 'literary' version was that, despite his own creative limitations, he was able to channel his hagiographical 'treatment' into the traditions of folklore and the lives of the saints. We can see the author's unambiguous orientation towards the level of mass consciousness in his own time of people who had scarcely freed the 'dark' sacral side of their characters from the influence of traditional ideas. Thus the scriptwriter, caught between the two magnetic fields of group ideology and popular mentality, produced a 'contraband' of class 'values' combined marvellously with the folklore model.

The first part of the 'literary' version of the script, which served as an exposition for the subsequent action, was specifically modelled on the oral folk tradition, like the prologue to a folk story or a fairy tale [*priskazka*, or *skazochnyi zachin*].[23] The description of the life of the people in pre-Revolutionary Russia, despite the use of some Marxist terms ('capital flourishes', 'capital accumulates', 'life determines consciousness', etc.), is conveyed in precisely the same form and precisely the same images as those familiar from the folk tale.

> Strongly influenced by this canon, the finale of the film fairy tale about Lenin overtly verbalises its link with the folklore model in the quiet of legendary surroundings, the great leader of the proletariat is himself gradually transformed for the whole wide world into a fairy tale, a symbol, a legend.[24]

In Voyevodin's script we can see equally clearly the generic features of the traditional lives of the saints. This is demonstrated above all in the author's attitude towards his hero. His depiction, born of contemporary events, is a mirror image of the depictions in medieval Russian literature, which people had continued to read, either in their original form or in imitations or stylised versions. As a crude generalisation, and leaving aside what was for the author the deeply obscure sphere of cinematic imagery, his script represents another pure example of the imitation of an archaic tradition executed in exotic form – a chain of poorly connected events, recreating in mediated form the earthly path of the hero. In the 'directing' script the seventy-one episodes of the 'literary' version were reduced to ten scenes. Voyevodin managed in effect to deprive Lenin's image of its individual humanity, replacing it with a name-mask performing a sacred feat of self-sacrifice against a minimum of historical background. Several speech constructions, retained in both versions, reproduce in modernised form the style of irrational apologia of the heroes of the saints' lives. Consider, for instance, the following in the 'literary' version: 'From factory to factory stretch the thousand magic threads of Ilyich's eagle eye: with a firm hand he steers the rudder of the new history';[25] and 'Through the fire and tempest of Civil War, fatally wounded by the bullet of a woman [Fanny Kaplan] blinded by folly and led astray by falsehoods, Lenin strives ever onwards and upwards towards universal human happiness and freedom.'

In analysing Voyevodin's script, it is thus appropriate to employ current evaluations of medieval Russian literature, such as that of Dmitri Likhachev, the most eminent scholar in this field:

It is not the deed or feat itself which is of paramount importance, but the attitude the author expresses towards that feat: the emotional characteristics of the feat are always heightened, almost exaggerated, while at the same time remaining abstract. The facts themselves are exaggerated, good and evil are expressed in absolute terms, never appearing in any partial form. There are only two colours on the author's palette: black and white. This explains the author's predilection for various exaggerations, for expressive epithets, and for a psychological characterisation of the facts . . . If the author employs comparison, he is not concerned as to whether it is concrete, visual or perceived. For him it is the inner sense of the events that is important, not external similarity . . . It is not the similarity in external appearance that interests the author, but the similarity in the actions, the sense behind these actions. The visual, concrete image of a human being is simply absent . . . This method of characterising a person is very far removed from our artistic consciousness, but it may be fully explained by the artistic consciousness of its own time: the individuality of a person was abstract and unclear, the character of a person had not yet been discerned, so that it was not the man himself who was being compared, but merely his works, his deeds, actions and feats – and he was judged according to those . . . Thus it was important to bring out the significance of an action, to underline its significance, the impression it made on people, rather than to describe it in concrete terms. Details were omitted because they were regarded as inessential, so that the actual action appeared exaggerated, as was its psychological effect. The only details that were included were those that contributed to this effect. Hence it was common in literature of the time to pile horror upon horror . . . and indulge in all sorts of hyperbole.[26]

There is another level in the relations between Voyevodin and his hero outside the bounds of the actual text under examination but which to some extent makes up for its laconic (and at the same time, archaic!) structure. This is provided by Voyevodin's memoir accounts of his meetings with Lenin. The earliest of them date from the time before he had begun work on the script and they preserve an immediacy of perception, without the least trace of the self-censorship that characterises later memoir texts. In them we can ascertain several features and details of the living, rather than the imagined, Lenin.

In the spring of 1918 Voyevodin, then one of the leading Bolshevik activists in Western Siberia, had come to Moscow on business and met Lenin for the first time in his life.

> I was in the room where the Council of People's Commissars met. There it was: the holiest of holies of workers' and peasants' power, the place where the spirit of the dictatorship of the proletariat permeates everything and reigns supreme! . . . For the first time in my life I saw at close quarters beside me the man I had followed, despite all odds, for twenty years of my life. I saw his lively, penetrating little eyes, sly but with a hint of benevolence and amusement, and the bald spot on his muzhik's head. I heard his voice, sometimes harsh, sometimes whispering, but clear and gradually capturing the listener's full attention . . . Alongside many People's Commissars he looked plain, thickset and very poorly dressed, but soon Comrade Lenin's business-like and amusing speech, with its news of the situation on the Republic's border with the Ukraine, where the Germans were putting pressure on us at the time, attracted my full attention, and I listened to Comrade Lenin's words with admiration. The amusing tone of his remarks about the Germans revealed an excellent knowledge of the international situation and a confident analysis of the events unfolding, subjects in which Comrade Lenin felt like a fish in water.[27]

It was then that Voyevodin had his first conversation with Lenin. The subject of that conversation and Lenin's reaction to it are of some interest.

> I told him about an occasion when there had been a big argument among our comrades in the organisation. It was over the problem of how to sell the vodka which had been stored in vast quantities in warehouses in Siberia. The problem was discussed at the Congress of Soviets of Western Siberia but nonetheless we failed to resolve it properly. When the problem was discussed in Party circles, some people, including me, suggested that we should sell the vodka to the peasants in exchange for

grain. Only three Party members supported my suggestions. Ilyich said: 'The fools! What fools! Why didn't you do that? You are after all an Old Bolshevik. You are in charge of economic affairs. And there is another Old Bolshevik, Kosarev, who's head of the Executive Committee. And other Old Bolsheviks there too. Why didn't you push it through?' Then Lenin said: 'But could you have sold that vodka abroad?' I said that we could have kept France supplied with spirits for fifteen years. Then Ilyich asked, 'But could you actually get the vodka out?' There were some absurd ideas going the rounds. I told Lenin that we couldn't have transported it all down the River Ob because we didn't have the tanker barges or appropriate containers. What was more in the lower reaches of the Ob we'd have had to transfer all of it on to sea-going steamers. After reflecting, V. I. said, 'It's a pity you didn't sell it to the peasants. You should have ordered it. It ought to have been done.' I started to explain that it was not for us to decide to do it off our own bat. Ilyich said, 'If you'd done it, we'd have approved it.' I laughed and asked him, 'And then you would have condemned us?' Ilyich began to laugh, 'That's all right! We'd have condemned you for it, but you'd have done the right thing.'[28]

In tracing the origins of Voyevodin's film, we should note that it had already been announced in the press at the end of November 1921, while work on the film *In the Heat of the Revolution* was still in progress. The advertisement suggested that Lenin himself would participate in the outdoor shots.[29]

We now know that this was merely a statement of intent conceived in the style of the film press of the pre-Revolutionary period. Nothing more existed at the time than the rough title and the author's broad outline of the script. Voyevodin meanwhile pursued his research:

Meeting Vladimir Ilyich on several occasions at various congresses and hearing him speak, I saw what magic winning-power he exerted over people. Several times in those years, after experiencing personally the powerful educational effect that Vladimir Ilyich had on me,[30] I set myself the task of producing a cinematographic representation of Ilyich's multifaceted life . . . There were no published details of Lenin's private life at all. Nor at that time were there any stories in the press from people who had met him. I was left with just the personal and individual impressions I had of my meetings, conversations and observations. A couple of attempts to talk to Vladimir Ilyich about my desire to write his biography produced nothing. Ilyich reacted to my biographical questions with delicacy and seriousness: 'It's still too early to write about that and, as far as history is concerned, it's more important to make it than to write about it.'

Even in response to the question that I somehow managed to put to him casually about the origin of his name 'Lenin', Ilyich said nothing but very gently and efficiently diverted my attention ... to other subjects ...

Nor did I manage to get the information I needed from my conversations with Nadezhda Konstantinovna [Krupskaya] on the subject.[31]

Lenin's unwillingness to enlarge upon his personal biography to strangers can be explained as much by his character as by the conspiratorial reflexes of a revolutionary. The subject was taboo even to his closest circle. The biography of the leader had from the beginning to be completely identified with the history of the political organisation that he created and led. Nikolay Valentinov [N. V. Volsky] met with a similar response to his attempt to cross-question Lenin as early as 1904.[32]

Since he got nowhere with Lenin, Voyevodin turned to more accessible sources, in particular Mikhail Olminsky, the head of Istpart.[33] As early as May 1917 Olminsky and others had set off a 'tidal wave' of mass popularisation of the figure of Lenin.[34] Hundreds of thousands of copies of biographical sketches, articles and pamphlets devoted to Lenin were in circulation by 1921 in which we can already see the image of the leader of the Party and the Revolution that was fairly close in terms of stereotype to what was taking shape in Voyevodin's imagination. Lenin's individual personality was quite absent from general consciousness and had been replaced by something like a faded but heavily retouched photograph hanging on the wall. Mikhail Koltsov,[35] one of the leading 'drummers of the period', who had often observed the leader with his own eyes, commented in 1927:

We know that:
1. He likes children.
2. And cats.
3. He often laughs.
4. He is modest in his dress and his way of life.
5. He is a good chess player.
6. He likes cycling.
That is almost everything. We know a little bit more, but not very much, about him ... Isn't this strange. How much we admire him, how much we love him – and how little we know about him as a person. We already have a Lenin Institute, which is collecting every scrap of paper he ever wrote on, but Lenin himself still remains quite unfamiliar and unintelligible.

Napoleon, Cromwell, Garibaldi have left us portraits, anecdotes, dust-covered gloves under glass in museums. Lenin has left us great historical achievements ... because the genius of Lenin is thoroughly utilitarian, profoundly intertwined with his Party, his class and his era ... That is why his appearance is so strange, so protectively bland, that is why he has merged into the working class . . .

And that is why in Lenin, the first of the men of the future, we cannot and *must not* [my italics] look for petty personal characteristics, gestures and phrases . . .[36]

Towards the beginning of February 1922 Voyevodin finished work on the script and discussed it with an adviser and with professional film-makers. According to some sources, work had already started by then on the selection of newsreel material.[37] There remained the last and most important thing – getting the approval of the hero of the film and, assuming a favourable outcome, getting his agreement to take part, as previously announced, in the shooting. On 4 February Voyevodin sent Lenin two copies of his script with the following letter:

Dear Vladimir Ilyich,

I feel obliged to present for your approval a script that I have written, and which I feel is important for our cause, for an agitational historical– Revolutionary feature film, *Vladimir Ilyich Lenin*.

This script has been approved from the technical and artistic point of view by the VFKO Artistic Council, composed of authoritative specialists – directors, artists and writers. As for the purely ideological interpretation and political consistency, I have been governed solely by my own political sensitivity and experience and I may submit my script for production when I receive your decision and approval.

Apart from my pride as the author (this is the first attempt at artistic representation in this field in general and in particular of the workers' movement in Russia during the past forty years with your direct participation and under your leadership), and apart from my material interest (the film might be sold to other countries as well), the most important thing in this instance is that I have a correct understanding of the historical process and a correct interpretation of the role and personality of the leader of the proletariat during the struggle with our class enemies.

As one of your pupils who has now been following you for more than twenty years since early childhood, your opinion and your decision about my work and your agreement to accept my dedication to you, are important to me, not just as strict comradely criticism, but also as corroboration of the need to begin the work that I am now doing on the history of our Party for Istpart.

I implore you, Vladimir Ilyich, to excuse me for disturbing you and to write a few lines about this work here presented to you by a self-taught worker-author, who wishes, in this sphere too, to serve our common proletarian cause.

Yours, with sincere respect,

Pyotr Voyevodin

... I should be very grateful if you would intercede with Comrades Chicherin and Litvinov to have Comrade Tisse, an experienced and trustworthy cameraman from VFKO, sent to the Genoa Conference, which is very important to our story.[38]

When he sent his script off for comment, Voyevodin apparently felt almost certain of a favourable response because, without waiting for Lenin's answer, perhaps taking a week's silence as a sign of approval, he signed a contract on 11 February 1922 with the Kinotrud company for the script and for a film based on it, *Through Obstacles Onwards and Upwards*. The author's contract stipulated a fee of 1,000 gold roubles and, in addition, an author's royalty on each copy in distribution – for Russia a minimum of ten copies was specified.[39]

Meanwhile, the delayed comments arrived. By family convention they were made by Krupskaya who as head of Glavpolitprosvet [Principal Political Education Committee of Narkompros] was Voyevodin's superior. Her comments amounted to this:

The author of this dramatisation wants to depict almost the entire Revolution. The selection of facts is often arbitrary. Many biographical details are incorrect.

The production is extremely complex, requiring masses of participants, it will cost a fantastic sum, be badly executed and resemble a bad *lubok*. The technical resources of our cinema are very poor and it is incapable of providing what the author wants. The script is scarcely acceptable.

N. Krupskaya

On 18 February Lenin penned a postscript to this note: 'Reject completely on the basis of this comment' and passed it to his secretary Fotiyeva for action.[40] On the very same day one copy of the script Voyevodin had submitted was returned to him with what are probably Krupskaya's marks and comments on it. It was accompanied by the following letter from Lenin's office:

Comrade Voyevodin,

In response to your letter, on the instructions of V. I. Lenin, I must inform you of the following:

The organisation of your picture is extremely complex, it requires masses of participants and enormous expense, its execution will be unsatisfactory because the technical level of our cinema is very low, and the events that you depict are partly untrue and partly should not be included in the script.

For this reason Vladimir Ilyich deems it necesary to reject your proposal that your script be produced.[41]

It is at this point that the known history of the first film about Lenin suddenly stops but there was a sequel which cast its shadow in the most surprising directions. The response to Voyevodin was probably unexpected and quite disheartening, coming as it did when he was already under a contractual obligation to the studio. Voyevodin immediately sought a meeting with Lenin, who told him:

'Well, perhaps it is necessary to make a film like this, but it is too early as yet. Too early to produce something like this, given our current international situation.'

Ilyich accompanied me out of his office and, as if to console me, added: 'Cheer up! A time will come when a film like this can be made. But at the moment it's early, too early!'[42]

A meeting with Krupskaya was also fruitless:

... I tried once more to convince Nadezhda Konstantinovna that, despite all VFKO's difficulties, we nevertheless ought to make a film of this kind and I told her of the enthusiasm with which all my colleagues dreamed of making a film about the life and work of V. I. Lenin ... Nadezhda Konstantinovna said sympathetically, 'I have faith in you and I do believe that you and your film people [*kinoshniki*] will make a film like this but, once Ilyich had said that it was too early, we all had to bear this in mind. You must understand that Ilyich did not turn it down as a mere caprice but only out of consideration for the general situation of our state. Don't be upset ... You and your VFKO have enough to do as it is ...[43]

Hence Voyevodin's persistence went unrewarded: the aesthetic reasons for the rejection of the script concealed highly political considerations. The reasons lay much deeper than the particular strengths or weaknesses of the script as a literary text. As the film was specifically intended for sale abroad, Lenin was probably apprehensive that it would be interpreted by international public opinion as an attempt by the Bolsheviks to confirm their position over the dead bodies of their opponents. This could alter the delicate balance of opinion and counter the conciliatory impact of the introduction of the New Economic Policy (NEP) and the preparations for the Genoa international conference, particularly as at the same time Lenin and his colleagues had already committed themselves to new measures against internal opponents. Despite the façade of constitutionalism, the first fundamental peacetime purge of disloyal elements was being prepared: the fate of a large group of professors, doctors, agronomists, writers and social activists was being decided, and soon they would be exiled abroad.[44] The decision had already been taken to begin the legal and extra-legal persecution of the remnants of the non-Bolshevik socialist parties – the Socialist Revolutionaries and the Mensheviks – and there is no doubt that Lenin was one of the moving forces behind it.

Meanwhile, Voyevodin suffered a further disappointment. The film project *In the Heat of the Revolution* was completed and had an unusual premiere: it was shown to the delegates to the Eleventh Congress of the Bolshevik Party on 31 March 1922 in Lenin's presence. The reaction of this first audience was unanimously hostile.[45]

After so many decades it is difficult to reconstruct the precise nature of the audience's complaints against the makers of the film (which has also not survived in its entirety). One scholar, who has devoted many years to the study of the early history of Soviet cinema, tells us:

> The film, of course, was a complete failure in the Congress hall: more than two-thirds of the delegates – those who had the decisive voice – had been Party members since before the Revolution, and half were workers. Hundreds of people who had until recently been leading strikes and taking part in them did not, it seems, take seriously Zoya Barantsevich's disguises or the flat agitational tempi used by the film-makers.[46]

Another no less authoritative scholar (who was, in addition, an eye-witness to the events of those years!) nevertheless felt intuitively that the release of this kind of film had its own justification: 'The best of them, by popularising the basic slogans of Soviet power in simple and accessible form, inspired the workers and roused the people to the struggle for a better future.'[47]

If we are seeking an ideal figure to represent the tastes and group enthusiasms of the Party audience, we can do no better than choose Lenin himself. Despite the paucity of concrete evidence, it is quite obvious that the fiction films of Lenin's day found practically no place in the scale of his aesthetic values. He judged cinema, and indeed any other art form, in purely utilitarian terms: from the standpoint of its usefulness or its unserviceability for the aims of the political struggle and the agitation and propaganda treatment of the masses.

Was, let us say, Alexander Panteleyev's film *The Miracle Maker* [Chudotvorets, 1922], which Lenin saw in the last months of his life, of higher aesthetic merit than *In the Heat of the Revolution*, the film by Chargonin, who was considered to be one of the original masters of the Russian school of cinema? Nowadays this seems unlikely. Lenin's positive comment on *The Miracle Maker*, recalled by eye-witnesses,[48] is rather confirmation of the politicised attitude to art that we have already mentioned, and in essence bears no relationship whatsoever to the cinematic virtues of this celebrated anti-religious film.

Another feature of Lenin's reception of cinema, also noted by eye-witnesses during the last period of his life, is linked to the fact that he tired easily of full-length feature films. In my view this was not just a consequence of his last illness, but a sign that betrayed his long-standing 'anticinemism'.[49]

Lenin's famous conversation with Lunacharsky about the prospects for cinema's development took place at the same period.[50] Lenin's remark that 'the production of new films imbued with Communist ideas and reflecting Soviet reality should begin with the newsreel' and 'that, in his view, the time to produce films of this kind had perhaps not yet arrived' was directly connected to the grand political game in general and to Voyevodin's script in particular.[51] It is possible that Lunacharsky apprised Voyevodin of the contents of the conversation, at least as far as Lenin's wishes for the priority areas in the development of Soviet cinema were concerned. Voyevodin apparently perceived these as a guide to action and as an opportunity for official rehabilitation. But it was an unexpected factor that made it possible to turn these efforts into practical action.

Lenin's health was already deteriorating at the end of 1921 and beginning of 1922 and the Party authorities had to order him to take leave in Gorki, just outside Moscow, until 7 March 1922. He suffered his first stroke on 25 May 1922. The fact of his illness was not widely proclaimed at the time but it probably received fairly wide publicity in the higher echelons of the Party and in some way reached Voyevodin's ears. This persuaded him to devote himself with renewed energy to the realisation of the project that was so close to his heart. Lenin's recent rejection of the script became meaningless because a film about the leader might immediately become ammunition for the propaganda machine and fulfil its purpose in the best possible way. Lenin's possible anger at the breaching of his ban would be cancelled out by the Napoleonic principle, which had imprinted itself, not entirely by chance, on the consciousness of his loyal student: 'We'd have condemned you, but you'd have done the right thing.'

Evidently Lenin's preference for newsreel film at the expense of other types and genres of screen art had a decisive significance in the reworking of Voyevodin's script: Voyevodin yielded first place to a professional, Grigori Boltyansky, an enthusiastic scholar and avid collector of the film annals of the Revolution. The second version of the script seems, in essence, to be a cue sheet for the film, and Voyevodin's role in it was confined to the authorship of the politically consistent intertitles, which largely repeated the pathos of the original version. But at the same time the conceptual contours of the script were altered. In the surviving 'Explanatory Note to the Budget', put together by Boltyansky himself, he noted: 'I propose that we use a total of eight newsreels, 300–450 metres each in length, namely: 1) Lenin; 2) Trotsky; 3) Kalinin; 4) Zinoviev; 5) Lunacharsky; 6–7–8). Three different compilations, in all about 3,000 metres . . .' The total expense of each copy, including scriptwriting, direction, editing and additional filming, plus the cost of the negative film stock, came to 162 gold roubles.[52]

Boltyansky himself prepared a report for Voyevodin which listed every aspect of the preparatory work on the Lenin film:

	Completed Work
BOLTYANSKY	1) Viewing of the selected positive material. 2) Viewing of all the negatives and selection for printing, with Comrade Lenin. 3) Compilation of a script plan, with Comrade Lenin. 4) Compilation of lists of negative and positive footage for the planned subject of the script (three reels).[53]
SVILOVA	1) Search for all the positive footage relating to the film, with Comrade Lenin. 2) Selection of all the negatives to choose the sequences and view them (with Comrade Lenin). 3) Selection of all the old *Kino-nedelya* [Cine-Week] negatives (for the October period) and the *Svobodnaya Rossiya* [Free Russia] negatives (for the February period). 4) Search for all the positive footage related to the film (from which there will inevitably be cuts). 5) Submission to the laboratory of the order for the printing of the negatives.[54]

In Voyevodin's archive other documents have been preserved which reflect the further progress of the project. Judging from the report by Boltyansky, who was patently being pursued by his boss:

There remains to be done:
  1) Submission to the laboratory for printing.
  2) Editing the positive into a continuous film.
  3) Compilation of the montage list? . . .
From the script we have to do:
  1) Lenin in emigration . . .
  2) Session of the Council of People's Commissars . . .
  3) a) under Lenin's chairmanship;
     b) Lenin's speech.
  4) The seizure of land by the peasants and of factories and plants by the workers.
  5) The session on the Treaty of Brest-Litovsk (from a photograph) . . .
  6) Towards the Genoa Conference (from a photograph) . . .
  7) The Tenth Party Congress. Lenin's speech (from a photograph) . . .

8) Lenin in a village in the Volokolamsk district (from a photograph) . . .
9) The Kremlin. General interiors and exteriors with the
churches and St Basil's Cathedral.
   The sound of the Kremlin bells (fortissimo).
   The government building and the traffic around it . . .

Judging from the careful calculation of the footage of negative and
positive film, when this report was compiled the film-makers had at their
disposal 255 metres of positive film with shots of Lenin collected by
Svilova. According to the list cited above, a further 65 metres had still to be
shot, but VFKO had in its stores a total of only 49 metres of negative. There
is a note in Boltyansky's hand on the report suggesting the possibility of
cutting Lenin shots out of existing films and sticking them into the film that
was in preparation.[55] In the end it was decided to abandon further shooting
completely and to confine work exclusively to the re-editing of existing
film material, and Boltyansky took this upon himself.[56] This time the
history of the Lenin film loses its documented thread completely, but we
have every reason to suppose that, in this radically transformed state, it
nevertheless did reach the audience in April 1922 in the guise of a special
issue of the newsreel *Goskinokalendar'* [Goskino Calendar], directed by
Dziga Vertov. For Boltyansky this work became the basis for his single-
minded pursuit over many years of newsreel film material of Lenin, which
was first summarised in his book *Lenin i kino* [Lenin and Cinema].[57]

Voyevodin himself was soon removed as head of VFKO in June 1922.
For some time he attempted a comeback, intriguing against the new heads
of the film industry[58] and submitting new scripts to the film studios, but all
to no effect.[59] In 1923 he tried to turn attention back to his Lenin project in
its original form as a feature film. Ever sensitive to ideological innovations,
Voyevodin the Party member found a new justification for the genre:

Now Americanism . . . must give way to a new device [*tryuk*].
   The Russian device.
   Russian, of course, not in the national, but in the class sense. Now
Russia is becoming the embodiment of a single class: the working
class.
   Our Russian device, the device of the Great Russian Revolution, will
replace the American device.
   Our device will be more powerful than the American. More inter-
esting. More profound. More valid . . .
   Every moment of our Great Revolution casts similar devices in our
direction . . .
   One example: the history of Our Great Leader . . .
   The poor student on the banks of the Volga.

The unknown émigré on the banks of Lake Geneva, immersed in books.

The German 'spy' in a sealed railway carriage.

The hatred and fear of hundreds of members of the bourgeoisie and the hope of millions of workers – in the house of a ballerina, the Tsar's mistress.

The worker at the Sestroretsk factory . . . And, finally, the support and hope of the workers and the brain of the worldwide proletariat in the Red Kremlin, the former cradle of the Russian tsars.

That is our Russian 'device' . . .

Is not the life of the majority of our Party members like this? Does it not resemble these changing features in the script? . . .

Our universal struggle, a life-and-death struggle between the two classes that have seized both hemispheres, provides us with an incalculable number of device opportunities that are enthralling, profoundly conceived and enormous in their agitational significance.

These devices on screen are our equivalent of Pinkerton. Our Red Pinkerton.[60]

In Voyevodin's archive there is one more document that bears witness to the fact that the failure associated with the Lenin film still rankled. At the beginning of 1939, when the myth of the leader had been purged of all unnecessary details and particulars, and had in all its grandeur completely penetrated the popular consciousness, Voyevodin decided to remind the Party leadership about his longstanding work. His letter to the Party Central Committee is of interest, not merely from the point of view of an argument renewed, but also because it is clearly resonant with political motifs that had in the past been scarcely discernible:

As far as the script is concerned, I had the opportunity [to discuss it] personally with Vladimir Ilyich who, without raising any fundamental objection to the making of such a film, expressed his view that, bearing in mind our continuing struggle, both inside the country and in particular in the international arena, and the many facets of our Bolshevik activity, the time had not yet come to speak quite openly, even in a work of fiction or a film . . . Clearly, after what Lenin had said, I felt that it would be wrong for me to proceed to the production of my script and I showed my script to nobody apart from Mikhail Olminsky.[61]

Voyevodin felt that the time had come by 1939 to make films about the life of the leader of the Revolution and he undertook to freshen up his project in a new version.

He never received an answer to his suggestion and his testimony as eye-witness and participant in the history of the Revolution had by that time become an irrelevant detail. The myth of the leader had been given its full-blooded formulation by other masters who had proudly declared that 'by making films about the Great October Socialist Revolution and its leader, Soviet cinema has responded to the deepest requirements of the Soviet audience and has demonstrated the ideological and creative maturity of its masters'.[62] Thus it was that the man who had laid the foundation stone for the myth of the leader fell by the wayside.

Chapter 3

The 1930s and 1940s: cinema in context

Maya Turovskaya

THE CULTURAL CONTEXT: A PHENOMENOLOGICAL DESCRIPTION[1]

The cultural situation in the USSR in the 1930s and 1940s is usually studied in the context of the dominant totalitarian doctrine of these decades. This was consolidated organisationally by the First Congress of Soviet Writers and the establishment of the Union of Writers and theoretically by the formulation of the normative postulates of Socialist Realism, which extended to all art forms. These postulates were certainly nominally dominant: they furnished the basis for teaching in schools and higher education institutions, served as the criteria for the work of publishers and journals and for numerous 'officially approved' works in the figurative arts, stage shows, films, etc. At the institutional level – be it the organs of state power (the Committee of Artistic Affairs and its offshoots), the Party, or leading public organisations (such as the creative trades unions) – ideology 'commanded' the kind of culture in which it had an interest. But did ideology in fact take hold of the entire gamut of culture as it actually functioned on a day-to-day basis in society?

Alexander Herzen once said that there was only one salvation from bad Russian laws and that was to carry them out equally badly. This applies in full to the sphere of ideology. It could 'command' culture at its 'point of departure' and check up on it at its 'point of exit', but the real presence of culture in society was only partially subordinated to this dictate. In actual fact culture was more complex, more multilayered and more 'pluralistic', as people say nowadays. We must remember that, even officially, Soviet society was still considered to be a 'class society' right up to the Stalin Constitution of 1936. If we are to reflect its practice more exactly, it would be more correct to call it 'multistructured'. Powerful processes of population migration were at work in society in the 1930s: both forced ('dekulakisation') and natural, geographical and social (urbanisation). In the process of the formation of the Soviet Party-state numerous transitional microconditions emerged. People who had yesterday been peasants went into the factories and studied in the technical colleges alongside the children of 'white-collar workers', who in turn were excluded from institutions of higher education because of their social origin: it was easier for a worker or a peasant to obtain higher education. From amongst the 'dekulakised' peasantry came the 'domestic servants', without whom it is impossible to imagine life in the 1930s. These Soviet 'Arina Rodyonovnas'[2] brought their rustic preconceptions into the home; they took the children to church and even had them secretly christened. On the other hand the 'disenfranchised' people who had once 'been somebody' went to work in official institutions, bringing their culture with them, or taught music and foreign languages to children. Music lessons, nursery governesses and German-language groups were just as typical of the time as domestic servants. In everyday life there remained many areas of private enterprise, such as suburban milk ladies, tailors and cobblers. The composition of the Party and state leadership changed. Workers who had been promoted [*vydvizhentsy*] took the place of revolutionaries with experience of pre-Revolutionary underground work. Vertical mobility in society was in fact much greater than it is today. Society was crisscrossed in all directions by these marginal groups, these petty strata, who were in addition forced to coexist in communal flats where they were only rarely able to choose their neighbours by voluntarily giving up part of their own accommodation; they usually had strangers imposed upon them. After all, even Eisenstein lived in one room in the once huge flat of Dr Strauch.[3]

Everyday life was, like these different social groups, thrown into the melting pot. The village brought to the town country amusements such as outdoor singsongs and dancing to the accordion in the yards and areas around the communal flats, customs which still exist today on the periphery of the big cities. Utopian socialism was realised here and there in the form of Constructivist clubs, communal houses (which very soon became hostels) and factory kitchens. But, on the whole, daily life consisted of the remnants of pre-Revolutionary material culture – in the village more than in the town, and in the provinces more than in the capital.

It may be supposed that life in the 1930s was morally without direction, at least from the point of view of guiding values. But the environment of material objects also forms part of any culture and shapes aesthetic norms and criteria, if not on the conscious, then at least on the deeper, unconscious level. However 'futuristic' (focused on the future) *consciousness* is, *emotion* values the commonplace and canonises the familiar. The theoretical aspiration for the future, on the one hand, and practical entrenchment in the past, on the other, constituted one of the many paradoxes of social consciousness in the 1930s.

This was not confined solely to material culture. A similar paradox arose from the yawning gulf between the extremely high level of *personal* morality (a creative attitude towards work, honesty) and the unprecedented cynicism of *public* life. This was not just a question of blind belief and enthusiasm, nor mere fear. It was a matter of this same duality – theoretical aspirations for the future and practical entrenchment in Christian morality, which in turn was much more conservative than consciousness. In order to understand this we must introduce the concept of a moral seam that is gradually being exhausted.[4]

There was also the range of reading matter that was available. The collections of private and public libraries retained the accumulations of different epochs including the 1920s (the volumes produced by the celebrated Academia Press, the translated literature of ZIF, etc.[5]). But quantitatively these collections consisted largely of pre-Revolutionary publications. At the turn of the century, book and journal publishing had developed rapidly and enabled people of average means to collect books. So there was a wide and diffuse range of material available to the reading public, which in turn influenced their cultural interests.

Hence, before we talk about cultural attitudes, we must introduce one further concept: the seam of material culture. The ecology of culture (as of nature) depends upon its complex composition, its profusion of resources and, quite simply, its capacity. Whereas the Russian cultural stratum was in many ways deformed and ruined by the Revolution, it was at the same time essentially augmented and enhanced by it. What is more, the shake-up in daily life made it, in a certain sense, more visible. In the 1930s this material-cultural seam was in any case no more exhausted than were natural resources.

At the crossroads between the generations and at breaks between the social strata culture functioned radially from the ideological centre through the educational and training system (the network of Party education, all sorts of 'circles' and programmes like the 'GTO complex',[6] the press, etc.) but it also functioned in scattered units at the grass roots. In fact the autonomy of the micro-institutions (from children's groups, the Leningrad journals *Yozh* and *Chizh*,[7] particular schools and amateur theatrical groups up to organisations like the humanities-based Institute for Philology, Literature and History and the half-destroyed scientific schools) was relatively great at the beginning of the 1930s and diminished more gradually than the totalitarian authorities would have liked. Hence for instance the various ideological 'campaigns' (like that for the destruction of 'Formalism', for example) in the mid 1930s.

Thus, culture in the 1930s was not poverty-stricken: it was rich, multilayered and complex. Unification (including unification of perception) had not yet been achieved: it was a process that was stretched out in practice to the end of the Brezhnev era. Within this process various orientations functioned on both the general everyday and individual level, without any public declarations or manifestos.

The escapist conservative tradition was noticeable: it was orientated towards the beginning of the century and the ideals of the classics, and it was still embodied in living people who were the bearers of that culture and in the museums and 'old' theatres like the Bolshoi and the Moscow Art Theatre. The tradition of the half-destroyed 'avant-garde', wanting to 'make a new life', was still alive, with its orientation towards new ways of living, towards Revolutionary art, towards the theatre of Meyerhold and our distinguished montage cinema.

Strange as it may seem, in my generation there emerged a decisive rejection of anything connected with the Revolution, not only of its forms (say in music or in painting) but also of the whole complex of its ideas. This was a kind of 'neo-escapism' and as a result literary and theatrical tastes were distinctly conservative, looking to the culture of the 'Silver Age', the Moscow Art Theatre and Bulgakov.[8] These conservative orientations were also a result of cultural autarky. We knew little about other cultures, and 'Westernising' orientations were also by their very nature escapist.

There was of course also the widespread, low-level, 'petty-bourgeois' culture with all its attributes, from the accordion to little rugs with swans on them,[9] which only very gradually, reluctantly and partially fused with official mass culture and exercised a permanent influence on it. This phenomenon has existed right up to the present day.

It is only against this heterogeneous background that we can study the establishment of the official culture of the period from the 1930s to the 1950s, which replaced that of the 1920s. The change of paradigm, which had a universal character, was accompanied by a shift towards totalitarian structures. Autarky (that unique construction, the Iron Curtain, was erected) and monopolisation became the 'objective circumstances'. Cinema, in particular, with the abolition of the last remnants of private enterprise in production and distribution at the beginning of the 1930s, became a complete state monopoly.

The culture of the period from the 1930s to the 1950s, which began to take shape when the avant-garde of the 1910s and 1920s was in decline, was, at first naturally and then forcibly, orientated towards stabilisation, which in time was complemented by a complex of 'restoration' – the expression 'Stalinist Empire' is no accident.

Universalism and the construction of a new way of life, the rejection of the past in favour of the Utopia of the future, and deconstruction, the search for new forms, pluralism and the competition between the 'isms', involvement in the world cultural process – all these gave way to pragmatism, to the embodiment of the idea of the imperial state, to unity of method ('Socialist Realism'), to an orientation towards the past: the legacy of the classics, the search for national roots, the ideal of beauty, popular accessibility, clear plot structures and the image of 'living man'.

Step by step this state hierarchy became entrenched in the arts. In 1936 titles were introduced for actors such as 'Honoured Artist' and later

'People's Artist'; in 1941 Stalin Prizes of various classes were established for cultural figures. In 1935 Mayakovsky was posthumously granted the official status of 'the Best and Most Talented'; the centenary of Pushkin's death in 1937 was celebrated with political pomp.[10] The Moscow Art Theatre – which until the end of the 1920s had retained the character of a private company – became not just an academic theatre but also the model theatre for the country as a whole; Stanislavsky's 'Method' was integrated into the framework of Socialist Realism.

The performing arts were, generally speaking, the most favoured in those days: they constituted the façade of the period. It was a time when the Bolshoi Theatre really flourished: both the ballet and opera corps performed with brilliant companies. The emphasis on might and majesty, even if it did not promote the modernisation of these court genres, at least proved beneficial for the grand style of Marina Semyonova in the ballet and Mark Reizen in the opera. International prizes for musicians such as Emil Gilels and David Oistrakh confirmed this same grand style. Yevgeni Mravinsky's hallmarks as a conductor were also might and majesty. The performer's craft was in its turn the 'favourite of the era'.

The national republics, irrespective of their traditions, were obliged to reproduce the same pyramid: if the particular national culture had no tradition of opera or ballet, one was conjured up like a homunculus. In the drama theatre cultures based on different languages and even different faiths found in Shakespeare something in common which was 'consonant' with the epoch. *Othello*, for example, became a classic for a variety of cultures. These are, of course, just a few examples, but they are symptomatic.

The reintroduction of military ranks (Marshal in 1935, General in 1940), the revival of dress uniforms, of epaulettes and of rituals marked the rebirth of the imperial idea. On the level of the 'living man' who was restored by the art of the 1930s, this meant that his interests had to coincide with the interests of the state, or, if they did not completely coincide, they had at least to harmonise. They had to be sacrificed – right up to their own self-sacrifice – if the state required it. Any conflict with declared public interests, any non-convergence or even deviation was constituted into the universal figure of the 'enemy of the people', who, according to the well-known formula, was destined for elimination. Such was the simple but wide-ranging algorithm of art in the 1930s. But it should not be forgotten that it did not emerge fully armed from the head of Zeus, but came out of the crucible of the so-called 'reforging' process; and that, on the common human scale of valour, exploits and glory, the ability to sacrifice oneself (and others) in the name of a higher ideal had always been one of the most attractive notions; might and majesty were seductive to the artistic imagination.

These, in very general terms, were the parameters of official culture.

While it was deliberately and officially hierarchical (actors in academic theatres received higher pay than those in ordinary theatres, for instance, and actors with titles received more than ordinary actors), this culture was nonetheless orientated towards the idea of popular accessibility and, in that sense, towards homogeneity. People lived in cramped conditions in communal flats; special 'supplies' still continued to exist even after the end of the rationing system (which had also been hierarchical with its 'A' and 'B' categories, etc.[11]), but in theory everyone had equal rights. The idea of equality was realised through the mechanism of a unique kind of representation, formulated in the words of the popular song: 'When the country orders us to become heroes, any one of us can become a hero.'

Groups of collective-farm shockworkers and of Stakhanovites passed through the Kremlin and were given the opportunity to go to the ballet, opera and drama. The best representatives (the heroes) might be provided with cars or individual flats, whether they were polar explorers, pilots, Stakhanovites or distinguished musicians. The 'wedding-cake' skyscrapers or the post-war showcase reconstruction of Gorky Street in their own way 'represented' the construction of living space for the people. The All-Union Agricultural Exhibition (later the All-Union Exhibition of Economic Achievements) was established with its sections and national pavilions for the display of the greatest achievements of the collective farms.[12]

The method of Socialist Realism – what really was plus what ought to be – provided a means for comparing art with reality without anguish: the might of the state and the level of its 'best representatives' personified each and every one. This was a symbolic culture, a compensatory mechanism, which had worked with enviable effect in the case of large-scale prefabricated buildings.[13] This Stalinist culture was not the caprice of one man, or even of a clique. It embodied all the hallmarks of totalitarianism – the similarity to German practice is not accidental – hence, like all large-scale systems, it had its own logic of development.

In fact there was of course never that unity or homogeneity of culture ordained by the First Congress of Soviet Writers, because such a thing can never exist. As I have already suggested, the culture of the period from the 1930s to the 1950s was more than merely officially hierarchical. Like any system it was structured vertically and horizontally. Along the horizontal lines were art, science, performance, design, fashion, comfort, etc.; and it was structured vertically inside each sub-system. Even though the Meyerhold Theatre offered free tickets to shockworkers, even though the Moscow Art Theatre 'adopted' a factory, society was nevertheless in reality divided into cultural strata, into communities and groups that demanded their 'own' culture, including very high culture. This 'own' culture, as always, fulfilled a variety of different functions. It had escapist and socialising functions, compensatory, informative, recreational, prestige, aesthetic, emotional and any other functions you like. It was far from *only* having that

Figure 1 Manufacturing Socialist Realism: filming *Chapayev* (1934) in the summer heat.

Figure 2 Yefim Dzigan filming *We from Kronstadt* (1936).

agitational-mobilisational and, worse still, that 'eye-wash' function that people sometimes imagine today was the case. In addition, it simply helped people to survive. Everyone had their 'own' culture and their 'own' art exactly like that old recipe of Kozma Prutkov:

> Some may think Berlin is great,
> But I prefer Medyn . . .
> To you horseradish tastes as sweet
> As raspberries and cream . . .[14]

Individual factors naturally came into play here: family traditions, educational level, actual opportunities, the chance factor of environment, and so on. Of course all these subcultures led a semi-legal existence on the frontiers of totalitarian culture. If they did not have their *samizdat*, there were at least 'informal' relationships which were sometimes very curious. It goes without saying that they were all in one way or another deformed by totalitarian culture.

A purely personal example will illustrate the point. The universal obligation to a single philosophy and aesthetic theory taught me and many of my generation to avoid philosophy and theory and to keep 'close to fact', to use Dostoyevsky's phrase, and to look for general ideas in areas other than the humanities, for instance in the books of Einstein, Nils Bohr, Schrödinger and Freud. Of course this is a fundamental deformation, just like that loathing of quotations and of Aesopian language that our entire once-censored culture now suffers from, just as divers suffer from the 'bends' when they surface too quickly. However, if these subcultural phenomena had not existed, it would now be impossible to re-establish the links between different epochs and to make any further progress.

The study of totalitarian cultures as systems has now become practicable, not only factually, but also emotionally. This is an important task because their mechanisms are still active and the temptations to revive them are enormous.

AUDIENCE PREFERENCES IN THE 1930s

> The public's taste will not be improved by purging films of tastelessness, but the films will get worse. Because who knows what gets thrown out along with the tastelessness? The bad taste of the public has deeper roots in reality than has the taste of intellectuals . . .
>
> Bertolt Brecht[15]

The elucidation of audiences' film preferences in the 1930s is an extremely complex problem for two disparate reasons. The 1930s were specifically a period of practical monopoly over the production and distribution of films in conditions of almost complete autarky. The importation as well as exportation of films was reduced to a minimum. The Soviet Union opted out of the world film process and inside the country Soviet films experienced virtually no competition. Distribution ceased to be 'patchy' and became unified and 'linear': the number of titles per week fell sharply as the number of cinemas increased. So the audience had almost no choice: they had to watch what was offered. The change in the pattern of distribution over the decade makes this clear:

Year	No. of Cinemas	No. of Titles per Week		
		(Total)	(Soviet)	(Foreign)
1927	17,000	31	11	20
1937	31,000	11	11	0

In the 1920s what the state offered was still determined by economic considerations: club distribution for Revolutionary films, 'workers'' cinemas, cut-price tickets, special collective screenings, touring shows and so on. But in the 1930s there were no alternatives to what the state supplied. Audience penetration became much more complete but choice was more restricted. We can therefore formulate the situation of the audience in the 1930s as follows: *given a general shortage of entertainment facilities* (cafés, dance halls, 'parks of culture', sports grounds, etc.) *it was not specific films but cinema as a whole that became the target of increased demand.* As a result – in a situation in which 'everybody saw everything' – it is objectively much more difficult to isolate the indices of actual audience preferences.

The second problem is more specific, but is unfortunately also difficult to overcome. It is connected with the permanent 'secrecy' about statistical data, the chaotic storage of archival documents, the 'purges' of the archives and, quite simply, their inefficiency. The search for figures is like producing radium: 'a year of labour for a gram of output' and it depends mainly on the researcher's luck. That is why our statistics on the 1930s are for the moment very incomplete. In the final analysis it will not be *absolute* figures that interest us so much as *relative* ones. We hope to be able to provide a fairly full picture of the film process, providing information for each film on its distribution (in 'screen-days') and the income it generated (in roubles). Thus we hope to rank films in accordance with audience 'demand'. The research is, however, not yet completed but these tentative methodological comments need to be made.

The phenomenon of Soviet cinema in the 1930s as 'the most democratic of all the arts' was not born in a vacuum and was not self-generated. It was preceded by more general processes. First, the global change in cultural paradigms: leadership everywhere passed from the avant-garde of the 'roaring twenties' to a stabilised type of consciousness; that is to narrative, 'generally accessible' structures in art as a whole. Second, the technical revolution associated with the arrival and mastering of sound made this process in the cinema particularly inevitable and obvious.

In the Soviet Union the beginning of the 1930s was a turning point in various ways. In the social sphere, the peasantry was destroyed. In the economic sphere, the process of the industrialisation of the country on a monopoly basis was inaugurated. In the political sphere, the path was laid for the seizure of power by one man. In the ideological sphere, the ideas of the Revolution had to yield pride of place to the notion of imperial might and majesty.

In these circumstances a new paradigm of Soviet cinema emerged. As early as 1927 the future monopolistic structure had been formulated in an anonymous report in a fairly programmatic way:

> The critics attack those films that drive the workers and the progressive part of the intelligentsia into raptures . . . The slogan of Soviet cinema enterprises is: 'Our films must be 100 per cent ideologically correct and 100 per cent commercially viable.' Soviet film must be highly profitable. It can only be an instrument of Communist enlightenment if it is accepted by the audience with pleasure. We therefore declare that the 'commercially profitable film' and the 'ideologically correct film' are not mutually exclusive categories but rather complementary to one another.[16]

'Full servicing of the film market', according to the author of the report, required no fewer than 200 feature films a year. However, as the actual resources were only sufficient for fifteen to twenty properly produced films, these would also have to be ideologically successful. The remaining mass of cheaper pictures would have to be 'of a predominantly entertaining character'.

Thus, as the New Economic Policy (NEP) drew to a close, the author of the report outlined the future 'model' – as we would say nowadays – for a commercially profitable and ideologically effective cinema. This model foresaw not only the basic principles and quantitative indicators, but also the hierarchy of film types:

> The principal place in the repertoire must be occupied by heroic pictures. The aim of these films is to mobilise the masses. The second place must go to pictures on the problems of everyday life in the transitional epoch . . . In third place – less significant but more numerous – should be entertainment pictures, the aim of which . . . should be to attract the masses to cinema . . . to fight against the more harmful leisure activities of the population such as drunkenness, hooliganism and so on.[17]

In fact this change of paradigms, at a time when the class struggle was being overtly intensified, took on the sinister character of the 'destruction of Formalism', reaching a peak in cinema with the All-Union Creative Conference of Soviet Cinema Workers in January 1935. With the monopoly of production and distribution finally achieved, ideology acquired a decisive pre-eminence over economics. In qualitative terms, this was expressed by marginalising 'popular film' and gradually excluding it from the film process. In quantitative terms, it meant a general reduction in the number of titles.

At the end of the 1920s and beginning of the 1930s the highest feature film production figures were achieved: in 1927 – 119 films; in 1928 – 124; in 1930 – a record 128 films were produced. But 1933 shows a sharp decline with the production of only twenty-nine films.[18] The number of films produced in a year never again reached a hundred in the period until Stalin's death in 1953 and it varied on average from about four to five dozen. The fateful year 1937 provides a classic figure in this respect, with forty films. In the post-war years production fell to an average of two dozen films, reaching an absolute minimum in the late 1940s and early 1950s (the so-called period of 'film shortage' [malokartin'e]) during the next 'intensification of the class struggle'. Thus, in 1947 twenty-three films were produced, in 1950 only thirteen, and in 1951 a record low of nine.

This reduction in film output occurred at the expense of production in the second and third official film categories (everyday life and entertainment pictures, respectively) outlined in the theoretical model of 100 per cent ideologically reliable and 100 per cent commercially profitable production as proposed in 1927. In fact this model was never actually achieved. At the All-Union Conference on Thematic Planning in the transitional year 1933, Boris Shumyatsky, the head of GUKF [the Principal Directorate for the Cinema and Photographic Industry], labelled the 'quantitative drive' a 'left-wing error' and even 'sabotage', and named a number of films in which 'entertainment value . . . had been divorced from ideological content and become an aim in itself'.[19] Those films were taken out of circulation. As a result of this wilful decision by GUKF, even as commercial a studio as Mezhrabpom was unable to recover its expenditure on production and suffered losses on 'entertainment' films. For instance, the studio lost 163,100 roubles on Yuri Zhelyabuzhsky's Prosperity [Prosperiti, 1933] and 312,900 roubles on Kuleshov's Gorizont [1933]. Thus the relationship between ideology and profitability was in practice and for the duration decided in favour of ideology. In this situation Shumyatsky's idea for the establishment of a Soviet Hollywood could not be achieved, and withered away with his demise in 1938.

Nevertheless, 'entertainment value' became an essential element of the new paradigm, although this had no connection with communicability (i.e. popularity as measured by attendance). After the 1933 conference mentioned above, 'the leading model for entertainment film' was officially acknowledged to be Yutkevich and Ermler's Counterplan [Vstrechnyi, 1932] which, in the terminology of 1927, dealt with 'the problems of everyday life in the transition period' and which was made 'by special instruction of the Central Committee of the Party for the fifteenth anniversary of the October Revolution'. In his report Shumyatsky also provided the following definition: 'By the entertainment value of a film we mean the considerable emotional effect it exerts and the simple artistry that *rapidly and easily communicates its ideological content and its plot to the mass audience*' [emphasis added].

For the moment we do not know whether *Counterplan* really became the favourite of the mass audience. Let us therefore look at the case of Nikolai Ekk's *The Path to Life* [Putevka v zhizn', 1931] – the Mezhrabpom studio's ultimate hit. It represented a sketch, a preliminary outline, of the specific relationships being established in the 1930s between the mass audience and cinema as a power in the land.

The Mezhrabpom studio had originally been founded on the basis of mixed Russian and German private capital as Mezhrabpom-Rus in 1923. From the very beginning it had been orientated towards profitability and export, and to some extent it retained this image of a 'joint-stock company' even in the new conditions. In its Rus period it numbered among its productions many commercial successes, such as Fyodor Otsep's three-part *Miss Mend* [1926], which earned 3,201,000 roubles; Konstantin Eggert's *The Lame Gentleman* [Khromoi barin, 1928], which made 1,346,000 roubles; Yuri Zhelyabuzhsky's *Dina Dzadzu* [1926], making 1,056,000 roubles; Lev Kuleshov's *The Two Buldis* [Dva-Buldi-Dva, 1929], 863,000 roubles; Yakov Protazanov's *The Man from the Restaurant* [Chelovek iz restorana, 1927], 852,000 roubles; and Eggert's *The Bear's Wedding* [Medvezh'ya svad'ba, 1925], 829,000 roubles.[20] This was the debit side of the success of 'petty-bourgeois films'. But there was also an accumulation of ideological films that had produced respectable commercial results, with such classics of Soviet cinema as Vsevolod Pudovkin's *The Mother* [Mat', 1926], which earned 556,000 roubles; his *Storm over Asia* [Potomok Chingis-khana, 1928], which made 537,000 roubles; and Protazanov's *The Forty-First* [Sorok pervyi, 1926], which brought in 516,000 roubles. The studio had the very best technical equipment including sound and it entered the new decade as the first to achieve the new paradigm: ideology plus profitability plus sound. *The Path to Life*, made on the orders of the Cheka, had earned 2,883,500 roubles for the studio by 1935.[21]

In analysing the studio's exceptional success with this film, however, the grain has once again to be officially separated from the chaff:

> The unprecedented success of *The Path to Life* did not depend on a few thieves' songs or the unfortunate scene with the drinking bout, as some have tried to argue, but on the subject matter and on the extremely powerful effect of simple but extremely dramatic and ideologically charged situations . . .[22]

The plight of many thousands of homeless children, orphaned during the Revolution and Civil War [*besprizornichestvo*], constituted a social drama that offered many opportunities to cinema and a vast number of plots and visual elements essential to the establishment of a mass genre 'store' of films, albeit with a didactic content; moreover, *The Path to Life* was the first Soviet sound film and this undoubtedly determined its exceptional success, even though by 1934 only 300 (or 1 per cent) of the 30,000 film projectors in the country were sound projectors. Films had to be made either as silent pictures or in silent versions: the well-known example of Mikhail Romm's Maupassant adaptation *Boule de Suif* [Pyshka, 1934] was not an exception. However, the trail blazed by Ekk's film was not explored further: no more films were made about these homeless children. The potential of the subject matter and the visual elements already 'explored' by the film, which went against the declared paradigm of 'entertainment value', were neither added to the armoury nor mastered. Instead they remained the attributes of an isolated case.

This was typical of the non-commercial model of cinema. The enormous potential for social criticism that this subject matter provided disappeared – along with the unrealised profits – into the sand. This is particularly obvious if we make a comparison with the commercial production model of cinema in the USA in a similar situation. During the period of Prohibition, the bootleggers became the same kind of social ulcer in America as the homeless children in post-Revolutionary Russia. A whole genre of gangster films was built around the bootlegger theme. With *Little Caesar* [USA, 1930] and its successor films, Warner Brothers not only made profits but also mastered the principles of the genre.

A genre-based mass cinema cannot emerge without continuity, without the elaboration of canons and methods, without a star system, and without everything that constitutes what we call the 'film industry'. It cannot consist simply of isolated instances of films by *auteurs*. Who knows what classics and what perspectives were lost to Soviet cinema when it failed to make use of the lessons of *The Path to Life*?

The only exceptions in the practice of the non-commercial and predominantly ideological Soviet cinema were films about the Revolution. As early as 1927 it had been proclaimed that 'heroic films must take first place in the repertoire' and that the aim of these films should be 'to mobilise the consciousness of the masses'. These heroic films, first and foremost, turned the principal focus for social criticism towards the past: as a result, numerous 'enemies of the people' were to be granted the status of 'birth-marks of capitalism'. Second, these films exchanged real history for required legend – and mythologised it.

It was in precisely this genre of legend that Soviet cinema was most successful, creating both a canon and a continuity, elaborating the stereotypes and methods that could later be transplanted to any time and place, for instance in the biographical films about Russian military commanders. It is in precisely this genre that we can also detect the 'serialism' peculiar to mass cinema (in the Maxim trilogy, for instance, in the Leniniana and later in the Staliniana),[23] which established the desired 'image of the hero' as well as the 'image of the enemy' that was necessary to his canonisation.

For this reason, therefore, we suggest that the historical-Revolutionary film not only represented a permanent category in the thematic plan but was also a genre in the fullest sense, in fact '*the* chosen genre of Soviet cinema' to use Bazin's expression.[24] It was here that ideology and commerce could finally meet and here that cinema could give them both of its best. The Vasiliev 'brothers'' *Chapayev* [Chapaev, 1934] revealed the formula for audience success that survived every succeeding decade right up to the 1980s.[25]

In the history of Soviet cinema *Chapayev* is usually considered in terms of the historical-Revolutionary film and its genre origins are overlooked. However, in terms of its structure – from primeval chaos to order – and in terms of its narrative conception, *Chapayev* is close to a conventional Western.[26] In this sense it could therefore be called an 'Eastern'. Both structures rely on the canons of the adventure genre developed over the centuries. The combination of the document – in the shape of Furmanov's book – and the canon of this genre created the phenomenon of *Chapayev*. The film was not conceived at all as a 'hit'. Indeed in the thematic plan for 1934 it was characterised as a run-of-the-mill 'defence film'. But it also became the first experiment in monopoly state supply, signalled by the famous leading article in *Pravda* on 21 November 1934: 'The Whole Country is Watching *Chapayev*.'[27]

The spontaneous audience reaction to the genre's successful formula was used for an extensive propaganda campaign:

> The film *Chapayev* develops into a political phenomenon . . . The Party has been given a new and powerful means of educating the class consciousness of the young . . . Hatred for the enemy, combined with a rapturous admiration for the heroic memory of the warriors who fell for the Revolution [*sic!*], acquires the same strength as a passionate love for the socialist motherland.[28]

The distribution policy that was to lie at the basis of the new structure of the film process and that has lasted far beyond the confines of the 1930s was also determined – the prevalence of supply over demand.

> The whole country is watching *Chapayev*. It is being reproduced in hundreds of copies for the sound screen. Silent versions will also be made so that *Chapayev* will be shown in every corner of our immense country: in the towns and villages, the collective farms and settlements, in barracks, clubs and squares.[29]

For a long time the number of copies of a particular title, determined in an arbitrary and bureaucratic manner, was given priority over the number

Figure 3 Cinema in context: *Chapayev* and *The Youth of Maxim* (both 1934) vying for audience attention in Kazan, 1935.

Figure 4 Peasants carted in to see *We from Kronstadt* (1936).

of titles overall. We have not yet fully researched the question of the export of Soviet films, or indeed the import of a small number of films in a context of almost complete autarky, but the surviving members of the 1930s audience can count those imported films on their fingers. Leaving aside the two Chaplin films, *City Lights* [USA, 1931] and *Modern Times* [USA, 1936], importation was fairly haphazard. The level of popularity of any foreign film could be seen from everyday fashion: for instance, the shape and name of the 'Malen'kaya Mama' hat which was popular right up to the war, was borrowed from Hermann Kosterlitz's film *Little Mummy* [Kleine Mutti, Austria/Hungary, 1934], starring Francesca Gaal.[30]

The transformation of cinema, like vodka, into a state monopoly,[31] the conferring on it of a propagandistic, predominantly didactic status, the universal 'indoctrination' of even those residual genre structures (the odd isolated comedy, one or two musicals, etc.) that had been relegated to the margins of the film process, and, lastly, the prevalence of arbitrary supply over demand in a situation where there was a general shortage of entertainment at the end of the decade – all these factors exerted a greater influence on audience demand than we might have expected.

In principle the audience's 'alternative taste' (a term that we have used in preference to the art scholar's notion of 'bad taste') was fairly stable. If we accept the semi-market situation of the 1920s in Soviet cinema as the norm, then the end of the 1930s shows the greatest divergence from it, not only due to the presence of politics in cinema, but also because of the general destabilisation of public consciousness.[32]

On the occasion of the next Revolutionary Jubilee in 1937 the parameters of audience demand demonstrated a noticeable shift. This was the only time when the leading films in terms of distribution were those that were recognised as representing artistic standards and, by force of circumstances, they became the ideological watchwords of the time: Mikhail Romm's *Lenin in October* [Lenin v oktyabre, 1937],[33] Eisenstein's *Alexander Nevsky* [Aleksandr Nevskii, 1938], and Romm's *Lenin in 1918* [Lenin v 1918 godu, 1939]. Ideological, aesthetic and box-office criteria coincided, revealing a genuine 'moral and political unity' in society.[34]

It is necessary here to introduce some precision into the concept of 'mass demand'. It was indeed 'mass' in so far as it manifested itself as box-office demand: i.e. it expressed itself through economic indicators. Yet – and this is particularly true in the context of a non-economic structure oblivious to marketing – it was at the same time very private, serving personal and even intimate needs. It is for this reason that, even in totalitarian conditions, mass demand could not simply be equated with state supply, no matter how arbitrary the latter was.

For this reason we have tried as far as possible in our project to clarify another differentiating indicator which acts as a corrective in calculating the index of the popularity of a film: this is the turnover per copy of the film. It is an essential indicator as it signifies demand only, independently of – and sometimes in contradiction to – supply, and it demonstrates that, even in the most monopolistic model, supply and demand, however closely they coincided, were nevertheless not identical. Viewers had their own private demands which, however microscopic, were not the same as those of the state.

When we use this indicator, we find that the leading titles are often those which are almost unknown in the history of Soviet cinema. In the Jubilee year 1937, for instance, *Lenin in October* was far outstripped by Artashes Ai-Artyan's little-known film *Karo*. *Lenin in October* made 774,600 roubles from 955 copies, giving a turnover of 767 roubles per copy, while *Karo* made 355,900 roubles from 198 copies, giving a turnover of 1,797 roubles per copy. *Karo* was an Armenian screen version of the short story *The School* by Arkadi Gaidar. It was a run-of-the-mill historical-Revolutionary film with a plot like a Western, magnificent 'adventure-film' mountain landscapes, with recognisable film references (mostly to *Chapayev*, right down to the girl machine-gunner) and a young hero who was easy to identify with. There is no doubt that young people of a similar age went to see the film over and over again. This is confirmed by the fact that following *Karo* in turnover per copy was another film for young people, Vladimir Legoshin's *The Lone White Sail* [Beleet parus odinokii, 1937]. Thus, the most active youth audience of all time was true not to fashion, but to nature, to common human values fixed in the stereotypes of the genre.

In 1938 the overtly ideological film *Alexander Nevsky* came first according to both indicators (it was Eisenstein's only box-office success), even though the same year saw the release of Grigori Alexandrov's comedy *Volga-Volga*, *The Vyborg Side* [Vyborgskaya storona], the third part of Kozintsev and Trauberg's Maxim trilogy, and Sergei Yutkevich's *The Man with a Gun* [Chelovek s ruzh'em]. But Vaska Buslai and Gavrila Oleksich, the folk-tale costume heroes of the battle-piece film, became characters in children's games just like Chapayev. This demonstrates yet again that a film becomes a hit when it satisfies deeper, non-aesthetic demands.

The phenomenon of the end of the 1930s, a maximum convergence between the three criteria – ideological, aesthetic and mass appeal – has never been repeated in the history of Soviet cinema. The war produced a noticeable 'privatisation' of demand, which corresponded to Vasili Grossman's paradoxical notion of the liberation of the inner world of Soviet man in extreme conditions.[35] In the portentous year of 1945 the top place among films was taken by Vladimir Petrov's *Guilty without Fault* [Bez viny vinovatye], a classical, theatrical melodrama which had no connection with the war whatsoever.[36] Its turnover per copy was only exceeded by Alexander Ivanovsky's artistically weak screen version of the operetta *Silva* [1944]. Films of all genres that were in any way connected with the war trailed behind: they included Friedrich Ermler's *The Great Turning-Point*

[Velikii perelom], Abram Room's *Invasion* [Nashestvie], even Sigismund Navrotsky's adventure film *Sigmund Kolosovsky* [Zigmund Kolosovskii, 1945] and Semyon Timoshenko's comedy *The Heavenly Sloth* [Nebesnyi tikhokhod]. Mass taste was never again to coincide with state supply.

From 1947 to 1949 the system of cinema autarky was, however, broken down in the most paradoxical way: so-called 'booty' films, captured from the Goebbels archive, were thrown into Soviet distribution on a mass scale, without subtitles and often under different names. They were mostly German films but the haul did include American films like Raoul Walsh's *The Roaring Twenties* [USA, 1939] (which was released as *The Fate of a Soldier in America* [Sud'ba soldata v Amerike]) and one of the *Tarzan* films. Given the small number of Soviet titles at that period, the share of these foreign films in distribution was enormous. Whereas in 1947 the four German films in circulation represented only 17 per cent of the twenty-three Soviet titles released, in 1948 the fourteen German titles constituted 82 per cent of the seventeen Soviet films, and in 1949 the seventeen German titles represented 94 per cent of the eighteen Soviet titles.

Thus it was that the 'generation of victors' was brought up on Nazi film production.[37] The basic mass of the films of course belonged to the non-ideological, entertainment genre such as *Snow Fantasy* [Snezhnaya fantaziya, released in the USSR, 1949; originally *Der weisse Traum* (The White Dream), 1943], the undistinguished *The Indian Tomb* [Indiiskaya grobnitsa, released in the USSR, 1948; originally *Das indische Grabmal*, 1938], *The Road to the Scaffold* [Doroga na eshafot] and others. But there were also key ideological films like *Transvaal on Fire* [Transvaal v ogne, released in the USSR, 1948; originally *Ohm Krüger* (Uncle Kruger), 1941] or *A Poet's Calling* [Prizvanie poeta, released in the USSR, 1949; originally *Friedrich Schiller*, 1939]. Alas, they too were accepted without any shame: the ideological message – whether it was revolution or the exposure of British imperialism – was the same.

In 1947 the unforgettable *The Girl of My Dreams* [Devushka moei mechty; originally *Die Frau meiner Träume* (The Woman of My Dreams), 1944], starring Marika Rökk, exceeded the turnover per copy of Boris Barnet's home-made Soviet hit *The Exploits of a Scout* [Podvig razvedchika]. The German film took first place with takings that were nearly five times greater: 103,800 roubles against 22,200 roubles for Barnet's film. Strange as it may seem, this should be seen as a relative normalisation of mass demand. The success of *The Girl of My Dreams* was evidence of the desperate absence of a normal sense of well-being, of a European standard of living (albeit in the style of kitsch) and, finally, of the eroticisation of women. When their own 'mass culture' is catastrophically inadequate, people find what they want where they can.

When the next 'intensification of the class struggle' occurred (on this occasion the struggle with 'rootless cosmopolitans'), the unity of the three criteria within this model – the ideological, the aesthetic and the box-office – was rudely shattered. The state, the intelligentsia and the mass audience had begun to choose different favourites. This laid the foundations for the protracted war between aesthetic criticism and, on the one hand, quasi-officialdom (which was unfortunately conducted only in the corridors until the Fifth Congress of Cinematographers in 1986) and, on the other hand, the 'bad taste' of the public – in the press.

The situation has not changed even now. Familiarity with the world film process (Neo-Realism, the New Wave) has made this 'alternative taste' more obvious. The 1970s passed with box-office success for undistinguished foreign films, such as those imported from India; the earlier, Western model of a film hit has apparently given way to the 'Eastern' model in audience preferences. This speaks volumes about the general condition of our society.

This is how an arbitrary state policy in the field of cinema in the crucial decade of the 1930s caused a deformation of the film process that still affects us to this day. Its key features were: (a) monopolisation; (b) autarky; (c) the establishment of a single model of quasi-popular, propaganda cinema; (d) the unifying perception of the principle of Socialist Realism.

The principal characteristics of this deformation are as follows:

(a) a neglect for the natural, heterogeneous structure of demand – a model of cinema development that had emphasised the aesthetic (spiritual), the political, the entertainment and other functions – and its replacement by a homogeneous model of propagandistic (didactic) quasi-popular cinema, whose ideal embodiment was the great cinema of the 1930s;

(b) a training in one-dimensional didactic perception resting initially on the postulates of Socialist Realism with a requirement 'to verify cinema against life' irrespective of genre. This didactic one-dimensionality in a paradoxical way unites both extremes –the Party state and aesthetic criticism – against 'alternative taste', putting that taste outside the law;

(c) an artificial suppression of the 'popular cinema' that had in the 'market' era been developing as a branch of the industry.

However, insofar as the structure of demand remains heterogeneous, while the foundations of 'alternative taste' are apparently laid much more deeply than we imagine, the real functioning of cinema in society cannot be completely subordinated even to the most arbitrary supply.

I therefore draw the following provisional conclusions:

(a) the mass audience chooses its favourite films more often than not from those foreign cinemas in which popular film is firmly established ('American cinema', 'Indian cinema');

(b) neither Party-state power nor aesthetic criticism nor the cinema audience has any instrument with which to study 'alternative taste';

(c) the current situation in Soviet cinema at the moment of its transition to a new model remains unknown and unknowable.

Chapter 4

Soviet cinema in the age of Stalin[1]

Peter Kenez

At the end of the 1920s Soviet film enjoyed a well-deserved worldwide reputation but within a short time the fame and influence of the great directors was lost: the golden age was brief and the eclipse sudden and long lasting. The coming of the sound film made the famous 'Russian montage' outdated, and it was therefore a factor in the decline. But far more important in destroying the reputation of Soviet cinema were the political changes that took place in the early 1930s.

The New Economic Policy (NEP) system collapsed under the weight of its own contradictions, but what would take its place was not clear even to those who actively participated in its destruction. The change from the cultural pluralism of NEP to orthodox Stalinism came about in two stages. The first period, called by Soviet publicists 'the Cultural Revolution', was a time of genuine enthusiasm on the part of many activists, a revival of the utopian and egalitarian spirit of the Civil War, but also a time of wild anarchy and of destructive attacks on institutions and human beings. By contrast, what followed was a period of vast changes in the social and economic structure of the country, extraordinarily cruel repression, the establishment of a new orthodoxy and with it the creation of a conservative social and artistic order. The artists were cajoled and coerced to come up with principles and methods that would be suitable in the new order. Only rarely were they passive victims: most of the time they actively collaborated.

Although in its golden age Soviet film was widely admired, the Stalinist leadership was dissatisfied. The Bolsheviks considered film to be an excellent instrument for bringing their message to the people, and they intended to use it, more than any other medium of art, for creating the 'new socialist man'. These excessively high expectations were bound to lead to disappointment: films that were artistically successful and made in a Communist spirit did not attract a large enough audience. The Bolsheviks wanted artistically worthwhile, commercially successful and politically correct films. It turned out that these requirements pointed in different directions and no director could possibly satisfy them all.

The Cultural Revolution in cinema aimed to remedy what seemed a major fault to the Bolshevik leaders: the artistically most interesting and experimental works remained inaccessible to simple people. In order to make an impact on workers and peasants, they had, of course, first of all to be attracted to the cinemas. Bolshevik policies brought about some of the desired results and in the course of the 1930s movie-going for the first time became a part of the life of the average citizen. In the 1920s cinema was basically an urban entertainment, whereas the bulk of the population lived in villages. Now the peasantry was coerced into joining collective farms and the collectives were pressured to buy projectors. From 1928 to 1940 the number of installations quadrupled and the number of tickets sold tripled.[2] Soviet industry was also finally successful in producing its own raw film stock, projectors and other equipment. Although the technical quality of Soviet studios remained very much behind the West, this was nonetheless a considerable achievement. The coming of the new sound technology was very attractive to the propagandists, for simple ideas could of course be better conveyed with sound than with images. On the other hand, the technological burden of reorganising the industry was great. Even during the Second World War the Soviet Union was forced to make silent versions of most films, because the industry lacked projectors capable of reproducing sound.[3]

The choice available to movie-goers in the 1930s greatly diminished. The import of foreign films, by far the most successful ones in the previous decade, for all practical purposes stopped. Only a handful of foreign films were shown in the Soviet Union in the 1930s and these were a haphazard collection, by no means the best, the most successful or the most desirable.[4] The number of domestically made films also greatly declined. The industry drew up ambitious plans, explicitly aiming to match the output of Hollywood, but the studios made no more than 20 to 30 per cent of the planned films.[5] While in the late 1920s the industry produced approximately 120–140 films a year, by 1933 the output had declined to thirty-five, and in the rest of the decade it remained stationary. Perhaps there was no other branch of the Soviet economy that remained so far behind the planned targets.

The numerical decline went hand in hand with a reduction of stylistic variety, because Stalinist leaders imposed Socialist Realism on all Soviet artists. Socialist Realism is a simple yet much-debated political-artistic principle. It is best understood in negative terms: by replacing genuine realism with an appearance of realism it prevents the contemplation of the human condition and the investigation of social issues. In order to accomplish its task, Socialist Realist art must have an absolute monopoly, for it must convince the audience that it alone depicts the world as it really is. This art form can exist, therefore, only within a definite political context. No country has ever had Socialist Realist art without at the same time having concentration camps.

Following Katerina Clark, we may establish a master plot that is to be found in Socialist Realist films as well as in Socialist Realist novels.[6] A Socialist Realist novel is always a *Bildungsroman*: that is, it is about the acquisition of consciousness. In the process of fulfilling a task, the hero or heroine, under the tutelage of a Party worker, acquires an increased understanding of self, the surrounding world, the task of building Communism, the class struggle, the need for vigilance, etc. Socialist Realism is middle-brow, formulaic art that excludes irony and, above all, ambiguity. It is bitterly hostile to experimentation with form, for this would impede immediate comprehension by the half-educated and therefore lessen the didactic value of the product. More importantly, stylistic heterodoxy is bound to lead to ambiguity of meaning, and that is something that a totalitarian political order cannot tolerate.

Between 1933 and 1940 inclusive, Soviet studios made 308 films.[7] Of these, fifty-four were made for children, including some of the best films of the decade such as Mark Donskoy's Gorky trilogy of 1938–40. These films were didactic and aimed to educate children in the spirit of Communism by showing the difficult life of children in capitalist countries, their heroic struggle and, most importantly and frequently, the importance of the collective.

Historical spectacles became especially frequent in the second half of the decade, as the régime paid increasing attention to rekindling patriotism by old-fashioned and non-Marxist appeals to national glory. These films were made about heroes such as Prince Alexander Nevsky [dir. Sergei Eisenstein, 1938], Peter the Great [*Peter the First* (Petr Pervyi), dir. Vladimir Petrov, 1937–9] Marshal Suvorov [dir. Vsevolod Pudovkin and Mikhail Doller, 1940] and Pugachev [dir. Pavel Petrov-Bytov, 1937], and they were shamelessly anachronistic. Pugachev and Stenka Razin, two Cossack rebels, are shown, for instance, analysing class relations in Marxist terms and, before their executions, consoling their followers by predicting the coming of a great and victorious revolution. Another film-maker set a Pushkin story in the middle of the Russian Civil War.

Sixty-one films in this period dealt with the Revolution and Civil War. These included such well-known films as *Chapayev* [Chapaev, dir. the Vasiliev 'brothers', 1934], the Maxim trilogy [dir. Grigori Kozintsev and Leonid Trauberg, 1934–8] and *The Baltic Deputy* [Deputat Baltiki, dir. Iosif Kheifits and Alexander Zarkhi, 1937]. Each national republic that had a studio made at least one film on the theme of the establishment of Soviet power.

The rest of the films were set in the contemporary world. Of these only twelve took place in a factory, which is a remarkably small number when one considers the significance of economic propaganda and Stakhanovism on the Soviet agenda. One suspects that directors found it difficult to make interesting films about workers and therefore tended to avoid them. Seventeen films took place on collective farms. In contrast to the construction dramas, these were more likely to be musical comedies. A Soviet person who received all his or her information from movies might have thought that life in the countryside was a round of never-ending dancing and singing. Directors, and presumably audiences, liked exotic locales and therefore a large number of films were made about the exploits of explorers, geologists and pilots. Between 1938 and 1940 alone there were eight films that had pilots as heroes.

The directors lent their talents to the creation of an atmosphere of hysteria and paranoia. A recurring theme in films dealing with contemporary life was the struggle against saboteurs and traitors. It was, after all, an age of denunciations, phoney trials and exposures of unbelievable plots. The scenarios closely resembled the tales of the most vicious story-teller of them all, Andrei Vyshinsky, the Chief Prosecutor at the purge trials. In the films, as in the confessions at the trials, the enemy perpetrated the most dastardly acts out of an unreasoned hatred for decent socialist society. In fifty-two out of the eighty-five films dealing with contemporary life (i.e. more than half) the hero (for it was usually a man) unmasked hidden enemies who had committed criminal acts. The hero could never be too vigilant. The enemy turned out sometimes to be the hero's best friend, sometimes his wife, and sometimes his father.

At the end of the period, in 1940, a curious phenomenon occurred. Of the thirty films dealing with contemporary life in 1940 not one focused on traitors. The internal enemy completely disappeared and was replaced by foreigners or agents of foreigners. The country was preparing to face a foreign foe: instead of ferreting out non-existent internal enemies, the films now preached how the nations making up the Soviet Union must work together for the common good.

All through the 1930s the films depicted the outside world as undifferentiated, threatening and uniformly miserable. In this world, people were starving to death, brutal police were repressing the mighty Communist movement, and the ultimate concern of foreign workers was the defence of the Soviet Union, the motherland of socialism. A recurring theme was that of foreigners coming to the USSR and finding there a happy and rich life. On the basis of these films one might have thought that the Soviet Union found difficulty in keeping out all those people who wanted to come and live there. Twenty films were set entirely or partially outside the Soviet Union. The choice of locales changed to reflect the twists and turns of Soviet foreign policy. Before 1935 an unnamed foreign country was usually portrayed. Ivan Pyriev's *The Conveyor-Belt of Death* [Konveier smerti, 1933], for instance, took place in a generic West: street signs were in English, French and German interchangeably. In Pudovkin's *The Deserter* [Dezertir, 1933], where Germany was specified, not only was there no comment on fascism, but the Social Democrats were depicted as the main enemies of the Communist workers. Six anti-Nazi films were made between 1935 and 1939 after the shift in Comintern policy. The best and most prominent of these were: *Professor Mamlock* [dir. Gerbert Rapoport, 1938] and *The Oppenheim Family* [Sem'ya Oppengeim, dir. Grigori Roshal, 1939].[8] In 1940 audiences could see how the Red Army brought the good life to Ukrainians and Belorussians, just liberated from Polish oppression.

The Bolshevik leaders, dissatisfied with the small output of the studios, reorganised the industry time and again, but nothing seemed to help. Heads of studios and other leading cadres of the industry, including the most important figure, Boris Shumyatsky, became victims of the purges. Constant reorganisation and changes in personnel – caused by the arrests – created chaos. However, the fundamental cause of the decline in the number of films made and exhibited in the Soviet Union was not disorganisation, but the fact that the authorities set ever more difficult requirements for film-makers. Completing a picture in the Soviet Union took several times longer than in the West, and it also took much longer than it had in the 1920s.

We are accustomed to talking about censorship in Soviet cinema. The use of that concept, as it applies to the Stalinist 1930s, is, however, misleading. When we think of censorship we conjure up the image of the artist struggling against a political authority that is limiting his freedom of expression by forbidding the discussion of some topics. What is wrong with this picture? First of all, the problem was not that certain topics could not be discussed, although of course that was true, but that the requirements that the artists had to satisfy were prescriptive. The artists tried to produce works that were in fact essential for maintaining the régime in its given form. It is no exaggeration to say that the Soviet system as we know it could not have existed without Socialist Realism. An alternative reality had to be created to take the place of the unsatisfactory actual reality. Artists of all kinds, but especially film-makers, had a vital role to play.

Second, there was hardly any conflict between the two sides. The régime and the artists combined their talents to produce works that were needed for the maintenance of the system. It is not only that the representatives of the régime and the artists were not enemies: they were collaborators. Artists became state functionaries with a well-established hierarchy, and Party functionaries became co-authors. The artists, as far as we know, were willing collaborators. Eisenstein, for example, cheerfully accepted the removal of Trotsky from his chronicle of the Revolution, *October* [Oktyabr', 1927]. This is a powerful example, first of all because it came before the age of the bloodiest terror and second because Eisenstein was, and remained, the most independent of directors.

There is, however, one instance that is worth noting precisely because it is so unusual. Lev Kuleshov made *The Great Consoler* [Velikii uteshitel'], a film about artistic freedom, in the relatively balmy atmosphere of 1933. In it the gaoled author – in America, to be sure – addresses the audience: will the time come when we can speak the truth? It is the only film of the time that attempted to use Aesopian language, a language that was so well known to artists of an earlier age. The controlled passion of the film should be obvious even to the modern viewer, far removed from the time when it was made. The great irony of the situation is that this film, the only anti-Stalinist product of the period, was shown and widely reviewed, while others made by fawning directors who tried to work in the Stalinist mode of expression were rejected. No one dared to say that they understood the film's subversive message; only an enemy of the régime could have thought that the film was relevant to the Soviet Union. The very thought that the Stalinist régime suppressed freedom of expression was horrendous.

To the question, often asked by Soviet publicists at the time, why could the industry not fulfil its plans and provide the public with enough films, there was an easy answer. It became almost impossibly difficult to make a film in the Soviet Union. None of the difficulties faced by the artists was entirely new: Glavrepertkom, the State Repertoire Committee, as early as February 1923, had ordered the studios to submit every completed film for approval, and no changes in the finished work could be made without its agreement. Nevertheless, in the 1920s, at a time when state-owned and private companies were competing, when several artistic trends could coexist, considerable creative freedom remained. The great deterioration began with the Party Cinema Conference in March 1928. The Cultural Revolution in cinema meant the purging of every film organisation and a merciless attack on artistic experimentation in the name of the struggle against 'Formalism'. It was at this time that the number of Soviet films began to decline.

Although script hunger [*stsenarnyi golod*] was as old as the film industry itself, in the 1930s the problem became more serious. This deterioration happened partly because the issue became entangled with a theoretical discussion concerning the relative importance of directors and scenarists in film-making. What took place could not accurately be described as a debate, for only one side could be articulated. Times favoured the screen-play writers. Publicists denounced as 'Formalist' the idea that the film primarily belonged to the director.[9] There were two main reasons why the Stalinist politicians objected to giving primary responsibility for the artistic product to the director. First of all, as Socialist Realist film developed, more and more precise stipulations as to what constituted an acceptable storyline were set for film-makers, and only the scriptwriters could satisfy these additional demands. Second, if directors were given a measure of artistic freedom, there was a danger that at least some of them would experiment, put their own individual stamp on the product or, according to the terminology of the time, produce 'Formalist' cinema.

In a 1933 editorial the journal *Sovetskoe kino* expressed this clearly:

We are struggling for a great, full-blooded art, an art of great social content. Is this not, above all, a struggle for scenarios? It is obvious that it is the scenario that first and foremost determines that circle of ideas that will be fixed in the future film, and it is the scenario that gives the director material whose ideological quality determines the political correctness and artistic persuasiveness of the film.[10]

Four years later it proved necessary to repeat the correct line. N. Otten wrote in *Iskusstvo kino*:

The very understanding of the role of the scenario is different in different stages of the development of cinema. The scenario was developed as a service for the director at the time of shooting, as a notebook prepared for him by his literary co-worker, his assistant. But, in the final stage of the development of cinema, the scenario becomes an independent, complete literary product, indicating what should be expressed on film, describing frame by frame the ideas, the characters and their development ... This struggle [for recognition of the importance of the scenario], despite the abundance of fine words from all sides, is far from finished. The struggle continues above all against the survival of Formalism, which asserts the unconditional priority of the director against all other creators of the film, and primarily against the scenarist and the actor.[11]

It was intolerable for the director not to follow precisely the script that had been evaluated so exhaustively. When the director disregarded a scenario, this led to a large number of films being made but not exhibited, and consequently to the loss of a great deal of money. No wonder the industry failed year after year to live up to the financial plan. It was necessary to cut the director down to size: the scenarist was to get equal credit, and carry equal responsibility. The official Soviet emphasis on the primacy of the script (the written word) over the work of the director (the visual image) was profoundly antithetical to the very notion of cinematic art. None of the outstanding figures of the silent era could produce first-rate work and at the same time satisfy the political demands which called for nothing more than providing illustrations for a written text.

The bulk of the films of the early 1930s were written by the directors themselves, but this arrangement was considered unsatisfactory by the authorities. They would have liked to attract well-known writers for the task. They had attempted to conclude agreements with authors concerning the delivery of screenplays, but this campaign did not bring sufficient results. Not enough material was delivered and many of the completed scenarios were not passed for shooting. Between 1929 and 1933 Sovkino and its successor Soyuzkino drew up fifty-eight contracts with writers, of which only seven became completed films.[12] In 1933 Soyuzfilm paid out advances for the writing of 129 scripts: of these only thirteen were accepted for production.[13] Nevertheless, as time went on, it became increasingly rare for directors to write their own scripts. Indeed, GUKF [the Principal Directorate for the Cinema and Photographic Industry] considered passing a regulation that would have forbidden directors to write their own material. This did not happen, for there were so few scripts that the industry could not afford to impose further restrictions upon itself.[14]

The task of the scenarist was not an easy one. The number of steps between developing an idea and seeing the finished product was considerable. The writer first submitted a synopsis to the scenario department of the studio. These departments, set up in December 1929, included representatives from the district Party committee and the Komsomol. According to the regulations, Party and Komsomol representatives were to make up at least a third of the committee. In addition, there were people from ODSK [the Society of Friends of Soviet Cinema], and from ARRK [the Association of Workers of Revolutionary Cinema] – as long as these organisations existed – and from the Party, trade union and Komsomol organisations of the studios. Only after the synopsis had been approved could the writer proceed with the work. The finished script was then examined by another set of censors, known as editors and consultants.

In the course of the 1930s the extent of control and intervention became more and more extraordinary. From April 1933 onwards the scenario had to be discussed by the studio's Party organisation before it could go into production. Finally GUKF had to approve each and every project. After March 1938 the scenario department of the Cinema Committee had to approve every submitted project. If approval was given, the director could not change a single word in the screenplay without explicit permission.

Even so, on each occasion changes or additions would most likely be demanded, and the writer had no control whatsoever over the final product. In some cases, such as Ivan Pyriev's *The Conveyor-Belt of Death*, the film was remade fourteen times.[15] When one contemplates the control mechanisms that existed, it is not surprising that authors tended to shy away from cinema and that there was an inordinate amount of time lost between the conception of the film and its appearance in the cinemas of the country.

As the script problem remained unresolved, instead of simplifying the process the authorities set up more and more supervisory organisations. In 1937 they created special commissions from the representatives of the Party and of social organisations (such as the trade unions and the Komsomol). These commissions were placed within the scenario departments and had the task of passing on submitted film projects. Sometimes workers were invited to participate in the discussions. The Komsomol demanded the evaluation and discussion of all scripts dealing with the problems of youth.

The Ukrainian GUK [Principal Directorate for the Cinema] formalised this process in 1937 by ordering that all film projects be examined by representatives of these so-called voluntary organisations. In addition, from 1934 onwards, almost every issue of the monthly journal *Sovetskoe kino* [Soviet Cinema] included scenarios, published in order to encourage public discussion.[16] It is extraordinary – and yet revealing as to the extent of the controls that existed in the 1930s – that, even after all these discussions, the censorship, the evaluations, additions and deletions, a large number of completed films remained unreleased and were considered 'ideological rejects' [*ideologicheskii brak*]. How many films remained unreleased is unclear, for they were not included in the catalogue of Soviet feature films, but one may reasonably estimate that about one-third of the films completed were never exhibited. We know, for example, that in 1935 and 1936 alone thirty-seven films were declared to be 'ideological rejects'. These films cost the state 15 million roubles.[17]

One consequence of the large number of control and censorship bodies was that policy became altogether unpredictable. In 1936 Béla Balázs, the Hungarian film theorist and scriptwriter, made *Karl Brunner*, which dealt with the tragedy of a German boy who is left alone after his parents are arrested by the Nazis as Communists. The film had to be taken off the screens. Someone maintained that it was based on the true story of the son of Ruth Fischer, a Trotskyite. Balázs argued in vain that he did not even know that Fischer had a son.[18]

The politicians set up extraordinarily complex control mechanisms because they were absolutely certain that cinema possessed great power. Problems in film-making were treated as issues of the greatest significance and many of the top leaders, including Stalin himself, were not too busy to devote their attention to films. Jay Leyda, for example, who was in the Soviet Union in the 1930s and was acquainted with many of the prominent directors, tells us that Sergei Kirov, the head of the Leningrad Party organisation, concerned himself personally with the making of *Counterplan* [Vstrechnyi, 1932] from the very inception of the project and gave 'advice'.[19] We learn from Shumyatsky that in this same film the idea for the famous episode in which the Party secretary drinks vodka with the old worker came from the leadership of Soyuzkino.[20]

Although Stalin was very much interested in movies, he had not the slightest understanding of this medium of art. He did not comprehend the visual aspect of film-making and considered the word to be of primary importance. In his view the director was merely a technician who carried out the instructions of the scenarist. Directors benefited from Stalin's misunderstanding: with few exceptions, they survived. By contrast, scriptwriters and officials of the industry lived in a dangerous world and dozens of them became victims of the Terror.[21]

Stalin lavished an extraordinary amount of attention on cinema. From the mid 1930s to the end of his days he was the chief censor. He personally viewed and approved every film exhibited in the Soviet Union. Just like his German colleague Joseph Goebbels, he micro-managed the film industry: he suggested changes, altered titles, reviewed scripts and recommended topics. His extraordinary preoccupation with cinema is shown by the fact that, when the editors of the fourteenth volume of his collected works, as yet still unpublished, gathered material for 1940, they found that for that year only three pieces of writing had survived, and all these dealt with Stalin's views on film scripts.[22]

Stalin alone could afford to be liberal. Perhaps the most morally reprehensible Soviet film of the 1930s was Ivan Pyriev's *The Party Card* [Partiinyi bilet, 1936]. The film was about the need for vigilance. The enemy, the son of a kulak, hides his real essence and feelings, pretending to be an honest Soviet citizen. He steals his wife's Party card, which is then used for a nefarious purpose. The film was made at the time of the national campaign for exchanging Party cards and thereby purging unstable elements. One of the aims of the film was to contribute to the cult of the Party card, the loss of which was considered to be a major infraction of Party discipline. Many Party members carried their cards in a little canvas bag on a chain round their necks.[23] The enemy is unmasked at the end by his wife. For some reason the leadership of the Mosfilm studio found this film 'unsuccessful, false and distorting Soviet reality'. Stalin had a different opinion: he changed the title of the film from *Anka* to *The Party Card* and approved its distribution. Pyriev's next film, *The Rich Bride* [Bogataya nevesta, 1938], met exactly the same fate. Shumyatsky shelved it without comment, and the director once again successfully appealed to a higher authority.[24] The appearance of the film in cinemas coincided with Shumyatsky's arrest. Leyda informs us that Stalin himself intervened in order to permit Eisenstein, after the *Bezhin Meadow* [Bezhin lug, 1935–7] fiasco, to make *Alexander Nevsky*.[25]

Another illustration of Stalin's personal involvement in film-making comes from Alexander Dovzhenko. Having been severely criticised for his previous work in *Earth* [Zemlya, 1930] and *Ivan* [1932], he decided to turn to Stalin himself. As Dovzhenko tells the story, Stalin, Voroshilov, Molotov and Kirov received him twenty-two hours after he had posted a letter addressed to the General Secretary. He read to this distinguished company the entire script of *Aerograd* [1935]. Stalin made some suggestions and criticisms. On another occasion Stalin suggested to Dovzhenko that he make a film about the Ukrainian Civil War leader, Shchors. Then Stalin summoned him. Dovzhenko continues:

I want to write in greater detail about my second visit to Comrade Stalin. I want my comrades in art to be happy and proud and our enemies to have cause for reflection. Comrade Stalin summoned me to see him. It

Figure 5 'Thank you Comrade Stalin for a happy and joyful childhood': Young Pioneers performing at the Central Children's Cinema, Moscow, late 1930s. The on-stage slogan reads: 'To build, we must know, we must study (Stalin).'

Figure 6 Lenin as teacher and father of the people: Boris Shchukin and young friend in Mikhail Romm's cultic *Lenin in 1918* (1939).

was at the height of work on *Aerograd* when I was literally disappearing under the weight of the many newspaper articles about the making of *Shchors* that Joseph Vissarionovich had suggested to me. There was apparently a meeting going on in Comrade Stalin's office and I entered the room during the break when he was not in the room. A couple of minutes later Comrade Stalin came in and asked first of all whether I already knew everybody. It was only when I answered in the affirmative that he began to ask very detailed questions about work on *Aerograd*, about my creative state of mind, and about whether the Air Force was giving me enough help to film aircraft. In a word, I felt that whatever help I needed to complete the film was guaranteed. But surely he has not summoned me just for that, I thought.

'Now I will tell you why I summoned you,' Comrade Stalin said. 'When I spoke to you last time about *Shchors* I was giving you some advice, I was merely thinking of what you might do in the Ukraine. But neither my words nor newspaper articles put you under any obligation. You are a free man. If you want to make *Shchors*, do so – but, if you have other plans, do something else. Don't be embarrassed. I summoned you so that you should know this.'[26]

Needless to say, Dovzhenko carried out Stalin's suggestion without any hesitation.[27]

In the case of politically sensitive films such as Ermler's *The Great Citizen* [Velikii grazhdanin, 1939], which dealt with the purge trials, Stalin's revision of the script was so extensive that we might consider him as co-author. A letter that he wrote to Shumyatsky about the film in 1937 still survives. Once again, it is necessary to quote directly in order to convey the extent and nature of Stalin's interventions.

I read Comrade Ermler's script. I agree that there is no doubt that it is politically literate. Also it undoubtedly has literary virtues. However, there are some errors:

1. The representatives of the 'opposition' appear older both physically and also in the sense of the length of their Party service than the representatives of the Central Committee. This is not typical and did not correspond to reality. Reality gives us the opposite picture.
2. The depiction of Zhelyabov must be removed: there is no analogy between the revolutionary, Zhelyabov, and the terrorists and pigmies from the camps of Zinovievites and Trotskyites.
3. The reference to Stalin must be excluded. Instead of Stalin, the Central Committee of the Party must be mentioned.
4. Shakhov's murder should not be the centre and high-point of the scenario: this or that terrorist act pales in comparison with those that are being uncovered by the trial of Pyatakov and Radek.[28]

The letter continues with instructions on how the inner Party struggle must be presented.

Stalin's preoccupation with films was extraordinary. As he withdrew from the real world, in the sense of seeing actual factories, collective farms, villages and even the streets of Moscow, his view of the world came to be more and more determined by what he saw on the screen. Socialist Realist art aimed to do away with the distinction between 'is' and 'ought'. Through the medium of the film, 'reality' became what it was meant to be according to Bolshevik, Stalinist ideology. Of course, the Soviet people could not easily be taken in. After all, they experienced the dreadful conditions of the 1930s themselves, they knew how a collective farm in fact looked, and they knew what life was like in a collective apartment. But Stalin, ironically, allowed himself to be deceived by the lies of his own Party activists, lies that he himself had generated.

Film distribution was controlled just as strictly as film-making. Every year GUKF published a catalogue of all the films and newsreels which were allowed to be shown and those which were forbidden. The second list was usually considerably longer than the first. The list of forbidden films for 1936 contained most of the successful films of the silent era, including all the films of Kuleshov, several of the works of Dovzhenko, Protazanov, Kozintsev and Trauberg. Among the forbidden films were such significant ones as Kuleshov's *The Death Ray* [Luch smerti, 1925], *By the Law* [also known as *Dura Lex*, Po zakonu, 1926] and *The Happy Canary* [Veselaya kanareika, 1929]; Yakov Protazanov's *Father Sergius* [Otets Sergii, 1918], *Aelita* [1924], *His Call* [Ego prizyv, 1925] and *The White Eagle* [Belyi orel, 1928]; and Alexander Sanin's *Polikushka* [1919], Alexander Panteleyev's *The Miracle Maker* [Chudotvorets, 1922], Sergei Mitrich's *Yevgeniya Rozhnovskaya* [Evgeniya Rozhnovskaya, 1924], Vladimir Gardin's *The Cross and the Mauser* [Krest i mauzer, 1925], Konstantin Eggert's *The Bear's Wedding* [Medvezh'ya svad'ba, 1926], the Kozintsev and Trauberg film *The Devil's Wheel* [Chertovo koleso, 1926], Boris Barnet's *The Girl with a Hatbox* [Devushka s korobkoi, 1927], Abram Room's *Bed and Sofa* [also known as *Third Meshchanskaya Street*, Tret'ya Meshchanskaya, 1927], Friedrich Ermler's *The House in the Snowdrifts* [Dom v sugrobakh, 1927], Viktor Turin's *Turksib* [1929] and Alexander Medvedkin's *Happiness* [Schast'e, 1934].[29]

The authorities exercised tight control not only over films, but also over projectors. All of these had to be registered with the film distribution service, Soyuzkinoprokat. This registration was a complex process. A recognised body, such as a trade union, a Komsomol cell or a collective farm, assumed formal responsibility for each projector. That body had to certify that it had the appropriate technical personnel at its disposition and that the projector would therefore be properly cared for and used in accordance with the cinefication plan. The Soviet government thus spared no effort to prevent the showing of works that it considered ideologically dubious.[30]

The topic of film-makers' participation in the creation of a system that ultimately destroyed them as artists is a most delicate one. On the one hand, it is inappropriate to blame people who worked under cruel pressure in the shadow of mass destruction. On the other, it is obviously misleading to treat these people as innocent martyrs. The genius of the Soviet system lay in its ability to make almost everyone an accomplice, and the record of artists was neither better nor worse than that of other groups: film-makers denounced one another, just as most other Soviet people did. It is instructive, for example, to look at the minutes of the meetings held in 1937 for the purpose of denouncing Eisenstein's aborted film, *Bezhin Meadow*. Although people were forced to participate, it is nevertheless revealing to examine how individuals dealt with an obviously distasteful task. One finds a broad spectrum. Grigori Alexandrov, Eisenstein's previous collaborator, failed to show up for the meeting and for this act he was himself attacked. Esfir Shub spoke delicately, and Boris Barnet said something ambiguous. In the words of Dovzhenko, however, one senses genuine hostility. Pyriev went so far as to describe Eisenstein as not a 'Soviet person'. A certain Yu. Marian spoke with remarkable venom, saying proudly that he had felt hatred for all the works of Eisenstein, going back to *October* [Oktyabr', 1927].

Eisenstein's response was extraordinary. First he expressed contrition and asked the help of his comrades to overcome his errors. Then he made an ambiguous self-criticism that can be read as an attack on Stalinist art. He accused himself of believing that 'talent and glory gave me the right to have an original vision of the October Revolution. In *The Old and the New* I once again attempted to give my own special, as it were, independent view of the world. I thought I had the right, but it turned out that I did not.'[31]

By insisting on making every film accessible to even the least literate, by requiring the cessation of artistic experimentation, and by constantly denouncing individual style as 'Formalist', the régime destroyed the talent of great artists. This was the saddest irony of the history of Soviet film. The great film-makers of the 1920s – Kuleshov, Eisenstein, Vertov, Dovzhenko and Pudovkin – were not in fact Bolsheviks, for they had little understanding of or interest in Marxism. What drew them to the Revolution was a misunderstanding: they hated the taste of the 'petit bourgeoisie', and they hated philistinism. They were drawn to the Revolutionaries because the Bolsheviks promised a break with the old world and the old culture, which they understood to mean a transcendence of philistinism. They naïvely believed that they were the equivalents of the Bolsheviks in the realm of the arts. The Bolsheviks created in their minds an image of an ideal working class, one that had little in common with real-life workers, and they spoke in the name of this 'proletariat'. The film-makers did the same: they aimed to create a new form of art, one that would be appreciated by the proletariat. In fact very few workers showed interest in the films of the avant-garde, and to the extent that these directors found an audience – never a very large one – it was among the bourgeois intelligentsia. The irony was that the Bolsheviks, once they had destroyed cultural pluralism and extended their control over Soviet culture in the early 1930s, established a complete monopoly for the most 'petit-bourgeois' tastes, far worse than artists had experienced before the Revolution. The artists' misunderstanding was cleared up in the most painful fashion. It was the most 'revolutionary', the most 'leftist' artists who suffered the most. The wonderful originality of talented men like Vertov, Dovzhenko and Pudovkin gradually disappeared. Kuleshov stopped making films. Eisenstein was not able to complete a film between 1929 and 1938. But his individuality could not be destroyed and he was the only director who survived as an artist.

More specifically, film-makers contributed to the Terror by justifying it. In this respect no prominent director has a very good record, with the exception of Kuleshov, who made no more films after 1933. Eisenstein made his film *Bezhin Meadow* on the basis of the story of Pavlik Morozov. The purpose of the film was to justify a son's betrayal of his father. The fact that the film was never publicly shown had nothing to do with Eisenstein's intentions. Dovzhenko's *Aerograd* was about a man shooting his friend because he turned out to be a hidden enemy. In Pyriev's *The Party Card*, perhaps the single most distasteful film of the decade, the wife shoots her husband, who was the hidden enemy. Ermler's *Counterplan*, a film that he made together with Sergei Yutkevich, was about the necessity of fighting saboteurs. His *The Great Citizen* was the Stalinist version of the murder of Kirov and the great purge trials. While it was being shot, four people associated with it were arrested. We cannot know for certain, but it appears that there was not one single film-maker who sought a pretext for *not* making such films. Soviet artists contributed to the creation of the system that destroyed them all as artists, and it destroyed many of them as human beings as well.

Chapter 5

Red stars, positive heroes and personality cults

Richard Taylor

It is my intention here to raise questions rather than to provide answers. We are after all at a unique juncture in the study of Russian and Soviet history, at a point where we can at last ask not just difficult, but even awkward questions and hope to get some kinds of useful answers. We can at last also hope that those answers will be based, not on ideologically determined postures, but on solid empirical research, much of which has in recent years been, and is currently being, carried out principally by Soviet scholars working in Soviet archives and libraries in Soviet conditions. Even in the immediate post-Soviet era this will continue to be the case for, although physical obstacles to such research remain, and may indeed even have increased as the economic situation has deteriorated, the political obstacles have largely been removed.

The title of the July 1990 conference, 'Russian and Soviet Cinema: Continuity and Change', deliberately points up two of the central historical questions posed by the study of Soviet cinema.[1] The most important and also the most obvious question is: to what extent can we periodise the history of Soviet and pre-Revolutionary (or 'Russian', as recent Soviet scholarship has tended to call it) cinema usefully without distorting that history by pigeonholing it into our own – or other people's – retrospective preconceptions? The two key transitions here are those from tsarism to Bolshevism, through the Revolutionary events of February and October 1917 and the subsequent Civil War, and from Bolshevism to Stalinism, through the rapid industrialisation, forced collectivisation and 'Cultural Revolution' associated with the first Five-Year Plan of 1928–32. To question the conventional periodisation in cinema history inevitably raises even more provocative questions about the periodisation of Russian and Soviet history in general, particularly in the political sphere, and indeed the convention of historical periodisation itself. History is, after all, a process. To what extent do the institutions and practices that we associate with the post-Revolutionary régime, and above all with the phenomena grouped together as Stalinism, stem from the guiding ideology of Marxism in its Leninist interpretation (in however impure or pure a form), and to what extent do they stem from pre-existing Russian political and other traditions? This is, of course, the central unanswered question of perestroika. The question itself proved so difficult for the leading participants in the process to answer because it also proved almost impossible for them to ask it. To do so might cause the entire edifice to come tumbling down upon their heads because it could undermine the very legitimacy of the existing order.[2] This dilemma is a tribute, if that is the right term, to the power of historical myth, which is itself one of the central attributes of Stalinism and the personality cult. Political institutions may change, or appear to change, almost overnight, but historical myths and political cultures linger on.

In the creation and sustenance of the myth (using the word in this particular sense) of Soviet power, above all in Stalin's time, Soviet cinema has played a crucial role. Stalin himself remarked to the Thirteenth Party Congress in 1924 that 'Cinema is the greatest means of mass agitation'[3] and we know from Khrushchev's speech to the Twentieth Party Congress in 1956 how much the dictator came to depend on Soviet cinema for his own warped perception of the realities of Soviet life.[4] Indeed recent Soviet research has demonstrated that, in the period from the signature of the Molotov-Ribbentrop Pact in August 1939 until the unleashing of Operation Barbarossa in June 1941, while the rest of Europe was being rent asunder by war, Stalin devoted an extraordinary amount of time and energy to maintaining a detailed watch over the activities of Soviet film-makers.[5] This knowledge brings us to the second central question: to what extent is the history of Soviet cinema – and, furthermore, to what extent should it be – a history of cinema pure and simple, and to what extent has that history been determined by external factors?

Cinema does not, and cannot, have a history as cinema pure and simple. More perhaps than other art forms, all cinema has a history in context and that context has various strands: the aesthetic or artistic, the political, the social, the technological, the economic, and the industrial and/or organisational are factors that are all at play. Cinema historians, both East and West, have realised this better than cultural historians in other fields, principally those of literature who – at least in the West – have persisted in examining literary texts in isolation. It follows from this varied array of factors therefore that the history of Soviet cinema is to a considerable extent the history of its context. It would be absurd to deny that the overthrow of the tsarist autocracy in 1917 or the violent changes associated with the first Five-Year Plan had a major influence on the development of cinema. But we should not lose sight of the fact that external influences are always almost inextricably intertwined with internal factors. We shall probably never satisfactorily separate the two: indeed the search for a clear distinction between internal and external factors is somewhat reminiscent of the arguments about the role of the individual and of the psychology of the individual in history that bother historians from time to time and are never finally, or frequently even satisfactorily, resolved.

I have already mentioned the two key transitions in the history of Russian and Soviet cinema.[6] I want now to concentrate on the factors that are relevant to an examination of the second transition – from the 1920s to the 1930s, from the relatively pluralist climate of Lenin's New Economic Policy (NEP) to the centralised *dirigisme* that we associate with Stalinism and the doctrine of Socialist Realism. Readers will be all too familiar with the external factors that dictated general policy in this period and will, I trust, accept that those factors exerted a very considerable influence on the development of Soviet cinema. It is no coincidence that many films of the 1920s were peopled by characters who in some way 'typified' the mass of workers and peasants, whereas the representative films of the 1930s – and we can speak more accurately of representative Soviet films of the 1930s than we can of the 1920s – portrayed heroic leadership models, such as *Chapayev* [Chapaev, 1934], *Alexander Nevsky* [Aleksandr Nevskii, 1938] or *Peter the First* [Petr Pervyi, 1937–9]. The equation is not, however, that simple and I want to suggest, first of all, that there were factors *internal* to Soviet cinema that help to explain why *external* factors penetrated so deeply and effectively, and, second, to argue that, at least initially, those internal factors were independent of, if often parallel to, the external factors with which we are all familiar.

The most important internal factor shaping the development of Soviet cinema derives from the precise role in that development of the avant-garde film-makers. This is a hoary old problem, but the overwhelming majority of cinema historians on both sides of the old ideological divide will nowadays accept the argument that the entire population of the Soviet Union most emphatically did not spend the whole of the 1920s in a darkened auditorium watching the films of Eisenstein, Vertov, Pudovkin or Shub! That population, when it had access to a market-orientated cinema – and that itself was problematic, and in the countryside almost impossible – preferred the seductions of the popular entertainment films made by men like Yakov Protazanov,[7] Yuri Zhelyabuzhsky (who, incidentally, was Gorky's stepson)[8] or Konstantin Eggert[9] rather than aesthetic experiments designed to show that one particular style or form of film-making was inherently more authentic or realistic or Revolutionary than another. Eisenstein, Vertov and Shub all admitted as much – and bemoaned the fact repeatedly. For them, of course, the new forms in which the new content of Revolutionary art was to be expressed were the prime concern. When the time came, that in turn would expose them to the increasingly sterile, but nevertheless dangerous, stigmatisation of Formalism.[10]

There can, however, be no doubt that, in the towns and cities, where there *was* a choice between entertainment and experimentation (characterised more often than not as 'cash versus class' or 'commerce versus

Figures 7 and 8 The parallels of history as propaganda: Vsevolod Pudovkin's *Minin and Pozharsky* (1939) (Pl. 7) and *Suvorov* (1940) (Pl. 8).

ideology'), audiences repeatedly opted for glamour, comfort and escapism rather than a harsh confrontation with realities, especially where that was designed to shock them into a predetermined state of political awareness. The box-office receipts prove this for Soviet audiences in the 1920s as they do for other audiences in other places at other times.[11] But in the Soviet Union of the 1920s this brings us to Trotsky's conundrum: should Revolutionary art be a hammer or a mirror?[12] The so-called 'commercial' cinema network flourished, and was able to charge significantly higher seat prices than educational and agitational club houses, because it catered for the prevailing public taste like a mirror rather than trying to change it like a hammer. It often did this by offering a variety of attractions in addition to the films themselves. The grander cinemas frequently had an orchestra playing in the foyer that was larger than that accompanying the film inside the auditorium, and some even offered a range of additional facilities from chess and draughts to libraries and shooting galleries.[13] The popular films of the 1920s themselves tended to have straightforward and untaxing narrative structures, lavish sets, and heroes and villains whom audiences could easily identify with, or at least relate to.

We need to look more closely at the notion of a 'commercial' cinema at this time, because in fact the overwhelming majority of these outlets were owned, not by private entrepreneurs or 'Nepmen', but by branches of the state apparatus or political and social organisations like the trades unions and local soviets, which were using cinema as a money-spinning activity, as in some instances did charities and even collectives of the unemployed.[14] The clubs were the poor relations in this family and they were usually forced to show films that could not command a commercial audience because they were too overtly political, too obscure, too badly made, or because the print itself was too old or badly worn.

This mattered above all else because of cinema's potential as a propaganda weapon: as Lenin's well-worn quote put it, 'Of all the arts, for us cinema is the most important.'[15] It mattered even more once cinema was centralised in 1930 and entrusted with the task of making films that were, to use that other cliché of the time, 'intelligible to the millions'.[16] The cinefication programme, designed to spread the cinema network across the countryside by equipping every collective farm with film-viewing facilities, exacerbated the problem. First of all, the scale of the expansion dictated certain economies: it was hardly feasible to cover one-sixth of the world with a network of 'cultured cinemas'[17] with potted palms and palm-court orchestras like those in the big cities – and in any case the peasants would hardly have felt at home in such surroundings, any more than most urban workers would have done. It is not therefore surprising that the major part of the cinefication programme envisaged a rapid increase in the number of club cinemas, like those poor cousins in the towns. The rural audience did not therefore have a choice of film outlets to patronise: indeed most peasants had never seen a film before. Such an unsophisticated audience could not safely be exposed to unintelligible films, which would be counterproductive: when large sections of the forcibly collectivised peasantry were already hostile to Soviet power, the risk was obvious. As Lunacharsky had pointed out, 'Boring agitation is counter-agitation.'[18]

Hence the need for entertainment films became paramount: but they had to be entertainment films that were politically safe. There was nothing new in this. Although the driving force for the production of Soviet entertainment pictures in the 1920s had been the joint-stock company, Mezhrabpom-Rus, which became Mezhrabpomfilm in 1928, state-owned production companies in the 1920s had also delivered a diet of entertainment films – and been severely criticised for so doing – and state-owned cinemas had shown those films to delighted audiences. What was new in the 1930s was that the avant-garde ceased to receive the same degree of generous funding because control over that funding was now rigorously centralised and the criteria that were applied to its allocation were both more functional and more ideologically determined. They were also more closely monitored through the annual thematic plans and through the presence of Party cells in the studios.[19] This development hit documentary film-makers particularly hard, because their films had never attracted large audiences even when they were widely shown. Again this is an experience that was not confined to the Soviet Union,[20] but in that country's historical context the 'intellectuals' were deemed to have failed in their historic task. In the early summer of 1931 one leading critic described the Cultural Revolution in cinema as a move 'From Intelligentsia Illusions to Actual Reality'.[21]

Of course, to a considerable extent the avant-garde provided a convenient scapegoat for politicians seeking to explain why Soviet cinema-goers preferred a diet of salacious love intrigues to edifying stories of socialist construction. But it also provided a convenient whipping-boy for younger and/or less talented film-makers who saw their own career opportunities improving as the careers of the great names slipped into decline. We must not underestimate the self-interested actions of human beings caught up in a struggle for their own survival. This internal factor, unpleasant as it is to contemplate, has too often been overlooked. It comes out all too clearly, however, in the polemical remarks of Pavel Petrov-Bytov in his 1929 article 'We Have No Soviet Cinema':

> When people talk about Soviet cinema they brandish a banner on which is written: *The Strike* [Stachka, 1924], *The Battleship Potemkin* [Bronenosets Potemkin, 1926], *October* [Oktyabr', 1927], *The Mother* [Mat', 1926], *The End of St Petersburg* [Konets Sankt-Peterburga, 1927] and they add the recent *New Babylon* [Novyi Vavilon, 1929], *Zvenigora* [1927] and *The Arsenal* [Arsenal, 1928], *Do 120 million workers and peasants march beneath this banner? I quite categorically state that*

they do not. And never have done. I am not denying the virtues of these films. These virtues do of course exist and they are not negligible. Great formal virtues. We must study these films just as we study the bourgeois classics. But making them the banner of Soviet cinema is premature . . .[22]

There is something of this attitude in the speeches made by some of the lesser figures at the January 1935 conference of film-makers at which Lev Kuleshov, the 'father of Soviet cinema', and Eisenstein, the 'old man', were criticised for failing in their Revolutionary responsibilities.[23]

The obvious model for entertainment cinema in both the 1920s and the 1930s was that provided by Hollywood. Even though its ideological pre-conceptions were anathema, it was pre-eminently clear that Hollywood was successful in giving its audiences what they wanted, or at least in giving them the feeling that they were getting what they wanted. It is small wonder then that, in his search for the creation of a popular Soviet cinema, the head of the industry, Boris Shumyatsky, should have gradually come to the conclusion that he needed to create a *sovetskii Gollivud*, a 'Soviet Holly-wood', which would use the same production-line methods as the original. After leading a delegation to Western Europe and the USA in 1935, Shumyatsky planned the reorganisation of the Soviet film industry along what he took to be American mass-production lines, even adopting American terminology, such as 'producer', and promoting the imitation of American film genres.[24] Yet this was very much a continuation of the traditions of mainstream popular cinema, as exemplified in particular in the output of the Mezhrabpomfilm studio over the previous decade. Indeed more recently Soviet cinema had already produced its own equivalent of the legitimising Western with *Chapayev*, directed by the Vasiliev 'brothers' in 1934, and Grigori Alexandrov's chain of massively popular musical comedies had already begun with *The Happy Guys* [Veselye rebyata] in the same year.

The imitation of Hollywood further entrenched the rejection of the avant-garde and its experimentation: conveyor-belt production of mass entertainment was to become the be-all and end-all of Soviet cinema. But the imitation of the model did not end there: central to the success of Hollywood from its earliest days to its dominance of the world market was its creation and assiduous cultivation of the star system. Indeed Soviet cinema had offered a somewhat insipid imitation of this itself in the 1920s when *amerikanshchina* ('Americanism' or 'Americanitis') had been all the rage. The anti-heroine of Kuleshov's *The Extraordinary Adventures of Mr West in the Land of the Bolsheviks* [Neobychainye priklucheniya mistera Vesta v strane bol'shevikov, 1924], Alexandra Khokhlova, was the subject of a pamphlet and numerous articles (includ-ing a eulogistic one by Eisenstein),[25] and two pamphlets were written about the popular comedian Igor Ilyinsky.[26] The actress Nina Lee, billed as 'the Russian Mary Pickford', took an English-sounding name in the same way that British ballerinas once took Russian-sounding names to endow themselves with the aura of greater authenticity.[27] But the attentions of the film press in the 1920s had been largely confined to the American stars themselves, above all to Pickford and Fairbanks, but also to Chaplin, Keaton and the rest. When 'Doug and Mary' toured Europe in 1926, their reception was just as enthusiastic in Moscow as it had been in Berlin. Indeed the whole star system and the hysteria it evoked were sufficiently familiar to Soviet audiences (and perhaps dangerous to those who wished to control those audiences) to provoke satirical treatment in two films at the time: Sergei Komarov's *The Kiss of Mary Pickford* [Potselui Meri Pikford, 1927] and Nikolai Khodatayev's animated short *One of Many* [Odna iz mnogikh, 1927].[28] Both these films were made for the Mezhrabpom-Rus studio, and *The Kiss of Mary Pickford* was a joint production with the state-owned Sovkino studio. It is perhaps small wonder that the Lef group, in particular, railed against the 'Pickfordisation' of Soviet cinema.[29]

In the 1930s, however, this satirical treatment would not have been possible. This was in part the direct consequence of ideological considerations: not everyone shared Alexander Medvedkin's view that satire was legitimately 'a weapon that attacks shortcomings, that lashes like a whip, that lashes everything that interferes with life'.[30] In the 1930s satire was increasingly seen as dangerous, precisely because it was inherently subversive of the established order. As society moved towards greater conformity and proclaimed stability, the only whips allowed were those that lashed from above, weapons of punishment like the old knout. A similar fear of subversion, of alternative sources of knowledge and power, also dictated that Soviet audiences should no longer have direct access to American films, so that Hollywood stars as individual icons became a fading memory for some and a completely unknown quantity for others. Hence in the 1930s Shumyatsky's attempt to establish a popular Socialist Realist Soviet cinema through at least a partial imitation of the Hollywood model necessitated the creation of a new system of what we might call 'red stars'. Ironically, some of them had made their names in the semi-commercial hits of the 1920s made by the Mezhrabpom studio (which Shumyatsky closed down as an anachronism in 1936) and were therefore already genuinely popular with audiences without any form of encouragement from above. There was thus significant continuity here: Igor Ilyinsky, for instance, had enjoyed broad popularity since his début in Yakov Protazanov's comedy *Aelita* [1924], which had involved a romantic fantasy about a workers' uprising on the red planet Mars, and yet re-emerged as a 'red star' in 1938 after his performance as the bumbling bureaucrat Byvalov in *Volga-Volga*.[31] The emerging star system of the 1930s did not in fact build directly upon the Hollywood model: rather it built primarily upon that model as refracted through the Soviet experience of the NEP period, when studios such as Mezhrabpom had in turn built upon the model of pre-Revolutionary Russian cinema.[32]

The advent of sound cinema reinforced the rejection of montage, as Eisenstein, Pudovkin and Alexandrov had predicted in their celebrated 'Statement on Sound' in 1928.[33] Sound facilitated the development of individual characters on screen, accelerated plot development through the use of dialogue and helped to restore the hegemony of conservative literary narrative structures. Sound also destroyed the universality of silent cinema and confined films more rigidly within linguistic, national and ideological boundaries, reinforcing what Maya Turovskaya refers to elsewhere in this volume as the 'cultural autarky' of the Stalin period, and that autarky in turn reinforced the ideological hegemony of the Party and ultimately of Stalin himself. It also meant that Soviet cinema had to provide audiences with its own iconic figures: as we shall see, Doug and Mary gave way to Boris and Lyubov.

In the early years of Russian cinema audiences had fallen under the spell of international stars such as Max Linder and Asta Nielsen. The Russian film factory production line had also spawned an array of home-grown stars, with Ivan Mosjoukine and Vera Kholodnaya foremost among them. Despite the aesthetic influence of montage, popular Soviet films of the 1920s also produced their stars: Igor Ilyinsky and Nina Lee have already been mentioned, but they were not alone. Similarly in the 1930s Boris Babochkin was fêted after playing the role of *Chapayev*, which Boris Shumyatsky rather extravagantly described as 'the best film produced by Soviet cinema in the whole period of its existence . . . a film that represents the genuine summit of Soviet film art'.[34] The character of Chapayev penetrated into popular culture and everyday life in a way that few other screen characters have done, even if only as a butt for schoolchildren's jokes. Babochkin was even recalled from theatre work in 1941 to recreate his Chapayev role in a little-known wartime morale-booster called *Chapayev Is with Us* [Chapaev s nami].[35] Nikolai Cherkasov and Tamara Makarova were similarly projected.

The greatest star of popular Soviet cinema in the 1930s, however, was the leading actress in Alexandrov's musical comedies – his wife, Lyubov Orlova, frequently dubbed the 'prima donna of Soviet cinema'. The Russian critic Sergei Nikolayevich has recently characterised her film image as that of 'the ideal woman of the 1930s, the *femina sovietica*, a contemporary Valkyrie in a white sweater with a severe perm'.[36] Comparing Orlova to both Marlene Dietrich and Greta Garbo, he argues that the strength of her appeal to audiences lay in its complex ambiguity. He illustrates his case with a quotation from the American character played by Orlova in *The Circus* [Tsirk, 1936]:

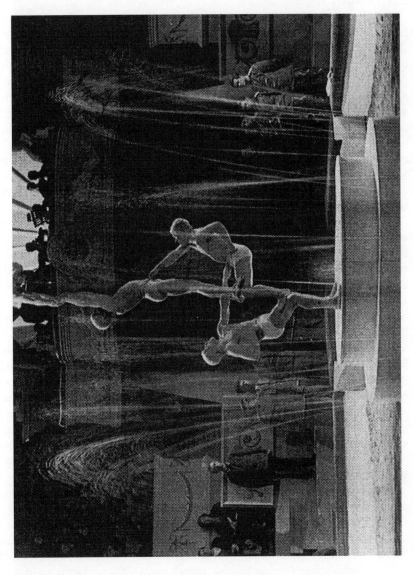

Figures 9 and 10 'I wanted to be happy in the USSR, but it's impossibly' [*sic*]: men and women mobilised to perform in unison in Grigori Alexandrov's *The Circus* (1936).

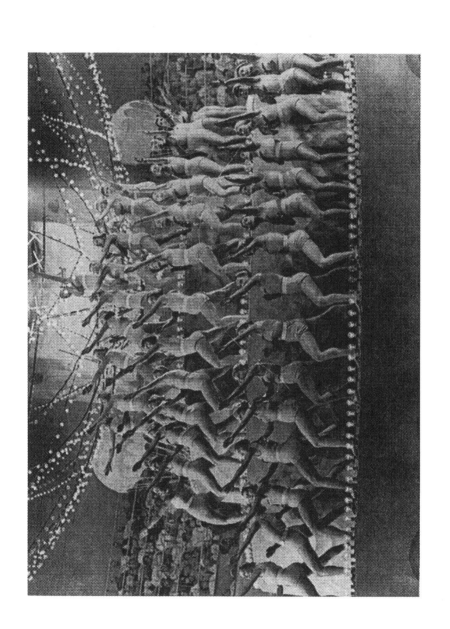

Figures 11 and 12 Light relief in the kolkhoz musical: laughter, love and music in Ivan Pyriev's *Tractor-Drivers* (1939).

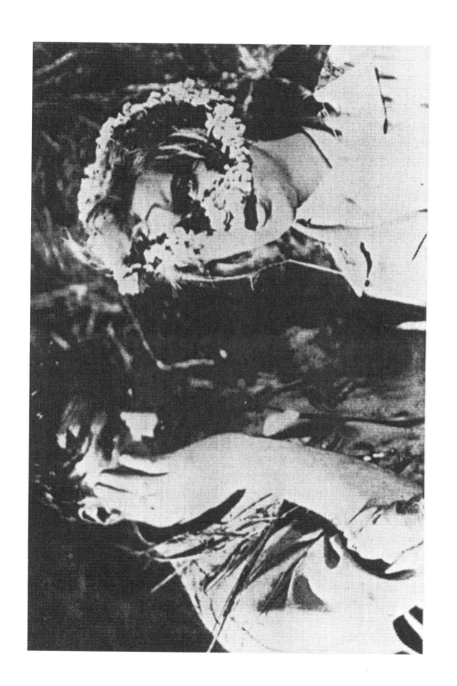

'I wanted to be happy in the USSR, but it's impossibly' [*sic*] – Marion Dixon's sorrowful refrain comes to mind when we think of the spiritual ordeals that Orlova and Alexandrov endured some decades later at the time of Khrushchev's rehabilitations. Nonetheless their films became what they themselves became for us all not just because they illustrated in a clear and accessible way a paradise that we could believe in, but also because they allowed us to laugh at that paradise. It is after all no accident that the co-authors of Alexandrov's musical comedies were Nikolai Erdman, Ilf and Petrov, and Isaak Babel. The pathos of self-irony brings this cinema closer to our own time, makes these films more alive and their leading actress more human.[37]

Nikolayevich has also made this extremely telling point about the nature of the appeal of Orlova's star quality:

It is naïve to think that people could be deceived, distracted or seduced merely by Dunayevsky's songs or Orlova's dances. There was a different phenomenon at work here, an actual willingness to be deceived, a boundless desire to be seduced.[38]

Records and video-cassettes of her films and songs still sell in Russia today and the quotation with which Masha Enzensberger ends her contribution to this volume is eloquent testimony to her continuing appeal.[39] Stars like Orlova were promoted through the familiar panoply of photographs, press articles and books. Cherkasov was the subject of two books in 1939 alone.[40] They were also held up as role models for Soviet citizens: they exemplified a popular cinema depicting heroes with whom audiences could easily identify. A slogan of the time had it that 'Any one of us becomes a hero when the country commands!' If Boris Babochkin could successfully defeat counter-Revolutionaries in *Chapayev*, if Marina Ladynina could extirpate inefficiency on her collective farm in Ivan Pyriev's *Tractor-Drivers* [Traktoristy, 1939], so too could the Soviet film-goer – at least that was the idea. This personal link between audience and screen character, facilitated by the restoration of straightforward conventional narrative and dialogue, was of course the complete antithesis of the montage cinema with which the avant-garde of the 1920s was so closely associated. As Eisenstein rather ironically noted after Shumyatsky's fall from grace in 1938, 'There was a period in our cinema when montage was proclaimed as being "everything". We are now coming to the end of a period when montage has been regarded as "nothing".' In the 1930s Eisenstein had pursued the theory of montage virtually alone.[41]

The stars, like compliant directors, were rewarded with the full panoply of patronage accorded to the Stalinist *nomenklatura*. They enjoyed privileged access to food supplies, welfare services, housing, fast cars, travel and holidays denied to the population at large. They received official honours and their films received official prizes, in particular the State Prize of the USSR and the Stalin Prize. In return they illustrated, and indeed populated, the mythic world of the cult of personality. But their role was not confined to the screen. Like all Soviet artists they were expected to tour factories and collective farms, workers' and peasants' clubs, to work in support of Soviet cinema and its message, to endorse on every possible occasion the official line and the status quo. Although the Hollywood system made similar demands on its stars, it is here that the red star system and its American equivalent begin to diverge. Apart from the obvious difference between the two countries in terms of the level of resources available for promotion, and of the level of sophistication of that promotion, Hollywood stars were first and foremost the property of an individual studio and a vital weapon for the success and wellbeing of that studio, just as European football players are nowadays a vital weapon for the survival and prosperity of their clubs. In short they functioned in a market economy: Soviet actors and actresses functioned in a centralised administrative-command economy. Red stars were in the final analysis the property of the state, of the Party, and ultimately of the leader. It is not perhaps too much of an exaggeration to say that red stars were expected to perform a similar function to that played in a constitutional monarchy by minor members of the royal family, and in a certain sense that is precisely what they were: minor functionaries at the court of King Joseph. As I have already remarked, cinema does not, and cannot, have a history as cinema pure and simple.

The emergence of the positive hero did, after all, have its external function as well in the promotion of the personality cult: Chapayev, Nevsky, Peter the Great and countless other characters can be taken as substitutes for the Great Leader of the World Proletariat. As the Stalin period wore on, it became increasingly difficult to make films that were not in some way touched by the leadership cult: indeed, as Maya Turovskaya has shown elsewhere in this volume, it became increasingly difficult to make films at all.[42] Nevertheless, even in the earlier years of Socialist Realism, it is possible to identify, at least tentatively, films that played a more precise role in the preparation for, or the promotion of, that cult. This is very much a preliminary ordering, and I do not want to be either too dogmatic or too schematic, but I think that we can begin to identify three distinct groups of films, which I shall here designate as *proto-cultic*, *quasi-cultic* and *cultic* proper. Of course, in real life, things do not fall into neat categories and we shall see that there is plenty of overlap between the categories, but I hope we shall also see that each group of films has a different focus and perhaps also a differentiated function in the mythic process.

Let us take the *proto-cultic* films first, as the name I have chosen suggests we should. Chronologically proto-cultic films do of course also come first, as they provide the bridge between the popular cinema of the

1920s and the films of the early 1930s and, in particular, of the early sound period. Even Grigori Roshal's silent *The Salamander* [Salamandra, 1928] might be included because Lunacharsky makes a cameo appearance as the heroic *deus ex machina*, except that the whole point about the personality cult resides in the general context. Rashit Yangirov suggests that the Lenin cult was at least presaged even before his death in January 1924.[43] While it is abundantly clear that the Lenin cult predates, parallels, coincides with *and* postdates the Stalin cult, it is the Stalin cult that we are here concerned with, and that cult begins to take off in earnest only after the officially promoted celebrations of Stalin's fiftieth birthday in December 1929.[44] Thus to describe a film such as *The Salamander* as proto-cultic, even though it had been made before that date and before the March 1928 Party Conference on Cinema had endorsed the call for films that were 'intelligible to the millions', would be to take the prefix 'proto-' too far and to falsify history in retrospect, a phenomenon all too familiar to the student of Stalinism!

Proto-cultic films have a linear narrative which revolves around a hero(ine) figure ('comrade living man') who is in some way transformed by the situations depicted and experienced as that narrative unfolds, rather like the hero of a *Bildungsroman*.[45] The film is usually set in the present day and the action unfolds against an everyday background – a factory, a collective farm, a tenement block, for instance. The message of the film, and the transformation of the main character, have political significance, but that significance is not as explicit, not as *foregrounded*, as it will be in the other categories. Typical films in this category might include the Kozintsev and Trauberg *Alone* [Odna, 1931], which depicts the struggles of a newly qualified woman teacher against the forces of darkness (including, but not confined to, male chauvinism) in the far-flung corners of the Altai mountains in Central Asia.[46] Although she never explicitly achieves her educational objectives and in her final confrontation does in fact suffer injury that necessitates evacuation, that evacuation is achieved through collaboration between the poor peasants whose interests she has promoted and the central powers who send a rescue aircraft. In her hour of need, therefore, the teacher is emphatically not alone and the long-term victory of her struggle as an individual fighting on behalf of the collective is implicitly assured. *Alone* therefore guarantees the happy ending that is *de rigueur* for all cultic films.

A rather more obvious candidate for inclusion in the proto-cultic category is perhaps Dovzhenko's film *Ivan* [1932], which deals with the transformation and awakening of the eponymous hero, a young peasant recruited to a vast hydroelectric construction project. Here he discovers the joys and disciplines of collective labour, fights saboteurs and wreckers, and eventually joins the Party. Membership will open the doors to further education and enable Ivan to realise his full potential as a member of the

Figure 13 The loneliness of the long-distance teacher: Yelena Kuzmina as the proto-cultic heroine battling against ignorance and superstition *Alone* (Kozintsev and Trauberg, 1931).

Figure 14 The hero as domesticated human being: Boris Babochkin as the quasi-cultic hero of *Chapayev* (1934), according to Boris Shumyatsky, 'the best film produced by cinema in the whole period of its existence'.

socialist working class. There are some similarities here with the character of Babchenko, who abandons vodka in favour of Communism and thus saves the day in Yutkevich and Ermler's *Counterplan* [Vstrechnyi], released in the same year. A fourth example could be Macheret's *Men and Jobs* [Dela i lyudi, 1932]. An American expert has been brought on to a large construction project to advise on improved methods of production: Zakharov, the hero, takes it upon himself to organise his own work brigade more effectively, thus outdoing the foreign specialist. His success is hailed as a victory for the workers. Another awakening of consciousness, another transformation, both lead to another *kheppi-end.*

The examples that I have given all come from the transitional period of the first Five-Year Plan and are proto-cultic in the true chronological sense of the word. But the spirit of this category of films continued to inform a large number of films throughout the Stalin era and indeed beyond, up to and including Brezhnev's period of stagnation. In the 1930s alone we can cite some of the most popular films in box-office terms, including at least two of Alexandrov's musical comedies, *The Circus* and *Volga-Volga*, both starring Lyubov Orlova, and Ivan Pyriev's kolkhoz musical comedies *The Rich Bride* [Bogataya nevesta, 1938], *Tractor-Drivers* and *The Swine Herd and the Shepherd* [Svinarka i pastukh, 1941], all three starring Marina Ladynina. Masha Enzensberger's analysis of Alexandrov's *The Radiant Path* [Svetlyi put', 1940] demonstrates that it also clearly fits into this category.[47] These proto-cultic films use the relatively straightforward conventions of plot structure ('goodies v. baddies') and of linear narrative familiar from popular cinema while introducing a political context and conveying a political message, sometimes implicitly and sometimes explicitly. It is this political element that marks them as proto-cultic, rather than non-cultic or pre-cultic films, because it is the political dimension that clarifies their function in promoting the concept of one-man leadership [*edinonachalie*] that is a crucial component of the personality cult. Nevertheless, as I suggested earlier, we cannot afford to be either too dogmatic or too schematic in our categorisation – and, in any event, the films I have mentioned by no stretch of the imagination constitute a comprehensive or definitive list – but we can say that these proto-cultic films represent one stage in the continuum from pre-Stalinist popular Soviet film to what I have termed the quasi-cultic and the cultic categories.

Quasi-cultic films build upon the model provided by the proto-cultic category by foregrounding the political. In this group the hero(ine)'s tale unfolds against an overtly political background: it might be the events of 1905 or even earlier, the October Revolution, the Civil War, the Communist International, or it might be a contemporary Party or government setting. Quasi-cultic films do not have to be set in the present day. The leading figure in a quasi-cultic film will *begin* from a standpoint of political commitment, whereas the hero of a proto-cultic film *acquires* political commitment in the course of the development of the plot. Inevitably there will be a happy ending, even if it involves a terminal sacrifice or political *Liebestod*. The Civil War film, which predates the Stalin period with its heroic myth legitimating the Bolshevik régime, plays an important part in this category. We must, of course, refer back to *Chapayev*, but we can also include Protazanov's *Tommy* [1931], Kuleshov's *Gorizont* [1932] (which concludes in the Civil War period), Dzigan's *We from Kronstadt* [My iz Kronshtadta, 1936], Ilya Trauberg's *The Year 1919* [God devyatnadsatyi, 1938] and Dovzhenko's *Shchors* [1939], which the director claimed had been made at the suggestion of Stalin, 'the artist's teacher and friend'.[48] Contemporary settings, in which the constant need for vigilance against enemies of the people, saboteurs and wreckers – or even just human weakness – was emphasised, are also frequently to be found in films in this category. The hero of Yuli Raizman's *Pilots* [Letchiki, 1935], Rogachov, played by Boris Shchukin, is described at one point in the story as 'a true Stalinist' and it is his quiet strength that wins through in the end against the flamboyant behaviour of his rival, Belyayev. The role of Stepan Glushak in Dovzhenko's *Aerograd* [1935] provides a more graphic example of the triumph of good over evil, while Sergei Gerasimov's *Komsomolsk* [1938] shares something of the same pioneering spirit. In all these films the leading characters are more or less ordinary people whose lives have been touched by the historic events around them. Here we should also include as classic examples of *Bildungsroman* (or rather *Bildungsfilm!*) the Kozintsev and Trauberg Maxim trilogy – *The Youth of Maxim* [Yunost' Maksima, 1934], *The Return of Maxim* [Vozvrashchenie Maksima, 1937] and *The Vyborg Side* [Vyborgskaya storona, 1938].

Further across the spectrum Boris Barnet's *One September Night* [Noch' v sentyabre, 1939], which deals with the Stakhanovite movement, allows the lives of its ordinary characters to be touched not only by the historical events around them, but also by an impersonation of a real historical personage, Ordzhonikidze, who had committed suicide at the height of the purges in 1937. The introduction of Ordzhonikidze into the plot structure sets the seal of official approval on the victory of the ordinary characters in their struggle against adversity. Other quasi-cultic films were actually based on the lives of prominent people: the Zarkhi and Kheifits film *Baltic Deputy* [Deputat Baltiki, 1936] was inspired by the life of the Russian scientist Kliment Timiryazev, who died in 1920, while the two-part *Great Citizen* [Velikii grazhdanin, 1937 and 1939] depicted a thinly veiled version of the life of Sergei Kirov, the Leningrad Party chief who had been assassinated in 1934, and Yutkevich's *Yakov Sverdlov* [1940] was devoted to the life of the first Soviet President, who had died in 1919. Indeed there was something of a sub-industry in the filming of the lives of people recently dead and therefore not merely no longer dangerous but also ideal subjects for the creation of a heroic myth: this includes that other trilogy of

1930s Soviet cinema, Donskoy's Gorky trilogy – *The Childhood of Gorky* [Detstvo Gor'kogo, 1938], *Among People* [V lyudyakh, 1939] and *My Universities* [Moi universitety, 1940]. Gorky had died in 1936, two years after sponsoring the guiding principles of Socialist Realism at the First Congress of Soviet Writers.

The creation of heroic myth on film was not, however, confined to the recently dead. The great figures of the past were also immortalised on film: after all, the further back into history the film-maker went, the more the absence of detailed evidence enabled him to use his imagination. Hence Eisenstein was able to create his own versions of both *Alexander Nevsky* [1938] and *Ivan the Terrible* [Ivan Groznyi, 1944–5]. We know from Leonid Kozlov's arguments that Ivan was intended as a representation of Stalin and he also demonstrates clearly the way in which, in Part Two of the film, Eisenstein managed to subvert the essence of the cultic myth and show Stalin the Terrible as a lonely and haunted man.[49] No other director had the courage, or perhaps the skill, to subvert the myth in this way. Other historical re-enactments are much more straightforward and more obvious cultic representations of the Great Leader. From Russia's history we can cite Petrov's two-part *Peter the First* [Petr pervyi, 1937–9] and his *Kutuzov* [1944], Pudovkin's version of the Napoleonic Wars *Suvorov* [1940], and many other examples. For the Ukraine there was Savchenko's *Bogdan Khmelnitsky* [1941], for the Bashkirs Protazanov's *Salavat Yulayev* [1940], and so on. It was only one small step from such historical quasi-cultic films to the full-blown cultic films which form our third and final category.

These *cultic* films lie at the heart of the personality cult in Stalinist cinema. They are placed later than the first category and emerge later than the second, because both the proto-cultic and quasi-cultic films were in a sense a preparation for them. In the early cultic films the hero is Lenin, although Stalin is there too as Lenin's closest confidant: for example, Romm's *Lenin in October* [Lenin v oktyabre, 1937] and *Lenin in 1918* [Lenin v 1918 godu, 1939] or Yutkevich's *The Man with a Gun* [Chelovek s ruzh'em, 1938]. The apotheosis of the Stalin cult in film is, however, to be found in the portrayal of Stalin by his fellow-Georgian, Mikhail Gelovani, in the films directed by another Georgian, Mikhail Chiaureli: *The Great Dawn* [Velikoe zarevo, 1938], *The Vow* [Klyatva, 1946] and the two-part *The Fall of Berlin* [Padenie Berlina, 1949], Mosfilm's gift to Stalin on his seventieth birthday. It is hardly surprising that all these films were awarded the State Prize of the USSR by the hero depicted in them. No words can adequately describe the full effect of these films: they quite literally have to be seen to be believed. The extent to which contemporary audiences did believe them is of course open to question: there are no accurate measurements, nor can there be, of the real effects of such overt propaganda in such a closed and atomised society.

The three categories that I have outlined do of course overlap and the home category I have allotted to each film is, as I have suggested, in most cases at best tentative, always debatable, and sometimes possibly mistaken. In particular, in the case of the proto-cultic films, I may be reading into them – in this case with the disadvantage of hindsight – things that are not there, and many films legitimately fit into more than one category. It is better to see these three categories as lying on a continuum from the popular entertainment films associated in particular with the Mezhrabpom studio to Gelovani and the apotheosis of the cultic film, each stage or layer in the propaganda process reinforcing the others. Central to that continuum is the role of the positive hero(ine) as a model to be followed by the audience, be it the extraordinary ordinary people like Tanya in *The Radiant Path*, the swine herd and the shepherd, Vasili Buslai and Gavrilo Olexich in *Alexander Nevsky*, Natasha and Alyosha in *The Fall of Berlin*, or historical figures like Chapayev, Nevsky himself and ultimately the ordinary extraordinary figure of Stalin.

The centrality of the hero figure and the need to provide a focus for audience identification determined the centrality of actors and actresses in Soviet cinema of the Stalin period. At the summit of the profession were those red stars, those 'favourites of the epoch' – to use the contemporary phrase – like Babochkin, Cherkasov, Ladynina or Orlova, who embodied the hopes and aspirations of the masses, who gave audiences a focus for their loyalty and their adoration and who made the ideological message of the time intelligible to the millions. Yet the summit of the screen world marked only the foothills of the real world, whose own summit was at first obscure but steadily became clearer. In that world there was and could be only one actor and one positive hero and that was that red star of stars in the Kremlin, the focus of the personality cult – Stalin the Red Tsar.

Chapter 6

Forbidden films of the 1930s

Ekaterina Khokhlova

One of the distinctive features of Soviet history, be it the history of the Party or the history of art, consists in the fact that throughout its existence various events, people and phenomena have constantly been 'left out' of it. In this respect the history of cinema is no exception. With the advent of perestroika, the films that were 'shelved' in the 1960s and 1970s have become the subject of numerous publications and discussions. The people who made these films have had the opportunity to provide their own accounts of the events of the past twenty years, while many of the immediate participants in those events are still active to this day.

However, the unhappy tradition of 'shelved' cinema is not confined to recent decades: its roots go back into the distant past. Since the end of the 1920s the history of Soviet cinema has existed, as it were, in two versions: the official version, in which it was treated until recently as the history of the progressive development of film art; and the realistic version, in which unfinished and banned films occupied an extremely important place. Very few of these films are mentioned in academic works on cinema, the most frequently cited being Eisenstein's *Bezhin Meadow* [Bezhin lug, 1935–7] and Abram Room's *A Severe Young Man* [Strogii yunosha, 1934].

Until now Soviet cinema specialists have mainly taken the view that it was not worth attaching too much significance to this 'off-stage' aspect of the cinema process. The proponents of this view have maintained that, since the majority of banned films have not been preserved, we cannot properly evaluate their quality and their significance for the history of cinema.

In actual fact, cinema is at a disadvantage in comparison with literature which has, however, also met a similar fate. But many of the literary works that remained unpublished or were banned at one time in the Soviet Union have nevertheless circulated in manuscript form, appeared in *samizdat*, or returned to their native land in Western editions. Although school textbooks on literature have until now given pride of place to the classics of Socialist Realism, the memory of the work of disgraced writers and poets has nevertheless to some extent been preserved in the consciousness of various generations of the Soviet intelligentsia.

But, in contrast to this, banned films quite simply ceased to exist from the moment they were banned. Even the people who made them have been reluctant to recall them because, as a rule, the act of banning a film was accompanied by a destructive diatribe that was fraught with the most unpleasant consequences for those involved. It is difficult nowadays to reconstruct a complete list of these films and the credits for many of them: the documentation was frequently destroyed at the same time as the copies of the films. The titles of banned films are mentioned neither in histories of cinema nor in monographs devoted to the work of individual directors. Furthermore, in those cases where the authors of monographs published in recent years do mention these films, they often, wittingly or unwittingly, repeat the conventional judgements: the film was not released or was taken off because it was 'unsuccessful', 'weak' or 'did not work out'.

However, a detailed reading of the press of the period (not to mention a familiarity with the minutes of discussions, official and private correspondence and other documents) is enough to make us realise that the banning policy implied quite specific goals, the most important of which was the total ideologisation of art, including cinema.

The effort of the state to intensify its control over cinema and to subjugate it to its own ends can be traced back to the early years of Soviet power. The numerous decrees, resolutions and instructions that dealt with cinema, beginning with the decree passed in March 1918 that introduced control over private cinema enterprises, were all directed towards precisely this end. The Agitprop Department of the Party Central Committee, created in 1920, gave a political rating to every script and film. After February 1923 not a single film was released without a certificate of authorisation issued by Glavrepertkom, the State Repertoire Committee, and it was only with the permission of this committee that any alteration to an already completed film was possible.

Nevertheless, the political and economic situation in the first half of the 1920s allowed for relative creative freedom. In conditions of competition between private, commercial and state enterprises it was certainly not ideologically motivated films that enjoyed commercial success, and this caused persistent disquiet among Party and state leaders.

From 1926 on, changes in the overall situation were inevitably reflected in the policy of those who ran cinema. Up to this time the activity of Glavrepertkom in controlling the cinema repertoire consisted in the banning of 'harmful' foreign films, mainly those with detective and crime themes. A struggle was going on to increase domestic film production in which left-wing film-makers took an active part. It was these very individuals who a few years later were to be labelled 'Formalists'. However, more and more often voices were raised claiming that the Soviet films being made failed to keep abreast of real life and did not reflect the problems involved in the building of socialism. Increasingly the criteria for the evaluation of a film came to be not its artistic quality but its ideological stance and its suitability for the working-class audience. Increasingly, too, Lenin's precepts on cinema were recalled: the obligation to observe the appropriate proportion between entertainment and educational-agitational films showing the revolutionary struggle and the struggle with religion and the need for the masses to take possession of the cinema.[1] In January 1928 ODSK, the Society of Friends of Soviet Cinema, declared that Lenin's 1920 statement on cinema should be taken as a basic directive for Soviet cinema organisations: 'pay attention to the need to select films carefully and take account of the impact of every film on the population while it was being shown'.[2]

The attack on Soviet films did not begin with the general distribution network, which was still not completely under state control, but with distribution for the Red Army clubs. Among the films rejected by a special commission of the Red Army's Political Directorate was one in particular: Lev Kuleshov's *Your Acquaintance* [Vasha znakomaya, also known as *The Female Journalist* (Zhurnalistka) 1927], which was criticised – as were other films – for alleged 'philistine tendencies'.

The turning point for cinema was the first Party Conference on Cinema in March 1928, which determined the line of development of Soviet cinema for the following decades. Cinema, as 'the most important of the arts', was given pride of place in the task of 'organisation and education of the masses round the slogans and tasks of the Party and their artistic education, wholesome rest and entertainment'.[3]

At this conference there was an open call to carry out immediately 'a purge of the entire repertoire through the Repertoire Committees and to remove from the screen those things that are obviously alien to us and actively harmful to the USSR'.[4] The head of Agitprop, Alexander I. Krinitsky, who expressed this view, defined the purging of the repertoire as a practical task of prime importance:

> We must also do the same if we find that similar things are being prepared in the USSR but have not yet been released for viewing. It is better to suffer financial losses than to allow these things on to the screen. In other words, from tomorrow we must begin to turn the decisions of the conference from words into actions.[5]

On 15 May 1928, exactly two months after the opening of the Party Cinema Conference, the newspaper *Kino* [Cinema] reported that eighteen films, thirteen foreign and five Soviet, had been taken out of circulation. A Glavrepertkom report pointed out that the foreign list had been drawn up from the releases of various years in a selective manner based on the following considerations:

> the idealisation of the pathological and decadent moods of the decaying bourgeois class; the popularisation of latent prostitution and depravity;

the romanticism of pure stunts and criminal acts; the showing of unjusti-
fied cruelties and sadism intended to test the nerves and the unhealthy
interests of a philistine audience; the propagation of bourgeois morals,
of mysticism and so on.[6]

In a leading article under the heading 'About Time Too!', published in the
same issue of *Kino*, the editors called on Glavrepertkom not to stop short at
what it had done so far but to draw in the 'general public' to help it in its
work.[7] It was this impersonal and ill-defined concept that for many years
provided the occasion for subjecting everything which in one way or
another did not conform to the official doctrine of the construction of the
socialist state to criticism, which was frequently very cruel and crude.

In 1929 the slogan 'ideological planning' was promoted. This meant the
introduction of annual thematic plans in every studio. On 7 December 1929
the Council of People's Commissars [Sovnarkom] adopted the decree 'On
Strengthening the Production and Exhibition of Political-Educational
Films' which involved a 30 per cent reduction in the production of fictional
feature films: from now on the most severe demands were to be made on
these films.[8]

Immediately after this in January 1930, on the pretext of removing alien
elements, eradicating bureaucracy, red tape and mismanagement, a purge
began in every cinema organisation. This purge was called an 'ideological
mirror'. All cinema workers were subjected to a most detailed cross-
examination by the Purge Commission. This included questions about their
origins, their political views and their attitude towards Formalism and anti-
Marxist positions in cinema. 'Anti-Marxist teachings' included in particular the theoretical views of Eisenstein, Kuleshov, Shklovsky and the other
'Formalists' of the 1920s.

Film production was subjected to a purge by Glavrepertkom, which
fulfilled the functions of principal censor in the field of cinema. Of the 111
Soviet feature films made in 1929 and early 1930, seven were banned,
thirty-six placed in the fifth distribution category and thirty-five in the
fourth. Films in the fourth and fifth distribution categories were thought to
be of little use and hovered on the brink of being banned. The number of
banned films continued to increase: between 1 January and 15 September
1931, of 144 feature-length fiction and agitprop films, only ninety-five
were approved and, of these, twenty-six were still in the process of being
made and twenty-nine were sent for alteration and correction.

The banning of films took place in conditions of glasnost, or more
precisely of 'super-glasnost' [*gromoglasnost'*]: screenings and discussions
were arranged in ARRK [the Association of Workers of Revolutionary
Cinema], ODSK and workers' and Red Army clubs. Typically, these passed
devastating resolutions demanding that a particular film that was 'unintelligible to the workers' should be banned and that the management of

studios that had wasted resources on the production of anti-Soviet films should be called to account. Thus the artist was squeezed between ideological pressure from above, on the part of the authorities, and from below, on the part of 'the people'.

It was in this way, for instance, that Grigori Roshal's film *Two Women* [Dve zhenshchiny, produced by VUFKU] was banned in 1930, with the accusation that the audience might come away with the impression that women Communists made bad wives. L. Sheffer's film *Two Mothers* [Dve materi, 1931] was banned at the 'request' of workers who thought that the subject of the film – the rights of a mother who had abandoned her own child and the rights of the woman who brought that child up – was ideologically harmful. A similar thing happened to A. Solovyov's film *Five Wives* [Pyat' nevest, 1930] which was accused of distracting the proletarian audience from the tasks of intensified class struggle and of propagating the subject matter of bourgeois art (jealousy, rape, the relations between the generations in a Jewish milieu). From those same workers came the suggestion that 'harmful' films like this should be destroyed, regardless of the money that had been put into them. In effect this repeated the directions given at the Party Cinema Conference in 1928.

Increasingly, the fate of a film depended on the concrete statements of the Party and state leadership. This was the case with *My Motherland* [Moya rodina, 1932], directed in Leningrad by Iosif Kheifits and Alexander Zarkhi. Rapturously received by the critics, the film was ready for release at the beginning of 1933 for the anniversary of the Red Army but was banned after Stalin's speech to the January plenum of the Central Committee and the Central Control Commission, in which he asserted the Army's strength. Against this background, a film in which Red Army soldiers actually died was regarded as a very crude mistake.

At the beginning of the 1930s in cinema, as in other sectors of the economy, there was an intense struggle for economies. The word perestroika never left the pages of the newspapers, just as it was to be several decades later. In reality the plans were not fulfilled. There were shortages of film, of equipment and of construction materials. However, even in conditions of universal shortages, the leadership preferred to ban or to destroy 'ideologically unreliable' films, rather than allow them on to the screen. In August 1933 at the session of the Purge Commission dealing with the Soyuzfilm Party organisation, one of the speakers, referring to information received from Boris Shumyatsky, then the head of GUKF [the Principal Directorate for the Cinema and Photographic Industry], said that over the past few years 50 per cent of the films made had remained 'on the shelf'.[9] In 1932 alone film conservation cost the film industry eight million roubles.[10] In order to justify these losses in some way, the search began for the guilty people among the creative workers or the political leadership of particular studios.

By late 1933 the period of perestroika in cinema had almost come to an end. The political position of the cinema leadership had been strengthened by the Central Committee decree 'On the Restructuring of Literary and Artistic Organisations', adopted on 23 April 1932.[11] After that GUKF no longer had to hide behind the 'interests of the people': it alone took the decision as to which films the people should see, but it did of course take a backward glance at the Party line. Among other films banned as harmful from a class standpoint were: S. Timoshenko's *To Live* [Zhit', 1933], Alexander Udoltsev-Garf's *Anokha* [1933], the Lev Kuleshov and Leonid Obolensky film *Theft of Sight* [Krazha zreniya, 1934] and *A Severe Young Man*, mentioned above.

In addition to the ban on individual films and the failure to release them for exhibition, there was another form of reprisal against objectionable works: this was called 'removing them from the screen in order to regulate film distribution', which in effect also meant that the picture had been banned. In 1935 about 2,700 films made between 1922 and 1935, including newsreels, shorts and animated films, were banned. Of these, about 500 were full-length feature films. By 1935 the majority of films made in the 1920s and many of those made in the early 1930s had been taken out of distribution.

On 17 January 1936, the very day when the new All-Union Committee for Artistic Affairs was established and directly subordinated to Sovnarkom,[12] there was a meeting in the Bolshoi Theatre between Stalin and those involved in the production of the opera *Quiet Flows the Don*, based on the Sholokhov novel. Stalin used the occasion to make some negative criticisms of the Constructivist elements in the staging. This particular meeting gave rise to the campaign for the struggle against Formalism and Naturalism in Soviet art. *Pravda* published a whole series of leading articles, each criticising a specific production in one or other area of the arts. The chosen victim in cinema was the film *Prometheus* [Prometei, 1935], directed by Ivan Kavaleridze and made at the Ukrainfilm studios. Judging by the article in *Pravda* entitled 'A Crude Sketch Instead of Historical Truth', this criticism was mainly a result of the fact that Stalin did not like the way Georgians and the role of Georgia in the colonisation policy of the Russian autocracy were depicted in the film.[13]

In the course of the campaign, which lasted several months, *Prometheus* and seven other Ukrainfilm films were banned, as well as several films made at other studios. But, while most of the banned films were only subjected to the limited charge that they were 'ideological rejects', one of them, Abram Room's *A Severe Young Man*, was subjected to particularly harsh criticism. It was condemned for 'the crudest deviations from the style of Socialist Realism'. In its entirety it was labelled 'a lampoon' and its director was banned from film directing from then on.[14]

The accusation of Formalism still remained the gravest sin for film-makers even after the official summing up of the 'discussion' on Formalism and Naturalism in art. In March 1937 an enormous scandal erupted around Eisenstein's *Bezhin Meadow*. The director's creative method was declared to be Formalist and the conception of the film to be abstract. At the conference called to denounce *Bezhin Meadow*, Eisenstein was told that 'the combination of ideological poverty with ponderous form is the mark of Cain that distinguishes Formalism'.[15] The film *The Wedding* [Zhenit'ba] made at Lenfilm studios in 1937 by Erast Garin, a pupil of Meyerhold, was also condemned and banned because of its 'Formalist affectations' and 'Naturalistic squalor'.

'Ignorance of life' and 'escape from reality' were two of the main accusations in the 1930s when art – and cinema in particular – was supposed to create some kind of abstract ideal of 'the bright future', which did not exist in real life but had been proclaimed by the Party and the government. In this ideal world there was no place for individual doubts, hesitations or reflections and no place for any kind of individualism. The mass had to be uniform. The system instinctively rejected anything that opposed it in any way.

The artistic value of the banned films may be judged from those that have been preserved. *My Motherland*, Boris Barnet's *The Old Jockey* [Staryi naezdnik, 1940, released 1959] and Nikolai Shpikovsky's *Bread* [Khleb, 1930] undoubtedly influenced the film-makers who saw them at the time.[16] It is perfectly possible that cinematic craftsmanship was also used as a reason for banning many films precisely in order to conceal the true state of affairs, since alleged professional incompetence was so persistently under-lined. It was those films that displayed a personal principle, either that of the artist or of the artist's heroes, that provoked the greatest obloquy.

The noisy campaigns that accompanied the banning of films were imbued with the spirit of the political trials of the 1930s. They were used not merely for the moral persecution of their creators, but also as a warning to other film-makers, and indeed to artists in general. By no means every artist, even among the most talented, was able to withstand the full force of the pressure that the system exerted. Some consciously struck a bargain with the conditions laid down by the authorities, others came to naught, yet others tried to manifest their 'self' within the narrow confines of what was permitted. Looking now at the films of the 1930s, we must bear in mind the whole complex of circumstances in which they were made.

The mechanisms that were put into place in the 1920s and 1930s, including the banning of films, continued to exert an effect in later periods. Hence, many of the problems of contemporary cinema unwittingly coincide with similar problems of that time in the 1930s which, by an ironic twist of fate, is also known in our country as a period of perestroika.

Chapter 7

'We were born to turn a fairy tale into reality': Grigori Alexandrov's *The Radiant Path*

Maria Enzensberger

We were born to turn a fairy tale into reality,
To extend distances and space;
We've been given reason, steel wings for arms,
And a flaming motor for a heart.

'The Aviators' March', a popular Soviet song

In a recent article Maya Turovskaya raised the question of the relationship between style and meaning in Soviet cinema of the 1930s and 1940s. She demonstrated the fairy-tale-like structure of the musical comedies of Ivan Pyriev (*The Rich Bride* [Bogataya nevesta, 1938], *Tractor-Drivers* [Traktoristy, 1939] and *The Swine Herd and the Shepherd* [Svinarka i pastukh, 1941]) and their 'folklorisation' of themes drawn from contemporary Soviet village life. Her conclusion was that their 'embellishment' of Soviet reality should be regarded not as a 'distortion of the truth' – for faithfulness to life was never their aim – but as a standard and perfectly legitimate stylistic mode within popular cinema, the mode that elevates its subject matter into the realm of a 'dream' or Utopia, enabling the spectator to 'rise above' reality and regard it in a more sublime and optimistic manner.[1]

The purpose of this paper is to extend the work done by Turovskaya into the analysis of another musical comedy from the same period: Grigori Alexandrov's *The Radiant Path* [Svetlyi put', 1940], originally entitled *Cinderella* but renamed on Stalin's suggestion. I intend to examine the way in which this story of a maid turned Stakhanovite weaver, and subsequently celebrated engineer and deputy to the Supreme Soviet, interweaves symbolic and realistic discourses into a powerful myth of the possibility of personal success in an ostensibly collectivistic society. It should be pointed out at once that the Stakhanovite movement provided a marvellous basis for such a reconciliation of 'capitalist' and 'socialist' ethics.[2]

There are several significant ways in which the Soviet musical of that period differs from its classical American counterpart. Whereas the latter tends to transpose its Utopia in time and space into some sort of 'golden age' or 'exotic community',[3] in which everyone (or so one is made to believe) spontaneously dances and sings, the Soviet musical enacts its Utopia in the here and now, the present-day Soviet reality in which everyone works and, for that matter, works miracles. One way in which this phenomenon is integrated into the fabric of the film is that dance numbers are frequently replaced with carefully choreographed labour scenes, made to appear equally liberating and cathartic. Work is thereby presented as fun and pleasure, and endowed with the same sexual overtones that dancing would carry in a Hollywood musical. As a consequence, dancing is almost entirely absent from the Soviet musical of that period. Songs, on the other hand, are often devised as natural concomitants of labour and are designed to uplift and glorify it, as in the girls' song in *The Rich Bride* or the 'March of the Enthusiasts' in *The Radiant Path*.

The other significant difference is that the Soviet non-backstage musical which we are discussing here (by which I mean a musical that is not concerned with the staging of a show) invariably privileges the female protagonist. Her sexual attractiveness, as in a fairy tale, is featured as an inalienable attribute of her high virtue, social awareness and extraordinary diligence, rather than as an asset in its own right. Presented as a model worker, fully integrated into the process of her country's reconstruction, it is this exemplary woman who sets up the standards which the hero must attain; hence it is she who pushes the narrative towards its inevitable resolution. Thus, it is not the female character who strives to win her male partner over by giving him what he wants, but the reverse – the male character strives to rise to the level of his miracle-worker bride by giving her what both she and the country demand from him.

Like a classic Hollywood musical, most of its Soviet counterparts have two central characters – the male and the female poles – so that the narrative, instead of following the fate of a single individual in a syntagmatic linear fashion, alternates between its male and female poles, bringing them into a paradigmatic relationship of parallelism and comparison.[4] But, while the Soviet musical also postulates marriage as a neutralisation of binary oppositions and a means of achieving social harmony, the nature of the male/female opposition acquires a dramatically different twist in view of the different status allotted to women. For the woman in a Soviet musical is portrayed outside the sphere of domesticity that is traditionally assigned to her and which includes an exclusive preoccupation with romance or any other conventional 'female' pursuits, such as clothes or physical beauty. In *The Radiant Path* the heroine is contrasted with a girl who is preoccupied with her appearance and the idea for a scene in which the heroine tries on a fur coat on arrival in Moscow was eventually abandoned.[5]

The Hollywood musical convention of supplying its central characters with substitute parents in place of the natural ones also acquires a different meaning in its Soviet counterpart. As a narrative device this phenomenon is characteristic of Soviet film from that period as a whole, for the substitute parents are invariably depicted as collective-farm chairmen or team leaders, foremen, factory managers or secretaries of Party organisations – in other words, the representatives of the Party and the state who 'replace' the natural parents, not only for the purposes of narrative intricacy, but also symbolically – as 'social' parents to their 'charges'. The latter are thus presented as the children of the Soviet state itself, the citizens conveniently freed from family ties and personal loyalties. (The absent family of the Soviet cinema of the 1930s and 1940s is a subject worthy of separate investigation.) The most extreme case of this is, of course, the betrayal of his father by Pavlik Morozov, the classic story read by all Soviet children, which was to be the subject of Eisenstein's aborted *Bezhin Meadow* [Bezhin lug, 1935–7].

Thus the rise to public success story does not merely parallel the romance in the Soviet musical: it becomes its inalienable concomitant, the indispensable condition for its successful resolution. Love and happiness, we are repeatedly told, are the rewards meted out to the outstanding, politically conscious workers, be they male or female. Laziness and philistinism, on the other hand, are vices punished by unrequited love. Thus, culturally conditioned sexual differences are played down in these films: their function as symbols of difference is assumed by minor social or occupational distinctions and the relationship of 'competition' between the protagonists. These supremely conscientious individuals are held apart for the duration of the film only by misunderstandings and the plotting of ill-wishers and rivals – hence the notorious *beskonfliktnost'* [conflictlessness] of the Soviet cinema from that period.

As in a fairy tale, characters in the Soviet musical are not personally delineated. The 'personal' is entirely submerged by the 'collective': virtue (i.e. the socialist attitude to work-cum-perseverance, represented by the central characters) is bound to triumph over vice (selfishness, philistinism or conservatism, represented by their antagonists). What is celebrated in the end is in effect the never seriously threatened harmony of the Soviet way of life: in *The Swine Herd and the Shepherd*, for example, the marriage of a record-breaking Vologda swine herd to an outstanding Daghestan shepherd, whom she met at the All-Union Exhibition of Agriculture, sanctifies, as the official cliché puts it, 'the friendship of the Soviet peoples'.

The representation of women as leaders in the sphere of production rather than consumption is both a realistic and a consciousness-raising device, for in the Soviet Union women have always been expected to work outside the home on a par with men. This representation is constructed in such a way as to allow for cross-sexual identification. The labour process, invariably depicted as 'competition' and 'record breaking', put the viewer into the position of a sports event or rather a sport-film spectator. The woman performing 'male' tasks (riding a motor-bike, driving a tractor or working on a shop floor) is dressed in male clothes – trousers, overalls, even a cap – yet she is never defeminised. Her androgynous image, like every case of carnival clothes reversal, serves to neutralise the male/female opposition threatened by the woman's entry into the traditionally male domain of public life. The woman's power and independence are nevertheless circumscribed within the narrative by the invariable presence of 'wiser' male superiors: she is the 'doer', never the most authoritative 'thinker' or 'decision maker'.

One of the most distinctive features of the Soviet musical of that time – and the reason for its wide popularity – is that it concentrates almost exclusively on the lives of the 'humble' and 'poor' and makes them appear 'powerful' and 'rich', proud rather than resentful of their lot. The Utopian sensibilities which the musical is uniquely equipped to unleash (Richard Dyer's categories of 'energy', 'abundance', 'intensity', 'transparency' and 'community' are fully manifested in those films[6]) uplift and sublimate the off-screen reality: people see themselves as they really are – i.e. workers and peasants – and, at the same time, as they would ideally like to be – glorious heroes and heroines, unique, powerful, prosperous and celebrated. It is this interplay of the symbolic and realistic discourses that turns those films into the most graphic 'documents of the emotions of their time' and enables them, in Turovskaya's words, to act 'not so much as the reflection of their time's objective reality, but rather as the reflection of the reality of its image of itself'.[7]

The Radiant Path departs from the dual-focus structure of the conventional musical discussed above: it concentrates on the fate of its central heroine following it through to its eventual triumph. Its genre can thus be best described as the 'rags-to-riches' or the 'ugly duckling' story. Romance, as fairy-tale conventions demand, serves both as a spur to success and as its traditional culmination.

The film's affinity with the Cinderella story is signalled from the very start by the heroine's ash-stained face and the song she sings in front of the mirror:

> The old fairy tale tells us
> About magic events:
> Once upon a time there were two sisters,
> The third one was Cinderella.
> I am miserable like Cinderella,
> Torn apart all day long,
> Yet I shall probably never encounter
> A wise old fairy.

Songs throughout the film complement and comment on the narrative, recapitulating the heroine's story as it goes along.

The film makes use of a number of traditional fairy-tale motifs, such as crystal (icicles and chandeliers), mirrors that can answer back, a dream castle and a wooden chest. Having dispensed with many details of the Cinderella story, *The Radiant Path* nevertheless retains its underlying themes: the growing-up process, the role of good and bad mothers, sibling rivalry,[8] the rewarding of diligence and the eventual reversal of fortunes.

The film opens with a shot of the sky: the title – *The Radiant Path* – flows across the screen, turning into an animated flock of cranes; one of them breaks away and continues its flight above a town surrounded by forest and lakes. A female voice sings:

> High up, under the cloud,
> Above the expanses of fields,
> A flock of cranes is heading
> Towards the south.

As the credits end, the crane reappears and the song continues:

> A strict order, bird after bird,
> Yet sometimes one of them
> Becomes timid and fearful
> And breaks up that strict order.
> Flying for the first time, it is afraid
> Of falling behind its comrades,
> Of breaking away from its girlfriends,
> Of getting lost in the grey clouds.
> I can't distinguish the way
> Through the storm and mist . . .
> I am afraid I'll fall behind,
> I am afraid I won't reach my destination.

The camera descends on to a small provincial town, zooming towards a wooden house: in close-up, a cockerel sitting on a painted board – 'Small Grand Hotel'. Through the window the camera introduces us into the interior of a guest-house, where a peasant girl, Tanya Morozova, works as maid to a pompous and capricious lady. The major themes of the film are thereby set in motion: 'sky' versus 'earth'; 'dream' versus 'reality'; lower versus middle class; striving and daring versus philistinism; the will to succeed and the fear of failure; the individual and the flock.

The film was originally conceived as a light comedy in which an exceptionally clever girl outwits everyone around her – the opening scenes of Tanya engaged in her chores retain that slapstick comedy flavour – but it was eventually decided that the fate of an ordinary girl-turned-Stakhanovite should be resolved in a more socially delineated manner.[9]

The narrative is set in motion by Tanya's encounter with a young engineer, Lebedev, who arrives at the hotel from Moscow. The arrival of the 'prince' is coupled with the arrival of the 'villain', an ex-kulak from

Tanya's village who later proves to be a wrecker. From now on Tanya wants to improve her lot. At this point another important character enters her life, a 'helper' and a 'good mother' (in effect a fairy godmother): the middle-aged woman, secretary of the local factory Party organisation, Pronina, sends her to study at a workers' school. Tanya's initial response is fear and self-doubt. Every major step forward in her life is punctuated by a song refrain:

O I am afraid I'll fall behind,
O I am afraid I won't become learned (succeed, and so on).

Tanya's every transformation is signalled in the film by a dissolve of her face, showing her new identity.

The fact that Pronina and all the other characters in the film are single (even Tanya's mistress, who has a child, appears to have no husband) and reside in a hotel or dormitory – the girls' factory dormitory is actually a converted monastery – is one of the devices by which the film suppresses the natural family, foregrounding instead the family of a socialist collectivity.

As Tanya and her mistress ('wicked sister'/'bad mother') vie for the attention of the young engineer, the mistress gets jealous and throws Tanya out. This is the first important moment in her growing-up process. The fairy-tale heroine is often thrown or teased out of her home to embark on her journey towards self-realisation. The breaking of the mother-daughter tie is usually enacted by means of displacement and projection: it is not the mother, but the stepmother – the mother substitute – who causes the daughter's departure. The rivalry between Tanya and her mistress also re-enacts sibling rivalry for the affection of the parents and later on the 'prince'.[10]

When Tanya finds herself homeless, Pronina takes her in, promising to take her to the textile factory next day. As Tanya sleeps on Pronina's couch, she dreams of a fantastic castle whose entrance is flanked by giant statues of a man and a woman bearing torches. The castle's gate dissolves into a noisy factory shop-floor where Tanya is entrusted with a broom (her first phallic symbol of potency, later replaced with a shuttle) and starts sweeping the floor.

'Dream' and 'reality' are intertwined into a vision of the factory as the 'entrance' into a 'new life'. The image of a modern factory as a symbol of the construction of a 'better future' is pervasive in Soviet cinema of that time: Pavel Petrov-Bytpov's *Cain and Artyom* [Kain i Artem, 1929]; Boris Shpis's *The Return of Nathan Becker* [Vozvrashchenie Neitana Bekkera, 1932]; Mikhail Romm's *The Dream* [Mechta, 1943].

Tanya's fate as maid-turned-industrial worker is both realistic, for this was the usual route for a peasant girl in those days, and symbolic of the possibility of social betterment in a developing society. The maid made good is a recurrent character in Soviet cinema of that period: Boris Barnet's *The House on Trubnaya* [Dom na Trubnoi, 1928]; Grigori Alexandrov's *The Happy Guys* [also known as *Jolly Fellows* (Veselye rebyata), 1934]; Romm's *The Dream*. It is interesting to note that, whereas in *The House on Trubnaya* the turning of a maid into a deputy to the Moscow City Soviet is still presented as no more than a mixed-identity confusion, in line with the more exalted spirit of the 1930s this same transformation is depicted as a 'real event' in *The Radiant Path*.

Tanya's rise up the social ladder reproduces the traditional fairy-tale plot of the reversal of roles and fortunes between the 'rich' and the 'poor', the 'strong' and the 'weak', the 'powerful' and the 'downtrodden'. This principle of role reversal was the inspiration behind the October Revolution itself, providing, in the words of the 'Internationale', the motto of the state that that Revolution brought about: 'We have been naught, we shall be all'. This may explain the symbolic significance attached to the social rise of women in the Soviet arts of that period: the social revolution that has taken place is epitomised in the rise of the traditionally most oppressed and vulnerable part of the population. In Medvedkin's comedy *Wonder Girl* [also known as *The Miracle Worker* (Chudesnitsa), 1937] the record-breaking milkmaid, who is called 'Tiny' [Malyutka], is outstripped by an even smaller and younger girl. The role-reversal principle is clearly expressed in the common Soviet oxymoron, noted by Turovskaya, which uses the word *znatnyi*, meaning 'distinguished' but with implications of nobility, in combination with occupations that are clearly not normally associated with the nobility: for example, 'noble milkmaid', 'noble weaver'. This privileging of women as tokens of social role reversal may also help to explain why 'wreckers' in Soviet cinema are almost invariably caught by women, and occasionally children: the 'weakest' in the community overpower the 'ghosts' of the past that threaten the new social equilibrium – Konstantin Yudin's *A Girl of Character* [Devushka s kharakterom, 1939]; Ivan Pyriev's *The Party Card* [Partiinyi bilet, 1936]; *Arinka* [1940], directed by Nadezhda Kosheverova and Yuri Muzykant; Antonina Kudryavtseva's *Lenochka and the Grapes* [Lenochka i vinograd, 1936].

The wrecker, another recurrent character in Soviet cinema of that time, is also both a realistic and a symbolic figure. Rather like a monster in a horror film, the wrecker is an embodiment of all the country's fears and obsessions. For purges were not merely an invention of Stalin, as some historians would make us believe: the whole country was seized by spy and wrecker mania. The reversal of roles brings in its wake the fear of reprisals.

In *The Radiant Path* Tanya's interception of a wrecker who has set a warehouse on fire helps her to overcome another of her residual fears and prove her resilience in the face of her first set-back at work when she is accused of breaking an already faulty loom. The intervening scene of her sitting alone amidst icicles in front of a skating rink full of gliding couples is reminiscent of another Russian fairy tale, *Frost*, which tells the story of a girl left in a winter forest by her wicked stepmother. At the same time, it anticipates the later scene of Tanya celebrating her success amidst the crystal chandeliers of the Kremlin.

Thus Tanya's growing-up process is marked by her gradual surmounting of all her anxieties and inhibitions. Not only does she master the skills of weaving but, in no time at all, she feels capable of operating simultaneously not just eight looms, like all the other women, but sixteen. Her zeal, however, comes up against the resistance of the conservative factory manager, Dorokhov. But Pronina and Lebedev rally to her support. (Lebedev's name, deriving from 'swan' [*lebed'*], is contrasted with that of a sluggish foreman's assistant Kurnakov, deriving from 'chicken' [*kuritsa*]. As Tanya's chosen 'prince', Lebedev is contrasted with the comic figure of the contender for Tanya's hand, the hotel receptionist, Taldykin, or 'windbag'.) Faced with a problem, Tanya writes to the Chairman of the Council of People's Commissars, Comrade Molotov – the conventions of comedy prohibited the appearance or even mention of Stalin in so light a genre – and she gets a reply congratulating her on her undertaking. The overcoming of another hurdle is marked by another dissolve of Tanya's face, transforming her yet again into a new person. Her ascent up the social ladder is signalled by the scene of her removal from the dormitory to a new flat (the attainment of better accommodation is one of the most significant status symbols in Soviet society) and by the song she addresses to her late mother: 'Mother, look, it's me, Tanya, No longer downtrodden, but business-like and famous.'

In the next scene Tanya is already aspiring to operate 150 looms, bringing to mind another heroine of Russian fairy tales, Vasilisa the Wise [Premudraya], who performed similar miracles. The scene of this demonstration of her remarkable skill is one of the climaxes in the film, and, through the use of camerawork, editing and the off-screen singing of the 'March of the Enthusiasts', the spectator is invited to identify with Tanya, as she deftly moves along the looms. The words, which include a paraphrase of Stalin's pronouncement, 'Labour in our country is the cause of honour, valour and heroism', are sung alternately by Tanya and a choir, and once again express Tanya's newly acquired sense of potency:

Whether you lean over a machine tool
Or drill a rock,
A beautiful dream, still indiscernible,
Calls you to go forward.
We have no obstacles in the sea or on land,
We are not afraid of ice or clouds . . .

The spectator is implicated in the action by the use first of direct address –

'you' (reminiscent of the same device used in the intertitles of Vertov's films and in Mayakovsky's poetry) – and then of the first person plural – 'we'.

No sooner does Tanya accomplish her feat than she finds herself yet again dejected by the news in the paper of the record set by another weaver Zvantseva (from *zvat'* meaning 'to challenge') who has mastered 200 looms. With Pronina's encouragement, Tanya announces her decision to work on 240 looms. Another important piece of news arrives at this point: Dorokhov has been removed from his post. In the original version of the film he was to be replaced by Pronina, but it was deemed more appropriate that Lebedev should be appointed as director.[11]

The Stakhanovite movement and the idea of 'socialist' competition are once again a tribute to the spirit of the time (the film was modelled on the achievements of the two famous weavers Dusya and Marusya Vinogradova) and a theme of profound symbolic significance (the spirit of sibling rivalry is clearly manifested here), for, like bootlegging for an American gangster from an émigré community, or boxing for a Black or Italian lad, Stakhanovism was the only way for an ordinary Soviet worker to outreach her or his rank. The material and social rewards were headspinning, as the next scene, in which Tanya learns she has been decorated, illustrates.

The concluding scenes in which Tanya first receives her order in the Kremlin and then, several years later, appears as an honorary guest in the textile pavilion of the All-Union Exhibition of Agriculture develop another theme characteristic of Soviet cinema of that time – the integration of the individual into Soviet society. Tanya's face cross-cut with the star on one of the Kremlin towers, like many similar cross-cuttings and combinations of an individual with symbolic state sites and buildings (mainly the Kremlin, the Exhibition of Agriculture – the apotheosis of Stalinist architecture – and Moscow as a whole; the town of Kostrov in *The Radiant Path* is sometimes made to look remarkably like Moscow), suggests the unity of the individual with the state, creating the image of a society that envelops the individual and fosters her or his prosperity. The message of Tatyana Lukashevich's *The Foundling* [Podkidysh, 1939] is that even a little child cannot get lost in Soviet society, but will be taken good care of and safely restored to her parents; the private life of Pyotr Vinogradov in the film of that name – Alexander Macheret's 'Chastnaya zhizn' Pyotra Vinogradova', 1935 – unfolds against the background of public buildings and recreation sites.

The Kremlin sequence in *The Radiant Path* contains a scene, conceivable only in a musical, of Tanya dancing in front of mirrors, each of which reflects an image of her as she used to be, engaging her in a dialogue with her former selves:

The fairy tale come true is being created by us,
And the inventions of old fairy tales
Grow pale before the truth of our time.

The next scene, a phantasmagoric flight of Tanya and her double in a car over the expanses of the Soviet Union (the narrative 'stops', giving way to a breathtaking, cathartic spectacle), indicates the passage of several years, during which Tanya becomes an engineer and a deputy to the Supreme Soviet. It is in this capacity that she appears in the concluding scene at the Exhibition of Agriculture.

Amidst the festivities of Soviet prosperity and abundance (created by people like Tanya – 'millions like us') Tanya and Lebedev meet again. He cannot at first recognise her in a scene parodying Eugene Onegin's meeting with that less fortunate Cinderella, Tatyana, in Pushkin's poem and Tchaikovsky's opera. Yet the traditional 'musical' marriage of opposites, in this case of hand and brain, of the peasantry, the working class and the intelligentsia (the scene ends in front of Mukhina's famous sculpture of the peasantwoman and the male worker outside the Agricultural Exhibition, which thereafter became the emblem of Mosfilm), of energy/enthusiasm and intellect/reason, has already been realised by Tanya's own personal accomplishments. It is with her own double, after all, that she 'flies' over the territory of the Soviet Union. All that marriage to a man can add to her existence is the fullness of being that, as every fairy tale maintains, can only be achieved by 'forming a truly satisfying bond with another', thereby dissipating the death and separation-from-mother anxieties.[12] Hence the image of sexual potency and fertility – the fountains and a relief celebrating animal procreation – that form a backdrop to the romantic reunion between Tanya and Lebedev.

Thus the film re-enacts in realistic images all the stages of the fairy-tale heroine's/hero's progress from 'once upon a time' through the inevitable stages of 'leaving home' and the anxieties of 'going into the world' and struggling there in temporary isolation, to the eventual 'finding of her/himself there', which culminates in the traditional ending 'and lived happily ever after'.[13] Thus, far from being a crude piece of propaganda, the film is in fact sufficiently rich in human content to be able to arouse the spectator's interest and empathy on both symbolic and realistic – referring to the socio-historical world outside the text – levels.

To demonstrate the film's extraordinary grip, not only on its contemporaries but also on subsequent generations of film-goers, I want to reproduce the letter that Lyubov Orlova, who played Tanya, received in the mid 1970s from the very people whose life the film was supposed to portray:

> Dear Lyubov Orlova,
>   We have just seen *The Radiant Path* on television. There were seventeen of us: weavers, spinners, foremen, engineers, metal workers, the secretary of the Komsomol organisation, and the former secretary of the Party organisation.

Figure 15 Lyubov Orlova as the Cinderella of the production line 'turning fairy-tale into reality' in *The Radiant Path* (1940).

Figure 16 Lyubov Orlova 'the *prima donna* of Soviet cinema', as the archetypal *femina sovietica* in Grigori Alexandrov's *Volga-Volga* (1938).

Dear Comrade Orlova, this film and you – our People's Actress[14] – are our life.

Our factory is the most revolutionary in Nizhny Novgorod. Together with the Sormovo workers, we were the first to raise the red banner and fight on the barricades in 1905.

Nowadays we have more shockworkers – weavers and spinners – than appear in *The Radiant Path*. One of them, Barinova, was among the initiators of the movement with Alexei Stakhanov and Dusya Vinogradova.

Comrade Orlova, we love you, you are a great actress and a remarkable person (with no conceit). We call our daughters after you – Lyubov is the most common and respected name in our factory.

You probably do not know that, whenever one of us is decorated or receives a bonus for outstanding work, even at weddings or when flats are allocated, we first of all ask ourselves how would our dear Cinderella, Lyubov Orlova, behave in this situation. Your name is for us the symbol of the Communist attitude to life. Do forgive me, but I am describing it all as it really is.

Comrade Orlova, if you are too busy to visit our Nizhny Novgorod, nowadays called Gorky, then perhaps you could send us your greetings. We have a museum in our club that is devoted to the glory of the Revolution and of labour. Among the other exhibits we display your photograph as both a Stakhanovite weaver and a world-famous actress who reflects our life, the life of ordinary people.[15]

Please forgive me for this clumsy letter, my education consists of the workers' school, the Great Patriotic War, seven wounds – four of them serious. I have two daughters and three sons and I have been decorated twenty-seven times. I am writing to you at the request of the women weavers and spinners. This morning the secretary of the Party organisation read out this letter at the factory. Everyone there wanted to sign it and even to write to the government, asking it to send you down here, but I posted the letter to avoid any argument.

I apologise once again. We, 4,000 weavers, spinners, metal workers, foremen, engineers, office workers, Komsomol and Party members, wish you, our favourite People's Actress, many long years of life and excellent health. We are proud of the fact that – along with Sobinov, Yermolova and Chaliapin – our Russian art has Lyubov Orlova.

On behalf of the workers of the Red October textile factory . . .

Nikolai Smirnov[16]

Chapter 8

The artist and the shadow of Ivan

Leonid Kozlov

In memory of Masha Enzensberger

> In life it is always possible to find the truth – if life is long enough.
>
> Sergei Eisenstein[1]

On 2 February 1946 Sergei Mikhailovich Eisenstein was in the cutting room at Mosfilm putting the final touches to the second part of *Ivan the Terrible*.[2] He never managed to see it again on the screen. That same evening he suffered a serious heart attack at Dom kino [the House of Cinema], where an official banquet had been organised in honour of those who had recently been awarded the Stalin Prize.[3] Eisenstein was among them, as the author of Part One of the film about *Tsar Ivan*.[4]

'By all the laws of science I should have died. But for some reason I survived.'[5] These words are from his memoirs, most of which were written in the Kremlin hospital and later in a sanatorium. Among the memoir materials published later there is one chapter without a title: in it the subject of suicide arises. Eisenstein confesses: 'I once attempted a rather complex means of roundabout suicide myself.'[6] Further on, in a series of free associations, there follow several phrases:

> I decided to work myself to death . . . The fuse of my intention was laid in the autumn of 1943 . . . This was probably the most dreadful autumn of my life . . . The beginning of 1946 reaped the fruits.[7]

Thus, in Dom kino on 2 February 1946 the 'fuse' that had been laid in Alma-Ata in the autumn of 1943 ignited. Why had that autumn in particular been the 'most dreadful' of his life for Eisenstein?

The history of the film *Ivan the Terrible* has many roots. Let us now turn to some of them.

In the middle of January 1941 it was suggested to Eisenstein that he make a film about Ivan the Terrible. The suggestion was made to him personally and directly by Andrei Zhdanov.[8] It was understood that cinema was now destined to play its part in the glorification of Tsar Ivan IV as a great and wise autocratic ruler that was already to be discerned in a number of works by Soviet historians and in the projects of playwrights and prose-writers. It was clear that, as 1941 dawned, the figure of Tsar Ivan was being subjected, not only to a justification, but also to official canonisation. That was what Stalin wanted.

The suggestion that Zhdanov communicated constituted in essence a commission and it was no accident that it was addressed to the director of the film *Alexander Nevsky* which, two years previously, had enjoyed not only a very broad success with the mass audience but also high-ranking official approval.

We have never known whether Eisenstein the artist had any hesitation about accepting the proposal. Judging by all the evidence, he was ready to accept this commission.

The previous year, 1940, which had on the surface been a good one for Eisenstein, was in fact a year of secret inner crisis – not so much creative, as spiritual, moral and existential.

So far we have found no mention in his diary of how he felt when he learned about the fate of his teacher Vsevolod Emilevich Meyerhold, whose death had been concealed behind the official formulation of a 'ten-year sentence with no right to correspondence'.[9] But Eisenstein's diary tells us about a lot of other things.

While he was waiting for the premiere of his production of Wagner's *Die Walküre* at the Bolshoi Theatre, working on his theoretical articles and on the script for his projected film on Pushkin (which he dreamt of making in colour if this were feasible), assuming that he would return to teach at VGIK [the All-Union State Cinema Institute], and undertaking the artistic management of Mosfilm, Eisenstein remained painfully and soberly aware of the situation that had arisen specifically for him as an artist, as the *author* of his own works. Behind him there was a multitude of 'unfinished business', of his own cinematic projects that had remained fatally unrealised. And the few films that he had completed, those that had brought him worldwide renown and recognition in his own country – from *The Battleship Potemkin* onwards – were all ones that had been made to order. The success of *Alexander Nevsky* (which had perhaps even saved his life – or at least his artistic life?) decisively confirmed the hopeless situation in which he now found himself in his relations with the man who had commissioned the work, the man who was by now the supreme ruler. His attempt to realise a new individual project in the film *The Great Fergana Canal* [Bol'shoi Ferganskii kanal, 1939] had been blocked by intervention from above.[10]

Now Eisenstein asked himself a cruel question: am I really an artist who has lost his individuality? Here are some of the entries in his diary for 1940:

10 March: I am 'searching' for my own subject and I cannot find it . . . Commissions have come ready-made, haphazardly and out of the blue. It was only afterwards that I 'realised' that they were things that I really

wanted to do. They 'grew up' . . . Careerist themes are *ausgeschlossen* [excluded] – they do not attract me. But don't I have any of my own?
8 April: I don't want a subject that takes a sledgehammer to crack a nut. The most successful things that I have done have been commissioned by the Government – *The Year 1905* [i.e. *The Battleship Potemkin* – Eds], *October*, *Nevsky*.
27 April: What lies ahead for us in cinema is absolutely unknown. What kind of films are we going to make? What about?
13 May: Is there anything in art that I would throw myself into the flames for? Yes or no? I fear . . . no. Was there ever? Yes, there was![11]

In these and other diary entries at that time Eisenstein's consciousness, failing to find that inner identity that he himself would probably have called by his usual name 'synthesis', unaccountably fragments. On the one hand there is the man who made *The Battleship Potemkin*, a man who has not renounced the ideals and principles of his youth, but who has subsequently been transformed into a 'state film director' (there had been no alternative) and who is doomed to hope that some higher power might acknowledge the need he felt for work that was worthy of his powers. On the other hand there is the artist who had come nowhere near realising his potential and who is overwhelmed by the terrifying danger of losing his own *inner freedom* and his spiritual will in the conditions of totalitarianism.

His embittered remark that there was nothing 'that I would throw myself into the flames for' was written immediately after he – inescapably possessed by a passion to complete something – resolved, after prolonged hesitation, to compromise. With the knowledge of the cinema leadership (and on the advice of his theatrical friends), he expressed his intention of filming the plot of a new play, *The Prestige of the Empire*, about the 'Beilis case', which had created a sensation in pre-Revolutionary Russia and which had been disproved and exposed at the time (in 1913) as an anti-Semitic political provocation – a Russian version of the Dreyfus affair.

Eisenstein approached this project with a troubled conscience, suspecting that he, as director, would be getting involved in something that was none of his business: 'Isn't it all just sensationalist muck-raking . . .?'[12] Nevertheless, for one reason or another, he resolved to take it on and began to mull over the way that he would tackle the film as director.[13] For him there were now months of exhausting and devastating waiting. Only the November premiere of *Die Walküre* brought him a feeling of achievement and success. But the fate of the project for *The Prestige of the Empire* remained unclear while his inner crisis became unbearable. 'I am quite inert,' he wrote in his diary on 2 January 1941.[14]

On 11 January Zhdanov telephoned him out of the blue and informed him that this proposed project 'is no longer of any interest'. In response to the question 'What status does it have?' Zhdanov had no answer and he asked Eisenstein to telephone him three days later.[15] Shortly afterwards they met for a discussion: the subject was the film that Eisenstein was expected to make about Ivan the Terrible.[16] Zhdanov explained the political 'supertask' of the film and guaranteed that Eisenstein would be given especially favourable working conditions.

Stalin needed this film because he needed Ivan the Terrible as a figure resurrected, rehabilitated and exalted in the mass public consciousness as the brilliant forebear of and, if you like, the 'prototype' for Stalin himself.[17] The image of a great autocrat, of a daemonic statesman, of a man whose punishment was implacable, who conquered territory and gathered a great empire together – not so much in historical reality as in the reality of myth – was an image that, so it seems, to a large extent corresponded to Stalin's own political self-perception: at least to the one that he had developed in that very year, 1940.[18]

The propagation of the 'personality cult of Ivan the Terrible' and the frightening ideological meaning of this cult very soon became obvious. On 4 February 1941 Boris Pasternak wrote:

> Our benefactor thinks that we have previously been too sentimental and that the time has come for second thoughts. Peter the Great is no longer an appropriate model. The new passion, openly confessed, is for Ivan the Terrible, the *oprichnina*, and cruelty. This is the subject for new operas, plays and film scripts. I am not joking.[19]

Eisenstein did not write or utter anything like this. As early as January he was working on the film script, in accordance with the proposal made to him, and he refused only one thing: to write with a co-author.[20]

The film *Ivan the Terrible* appeared to be necessary not just to Stalin but also – in its own way and to no less an extent – to Eisenstein. Why and what for? What motives and what impulses prompted him to a decisive 'yes', in contrast to Shostakovich, who had declined a suggestion that he should write an opera about Ivan the Terrible?[21] Was it the definitive nature of Stalin's commission deliberately directed to him, Eisenstein? Was it the guarantee of directing a large-scale film after an interval of two years, during which his own projects had been deemed to be 'not needed'? Was it an insatiable creative instinct tortured by a craving to complete something? Or was it artistic ambition? Was it the aesthetic spell of the character of Ivan the Terrible that had captivated him since childhood? The wealth of dramatic and staging possibilities presented by the actual material? Lastly, was it the temptation to pluck that 'disturbing string of cruelty' within himself that Eisenstein later spoke openly about?[22]

It is perfectly possible that all these things in one way or another hovered in Eisenstein's consciousness (and in his subconscious), confirming him in his decision to accept this commission. But all these factors were, or so it seems to me, joined together by one principal, decisive motive, which irrevocably defined his work on both the script and the film. This was the fact that in this work he saw the opportunity to turn a *commissioned* work into an *authorial* work, the opportunity to have his *own* say.

He conceived and began his script, taking as his starting point the idea of the figure of Ivan IV as the expression of a great state.[23] He himself, as both artist and thinking citizen, had little doubt about the notion of statehood (and of state unity) as historically both inevitable and necessary for the country. He realised that the path that had been suggested to him required from him an apologia for Ivan as a heroic figure. In this enterprise he had enough freedom to 'choose the right colours' and 'find the right angles'. In studying the variety of historiographical and artistic material relating to the time of Ivan, or addressed to it, he – as an artist – was free to find his own place on the borderline between history and mythology.

Here there was a great tradition. The historical memory of Ivan had for a long time been indistinguishable from the mythological memory, despite all the efforts of Russian historians to find some 'pure information' about the Tsar.[24] In the course of the centuries the myth of Ivan the Terrible had existed in folklore, poetic and historiosophical consciousness.

The image of Ivan the Terrible was perceived and recreated in various outlines and aspects, in various moral interpretations and evaluations: sometimes sublimely apologetic, sometimes in the guise of moral censure, sometimes displaying a controversial duality of the elevated and the base – but almost always preserving the characteristics of daemonic greatness.[25] The attempt to understand and interpret the figure of 'the first tsar of all the Russias' in the works of Russian artists and thinkers is a large subject and one which we can only touch upon here. The names are well known, as are the differences in interpretation. The 'shadow of Ivan' (as Pushkin put it)[26] has pursued many people who in the course of the past century and a half have tried to delve into the enigmas of Russian history in search of the laws that govern it.

Now the man who had only recently made such films as *The Battleship Potemkin* and *October* felt called to glorify a monarch whose name had become the symbol of Russian autocracy. This seems almost paradoxical. But history is a seamless garment, in all its antitheses and all its metamorphoses. The first person to put to Eisenstein the idea of making a film about the Russian monarchy (he had in mind such figures as Ivan the Terrible) was none other than Stefan Zweig, as early as 1928. After seeing the film *October* Zweig wrote Eisenstein a letter:

> I have been dreaming that you might make a large-scale historical film showing the rise of the tsars . . . to the colossal greatness of the Russian state, showing the hypertrophe of the idea of autocracy that arose from

the original cell of their stock and perished through their own malignant growth.[27]

It seems that in 1941 the artist's attitude towards Tsar Ivan had to be defined quite differently from the way it would have been in 1928 or even in 1935, when Eisenstein was working on the script for the film *Moscow*.[28] Nevertheless it was precisely in connection with his project for a film about the history of Moscow that he recalled one of his unrealised intentions: the making (since he was in America) of the film *Black Majesty* [Chernoe velichestvo] about Henri Christophe, the revolutionary and first emperor of Haiti. 'The Tragedy of the Degeneration of a Leader into a Despot' was how the hero's fate was described: it is with these words that the incomplete 'Foreword to Unfinished Affairs', written on 4 November 1933, breaks off.[29]

How did Eisenstein perceive the events of the second half of the 1930s when Stalinist totalitarianism was so obviously celebrating its victory in his own country? We can only partially judge from his articles and public statements of that time: in them there is expressed from time to time an apologia for Soviet state policy and in this context Stalin is mentioned. Half a century later it is easy – all too easy – to accuse Eisenstein of conformism, double-think (as Orwell puts it), and so on. Inevitably he was a man of his country, of his time, of his generation.[30] Apparently the figure of Stalin cast its hypnotic spell on him too, just as it did in various ways in the 1930s on the works and behaviour of many artists (including both Pasternak and Bulgakov). To what extent was he affected by this spell and how long could it have lasted? This is a question to which there is as yet no definite answer.[31] In Eisenstein's diary entries from the years 1928 and 1931 there are some far-from-flattering references to Stalin. Lines in his diaries and memoirs, often amazingly frank, conceal a vast store of thoughts and feelings that are never expressed. But what is not expressed *expressis verbis*, through written or oral speech, may be expressed, and may even have to be expressed, in the images created by the artist in accordance with the very logic of his imagination.

In the spring of 1941, when he had completed work on the general dramaturgical plan for the script – from Ivan's childhood to his campaign to gain access to the Baltic – Eisenstein published his article 'A Film about Ivan the Terrible', in which his conception of the projected film and his attitude towards the figure of its hero are set out in complete accordance with the official – that is, the Stalinist – point of view.[32]

At that time, however, nobody knew that the first scene of the film to emerge in Eisenstein's imagination as author was the confession scene:[33] Tsar Ivan turns to his confessor immediately after he has repented – a repentance that then, in the script version, developed into one of the principal climactic scenes. Let us recall it here:

after the bloody march of the *oprichniki* on Novgorod (where Alexander Nevsky had once been prince) Tsar Ivan, prostrated beneath the fresco of the Last Judgement in the Cathedral of the Assumption, offers the Heavenly Father his repentance for the evils committed in the name of the great cause . . . meanwhile in the choir of the church a monk reads an unending list commemorating all the people who have been repressed and put to death at the Tsar's pleasure.[34]

Thus the apologia for autocracy [*edinovlastie*] that had been expected of Eisenstein was transformed, from its very inception, into the tragedy of autocracy, while the idea of a great end justifying any means was changed, also from its very inception, into a question of the dreadful price paid for progress towards that great end. Eisenstein was prompted to this transformation because of his direct experience of the reality of contemporary life, the reality of the 'Stalin era' in which he was fated to live. It is in this, above all, that that 'new word' he felt free to utter consisted. It is this that explains why a film about Ivan the Terrible seemed so essential to Eisenstein. He was ready for this subject – the deeds and fate of a Russian autocrat – even before he received the order to make *Ivan the Terrible*.

As I have already indicated, 1940 was a crisis year for Eisenstein. 'I am "searching" for my subject and I cannot find it.' But these words were written a few days after he had started to elaborate his new project, a film about Pushkin. This project arose and developed spontaneously, independent of any notions as to its feasibility and seemingly despite all his agonised misgivings about being faithful to his inner creative self. By turning to Pushkin, Eisenstein acquired what Pushkin himself had called 'a secret freedom'. This project began to emerge immediately after Eisenstein had, on 4 March 1940, made a colour shot analysis [*raskadrovka*] of the famous episode in Pushkin's *Boris Godunov*, of Tsar Boris's monologue, 'I have achieved supreme power . . .' He mentally transferred the place of the action from the Tsar's palace to the Cathedral of the Assumption. The Tsar's monologue – pouring out in words his terrible premonitions, his horror of loneliness, and the torment of his troubled conscience – is represented as a confession before an invisible judge.[35]

Two days later this remark appeared on the last page of these drawings: 'Much better for "Pushkin".'[36] Eisenstein resolved that this imaginary film scene would find its realisation in his film about Pushkin; it is from that moment that the new project began to emerge. He did not yet know that Boris Godunov's monologue, that he had inserted into the drawings, was to become the original prototype from which his conception of the film about Ivan the Terrible would develop.[37]

When he was working on the script Eisenstein naturally did not forget that he was obliged in one way or another to embody the official ideological conception. In both the actual script and in the multiplicity of accompanying texts we find traces of the author's ingenious efforts to assimilate and interpret the official requirements in his own way, to combine – as far as was possible – his own attitude with the point of view of the man who had commissioned the film, or vice versa.

The apologia for Ivan did not come easily. Eisenstein strove to find his own 'keys' to the explanation and justification for his hero's actions – not merely historical, but also psychological and psychoanalytical[38] – without evidently missing any opportunity to portray the image of the 'good Ivan'. There is striking evidence for this in a note he made in his diary at the time he was finishing the script: ' "John" good – because personal *avant tout* – a mixture of oneself and the leading figure of our time.'[39] As we can see, the attitude of Eisenstein the artist towards the man who had commissioned his work was entirely deliberate within the limits of his working process and is reflected in things other than declarations intended for publication.

This, however, was only one of the reasons, only one of the motives for the organisation of the film's dramatic structure. 'The process of mastering [*osvoyenie*] the material, that is making the material *my own*'[40] followed several different paths simultaneously and the image of Ivan – Eisenstein's Ivan – was shaped by a variety of assumptions, and not just those that he wrote about in newspaper articles, or even in his diaries.[41]

Nevertheless, for one reason or another, Eisenstein, attracted by the dramatic possibilities of the project, was unable and unwilling (for the time being) to admit that the contradiction implicit in this work from the very beginning – the contradiction between the artist and the person who had commissioned the film – was to prove irreconcilable and insoluble, and that the realisation of his creative freedom *within* the limits of the conception of the commission (as had happened with *The Battleship Potemkin*) was by now no longer possible.

Subsequently critics and historians have often assumed that Eisenstein began by making Part One of the film, containing the apologia for its central hero, and then went on to make Part Two, in which Ivan the Terrible's deeds are portrayed in a negative light. But it did not happen like that. During the formation of the dramaturgical project and the writing of the script the film was conceived as an integral whole, which seemed to its author to be 'all-embracing'.[42] The contradiction 'between Parts One and Two' – or, more accurately, between the artist and the man who had given the order – increased as the artist came to grips with his project and as it took shape over several years during a time of great changes.

On 22 June 1941 Eisenstein was at work on the script. The war that was just beginning did not put a stop to this work. On 4 September – when Hitler's armies were already racing towards Moscow and Kiev – Eisenstein received an order: he was not to stop work on *Ivan the Terrible*. This order remained in force even after Eisenstein and other film-makers had been evacuated on 14 October from Moscow to Alma-Ata. As before, a script was still expected from him; as before, the anticipated production was guaranteed every possible 'privilege', and as before the 'caretaker' of Eisenstein's work was Zhdanov. The intermediary between Eisenstein and higher authorities was Ivan Grigorevich Bolshakov, the Chairman of the Committee for Cinema Affairs.[43] In January 1942 the script was finished and sent to Moscow for approval. On 14 May Bolshakov cabled to Alma-Ata: 'The historical conception of the script is basically correct.'[44] In September the text of the script, with corrections, was approved in full. The way was open: now he could get ready for the filming.

That is how the first year of the war appears on the surface in Sergei Eisenstein's biography. We can judge what was going on inside – that is, in the artist's mind – from several texts. On 25 July 1941, after German bombers had raided Moscow, he wrote in his diary:

If I survive, I must live differently.
More fully . . .
My life has been 'rolled up'.
In expectations. In eternal expectations. Of what?
The time has come. We've reached a watershed.
Soon there will be no time left for waiting.
War opens our eyes.
What if they suddenly blow us away tonight?
How would I appear before the Lord, if he exists?[45]

In the same diary, on the surrounding pages, he speaks of the instinctive and selfless devotion that emerged in people in the summer of 1941.

Another entry begins with these images: the July heat, the sense of danger, the threat of fire. Eisenstein is recalling the omens of that summer's day in Moscow when Meyerhold's stepdaughter, Tatyana Yesenina, asked him to take charge of the Master's archive. Eisenstein does not mention how he reacted – without any hesitation – to this request. This text was written three years later in 1944 and is headed 'The Treasure'.[46]

In the spring of 1942, after the script for *Ivan the Terrible* had been sent from Alma-Ata to Moscow, the first reactions from historical scholars reached Eisenstein. They scented danger: were there not too many executions in the film, 'wouldn't it be better to reduce the number'? Eisenstein noted in his diary: 'If I do that, the "bare teeth" of the epoch would be lost . . .' and, he added in brackets, 'of both!', both epochs – that of Ivan and the present day.[47]

This entry was made on 23 March 1942. His article, '*Ivan the Terrible. A Film about the Sixteenth-Century Russian Renaissance*' was written on 1 May 1942 and published in the newspaper *Literatura i iskusstvo* [Literature and Art] on 4 August of the same year. In it he remarks that the idea of absolutism, of personal autocracy, was necessary and progressive for *that* time, but not for the twentieth century. He also talks about the war that was going on against Hitler as a war of the nations against bloody and tyrannical obscurantism, the 'most beautiful and brightest' struggle, called upon to defend and affirm 'free democratic choice'. He also discusses the intention behind his next film:

> to do what every hero of the past has a right to: to show objectively the full scope and range of his activity. Because only this can explain all the characteristics, unexpected or murky, sometimes grim and often terrible, inevitably possessed by a statesman in an epoch as passionate and bloody as the sixteenth-century Renaissance, be it in sun-drenched Italy, in the England which in the person of Queen Elizabeth became queen of the seas, in France, Spain or the Holy Roman Empire.
>
> To show Ivan in the full range of this activity and in his struggle for the Muscovite state – that is what lies at the basis of this film.
>
> And it has to be said directly that the activity and the battle were immense and bloody.
>
> But we do not intend to wipe a single drop of spilt blood from Tsar Ivan's account.
>
> We do not want to whitewash him, but to explain.[48]

Thus the author's conception of the film turns out to have been presented from an unexpected angle: Eisenstein is essentially declaring that his film about Ivan the Terrible must not be transformed into an apologia for Stalin.

The fact that this article, published in Moscow, did not provoke any reaction from the ideological powers-that-be inevitably seemed to Eisenstein to be a good omen. He felt himself to be increasingly free.

In October 1942, while fierce battles were still raging in the ruins of Stalingrad, in Alma-Ata Eisenstein wrote the preface to the English-language edition of his book *The Film Sense*. Among the well-known Eisenstein texts this has no rival in terms of its pathos and its ecstatic power of expression:

> We cannot foresee or foretell the artistic paths that mankind will follow once it has risen from the mud and death of these years, cleansed by the everlasting heroism of its best sons, the warriors against fascist darkness . . .
>
> We are firmly convinced that victory over that darkness awaits us.
>
> Before us there is light.
>
> But we are not yet able to adapt to its rays, to discern the new life in its new rays, to move along the new paths that it illuminates.
>
> We have foresight, presentiment and premonition of it.
>
> But this light is only now coming to life in the truly apocalyptic madness in which the Universe is aflame . . .

Three things are left to us:
to wait,
to hurry,
to be at the ready ...

There is something thrilling in this waiting for a future fertilisation of art through a new phase and page of life.

In the consciousness of its numbness before the moment of its arrival.

This is the numbness in which young brides await the moment that they are given away to their unknown husbands, or the earth lies stretched out in fear and trembling for the fertilisation of the spring shoots.

There is something intoxicating, not just in the consciousness of the freedom of the spirit, but also in the sensation of a historical limit set to an obsolete stage of life, before it surges up again to give its blessing to a new stage in the development of art. It is at such moments that you sense the living step of the historical movement of the Universe.

May the candles in our hands as we await the light be pure and ready for the time when our arts are confronted by the need to utter this new word of life.[49]

In this monologue we see not just a faith in future military victory, but also a clear consciousness of the already approaching victory of light over darkness and the prophecy of the new world that is inevitably coming. The elevated style in which Eisenstein expresses this faith is obviously reminiscent of the style of biblical prophecies and evangelical eschatological parables. ('Let your loins be girded about, and your lights burning' (Luke 12: 35).) How can we explain this joy at 'freedom of the spirit' at the gravest moment of the war, this – almost mystical – premonition of the 'new, unparalleled era'?[50]

This was not just an expression of patriotic pathos or a feeling of the unity of the world powers fighting against fascism. This was an expression of something else: a special spiritual phenomenon that emerged precisely in this first period of the Great Patriotic War. 'Spontaneous de-Stalinisation' is how Mikhail Gefter has defined this phenomenon:

[The war] made both possible and inevitable actions outside the regulations and priorities of our 'peaceful' pre-war life. What is more, it defied them: in the tragic tribulations of the war there emerged – together with a feeling of personal responsibility for the fate of the fatherland – a personal view, or rather the embryo of a personal view of how it, the fatherland, should be both now and, even more so, in the future.[51]

Can we nowadays move forward through cycles of spasms and catastrophes with the same heroic enthusiasm as in 1941? ... Man, abandoned to the tyranny of fate, suddenly, at death's door, found the freedom to take control of his own life. Yes, freedom! As an eye-witness and historian I can testify to the fact that in 1941 and 1942 many situations and human resolutions manifested a spontaneous de-Stalinisation (and one whose deeply entrenched yet temporary quality has still, to this day, not been fully understood . . .) Yes, this was ours – Russian, all-Russian, Soviet – but it was also the World which became part of us then. When we lost what we had gained in those two terrible and great years, we completely lost both ourselves and the World.[52]

The first year and a half of the war, with all its catastrophes and countless sacrifices, did in fact lead Soviet people (millions of them) into a new existential consciousness of freedom of choice, freedom of action and freedom of decision. Hence the special spiritual atmosphere of that year and a half. 'De-Stalinisation' was not 'anti-Stalinism' in a direct sense: it was essentially different. From that moment of desperation at the end of June 1941, when it became obvious to everyone that this earthly god was not omnipotent, there emerged a tangible and recognisable realisation of human *independence*, of human sovereignty. The Stalin cult was not over-thrown, but its hypnotic effect weakened and the influence of ideological dogmas lessened. The intelligentsia felt significantly freer than they had been before the war.[53] As Pasternak later wrote: 'The tragic and difficult period of the War was a *living* period and in this context there was a free and joyful return of a sense of common interest with everyone else.'[54]

It was this mood that gave rise to that faith in an 'unparalleled future' that Eisenstein experienced while preparing to film *Ivan the Terrible*.

This 'de-Stalinisation' soon came to an end. The reverse process began as early as the first months of 1943, after the German surrender at Stalingrad. As the Soviet Army won new victories over Hitler's forces an imperial regimentation gradually entered the life of the country. The numerous portraits of Stalin in marshal's uniform were an embodiment of the way times were changing. Ideological control over ideas and their expression became increasingly severe and rigorous.

On 22 April 1943 in Alma-Ata the shooting of *Ivan the Terrible* began. In the autumn of 1943 Eisenstein was stricken by a grave inner crisis. In his diary entries at the time he does not once mention his revulsion at everything he saw. It was only three years later, in his memoirs, that he wrote about that autumn as the 'most dreadful' of his life, and compared it with those moments of creative catastrophe that he had experienced earlier with the failure of the Mexican project and the tragedy of *Bezhin Meadow*, forbidden and destroyed.[55]

What could have compared to these catastrophes? Only one thing: the failure of the idea behind *Ivan the Terrible*. Yet in the autumn of 1943 nothing happened that might have put in question the continuation of work on the film right through to its completion.

Eisenstein's confession, expressed in his memoirs, remained an enigma for a long time. The opportunity to unravel the cause of this crisis arose only recently. At first glance, but only at first glance, the clue seems paradoxical. It is provided by Stalin's comment on the script for *Ivan the Terrible*:

> To: Comrade Bolshakov
>
> The script has not turned out badly. Comrade Eisenstein has coped with the task. Ivan the Terrible, as a progressive force of his time, and the *oprichniki*, as his expedient instrument, have not turned out badly. We must start shooting this script as soon as possible.
>
> J. V. Stalin, 13 September 1943[56]

It was precisely this favourable comment by his august patron that threw Eisenstein into a mood of despair and disgust.

The period between January 1941 and September 1943 encompassed a whole epoch of suffering and hope that promised – for Eisenstein, but not for him alone – a renewal of the spirit, a reassessment of old values, the advent of a new world. In working on the script and the sketches for the film, Eisenstein was passing in his imagination 'from the realm of necessity into the realm of freedom', he was becoming himself again and was experiencing the happiness that comes with being true to oneself. Now, after all that, he had been praised as an artist who assiduously carried out orders: orders in which nothing had changed. As before, the talk was about the great progressive Tsar and the *expediency* of the human sacrifices carried out by his *oprichniki*: put simply, about a justification for tyranny and terror. It was obvious that Stalin had not detected anything to contradict this in the script that he had read – and he was not bothered about the 'number of executions'. The benevolence of his comment reflects that reader's imperturbable calm. In actual fact Stalin now felt himself to be in complete command of the victory won by the common people which had been decided at Stalingrad and Kursk. Now he, having received the leaders of the Russian Church in the Kremlin and having won the agreement of Churchill and Roosevelt to a meeting in Teheran, was once again interested in this project for a film about Ivan the Terrible.[57]

Eisenstein had hardly intended his script to provoke direct criticism from above. However, the approval that he received seemed to be worse than any criticism. Stalin had clearly paid no attention to those pages in the script where Eisenstein had openly – or so it seemed! – given expression to his own views as author on the tragedy of autocracy and the horrors of tyranny. By his résumé Stalin confirmed for Eisenstein his appointed place – that of Stalin's cinematic interpreter.

In September 1943 it was as if Eisenstein had been thrown back to January 1941. For him it would have been futile and fruitless to pose the question: had he deceived Stalin with his script, or had he in fact deceived himself? He took the decision to 'work himself to death', thus choosing the only 'way of committing suicide' that would allow him to carry on with his creative life.[58]

In surrendering himself completely to frenzied and self-destructive work making the film, Eisenstein did everything possible to broaden it in time and space in order to express and realise his *own* project. He replanned the second part of the film, as designated in the script, into two – a second and a third part. Hence Nikolai Cherkasov was to write that the second part was shot 'in accordance with the new version of the script that Eisenstein has developed',[59] although the plot structure of the script was not, strictly speaking, altered. It was the director's treatment that changed. The first and second parts were shot simultaneously, i.e. regardless of the chronological development of the action of the plot. But Eisenstein abandoned his earlier intention of preparing the first two parts of the film for simultaneous release.

To all appearances it was precisely then, in the autumn of 1943, that Eisenstein, fully conscious of his confrontation with Stalin, determined the strategy by which he would go on playing the game: he would present the anticipated apologia for Ivan the Terrible, as far as possible, in the first part of the film, and then, as early as the second part, he would carry out his plan to turn the film into a tragedy.[60]

Stalin's approval gave Eisenstein practical opportunities that he was quick to seize: he wanted to use them for his own ends. When permission was granted to publish the text of the script as a separate book, he resolutely insisted (albeit without success) that the volume should include a genuinely historical commentary and also – and this is very important – his drawings for the film, as an essential supplement that would help the reader to conceive more accurately the characters as the author imagined them. The drawings were to be accompanied by a commentary in which Eisenstein half revealed the way in which his conception of the film had developed and directly indicated that the Tsar's confession had been his starting point.[61]

In December 1943, when he was forced to rest after thirty-two nights' shooting, he wrote in German in his diary: 'Haßzustände. Haß zu Johannes dem Schrecklichen. Dann Ehrgeiz' [Feelings of hatred. Hatred for Ivan the Terrible. Then ambition].[62] His creative mood at that moment was truly ambivalent.

While continuing with the production, in his correspondence with the cinema authorities in Moscow he presented himself to the leading administrators as a responsible person enjoying the complete trust of the state. When the deadlines that Bolshakov had categorically insisted on turned out to be hopelessly unrealistic, Eisenstein appealed on 20 January 1944 to Stalin in a personal letter in which he asked him to 'intercede for me with Comrade Bolshakov and relieve him of his responsibility [*sic!*] for the deadlines for the release of my film *Ivan the Terrible*'.[63]

Those who worked with Eisenstein, those who witnessed his work, his friends, have subsequently recalled time and again his mood of fearlessness and passion at that time.

' "Taboo" is falsehood,' he wrote at the time, 'if you do something *with your heart's blood* you can say *everything*.'[64]

It was in this frame of mind, obeying only his 'daemon', as he was later to say, that he realised the scenes and episodes in the script in a way that puzzled and alarmed those who saw the rushes. In answer to the misgivings expressed by his friends, he gave them to understand that he had not forgotten his august viewer.

In the summer of 1944 he showed a large number of scenes from both parts of the film to Mikhail Bleiman and asked him for his opinion.[65] Bleiman, distinctly sensing 'trouble or, rather, danger', began to talk about the theme that, he thought, came through on the screen. This was:

> the ways in which the unity of the state had been achieved, the spiritual price that had been paid in the struggle. What emerged was an inner struggle, doubts, a review of deeds done. What emerged was the tragedy of power and retribution.
>
> 'Well . . .? Go on . . .!' Sergei Mikhailovich prompted encouragingly and without any sign of anxiety.
>
> 'It is a Pushkin theme.' I conceded. 'But, at the same time it could be understood as a contemporary theme.'
>
> Without looking at me, he said very seriously and simply, as if to cut me short: 'And what if that is just what I want?!'[66]

The actor Mikhail Kuznetsov recalled shooting the confession scene (which had been moved into the third part of the film):

> I said, 'Sergei Mikhailovich, what's going on? Look, 1,200 boyars have been killed. The Tsar *is* "Terrible"! Why on earth is he repenting?' Suddenly Eisenstein said, 'Stalin has killed more people and he doesn't repent. Let him see this and perhaps he'll repent . . .'[67]

At this point an association with Hamlet's play within a play, 'The Mouse-trap', naturally springs to mind. This is justifiable, not just in relation to the famous scene of the 'Burning Fiery Furnace' in Part Two of the film,[68] but also in relation to Eisenstein's whole schema.[69]

Of course in Eisenstein's mind the film he was making was not 'addressed' merely to the one man who had commissioned the film. He wanted to appeal to everyone: 'We shall have to have a lot of screenings – historians, writers, artists – and mass screenings, with thousands of people watching the film simultaneously, so that they will understand it better . . .'[70]

But then he was talking about Part Two.

Work on Part One was completed, back in Moscow, in November 1944.

Figure 17 The 'Burning Fiery Furnace' scene in Sergei Eisenstein's *Ivan the Terrible.*

During the final editing Eisenstein deemed it necessary to make a sacrifice: at the request of the cinema leadership he cut the Prologue (the scenes of Ivan's childhood) from the film. Now the action began with the coronation scene, in which the political theme of the film was unambiguously and insistently formulated. At that very moment it was particularly important to Eisenstein that his ship should not run aground.

His precautions were not in vain. On 7 December 1944, at a session of the Artistic Council of the Committee on Cinema Affairs, Part One provoked considerable discussion. It was reproached for its rationalistic coldness and inhumanity – meaning that the hero did not arouse spontaneous human sympathy.[71] Before long Pyotr Pavlenko, an influential literary figure and formerly Eisenstein's co-author for the script of *Alexander Nevsky*, wrote a hostile review of *Ivan the Terrible* but it never appeared. *Pravda* published a favourable review by Vsevolod Vishnevsky.[72]

The fate of the film, and its critical evaluation, had obviously been decided in the Kremlin after the screening on the night of 25 December. In January 1945 it became clear that the film would actually be released. A few weeks later, at the end of March, Bolshakov granted Eisenstein official permission to convert his two-part film about Ivan the Terrible into a trilogy.

It was that very winter, soon after the memorable discussion in the Artistic Council, that Eisenstein wrote an autobiographical essay in which, combining a defiant openness with exquisite irony, he subjected his own work to psychoanalysis, representing himself as an 'inhuman' artist and the subjects of his films as a form of sublimated sadism. In this regard, he remarks, 'it appears to be no accident that for a considerable number of years the man who has occupied my thoughts, my favourite hero, has been none other than Tsar Ivan Vasilevich the Terrible himself'.[73]

'*The man who has occupied my thoughts, my favourite hero . . .*' The man who occupied his thoughts? Probably. But several months later, in the summer of 1945 shortly after the end of the war, he wrote a quite different article, a rapturous declaration of love for John Ford's *Young Mr Lincoln* [USA, 1939], a film to which he directed exceptional and incomparable praise: 'of all the films made to this day it is *this* one that I should most like to have made myself.'[74] After spending several pages expressing his boundless admiration for the historical Abraham Lincoln, he turns to John Ford's film, which he had first seen before the war and which had captivated him 'above all by the way Lincoln himself was depicted', and says that his love for this film has not cooled to this day: 'On the contrary, it has grown and strengthened, while the film itself has in some way grown dearer and dearer to me.'[75] Essentially this is the best possible commentary by Eisenstein on his own statement that Ivan the Terrible was his 'favourite hero'. It is not difficult to imagine what his ambivalent love-hate relationship with his daemonic character cost him.

Eisenstein's widow, Pera Moiseyevna Atasheva, once related a conversation that she had had with him in their dacha at Kratov in that same summer of 1945. Like others who were close to him, she was worried about the risky turn his work had taken with his decision to make *Ivan* in three parts, rather than two, and she tried to instil some common sense:

> Why've you put the finale off to Part Three, old man? Why're you getting involved in this boyar's plot? Uncle Joe won't forgive you! This is the year of victory and he's the victor. Stick everything that's left into one part, get your Ivan to the sea shore more quickly – and you'll be the victor as well![76]

Eisenstein's answer was cold and sharp and indicated his disagreement. In the draft of *Nonindifferent Nature* (he was working on this manuscript that same summer) there are some quickly scrawled lines: '*Beyond my will-power* I am hymning Ivan as he was filmed. I am going *beyond* my inspiration and setting everything out as it dictates it to me.'[77]

In February 1945 Alexei Tolstoi died. His last completed work was the second part of a dramatic trilogy about Ivan the Terrible. So Tolstoi, the most successful of Soviet writers, never began the third part that he planned: he realised that it would be impossible to carry his extended apologia for Ivan the Terrible ('Ivan the Sweet', to use Eisenstein's English expression) through to the final years of the life of the historical Ivan IV. The Moscow Art Theatre was preparing to stage Tolstoi's second play about Ivan. In November, in the midst of dress rehearsals, one of Eisenstein's favourite actors, Nikolai Khmelyov, who was playing the leading role, suffered a fatal heart attack, while wearing the costume and make-up for Ivan the Terrible.[78]

Eisenstein continued work on his own Part Two. On 26 January 1946, a few days before it was completed, the radio announced that Part One of *Ivan the Terrible* had been awarded the Stalin Prize. This came as a surprise, since it was well known that the Stalin Prize Committee had excluded Eisenstein's film from the recommended list. The Prize had been awarded at Stalin's personal insistence. When he heard about the award, Mikhail Kuznetsov telephoned Eisenstein straight away to congratulate him:

'Well, old man, we took the right road!'

'No,' Eisenstein replied, 'we took the wrong road, but by chance it turned out to be the right one.'[79]

At about the same time Part Two, almost completed, was shown to a group of film directors at the Ministry of Cinematography. According to an eye-witness account by Mikhail Romm:

they felt the same alarm and the same sense of too dreadfully obvious allusions as did the Ministry officials. But Eisenstein behaved with impudent gaiety. He asked us:

'What's up? What's wrong? What do you have in mind? Come out with it!'

But no one could bring themselves to say directly that in Ivan the Terrible they keenly sensed an allusion to Stalin, in Malyuta Skuratov a reference to Beria, and in the *oprichniki* an allusion to his myrmidons. We sensed much else besides but we could not bring ourselves to speak.

But from Eisenstein's impudence, from the gleam in his eyes, from his provocative and sceptical smile, we felt that he knew what he was doing and that he had decided to go for broke.

It was dreadful.[80]

On 2 February 1946 Eisenstein finished editing Part Two and ended the day in hospital, miraculously still alive.

A month later, on 2 March 1946, the Minister of Cinematography, Ivan Grigorevich Bolshakov, decided to show Part Two of *Ivan the Terrible* in the Kremlin. When the film came to an end, Stalin reacted immediately: 'This isn't a film – it's some kind of nightmare!' Beria was more specific: 'It's a bad detective story!' Both of them gave vent to their extreme irritation at the depiction of the *oprichniki*: Beria compared the scene of the feast and dancing to a Witches' Sabbath, while Stalin likened it to the Ku-Klux-Klan (which would seem to reflect his acquaintance with American films). Beria: 'But Ivan the Terrible is depicted as a pitiful neurotic.' Stalin: 'Ivan the Terrible is depicted as a weak-willed and spineless character – like Hamlet.' At the end of the discussion Stalin told Bolshakov of his dissatisfaction with the state of mind of Soviet film-makers: 'During the War we didn't have the time, but now we'll lick you into shape.'[81]

Eisenstein was still in hospital when he learned that Stalin had turned down Part Two. 'He took the news unexpectedly calmly. He had anticipated it, he knew that it would happen.'[82]

The Orgburo [Organisational Section] of the Party Central Committee met on 9 August 1946 under the chairmanship of Zhdanov and in the presence of Stalin. It dealt first with the question of the Leningrad literary journals – and, individually, with the cases of Anna Akhmatova and Mikhail Zoshchenko[83] – and, second, with the quesion of 'ideological errors' in the films *The Great Life* [Bol'shaya zhizn'] Part Two and *Ivan the Terrible* Part Two.

On 4 September the Party Central Committee's resolution 'On the Film *The Great Life*' was published. It stated in particular that:

> The director S. Eisenstein has displayed ignorance in his depiction of historical facts, representing the progressive army of Ivan the Terrible's *oprichniki* as a band of degenerates, like the American Ku-Klux-Klan, and Ivan the Terrible – a man of strong willpower and character – as weak-willed and spineless, rather like Hamlet.[84]

Thus, Eisenstein forced Stalin to take back the approval that he had given in September 1943. The letter that Eisenstein wrote to the editors of the newspaper *Kul'tura i zhizn'* [Culture and Life] admitting his 'errors' was an unavoidable ritual act.[85]

But there was another letter, written by both Eisenstein and Nikolai Cherkasov and addressed to Stalin, asking for a personal meeting.[86] The ostensible purpose of this meeting (Cherkasov was more than a little worried about arranging it) was to enable them to receive their instructions for the reworking of Part Two. There is reason to suppose that Eisenstein's real purpose was to win time to preserve Part Two in its earlier form. This aim was achieved.

On the night of 24/25 February 1947 Eisenstein and Cherkasov were received in the Kremlin. The content of the conversation is well known and several accounts of it have been published.[87] The judgements and recommendations made by Stalin (and indeed by Molotov and Zhdanov)

Figures 18 and 19 Ivan's awe and repentance in the cathedral: Nikolai Cherkasov in *Ivan the Terrible*.

contained nothing unexpected. But the path of this lengthy conversation was by no means smooth. Eisenstein did not display his characteristic diplomatic and pedagogical skills and his utterances (especially at the outset) provoked evident dissatisfaction on Stalin's part, so that it was only Cherkasov's intuitive genius as an actor who knew how to charm and entertain his hosts that saved the situation. (As we know, a day later a decree was published awarding Nikolai Cherkasov the title of People's Artist of the USSR.) The practical result of this Kremlin meeting was the best possible one: Eisenstein was given time to reflect on and prepare changes in Part Two and given permission to show it to his friends and to the students at VGIK.[88] Eisenstein remarked to Bleiman, 'Went to see Stalin yesterday. We didn't like one another.'[89]

After Part Two had been shown to the students at VGIK Eisenstein delivered two lectures. He paid particular attention to the scenes of the feast of the *oprichniki* and the murder in the cathedral:

> You should bear only one thing in mind, comrades: you know what happened to Part Two? You know where it went wrong and I do not need to tell you again. You should look at something else. You know that in Part Two the *oprichnina* and that scene are not properly done – not from the point of view of the idea that I am depicting there, but from the point of view of the actual staging. You absolutely must remember this. Let us admit that I made the *oprichnina* savages, like the Ku-Klux-Klan – as it said in the decree – and I viewed them from a false historical perspective. But, from the point of view of the idea that I was depicting, it's 100 per cent correct. That's the whole problem. As I conceived it, so I made it. You need to look at it from the point of view of how I imagined it and how this was conveyed. And, remember that I imagined it wrongly. This does not mean that I imagined it correctly but that, because of Formalistic or other deviations, it did not turn out right. The error was more deep-rooted. You must remember and look at this as an idea that we consider wrong executed to the limits of the expressiveness of its raw material. Is that clear?[90]

Eisenstein told his friends that he was not going to rework the film.[91] He realised that he had expressed what he wanted to express and done it in the way he had wanted to do it, as 'his inspiration had dictated'.

If we can say of Part One that in it Eisenstein was rendering unto Caesar the things that are Caesar's, then Part Two represents the revolt of the artist ... The day after the screening of Part Two Eisenstein was talking to Iosif Ilyich Yuzovsky:

> 'I've even heard that, as an intellectual, I couldn't manage without the Hamlet tradition – I've dragged myself in, not Ivan.'
> 'There is a tradition, but it's not Hamlet's.'

Eisenstein's face became extremely serious. His eyes seemed to be piercing into me. 'So you think there's some kind of tradition there?'

'I even think I know which one . . .'

'Well, tell me . . . but briefly . . . no, it's impossible!'

'Boris Godunov.'

Eisenstein burst out laughing and then crossed himself. 'Lord, can you really see it? I'm so happy, I'm so happy! Of course it's Boris Godunov: "Five years I have governed in peace, but my soul is troubled . . ." I couldn't make a film like that without Russian tradition, without that great Russian tradition, the tradition of conscience. Violence can be explained, legalised, validated, but it cannot be justified. If you are a human being, it must be atoned. The destruction of one man by another: I say yes, but, whoever I am, I find it painful, because man is the highest value. Violence is not an end, and the joy lies not in achieving that end – as it did for other classes, epochs, states . . . even peoples. The Russian will know no mercy in his just anger, but the blood he sheds will bring bitterness to his heart. To say otherwise would be to debase the nation, the human race and the great idea of socialism. This, in my view, is the most stirring tradition of the people, the nation, and the literature . . .'[92]

The climax to Part Two, the focus of its meaning, is to be found in the scene of the procession in the cathedral and the murder of Vladimir Staritsky. On 15 November 1941, long before it was made, Eisenstein had made a note to himself that Vladimir's murder was the most important, the key scene in the script.[93] Subsequently, in his notes for 28 August 1947, he judged the scene in the cathedral to be the best that he had made in his entire life. ('. . . the murder of Vladimir is perhaps the best thing in my *opus*.')[94] The final journey and the death of Vladimir, the most insignificant of the characters in the plot, is depicted on the screen on a grandiose and tragic scale. The terrible Tsar, by the will of the author, yields his place as protagonist to his victim. But one of the last shots in this scene – Yevfrosinia Staritskaya with her son's corpse – is a direct paraphrase of the famous shot in *The Battleship Potemkin* of the mother with her murdered son on the Odessa Steps.[95] Eisenstein had managed to bring the tragic theme of his art to a new and perfect realisation.

As for the 'reworking' of Part Two, that was envisaged for 1948, the year for which Eisenstein had a premonition of his own death.

Four years later Stalin gave orders that the leading Soviet film directors should be commissioned to work on new films devoted to the great figures of the historical past. The task of making a new film about Ivan the Terrible was given to Ivan Pyriev.[96]

The execution of this order was interrupted by Stalin's death on 5 March 1953. After another five years Part Two of *Ivan the Terrible* was released on to the world's screens.

Chapter 9

Soviet films of the Cold War

Maya Turovskaya

The subject of my analysis in this paper is not films themselves, but the relationship between film and its changing socio-political context. I begin from the premiss that not even the most objective method can guarantee an exhaustive description of a film, because even the most primitive film is a multilayered structure containing various levels of latent information, which are revealed only in interaction with that film's socio-political and psychological context.

Perhaps this approach is not sufficiently 'art historical', but the object of my interest has always been 'sculpted time' [*zapechatlennoe vremya*],[1] rather than the medium of cinema itself. In its time my generation has lived through so many cataclysms, so many different lives, that our distingushing characteristic must be our experience – experience mainly of a negative kind, if you believe that 'we are born for inspiration, for sweet sounds and prayers'.[2] What is more, this experience must not be repudiated.

I know from my own experience that, however tendentious or, on the contrary, dispassionate, directors of film sculpt their work into many more aspects of their time than they think and recognise, from the level of technology employed to the ideological myths reflected. In Soviet state monopoly cinema this relationship between an 'order' in the literal sense and the intentions of the artist is so complex that to study it would require a special programme rather than a hurried 'list of plus points' and its opposite.

I have chosen for my analysis a group of 'anti-American' films relating to the late Stalin, post-war or Zhdanovite period of our culture, precisely because this was the worst – the most false and mendacious – of any period, when artists could scarcely plead 'ignorance' or appeal to their 'faith'. These films are: Grigori Alexandrov's *Meeting on the Elbe* [Vstrecha na El'be, 1949], Mikhail Romm's *Secret Mission* [Sekretnaya missiya, 1950], Mikhail Kalatozov's *Conspiracy of the Doomed* [Zagovor obrechennykh, 1950] and Abram Room's *Silvery Dust* [Serebristaya pyl', 1953].

This is only a small number of films, but we must remember that these were the years of film shortage [*malokartin'e*]: eighteen were produced in

1949, thirteen in 1950 and only nine pictures at the low point in 1951.[3] So the relative weight of these films compared with the repertoire as a whole was significant. They appeared against a background of acute ideological crisis.

We must remember that the self-awareness that was on the point of emerging during that war that we can unequivocally call 'patriotic' very quickly ran up against a new and all-pervasive discrimination. Questionnaires asked things like: 'Have you been a PoW?' 'Have you been in occupied territory?' and so on. However, openly declared ideological terror was unleashed directly against culture. Even the nominal 'moral and political unity' of anti-fascism was violated, and there was, at the very least, a schism among the intelligentsia. In addition, the war had also physically violated the ecology of culture.

On the other hand, as I argue elsewhere in this volume, it was in precisely this post-war period that the aesthetic system of Stalin's 'Empire' was constituted and acquired its definitive form. The style of a resplendent and victorious Great Power became the aesthetic norm. This was essentially a phenomenon of *style* – rather than life which was characterised by ration cards, so-called commercial shops and almost universal shortages. In everyday life, alongside the term 'captured' [*trofeinyi*] ('captured' films, 'captured' watches and nightshirts), the notion of another life, one that was 'beautiful' and 'abroad', emerged.[4] It too was more a notion than a fact of everyday life, but as a notion it was nevertheless current.

Cinema as a state-monopoly branch of culture had to, and did, respond to the style of the Soviet Empire. A substantial part of production consisted of historical biographical costume films. Although the films about the Cold War proposed in the 'thematic plan' were put forward as a pointedly contemporary, publicistic counterpoint to the historical, they did in fact also represent the very same 'costume' part of the repertoire. Between the press, the agitational topicality of the task and the individual signature of the director (and they were held up as 'masters'), there was a layer of ideologically inspired aesthetic stereotypes, which can be dated very precisely to the last Five-Year Plan of Stalin's rule.

The agitational task of the films was to represent yesterday's ally in the anti-fascist struggle as the enemy.[5] Hitler, who was a great expert on propaganda, had already said in *Mein Kampf* that all enemies of the people should be depicted at the same level, so as not to frighten the man in the street or provoke him into feeling that he had been abandoned. It was precisely in this kind of set-up that all the networks of enemies of the people were ranked equally with one another and this, together with the concept of absolute evil, established a monotonous plot structure for these films. The transformation of recent allies into the 'image of the enemy' was achieved in terms of plot through secret links between Americans (class enemies, naturally, like generals, senators, businessmen or diplomats) and

Nazis. The identification of the Americans with the Nazis was the only 'secret ingredient' of the whole package of Cold War films, while in *Conspiracy of the Doomed*, East European Social-Democrats were actually equated with the Americans, as if with absolute evil.

However, insofar as it was also a matter of class doctrine and the man in the street not being allowed to feel abandoned, the 'negative' American was inevitably contrasted with the 'simple' American who, if he was not actually a Communist, was at least a sympathiser. If the 'bad' American (or German, or foreigner, or class enemy) was individualised at least within the limits of his function or 'image', then the only function of the 'simple' American (or the black or the Czech) was to believe in the Soviet Union. He was not a personality in his own right but a delegated representative of the people (an 'idealised role').[6]

In *Conspiracy of the Doomed* there are four such representatives and, even though they are all played by actors who were popular – Pavel Kadochnikov, Vladimir Druzhinikov, Rostislav Plyatt and Maxim Strauch,[7] the roles still remained 'idealised'. Naturally, in this Socialist Realist typological structure almost everybody who was not 'one of us' was in practice depicted as an 'enemy of the people', and vice versa. The function of the 'wrecker' could be played, according to Plyatt, by a senator or an American ambassador in an Eastern European country, not to mention a general. But it was only on the periphery of the action that a representative of the CIA as a professional intelligence officer appeared. The genre structure of these films was therefore considerably weakened: the spy intrigue provided the framework for the plot rather than motivating the action. It was for this reason that the authors of a film willingly gave spy roles to women: it allowed them to enliven the action with unexpected plot twists and striking outfits, and sometimes to secure a role for the wife of the director. Even *Secret Mission*, which is the only film in which an intelligence officer appears on the Soviet side, hardly moves away structurally from the typology of anti-American films. While it did not change anything in the group of Cold War films, *Secret Mission* did contain in embryo the situation and approach of the only real contemporary Soviet spy hit, the television series *Seventeen Moments of Spring*.[8] But that was shown in a different period when the ideological foundations were breaking down.

In a paradoxical way the entertainment potential of these 'thrillers' can be calculated not so much from their genre as from their cast of actors and their settings. The films made by the great directors were for the most part 'actors' films'. The dominance of actors was not accidental in the developed Stalinist cinema aesthetic: actors were the favourites of the time. First, at that time people generally preferred the idea of high-quality performance to the image of the artist-demiurge. (Eisenstein could only be tolerated within the limits of his realisation of Stalin's own spiritual command.[9]) Second, the actors were in a precise sense the *face* of the time.

The repersonalisation of history and its mythologisation were achieved in 1930s cinema not just on the level of plot or director but rather on the level of physiognomy. It was not only the Party leadership that changed but also the typology of the characters portrayed on the screen. In the notorious political trials of the 1930s anyone sporting a beard, a pince-nez or even simply an intelligent-looking face typical of the first generation of Revolutionaries became on screen a visual symbol of unreliability – the face of the enemy. The Revolution had to have a proletarian face, and this face was actually found – in Chirkov's portrayal of the title role in the Kozintsev and Trauberg film, *The Youth of Maxim* [Yunost' Maksima, 1934], for instance. The social priorities of this period were also those of physical labour and film-makers selected worker and peasant types, such as Nikolai Kryuchkov, Boris Andreyev, Pyotr Aleinikov, Boris Chirkov and, to take an extreme case, Nikolai Bogolyubov.[10] The Great Patriotic War changed things in this regard and we shall return to this later.

However, for the supposedly anti-American films different, intelligent-looking faces were required and they had to be recruited from theatre. A quite different kind of actors' 'group' gathered around these films. At this point we should remember that, although cinema was popular, theatre was more highly regarded in the general scale of values. Paradoxically, the best actors were invited into cinema to be the 'worst' enemies. Stage actors (among whom were students of the 'conventional' theatre such as Rostislav Plyatt, Erast Garin, Maxim Strauch and Alexander Vertinsky)[11] brought with them 'an attitude to the character', a tradition which had not been completely dissolved in the Stanislavsky 'Method'.[12] All this contributed to a noticeable theatricalisation of the films. Two decades later this theatricalisation was to return to world cinema in the form of the conscious device of 'alienation'.

Theatricality contributed also to the principles of scriptwriting. Although the action of anti-American films was contemporary, the geographical – not to mention the ideological – frontier between the two worlds had a metaphysical quality. The reversal of time and space on the screen allowed the transformation of films which were intended as reportage into 'costume' and 'situation' films, similar to historical films: the spatial distance interfered with the temporal. These pictures were filmed, whether the plot required it or not, in the interiors of palaces, retreats and villas, against a background of diplomatic entourages and receptions, or in evening dress that had no connection whatsoever with the everyday experience of the audience.

Genetically this descended partly from the 'linking' formula of the theatre of the 1920s, the device of 'Meanwhile the bourgeoisie was decaying'. But, to an even greater extent, this theatricality corresponded to the emerging style of the late Stalin Empire, cloaked in the class postulates of 'Socialist Realism' in accordance with the spirit of the time. These were not so much propagandist thrillers as pseudo-'foreign' films.

20

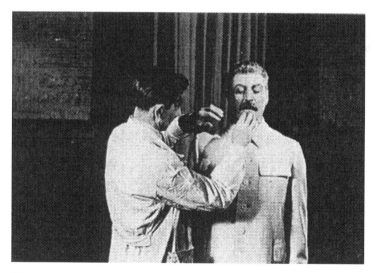

21

Figures 20–5 The hero of the cult: production shots of Mikhail Gelovani as Stalin in *The Fall of Berlin* (1949).

22

23

24

25

It would appear that all this combined to create constructs which were the most staged and unreal of any in Soviet cinema. That is precisely how the intelligentsia that broke away from 'semi-official' status regarded them. When I was writing about audience preferences I found it necessary to talk about a post-war division into three kinds of 'taste': 'semi-official', expert and mass. Our new socio-political context, in which much that had been kept secret has become open and in which the doctrine of confrontation with 'capitalist encirclement' has been transformed into collaboration, has removed the ideological tension between the viewer and the film and allowed us to look at the latent information which these films contain behind the conventionalism of their forms and to evaluate their relationship with the reality of their time on a different scale. It is precisely this coefficient of falsification, both ideological and aesthetic, that turns Cold War films into an accurate self-portrait of Soviet society in the Zhdanov era.

The Freudian analysis of cinema naturally operates on the basis of sexual symbols. In these films we are dealing with the emergence of a kind of 'social Freudianism'. The phenomenon of social Freudianism is characteristic of totalitarian art as a whole. However impeccable Utopian consciousness might be thought to be, within it there are powerful mechanisms of displacement and substitution at work. Nowadays it is hardly necessary to prove that the declared abolition of religion was compensated for by the sanctification of reality itself and the creation of cult forms which were much more universal and all-pervasive than the religious ones had ever been. This sanctification touched all forms of social life and found its apotheosis in cinema: Riefenstahl's *Triumph of the Will* [Triumph des Willens, Germany, 1935], all Staliniana from Dziga Vertov's documentary *Lullaby* [Kolybel'naya, 1937], with its rising spiral of montage, to Chiaureli's monumental 'icons' of Stalin.[13] These provide the most obvious text-book example, but in fact entire ideological structures were subject to displacement and substitution: the cultural layer, the moral layer and the layer of common human values were only gradually exhausted. The evident paradox of the 1930s lay in the fact that the hard work and personal honesty of the members of an amoral society derived not only, and indeed not so much, from a general faith in Stalin, but rather from this moral and cultural layer that had still not been exhausted. The wave of opposition to fascism was quite simply its practical expression. Totalitarian régimes exploit these human resources, just as they exploit the resources of nature. In this way the direct infringements of the taboo are displaced from the national consciousness and attributed to the 'enemy'.

We can cite a text-book example: the British concentration camp in Hans Steinhoff's anti-British film *Uncle Krüger* [Ohm Krüger, 1941] or the discrimination against the Germans in Gustav von Ucicky's anti-Polish film *Homecoming* [Heimkehr, 1941]. These only partially displayed

Figure 26 Stalin berates his advisers in *The Fall of Berlin* (1949).

propaganda methods in the sense of the Hitlerian 'lie, but all the more, so that something will remain from your lie'. To a significant extent, however, they did display a social-Freudian displacement of guilt in the national unconscious. This created that mirror effect on which the films of the Cold War were constructed: the genetic code of the system projected its own structures on to the material of the 'image of the enemy'.

Meeting on the Elbe is the creation of that 'Soviet Hollywood' of Alexandrov where the distilled style of Socialist Realism still experienced the pressure of reality (as in Wolfgang Staudte's *Murderers Are Among Us* [Die Mörder sind unter uns, Germany, 1946]) but it nevertheless depicted one peculiarity of the moment: the appearance of a new military generation that had been formed at the front in conditions of relative freedom. The theatre actor Vladlen Davydov,[14] in spite of his idealisation of the character, did reproduce the type of the intellectual front-line lieutenant quite precisely. The continuing post-war terror was also, to a significant degree, aimed at controlling that 'generation of victors'. We scarcely need recall Stalin's well-known order no. 270: behind the back of the officer at the front there always stood the behind-the-lines security battalions and SMERSH.[15]

The complex of themes devised by the scriptwriter Lev Sheinin, one of Vyshinsky's loyal henchmen, for *Meeting on the Elbe* about a similar lieutenant, a 'simple' American who, in his naïvety and loyalty to the allied cause, arrests one of his own American woman intelligence officers from the CIA, could well have served as an anecdote about the Soviet Union, didactically translated to the enemy camp. There is in any case no doubt that the level of dependence of the field officer on his own secret services was a mirror image of relations in the Soviet Army when it was abroad rather than in the US forces.

Whereas in *Meeting on the Elbe* this was a fragment of the structure, *Conspiracy of the Doomed*, scripted by Nikolai Virta and directed by Mikhail Kalatozov, demonstrated in its entirety the mechanics of that series of political transformations in post-war Eastern Europe from coalition socialist governments to party and personal dictatorships that Stalin realised within living memory.

Conspiracy of the Doomed has taken its place in Soviet cinema as the successor to Friedrich Ermler's *The Great Citizen* [Velikii grazhdanin, 1938]. In that film the aim had been to 'justify' the domestic show trials of the 1930s; here it was to do the same for similar trials in the countries of Eastern Europe (or the 'satellites', as they were called in the West). Just like *The Great Citizen*, *Conspiracy of the Doomed* was a talented work by an important director on a large scale with complex shot-by-shot montage and a first-class cast of actors. If proof were needed that the murder of Kirov was a deliberate provocation, then the existence of *The Great Citizen* provides it. This was a huge filmic 'repression' in the Freudian sense.

Conspiracy of the Doomed was something more. It showed, in quite a detailed and convincing way, the externalisation of the internal, transferring to a European country the mechanics of a plot that had already been executed in practice: the organisation of famine, subversion, the dispossession of the kulaks in the countryside, accusations of complicity by opposition parties in the plot, the dissolution of parliament, the establishment of the dictatorship, the vows to Stalin (with the prospect also of the trial of Rudolf Slánský, the execution of Imre Nagy, and so on).

It needed thirty years for the advantages of the Marshall Plan, which were successfully torpedoed not only in film but also in real life, to become obvious and for Eastern Europe to return to its own natural surroundings, while what had seemed to be the most 'progressive' intelligentsia – that stupid theatricalised farce in the spirit of Socialist Realism – was shown to be the true model of the mirror image.

After all the biggest sensation of *Conspiracy of the Doomed* for contemporaries was the appearance of Alexander Vertinsky on screen – the public went for the actors, the costumes, the sets, without noticing either the degree of dreadful authenticity or the social–Freudian complex that underlay their native cinema. Now the film can serve as a model, not just for cinema specialists, but also for historians.

Even such a feeble relic of the Cold War as Abram Room's *Silvery Dust*, with its exaggerated notion of the American outdoors filmed in Yalta, nevertheless conveys significant information about the time. Once, when we were viewing Nazi films for *Ordinary Fascism*, [Obyknovennyi fashizm, 1966] Yuri Khanyutin and I agreed on a working aphorism: these may not be documents of the time, but they are documents of the *emotions of the time*. *Silvery Dust* serves as just such a 'document of emotions'. Nevertheless the atmosphere of mutual suspicion, boorishness, cynicism, fear, complicity and alienation, together with the violence that embellished the last years of Stalinism and that was completely banished from domestic 'subject matter', could be realised only by constructing an 'image of the enemy'. The film-makers were scarcely conscious that they were displacing their own 'moral climate' to an imaginary America. Above all they were attempting to fulfil the social command;[16] but the displaced elements resurfaced in the 'image of the enemy'.

The lack of any opportunity to speak directly about experiments on people, about deliberately provoked disorders and arrests, about mutual blackmail – all this 'spiritual Chernobyl' has resulted from the totalitarian régime, from the exhaustion of the cultural and moral layers of society, from the natural resources of human beings. It should be said that the relationship between the artist and the régime in a totalitarian epoch is a separate subject for a substantial and interesting paper. It would touch upon the fundamental characteristics of mankind.

But, as I said, I was interested in the subject of 'cinema and its time'.

Chapter 10

Canons and careers: the director in Soviet cinema

Ian Christie

... a canon is not a list but a narrative of some intricacy, depending on places and times and opportunities.

Hugh Kenner[1]

Room was a tragic character because he felt he had no career.

Leonid Trauberg[2]

The wave of interest in 'canons' which swept literary and cultural studies in the early 1980s seems to have had surprisingly little impact in one field where its aptness is striking, namely Soviet cinema.[3] True, the canonicity in question was often of the less obvious variety, where the processes of formation and change were debatable and at least required expert elucidation. In such cases, there was also no evident controlling institution, unless it was the profession of critic-teachers, or a movement, such as 'Modernism', conceived as a kind of Althusserian ideological apparatus. Soviet cinema, by contrast, presents a more traditional instance of canonicity and I suggest that it may be by looking at it in these terms, rather than the more familiar historical-political ones, that we shall reach a better understanding of the special role assigned to the director in its 'classical' period of the 1930s.

I begin with some general observations on institutions and their relationship to canons, before addressing specific features of the Soviet cinema canon. Then follows an outline of the historical factors that tied the film-making profession to the Stalinist canon of 'masters of cinema', and an account of how Stalinist aesthetics both elevated and constrained the artist. Finally, I consider how Stalin's demise and the belated emergence of an intermediate institution – the film-makers' union – allowed Soviet cinema to gain critical distance from the interests of the state.

CANONS SACRED AND SOVIET

There are striking parallels between the early church's development of its canon and the Bolshevik legacy to the young Soviet state. Preoccupied with unity and unanimity in the face of constant threats of schism, both church and state identified heresy as their main enemy. The fusion of scriptures and dogma, invested with the full authority of the institution, provided a bulwark against this 'enemy within'.[4] The similarity between these institutions was equally striking in a non-Soviet context. For the Chilean film-maker Raul Ruiz, once associated with Salvador Allende's Popular Unity régime, there was an instructive parallel between the two institutions:

> I remember from childhood that the worst sin, far worse than murder or fornication, was not to attend Mass. It was not until later, when I had some experience of other institutions, that I began to understand this paradox of an institution more concerned with its own destiny than the morality of its members. I recall being very shocked when I read Gramsci for the first time and found that he compares the Party with the church, recommending the Jesuits as an example to be followed.[5]

The issue is not only one of doctrine, but rather of form and method. Any institution seeking the authority and efficiency of the church will effectively emulate or mirror its structure. In the case of Soviet cinema, we see a sub-institution 'willed to power' by its first exponents and adopted by the Soviet state as its *distinctive* artistic practice. While the traditional arts would all be canonised as 'Soviet' too, cinema can lay some claim to being the Soviet 'Ur-canon'. Unlike them, it could be interpreted as a wholly Soviet creation and could also plausibly be claimed to have had a worldwide impact.

Having linked the Soviet state's founder and its cinema in a 'sacred text' long emblazoned on studio and cinema buildings – 'of all the arts the most important for us is cinema' – the filmic texts of the resulting canon were circulated not only throughout the USSR, but also abroad through a subsidised and ideologically motivated international network.[6] These sacred texts were physically refurbished and, on occasions, secretly revised, in order to accommodate ideological shifts without ignominiously dropping components of the canon.[7] New works judged to be heretical were ruthlessly suppressed: some, like Nikolai Okhlopkov's *The Way of the Enthusiasts* [Put' entuziastov, 1930], Mikhail Kalatozov's *A Nail in the Boot* [Gvozd' v sapoge, 1932] and, most famously, Eisenstein's *Bezhin Meadow* [Bezhin lug, 1935–7], were apparently destroyed; others, like Abram Room's *A Severe Young Man* [Strogii yunosha, 1934] and in modern times Alexander Askoldov's *The Commissar* [Komissar, 1967; released 1988], long hidden from view. All of this 'canon maintenance', together with the vast corpus of writings that supported its officially approved interpretation and the harmonisation of any apparent contradictions, conforms closely to Frank Kermode's outline of the church's canonic practice in one of his many contributions to the modern 'canon debate'.[8]

The aspect of the Soviet cinema institution that concerns me here is the role of the film director as a 'value' within the Soviet canon. For this does not consist merely of films; each of the key works in the pre-war canon is inextricably linked with its director. Thus in a typical reiteration of the 'Ur-canon' – actually the preface to a sixtieth anniversary pictorial celebration of Soviet cinema, over the signature of the then Chairman of the State Cinema Committee [Goskino] Filip Yermash – we read:

> It is amazing how quickly the revolutionary cinema gained momentum – *The Truth about Lenin on Film* [*sic*] by D. Vertov, *Battleship 'Potyomkin'* by S. Eisenstein, *Mother* by V. Pudovkin and *Arsenal* by A. Dovzhenko marked the birth of a Soviet cinema new in its ideology, innovatory in its means of expression and able to capture the process of historical development from the viewpoint of the victorious working class and from the positions of a socialist world outlook.[9]

It is perhaps a feature of all cultural canons that they deal primarily in oeuvres rather than single works, in reputations rather than explications. In this sense, canons are more about relative value or hierarchy than about meaning or interpretation. Thus Kermode recalls the 'accession of Donne' to the canon of English literature as a relatively recent event, while Soviet cinema long excluded Kozintsev and Trauberg from its 'core canon', despite their prominence in the 1930s, and only admitted Boris Barnet in recent years.[10] Another consideration bearing on canon eligibility is that an oeuvre must in practice be able to support variant readings and valuations, including contradictory ones. In this respect, the cornerstones of the Soviet cinema canon have proved exemplary. Consider, for instance, the following sharply contrasted valuations of Eisenstein:

> The appearance on the screen of *Battleship Potemkin* stirred up a veritable revolution in feature film production. Not only did Sergei Eisenstein discover new potentialities of montage. He discovered his own country, her revolution and her people for the world . . . [Eisenstein's] historical films were profoundly modern – their problems were tied up with the present. Such was his *Alexander Nevsky*, where plastic directing, austere set design and musical expressiveness were harmoniously combined.[11]

> I think that these three films – *Strike, October* and *Ivan the Terrible* – are certainly Eisenstein's best, most extraordinary achievements . . . In *Battleship Potemkin*, the most famous sequence, the massacre on the Odessa Steps, is really an extension of the agit-guignol he had worked at in the Proletkult Theatre; other sequences of the film, beautifully composed photography, heroic postures, etc., look forward to the artistic disaster of *Alexander Nevsky*.[12]

What we have here is more than a difference of approximately contemporaneous critical opinion. The first account, by a Deputy Chairman of Goskino, is an 'official' interpretation of Eisenstein's place in the Soviet canon, which also asserts that canon's political significance for the Soviet state. The second is a 'heretical' interpretation of Eisenstein's career by Peter Wollen, then associated with the British 'New Left' (and himself a keen canonist), which seeks to reclaim Eisenstein from his settled canonic role and relocate him in an avant-garde tradition that was stifled by Stalin.

Behind these value judgements – perhaps inevitably in the Soviet instance – stand deeply opposed political positions. The former shows how an institution confers and in turn derives value from the texts admitted into its canon, while the latter implicitly attacks that institution precisely by devaluing the works it sets most store by and promoting instead works considered problematic. In these examples of the struggle between ortho-doxy and heresy over interpretations of Eisenstein, we can find a later riposte from within the institution which clearly seeks to challenge views such as Wollen's. The authors of a 1980 'history' of Soviet cinema intended for international distribution pause in their survey of the 1920s to chide foreign writers who

> idealise the twenties and place them in opposition to all other periods in the development of Soviet cinema, seeing this as a time of carefree experiments filled with fruitful innovations and discoveries. This atti-tude is expecially characteristic of 'New Left' film critics.[13]

These apologists go on to argue that much in the Soviet cinema of the 1920s must be considered 'negative' from their standpoint as licensed interpreters for the institution. However, they have to 'protect' the canonic Eisenstein from potential devaluation. Hence the claim that he was misinterpreted, then as now:

> This normative poetics were [sic] not, of course, created by that inspired, revolutionary artist Eisenstein, but by 'left' theoreticians who were genetically linked with pre-revolutionary decadent movements in art . . . 'The theory of "the emotional script" and "intellectual cinema" that grew out of the incorrect interpretation of Potemkin', wrote Sergei Yutkevich, 'was harmful to Eisenstein himself and to cinema as a whole, and hindered its progress for some time.'[14]

We shall return to the specifically Soviet feature of this ingenuous defence of the canon – the use of peer-criticism – but for the moment it suffices to illustrate, albeit crudely, a characteristic strategy in what Kermode terms 'the institutional control of interpretation'. Soviet cinema *needed* Eisen-stein as a key 'value' to secure the status of its canon; therefore he, above all, must be protected from heretical appropriation and revalidated.

FROM PIONEERS TO 'MASTERS'

The Soviet cinema canon was, of course, much more than an expression of cultural values. It was a formidable material and ideological reality, promoted and defended by a network of institutions owing direct allegiance to the Soviet state. Given this political and propagandist underpinning, many have wished to deny its aesthetic dimension – or, more commonly, to create an 'oppositional' canon based on a politico-aesthetic 'anti-state' scale of dissidence.[15] My concern here, however, is to explore further the paradox of the Soviet canon as an 'actually existing' structure – one that literally ruled the lives of Soviet film-makers from the late 1920s to the end of the Soviet era. When Abram Room complained that he had 'had no career', we can read this as recognition that he had been excluded from the canon, had been denied the promulgation of an exemplary 'career' as a concomitant of canonic status. That this exclusion may have enabled him to make more and better films than some of his canonised contemporaries is a judgement we may also make, but it is one which ignores what Harold Bloom has called the 'facticity' that necessarily constrains interpretation.[16]

How then can we acknowledge the 'facticity' of Soviet cinema's canonising era when this has been so assiduously mythologised? The key element in this 'creation myth' is the denial of pre-Revolutionary influence, well expressed by Eisenstein in an extended metaphor which has become famous:

> In the early 1920s we all came to the Soviet cinema as something not yet existent. We came upon no ready-built city; there were no squares, no streets laid out; not even little crooked lanes and blind alleys, such as we may find in the cinemetropolis of our day. We came like bedouins or gold-seekers to a place with unimaginably great possibilities ... something that had as yet no written traditions, no exact stylistic requirements, nor even formulated demands.[17]

Soviet cinema conceived as a 'newfoundland', discovered and settled by hardy pioneers, was a myth which satisfied both the Party and the emergent canon of 'masters of Soviet cinema'. It chimed with what Jeffrey Brooks has noted as an early Bolshevik 'aversion for the commercial popular culture of which pre-Revolutionary film was so much a part'.[18] Cinema in its Soviet manifestation could be presented as essentially a new invention: the combined product of nationalisation, a cleansing struggle (agit-film production and novel forms of 'front line' exhibition during the Civil War), propagandist realignment of existing forms (Vertov's militant newsreels) and scientific research (by Kuleshov's workshop). The *activity* of cinema – purged of its stars and producers through their emigration – could now appear quintessentially 'Soviet': the application of electricity to propaganda.

However, the material and ideological reality of the period 1918–24 now looks somewhat different from how it did under traditional Soviet historiography.[19] What production took place in these spartan years depended almost entirely on surviving elements of pre-Revolutionary cinema, whether this was the Rus Collective that produced *Polikushka* and would form the basis for the only true Soviet 'studio', Mezhrabpom-Rus, or even Kuleshov's workshop within the new film school, which was cofounded by Vladimir Gardin, one of that generally derided class, the pre-1917 'kings of the screen'.[20] Recent reconstructions of the long-ignored history of Russian cinema have tended to suggest that Soviet cinema's high cultural ambition in fact owed rather more to such tendencies already evident in the Symbolist and Futurist avant-gardes of the period 1912–17 than it did to any early Bolshevik recognition of cinematic potential.[21] It was the destruction of 'normal' cinema that provided a space for such tendencies to flourish and mutate as they encountered the multifarious avant-garde ideologies of the early New Economic Policy (NEP) era.

The concept of the film school, obviously inspired by the Bolshevik emphasis on education and noted admiringly by all early foreign observers, proved important in proclaiming the *difference* of Soviet cinema.[22] It proclaimed a message of egalitarian opportunity for new entrants to this most glamorous (and traditionally nepotistic) of professions. It also implied a rational and even scientific approach to what had formerly been considered 'magic' or mere showmanship. Henceforth, following in the image of Kuleshov, the Soviet director would be an educator in the broad sense and, specifically, a teacher of new generations of film-makers. The 'primal' teacher–pupil relationship between Kuleshov and his first workshop members, together with the lesser-known workshop of Room, established a master–apprentice pattern in Soviet film training which survived until recent times.[23] It provided a cultural-pedagogic legitimation of Soviet cinema as an artistic tradition that could boast direct links with its 'old masters' – as well as providing a convenient activity to which the latter could retire. It also permeated the organisation of the Soviet production studio, which came to resemble an extension of the film school, with leading film-makers (who were often also teachers) serving as overseers for groups of younger directors.[24]

Theatre also exercised a formative influence on the rhetoric and organisation of early Soviet cinema, despite strenuous efforts by proponents of the new medium to distance it from traditional theatre. Many of the first Soviet film-makers – notably Room, Eisenstein, Kozintsev and Trauberg, and Yutkevich – had started in the 'revolutionary' theatre movement before being attracted to cinema. They brought with them a commitment to working collectively, an iconoclastic, agitational mode of address and a design-conscious anti-naturalism, all of which contributed to the distinctiveness of early Soviet film-making.[25] Thus the first avowedly Soviet directors emerged, not as traditional *metteurs-en-scène*, but as impresarios of 'attractions', keen to make their mark in the highly competitive mixed economy of the NEP period. The competition at this stage was scarcely for audiences, since avant-garde Soviet production could not aspire to any mass circulation. It was rather for reputation and recognition in the ideological sphere.

As long as the Party remained neutral on the claims of competing styles and groups in the field of culture and continued to allow substantial imports of foreign entertainment films, the avant-gardes faced an uncertain future.[26] The Commissar with overall responsibility for cinema, Anatoli Lunacharsky, clearly had considerable sympathy for film-making which displayed 'brilliance, a variety of experiences, romance, beauty, rapid actions, an interesting plot', and this made him sceptical about an exclusive diet of 'films without a plot, without a hero, without eroticism'.[27] The Mezhrabpom-Rus studio, with which he had close connections, embodied his prescription for Soviet cinema to perfection. Supported in large part by the extensive Western connections of the International Workers' Aid, it employed film-makers from across the Soviet spectrum: veterans of the tsarist cinema such as Gardin and Protazanov; graduates from the Kuleshov workshop like Pudovkin, Barnet and Sergei Komarov (and eventually Kuleshov himself); and at least one of its young recruits, Yuli Raizman, would become a leading member of the 'modernising' generation that emerged in the 1930s.[28]

LEGITIMATING THE CANON

In the short term, the success of *Potemkin* served to vindicate the claims of an avant-garde which now faced increasingly serious domestic competition from its more audience-conscious contemporaries, especially at Mezhrabpom-Rus. The journal of the Association of Revolutionary Cinematography [ARK] proclaimed *Potemkin* in early 1926 'a victory for Soviet cinematography; for Kuleshov and Vertov who paved the way; for ARK which praised *The Strike*. Long live *Potemkin*, the greatest achievement of cinematography in the USSR.'[29]

Here *Potemkin* elegantly – if implausibly, given the differences between those yoked together – legitimised a genealogy and a structure: in short, a canon. Both *The Strike* [Stachka, 1924] and Vertov's *The Cine-Eye* [Kino-glaz, 1924] had won awards at the 1925 Paris Exposition des Arts Décoratifs, but this did little to promote further interest in them either internationally or at home. Vertov continued the struggle to secure his radical 'factographic' position by securing a commission from the state trade organisation Gostorg and a premiere at the Fifteenth Party Congress for *A Sixth Part of the World* [Shestaya chast' mira, 1926]. But it was Eisenstein's resounding international success with what had started as a 'voluntary commission' to commemorate the 1905 revolution that led to the cherished goal of true *state* commissions, such as those to mark the tenth anniversary of the Revolution in 1927 which produced *October* [Oktyabr', 1928] and Pudovkin's *The End of St Petersburg* [Konets Sankt-Peterburga, 1927].[30]

How might Soviet cinema have developed if *Potemkin* and its immediate successors had not caught the world's attention in the late 1920s? This hypothetical question is worth considering if only to remind ourselves of the extraordinary pivotal significance attached to a handful of Soviet 'classics' (imagine, for instance, if United States politicians and officials regularly invoked *The Birth of a Nation* as exemplary of *post-bellum* America's founding ideology, or if *La Marseillaise* played a similar role in France). In one of the official histories quoted earlier, there is a revealing trope which equates the fate of *Potemkin* with that of the young Soviet state itself:

> The insurgent ship with the flapping red flag on its mast (at that time the flag was hand-painted red on each of the film's copies) stirred the hearts of film-goers everywhere. Soviet Russia itself was like a ship sailing into the unknown over the waves of a stormy ocean hourly threatening it with disaster.[31]

The international *succès d'estime* of early films by Eisenstein, Pudovkin, Vertov, Kuleshov and Dovzhenko did not decisively reorientate Soviet production in the long term. For it was other film-makers who tackled the problems of creating a workable discourse between rulers and subjects as the authoritarian nature of the Stalinist state emerged. But foreign recognition for what became known as 'The Five' did bequeath a continuing problem to the ideologists of the Soviet canon.[32] How were such exceptional and idiosyncratic works – clearly betraying elements of Symbolism, Futurism, nationalism and many other proscribed 'isms' – to be cast as the cornerstones of a functional, disciplined structure, namely 'Soviet cinema'?

The solution that eventually emerged was to portray these five as a range of archetypes, each differentiated by an attribute regularly associated with them. Their common ancestor was declared to be D. W. Griffith, a protean 'primitive' credited as the pioneer of parallel editing and epic scale.[33] Eisenstein was be cast as the 'genius' – learned, wayward, professorial; Pudovkin as the 'propagandist' who lent passionate conviction to timely and varied subjects; Kuleshov as the 'teacher' and experimenter, prone to being led astray by his laboratory work; Vertov as the 'chronicler' who transformed newsreel into documentary; and Dovzhenko as the 'poet' who, as a Ukrainian, also played the part of 'good national', subordinating his national character to a 'Soviet' identity. When Room lamented his lack of a 'career', he was perhaps recognising that he had no place in this pantheon of Jonsonian 'humours'.[34]

HEGEMONY AND DEPENDENCE

By 1928 there seemed a real possibility that the appeals for serious state recognition and support, which had been made since 1922, would at last be met. A group of leading avant-garde (and non-Party) directors called on the

Figure 27 The cover of Viktor Shklovsky's 1929 booklet on Abram Room, described by Leonid Trauberg as 'a tragic character because he felt he had no career'.

Figure 28 Mikhail Romm and Sergei Eisenstein at the Mosfilm studio in the 1940s: in different ways both found their own niches in the canon and career structures of Soviet cinema.

first Party Conference on Cinema, held in March 1928, to create 'a political and cultural organ that is directly linked to the Central Committee of the Communist Party'.[35] The task of this new organ would be 'to present producers with comprehensive tasks of a political and cultural nature', for which it must seek to 'involve as many directors as possible as the cultural force on which the actual realisation of these plans has depended in the past, does depend and will continue to depend'.[36]

These signatories must have been gratified to hear the conference open with an acknowledgement of their claim by no less than the head of the Party's Agitprop Department:

> The Soviet cinema must not follow in the wake of the audience, but must move ahead of it; must lead the audience, support the beginnings in it of the new man, instil into it new views, tastes, habits which correspond to the task of the socialist reconstruction of the whole of society.[37]

The stage was now set for the pioneers to inherit the task that they had long coveted – together with the heavy responsibilities which accompanied a shift from the status of 'unacknowledged legislators' to that of 'servants of the state'.[38]

Some indication of the price to be paid in the Faustian pact now being struck between film-makers and the state had already been discovered by Eisenstein and Alexandrov. During the editing of *October* in late 1927, Stalin visited the cutting room and after viewing the work in progress insisted on the removal of nearly a quarter of the footage – including all references to Trotsky – which may indeed mark the first recorded instance of a political leader personally adjusting the filmic image of his legitimation.[39] That films based on major historical events and characters should reflect current interpretations and partisanship was a trend by no means confined to Soviet Russia: there were already numerous instances from America and France.[40] But the idea of cinema as a 'weapon', a direct contribution to the propaganda battle, was distinctively Soviet – perhaps specifically Stalinist – and would soon inspire the cinematic arming of Nazi Germany and fascist Italy.[41]

There is a distinction to be drawn between legitimation through foreign recognition (intensified in the Russian case by a tradition which regarded Western Europe as the seat of civilised values) and the estimate of actual propaganda impact. Reading the published polemics of the 'Cultural Revolution' period of 1928–30 and later homilies raises the suspicion that the latter may have been invoked in order to disguise or reappropriate the former. Consider, for instance, Alexandrov's account of how he and Eisenstein were summoned (while actually teaching at the state film school!) for a discussion with Stalin about their newly completed *The General Line*. The 'great leader of the people' expatiated:

> The significance of Soviet film art is very great – and not only for us.

Abroad there are very few books with communist content. And our books are seldom known there, for they don't read Russian. But they all look at Soviet films with attention and they all understand them. You film-makers can't imagine what important work is in your hands. Take serious note of every act, every word of your heroes. Remember that your work will be judged by millions of people.[42]

Despite Alexandrov's reputation as a notoriously unreliable witness, it seems likely that some such meeting took place in early 1929, since further changes to the film followed. It could be considered primarily a self-serving gloss written from the vantage-point of 1939, by which time it was almost obligatory to invoke Stalin's personal involvement in cinema affairs. But does it amount to 'evidence' that Stalin already believed in cinema as a prime instrument of international propaganda?

The foreign reputation of Soviet cinema in the late 1920s was certainly important and the tribute paid to the Soviet 'Five' undoubtedly a vital source of its, as of their, domestic status. But it also justified the demand for discipline and submission to authority. Alexandrov's report on the 1929 meeting continues: 'Cde Stalin spoke heatedly about the slight acquaintance that masters of Soviet film art had with the works of Marx.'[43] Accusations of political ignorance went hand in hand with allegations of 'Formalism' (the all-purpose sin of the Cultural Revolution) and insinuations of grandiosity on the part of the 'Five' and their epigones. In an exculpatory article of 1930, under the evocative title 'What Do We Have to Do?', Kuleshov voiced the indictment of the moment:

our leading directors are confused: they want to produce something gigantic but they end up with pure Formalism.

One of our directors made a political hit of this kind and immediately ARRK [the Association of Workers of Revolutionary Cinema] and the press signed him up as a leading director. When I asked what he was going to make next I got the reply: 'There's nothing to make: I shall only make something when I find a *vast political theme*.' That kind of reasoning is not far removed from awaiting inspiration![44]

The leading critic Ippolit Sokolov had written earlier that year against what he termed 'The Legend of "Left" Cinema', trying amid the hysteria of denunciation and self-justification to make some distinctions. 'Left' – meaning essentially avant-garde – cinema, he argued, was no longer a unified movement; distinctions now needed to be made, especially in respect of the 'reactionary' Kuleshov and the 'aesthete' Yutkevich: '*We must fight to ensure that the inadequacies of individual, unsuccessful "left" films do not become the canon and norms of Soviet cinema.*'[45] Sokolov went on to argue that directors (clearly arranged in order of current approval) – Eisenstein, Pudovkin, Turin, Ermler, Dovzhenko, Room, Vertov, FEKS, Yutkevich and Kuleshov – must be considered on their individual merits; and he ended with a highly significant rhetorical trope – the triple repetition of a litany:

> Eisenstein's *The Battleship Potemkin*, Pudovkin's *The Mother* and *The End of St Petersburg*, and Turin's *Turksib* signpost the path for our cinema/ . . . are creating the style of Soviet cinema/ . . . represent a form which is intelligible to the millions.[46]

Here we can perhaps see the mechanism of the canon in action. The legendary canonic Eisenstein and Pudovkin are being separated from their living, fallible selves.

As always, Eisenstein marked both an exception to and an intensification of the rule governing his profession. In the familiar story of his disastrous Mexican venture of 1930–2 – a sadistic Soviet inversion of the parable of the Prodigal Son, where Eisenstein is frustrated by the Father from bringing home the fruits of his industry – we may also read Stalin's intention to demonstrate to all the 'masters of Soviet cinema' that even their greatest could not rely upon his international renown to succeed in a project independent of Soviet support. When this was denied, Eisenstein had no choice but to return emptyhanded to the changed cultural climate of the Five-Year Plan era.[47]

FROM ART TO STATE CULTURAL INDUSTRY

The latter years of the first Five-Year Plan saw a lull in polemic and the emerging contours of what would become recognisable as 'Stalinist culture'. The Cultural Revolution had achieved its aim of destroying old structures of legitimacy and creating a new, overriding obligation of loyalty to 'the Party', which meant effectively Stalin and those who owed their position to him. The gap between élitist 'export' films and those intended for domestic consumption was closed; and Soviet films now unambiguously addressed a Soviet audience, albeit an idealised 'proletarian' one. They placed the Party at the centre of attention and created a 'positive' mythology around it in such major ideological *and* box-office successes as *Chapayev*, [Chapaev, 1934] and *The Youth of Maxim* [Yunost' Maksima, 1934]. However, comedy and romance, hitherto low priorities on the avant-garde agenda, also blossomed.

What effect did these transformations have on the director's status and role? Paradoxically, this became both more and less prestigious than before. Structurally, Soviet cinema reached the level to which many within it had long aspired in early 1933. Under Boris Shumyatsky's leadership, Soyuzkino became the Principal Directorate for the Cinema and Photographic Industry [GUKF] which had the status of a commissariat or ministry, combining ideological and resource responsibilities.[48] This replaced the fragmentation of the 1920s and the uneasy tension between

Narkompros's ideological concerns and the quasi-commercial role of Sov-kino and its other client organisations. Now, for better or worse, there was a 'direct' link to the Council of People's Commissars through a senior minister. Soviet cinema had finally achieved its privileged status among, or above, the traditional arts, and its directors enjoyed a unique prestige.

How much this restructuring owed to the fact that sound-on-film technology emerged contemporaneously with the Five-Year Plan is difficult to judge. The realisation with Soviet resources of what had already been achieved in the West meant that sound cinema became linked both literally and, perhaps more important, symbolically with industrialisation and the drive to 'catch up with America'.[49] Thus early sound films with 'industrial' themes – like Room's *Plan for Great Works* [Plan velikikh rabot, 1930], Macheret's *Men and Jobs* [Dela i lyudi, 1932], Dovzhenko's *Ivan* [1932], Ermler and Yutkevich's *Counterplan* [Vstrechnyi, 1932] – demonstrated Soviet industrial prowess in a satisfyingly new form. The medium became the message. This allowed some, like Vertov, to try to appropriate the vogue for 'shockworkers' and portray his group's work on *Enthusiasm* (also known as *The Donbass Symphony*) [Entuziasm/Sinfoniya Donbassa, 1930] as a crusade against old-fashioned attitudes within the film industry and among film critics.[50] Others took up the theme of 'efficiency'. Kuleshov, who had suffered heavy attack during the Cultural Revolution, offered *The Great Consoler* [Velikii uteshitel', 1933] as the latest example of his 'rehearsal method' overcoming delay and extravagance.[51] Correspondingly, any who professed doubts about the new technology became suspect and could easily find themselves labelled 'saboteurs'.

Changes which affected the Soviet workforce as a whole from the beginning of the 1930s inevitably had consequences for film-makers. Just as shockworkers were given special housing and food privileges and expected to play a leading part in union and factory government affairs, so too directors began to be rewarded in relation to performance.[52] For a short period in the mid 1930s, they received cash bonuses based on the box-office earnings of their films.[53] Since this experiment coincided with the first major successes of Soviet film-making, the effect was little short of embarrassing. There is an evocative photograph dating from about 1935 of Kozintsev and Trauberg dressed in the height of fashion, standing proudly beside the new cars which had been bought with their bonuses from *The Youth of Maxim*. The new scheme did not continue. According to anecdote, Stalin noticed 'too many' Jewish names appearing on the list of beneficiaries and it was dropped, although bonuses were later reintroduced on the basis of distribution 'categories' and for longer films. However, by the mid 1930s film-makers were enjoying substantial privileges as members of the new cultural intelligentsia, as a note by the rejected Vertov makes clear: 'They will have better production and living conditions: apartments, cars, foreign trips, valuable gifts, higher wages.'[54]

While the 'shock movement' and the later Stakhanovite movement offered incentives for increased effort and discipline in the workplace, the 1930s also saw intermittent efforts to coerce the Soviet workforce as a whole. In 1930 there was a premature attempt to introduce the 'work book' [*trudovaya knizhka*] system.[55] Although this was temporarily dropped in the face of opposition, it was successfully reintroduced in 1938 and played an important – if to the outsider invisible – part in controlling the careers of all Soviet citizens, including film-makers, until the relaxations of the mid 1980s. Yuri Norstein, the animator, recalled in a recent documentary how the slang term 'wolf's ticket' was coined in the 1940s for those with an endorsement in their work book who were henceforth eligible only for casual, often menial work – a secret stigma which doubtless blighted many careers.[56]

Work books noted their owner's status – in Norstein's case, 'Film director, category 1' – and also any awards received, such as Norstein's 'Honoured Cultural Worker of the RSFSR' citation in 1986. State awards were introduced at the beginning of the 1930s as part of the 'incentivisation' of the Five-Year Plan and these also carried cash awards and material benefits. They were first given to film directors in 1935, as a climax to the All-Union Conference of Workers in Soviet Cinema and, notoriously, were used on this occasion to convey carefully graduated degrees of approval.[57] Hence the Order of Lenin was given first to Lenfilm Studio, as the source of the most highly approved recent films, and to the directorial teams responsible for these – the Vasilievs (*Chapayev*), Kozintsev and Trauberg (*The Youth of Maxim*), Ermler (*Peasants* [Krest'yane, 1934]) – as well as to the 'loyal' directors Pudovkin, Dovzhenko and Chiaureli, and to such leading industry figures as Shumyatsky and the sound pioneer Pavel Tager. The Red Banner of Labour went to a number of administrators; while the Order of the Red Star was awarded to Vertov, the Ukrainian director Ivan Kavaleridze, the Armenian Amo Bek-Nazarov, Yakov Bliokh and Alexandrov. The pre-Revolutionary veteran Gardin and the lead actor from *Chapayev*, Boris Babochkin, were named People's Artists; and at the lowest level, the scriptwriter Nathan Zarkhi, the cameramen Eduard Tisse and Andrei Moskvin and the directors Eisenstein, Protazanov, Kuleshov and Nikolai Shengelaya became Honoured Art Workers. Thus a new kind of domestic 'pantheon' was formalised in full public view, signalling differentials of status and introducing a variety of administrators, actors and technicians into what had previously been the exclusive preserve of the artist–directors. An 'art' was visibly becoming an 'industry'.

By the 1940s, awards were an integral feature of the stratification of Stalinist society. Margaret Bourke-White, the American photographer who worked in Russia during the war, offered an interesting insight into their everyday sociology in her account of how the 'royal family' of Soviet cinema, Orlova and Alexandrov, wore their decorations:

[Lyubov] Orlova, the movie star, has received both the Order of Lenin and the Badge of Honour, but she does not believe they look well on summer dresses. No one, of course, would appear at an official function without them, but Orlova's omission of these from her daily attire is more unusual than the failure of an American wife to wear her wedding ring . . .

Alexandrov, the movie director, has an Order of Lenin, received for one of the pictures in which he starred his wife, Orlova.[58]

Bourke-White apparently accepted at face value Alexandrov's tall story about the award of the Red Star for his exceptional services to Soviet cinema:

Alexandrov is the only civilian to possess the military decoration Order of the Red Star. He received this when he did a picture called *Moscow Laughs* [also known as *The Happy Guys* (Veselye rebyata)] in 1935. Until then all Soviet moving pictures had been serious. Stalin, when he saw the picture, said: 'That director is a brave man to do a humorous moving picture', and it was at the demand of Stalin that Alexandrov was given his military decoration.[59]

Film-makers were now not only celebrities and commanders in the propaganda services; for a short period, they were also academicians. From 1934 to 1938 the direction and screenwriting departments of VGIK [the All-Union State Cinema Institute] became an 'academy'.[60] This enhancement of status had previously been granted to the leading theatres in the 1920s, apparently to tempt back from exile and flatter prominent actors and directors by conferring on them the title of professor. Now it was the cinema's turn, and in 1936 'a group of VGIK lecturers received academic degrees without having to defend their theses. Eisenstein became a Doctor of Art Studies and a professor, and Kuleshov a Candidate of Art Studies and a professor.'[61]

This new status, however, debarred entrants who had not already completed higher education, which further limited recruitment to a profession already short of skilled personnel. In 1938 the Film Institute reverted to being a normal higher education establishment, with Eisenstein, Kuleshov and the other 'masters' continuing to combine teaching with their production work. From afar, at least, the Soviet profession appeared to offer a unique, ideal combination of the practical and the intellectual. In 1936, such disparate figures as the young Samuel Beckett and the weary Erich von Stroheim wrote to Eisenstein – the one asking to enrol at the Film Institute and offering his links with Joyce as a credential, and the other seeking work as an actor in an industry he felt might value him more than Hollywood.[62]

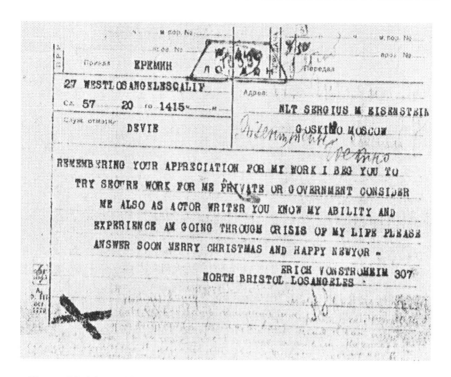

Figure 29 Job-seeking telegram from Erich von Stroheim to Eisenstein, mid-1930s.

CENSORSHIP, SELF-CRITICISM AND CO-AUTHORSHIP

While Soviet cinema became an industry during the 1930s, it also became a mass medium of entertainment, instruction and persuasion for the Soviet population. New film theatres appeared in the cities, featuring lavish decor and special foyers large enough to accommodate the jazz bands which provided popular entertainment before and after screenings. The shaping of this new-style 'cinema for the millions' was a complex operation which required a range of measures that cannot adequately be described as 'censorship'. Certainly, at the beginning of the decade there were several mass withdrawals from the repertoire of films from the 1920s. These included works by those who had since fallen into disfavour and a wide variety of films deemed 'Formalist' – including Protazanov's *Aelita* [1924] and Eisenstein's still-recent *The Old and the New* (as *The General Line* had been retitled) – as well as, one suspects, films that simply appeared old-fashioned or were no longer printable.[63] The redundancy of silent films was not yet a major issue in Soviet cinema, since sound projectors and cinemas were slow to spread outside the main cities and there continued to be a strong demand for silent films into the late 1930s.

Pruning the existing repertoire was perhaps the mildest form of control. More active intervention took the form of rejecting scripts, with the proportion of those turned down rising steeply during the Cultural Revolution. Scripts not rejected outright were subject to an increasing amount of comment and revision, while 'finished' films were viewed as candidates for 'improvement'. As early as 1928–9, when he had returned to *The General Line* after *October*, Eisenstein recalled bitterly how:

> the epic pathos of the 'rural theme' in cinema . . . was catastrophically smashed to pieces in the iron grill of prescribed demands of scenario departments and the Chief Repertory Committee [Glavrepertkom] for the cinema: 'Cooperatives not shown', 'weeding campaign not shown', 'the work of the Village Soviet is missing', etc., etc.[64]

Even such scrupulous attention to detail in those scripts that were allowed through proved insufficient to control the appearance of films deemed undesirable. The first major casualty of Stalin's willingness to see completed films 'shelved' was the directorial career of the distinguished actor Nikolai Okhlopkov. In 1930 his third film *The Way of the Enthusiasts* was banned and Okhlopkov thereafter confined himself to screen acting – notably in Eisenstein's *Alexander Nevsky* [Aleksandr Nevskii, 1938] – and to work in the theatre. In 1932, another career came to a temporary halt with the banning of *A Nail in the Boot*, though in the case of its director Mikhail Kalatozov there was to be a triumphant return in the aftermath of Stalin's death. After several ritual compromises and a spell in Hollywood during the 1940s as a diplomat, he made the key film of the Thaw 'New Wave', *The Cranes Are Flying* [Letyat zhuravli, 1957]. Among others who disappeared from the ranks of directors after one or two films were Albert Gendelstein, whose *Love and Hate* [Lyubov' i nenavist', 1935] has recently been acclaimed, and Mikhail Dubson, who made the remarkable *Border* [Granitsa] in the same year.[65]

By the mid-1930s fewer films were being produced and consequently fewer scripts were needed, but even these took ever more time to gain approval. Writing in 1938 in *Pravda*, G. Ermolayev castigated the leadership of GUK for denying studios the 'opportunity to build up a stock of scripts'. He went on to reveal the extent of the delays then common 'while the planned script was being completed [and] while the alterations and corrections were being done':

> The unfinished script for *A Great Citizen* [Velikii Grazhdanin, 1939] was 'planned' for the director Ermler in 1935 and 1936. But the script was not completed and approved until the beginning of 1937. The directors A. Ivanov and Ya. Bliokh waited almost two years for a script about the First Cavalry which never even went into production. The unfinished

script for *The Bridge of Terrors* was 'planned' for the director Barnet in 1937. Eight months later it was excluded from the plan . . . In 1938 the same fate awaits such masters of cinema as the brothers Vasiliev, Ermler, Ilya Trauberg, Sergei Gerasimov, and others.[66]

Such tortuous scripting processes were of course by no means exclusive to Soviet studios at this time. Hollywood could provide many equivalent examples of scripts endlessly rewritten, films postponed and talented direc-tors left idle. There, we assume the reasons were essentially 'commercial', resulting from intense competition between the studios, although it may be truer to say they too were 'institutional' and certainly followed no simple commercial logic. What lay behind the paralysis of Soviet production was ultimately Stalin's insistence that Soviet cinema should conform to his vision and taste, and that it should also play its part in the legitimation of his power and furtherance of his tsarlike image.[67] As a result, writers, directors, studio heads and ministry officials were all obliged to anticipate his reaction to projects and films, with the result that their caution became the major factor inhibiting Soviet cinema's fulfilment of even its modest production targets.[68]

Much has already been written about the fearful climate and immense waste of these years. But Soviet censorship was far from the clumsy, brutal and inefficient machine that is often portrayed (although it was often all of these as well); and to focus only on banning is to ignore its avowedly 'positive' intentions. The key to understanding these is the custom of peer-criticism, which evolved into a ritual of self-criticism during the Cultural Revolution and eventually into fully-fledged confession and recantation during the 1930s. Film-makers who gave expert criticism of their peers' 'errors' and confessed their own were not merely saving their careers, or even lives; they were also contributing to an ideology which lay at the heart of Stalinist aesthetics.

First came the transference of artistic responsibility from the individual to the Party. This should be understood in more than a weak sense: it meant not merely accepting advice, criticism, themes, but learning to say *and mean* 'yes' to anything the Party might will.[69] The film-maker, like artists in other fields, was invited to become a 'Soviet artist' or to give up his claims to being a professional artist.

Having made this fundamental choice, he next had to submit to a struggle against the traditions of his medium and indeed the very snare of art itself. For art is here opposed to 'life' – the latter being that which the artist is constantly urged to discover, learn from, embrace. Mikhail Yampolsky has convincingly analysed the theory implicit behind the rhetoric of this period:

What we have is the following schema: the artist whose task is to reflect life in his art at the very outset comes up against the norms which constrain him: form and language. He joins battle heroically with these and defeats them, thanks to an almost mystical fusion with the vital elements of life in all its diversity. In this way, censorship appeared as the bearer of these vital elements, as heroically fighting the withering pressure of the norms. It takes upon itself startling vital functions, whence the clash of censorship controversies, and whence the subtle therapy of the artist, which is supposed to lead him back to life.[70]

In support of his analysis, Yampolsky notes how often the Vasilievs and all who praised them spoke of *Chapayev*, the exemplary work of Socialist Realism in cinema, as a 'victory over' or 'blow against' Formalism. The use of the term 'Formalism' in Soviet rhetoric of the Stalin period is ultimately incomprehensible unless we equate it with *any* art which does not proclaim its allegiance to the Party.

The other term in the equation is 'life' – the quasi-mystical 'antidote' to the falsity of art. Again we can see that the imperative to 'learn from life' had its origins in the upheaval of the Cultural Revolution, and even before this in the anti-fine art ideology of Constructivism and 'production art' of the NEP period.[71] Before 1930 it meant leaving the big cities and discovering the reality of rural or construction scheme conditions. Increasingly, however, it came to mean accepting the Party's current themes and emphases – the official *interpretation* of events and conditions. Thus to 'learn from life' meant to pay explicit and ultimately visible attention to Party policy, whether on the rural, industrial, diplomatic or historical front.

The arch-Stalinist ritual of confession which evolved from self-criticism made public the artist's conversion from 'art' (characterised by Formalist concerns) to 'life' (as portrayed by the Party). This, however, he could normally not achieve without help; hence published criticism often took the form of earnest recommendations for self-reform, when it was not indignantly abusive. Yampolsky quotes one of the critics of *Bezhin Meadow* urging Eisenstein to

> Cast out what remains in you of Formalism, show the outstanding people of our epoch, learn to portray them with joyful love; then you will move forward with certainty, then the standard of the Revolution, which has fallen from your hand, will be recovered.[72]

When the reworking of *Bezhin Meadow* was found to contain the same 'Formalist errors' as its first version, Eisenstein was denounced for the grave sin of making an insincere confession and Shumyatsky took the opportunity to insist upon a distinction between self-criticism and true recantation through confession:

> More than once Eisenstein has verbally agreed with the criticisms made of errors in his work but he has not in fact drawn the necessary lessons from this . . . [he] had such faith in his indisputable authority that he cut

himself off from public opinion. Refusing to study life, ignorant of it, he laid store by his scholastic wisdom ...

S. Eisenstein disregarded one of the decisive conditions for the development of Soviet art: guidance. He 'recognised' it 'up to a point'.[73]

The artist, we may conclude, was considered *intrinsically* unreliable; needed for his rhetorical skills, for his ability to breathe life into mere policy – to create – but at the same time always tempted by Formalism, by self-will and by the lure of foreign reputation (domestic reputation being firmly under control).[74] Shumyatsky deplored the fact that Eisenstein 'promoted the constant hullabaloo of publicity around his name and did not confine himself to the USSR alone'.[75] Soviet art, like socialism, clearly should now be 'for one country'.

Artists who recognised this congenital weakness were those who constantly sought guidance and help. By doing so they involved the Party and ultimately Stalin in the 'co-authorship' that was the goal towards which mere coercive forms of censorship strove. While much of the activity clearly took place through the processes of script and final-cut approval, in Stalinist Russia it also involved two uniquely public ceremonial phenomena: the film-maker's personal audience with Stalin and the fictional portrayal of the leader on screen.

The personal audience obviously carried great prestige and publicised instances were therefore reserved for accredited 'masters' of the calibre of Eisenstein and Dovzhenko, as well as the newly promoted Alexandrov, pioneer of 'socialist comedy'. Dovzhenko, who had famously been mandated by Stalin to make a 'Ukrainian *Chapayev*', recorded what was probably the archetypal encounter with Stalin in 1937 and his article is worth quoting at length for the exemplary quality of its rhetoric:[76]

'Now I'll tell you why I summoned you', Comrade Stalin said. 'When I spoke to you about *Shchors* I was giving you some advice. I was merely thinking of what you might do in the Ukraine. But neither my words nor newspaper articles put you under any obligation. You are a free man. If you want to make *Shchors*, so do – but, if you have other plans, do something else ...

Joseph Vissarionovich told me this quietly and without smiling but with particular attentiveness and concern. In the midst of his work on matters of enormous state importance Comrade Stalin found the time to remember an artist, to check up on his state of mind and to relieve him of any feeling, however imaginary, that he lacked freedom, and to present him with complete freedom of choice.

I told Comrade Stalin that I was ready to make *Shchors*. I thanked him for the idea and consciously reproached myself on more than one occasion because I, a Ukrainian artist, had not thought of it myself.[77]

Here we see the intrinsic mechanism of Stalinist co-authorship laid bare

Figures 30–3 Now you see him, now you don't! Maxim Strauch as Lenin, with Mikhail Gelovani as his disappearing friend in Kozintsev and Trauberg's *The Vyborg Side* (1938) before and after revision.

with stark clarity. The film-maker's status on a par with with 'matters of state importance' is confirmed at the same time as his artistic 'freedom'. But this freedom can only be realised by his willing acceptance of Stalin's wishes. His volition has become, as it were, that of both Stalin and the state – and so the state has become 'co-author' of another exemplary film. There is also a further element in the case of Dovzhenko, long typified as the 'good Ukrainian'. Here he defers his own 'national' pedigree to Stalin's super-nationalism: readers of this 'gospel' are to understand that Stalin is *more* concerned with the culture and identity of the non-Russian republics than even their nationals – Dovzhenko confirms that 'Comrade Stalin's favourite Ukrainian songs are really the best songs'.

The representation of Stalin in a fictional context started in 1937, with Igor Goldstab portraying him in Mikhail Romm's *Lenin in October* [Lenin v oktyabre]. After 1939, when Mikhail Gelovani took over the role in Kozintsev and Trauberg's *The Vyborg Side* [Vyborgskaya storona] and Romm's sequel *Lenin in 1918* [Lenin v 1918 godu], it became customary to include scenes involving Stalin whenever possible and these soon became climactic.[78] In 1946, Stalin became a – perhaps *the* – central subject of Soviet cinema, with the release in that year of Friedrich Ermler's *The Great Turning Point* [Velikii perelom] and Chiaureli's *The Vow* [Klyatva]. Discussion of this theme was in fact materially hindered by the efficient removal of many sequences portraying Stalin and of the later canonic films of his cult *in toto* from accessible prints after the Twentieth Party Congress denunciation of the 'cult of personality'. Few scholars have thus been able to go beyond, or even fully appreciate, André Bazin's pioneering essay of 1950, 'Le mythe de Staline', lacking access to the films he discusses.[79]

Bazin's central hypothesis was that Stalin used his fictional representation to transcend the 'contradictions of subjectivity' and the contingency of his relations with Soviet politics in presenting an image of himself as 'History incarnate'. Bazin drew a telling contrast between the mummified figure of Lenin, at the centre of the Lenin cult, and the 'living mummification' of Stalin in cinema – which effectively gave him the magical attributes and powers of the film star: all-knowing, all-powerful, paternal, sexual, immortal.[80] Inevitably, most critical attention has focused on Stalin's rewriting of history through the later films of his cult, but what concerns us here is the effect this trend in Soviet cinema had on its makers.

By appointing them effectively court artists with a duty to glorify their patron, following the pattern established by Louis XIV, Stalin created an ever-increasing tension between the demands of narrative entertainment and of patronage.[81] This is not to say the resulting films lacked all aesthetic or cultural quality: on the contrary, many of them have an emotional power which, even if we qualify it as kitsch, can still evoke the 'aura' and compelling attraction of Stalin as a 'total artwork', in Boris Groys's evocative concept.[82] But this demand pushed film-makers increasingly towards the arts of spectacle and theatrical *mise-en-scène*, while further distancing them from the close involvement in scripting, casting and editing that had characterised the early phase of Soviet cinema.[83] Directors had become artificers of myth. Their status increased, while their actual power and freedom of choice narrowed drastically. The accredited 'masters' had to be protected from any tarnishing of their reputations upon which the Soviet canon depended. We can see how this constrained the later careers, not only of Eisenstein, Dovzhenko, Vertov and Kuleshov, but also of such later additions to the canon as the Vasilievs. After being conscripted to make *The Defence of Tsaritsyn* [Oborona Tsaritsyna], an early paean to Stalin's strategic brilliance in 1942, they were considered for an epic on the siege of Leningrad which was endlessly postponed.[84] Such 'model' film-makers could not be allowed to perform less than heroic tasks (any more than the hapless Gelovani could be allowed to play mere mortals).[85] In short, Stalin could not achieve his vision of a mythic cinema of self-projection without the co-operation of talented, pliable and also *convinced* film-makers; and the oft-quoted anecdote about him not consigning film-makers along with other artists to imprisonment or execution in the 1930s because he 'could not replace them' gains a grim credibility.

THE DIRECTOR AS DICTATOR/THE DICTATOR AS DIRECTOR

As Stalin insistently directed Soviet cinema towards the single overarching theme of his legitimacy and totemic power, even films that could not plausibly accommodate the 'little father' in their period or subject were made to echo his chosen motifs. He is clearly present in the dynamic moderniser of Petrov's two-part *Peter the First* [Petr pervyi, 1937 and 1939], as in the Russian folk heroes of Eisenstein's two historical films. Indeed we know from Eisenstein's copiously documented career that it was precisely Stalin's intervention that deflected the film-maker from his original intention to end both *Alexander Nevsky* and *Ivan the Terrible* on a sombre and submissive note. Nevsky, in the former, would have died after paying tribute to the Tartar Khan, knowing that he had paved the way for Russia's deliverance.[86] In the suppressed third part of *Ivan*, the Tsar would have ended his days with yet more blood on his conscience, alone and humbled before the all-seeing eye of God in a vast fresco.[87]

In both cases, Stalin was able to preserve the artistic thrust of Eisenstein's conception, while significantly modifying its final meaning. The cost of doing so was to enter into a complex relationship with Soviet cinema's favourite, if also perverse and wayward, son. For while Eisenstein detected in himself a tendency towards 'self-abasement' and a fascination with the Red Tsar (neither of these unique to him among the artistic intelligentsia), we can imagine that Stalin also grasped these vital traits in his most talented film-maker and knew how to play upon them. But, as indicated above, it would be wrong to assume that the balance of power was entirely tipped against Eisenstein. Having survived the loss of the Mexican film and *Bezhin Meadow* and committed himself to a conception of Tsar Ivan which would inevitably plumb the depths of Stalin's paranoia, he felt he had achieved a certain invulnerability.[88]

There is some support for these speculations and further evidence on Stalin's view of the director in the recently published account of another legendary Kremlin meeting. This was a discussion about the fate of *Ivan the Terrible* which took place on 25 February 1947 between Eisenstein, Cherkasov and Stalin, with Molotov and Zhdanov also in attendance.[89] The first part of the discussion more or less recapitulated criticisms of *Ivan* Part Two already announced when the film was banned in February 1946, namely that it misrepresented the *oprichniki* as 'a kind of Ku-Klux-Klan' and that Ivan was 'Hamlet-like'. Zhdanov and Molotov continued to voice criticisms which Stalin did not endorse; then he shifted to a tone of encouragement when Cherkasov promised that they would 'do better' in the proposed remaking of Part Two. In response to Eisenstein's enquiry about special instructions, he said, echoing the 'modesty before artists' motif already established in his meeting with Dovzhenko: 'I am giving you not instructions, but the reactions of a spectator.' And to the others: 'Give Comrades Cherkasov and Eisenstein the chance to complete the concept and the film.'[90]

Stalin's final question was about the ending which, it was clear to all by now, had to be different from that of the original published screenplay. Cherkasov assured him the revised film would end with the rout of Livonia and the march towards the sea, where Ivan would proclaim: 'We stand on the seas; and stand we shall.' Stalin approved and urged Eisenstein to take as long as necessary on the revision: 'If one and a half or two years, even three years, are needed to produce the film, take them so that the picture will be done well, "sculpturally".'[91] A director, Stalin went on to insist, must be 'adamant' and demand whatever he needs, whereas, he claimed, 'our directors yield too easily'.

At face value, this part of the conversation is absurd: it has the crazy logic of Stalin's celebrated telephone call to Pasternak in 1934, in which the dictator asked what literary people were saying about Osip Mandelstam's recent arrest. According to several later accounts, Stalin then reproached Pasternak, saying: 'If I were a poet and a poet friend of mine were in trouble I would do anything to help him.'[92]

Pasternak felt duly guilty – even though at some level he knew it was *Stalin* who was the real source of Mandelstam's problems! A Soviet director could only 'demand' to the extent that the officials and finally Stalin would permit such demands. Kozintsev's account of the first

Kremlin screening of that other 'model' film of 1934, *The Youth of Maxim*, confirms the essential naïvety of Stalin's outlook on cinema:

> We heard the voice several times during the screening. I listened hard to the words, trying hard to understand their meaning. It wasn't easy: sharp, at times even indignant exclamations were followed by approving interjections. But neither the anger nor the praise had any relation to the quality of the film. Gradually I realised that Stalin didn't watch movies as works of art. He watched them as real events taking place before his eyes.[93]

Other anecdotes confirm the accuracy of Kozintsev's perception. Lacking a conventional 'suspension of disbelief', Stalin treated cinema as the *representation* or *substitution* of reality. For the dictator who had shaped the whole Soviet state in his own image, cinema represented an equivalent superreality – the construction of which naturally required directors who could be as 'adamant' in the pursuit of their vision as he. It was only such a belief that enabled him to break the taboo on fictional self-representation which all other twentieth-century leaders instinctively respected.[94] Cinema provided Stalin with the 'living' image of his otherwise mummified state; thus his directors were as much court alchemists as practitioners of the modern craft of cinema – as when Chiaureli 'transported' Stalin to the ruins of Berlin in *The Fall of Berlin* [Padenie Berlina, 1949], so that his idealised self, Gelovani, could descend from the skies to receive the tribute of the grateful Soviet forces in an apotheosis which transcends mere propaganda and (on the basis of a recent screening) testifies to the blazing counterfactual conviction of all concerned.[95]

The price paid for such massive ideological investment was a slowing down of production during the last years of Stalin's reign almost to the point of standstill and paralysis in the cinema profession. The purging of many Jewish artists and intellectuals who had served on the Anti-Fascist Committee and the denunciation of 'cosmopolitans', both in 1949, further thinned the ranks of able directors.[96] Ivan Bolshakov, who had served as head of Soviet cinema since 1939 and the first Minister for Cinema since 1946, wrote in 1951 that 'the advancement of young directors has been at a standstill for the past ten to fifteen years'.[97]

His frankness was echoed by Ivan Pyriev, a specialist in the pre-war 'kolkhoz musical': 'Our art was ossified. Filming assignments went only to the most trusted directors . . . The road was barred to youth. During the last five years, no new names have appeared in our art.'[98] But it was only after Stalin's death that such complaints began to indicate a possible solution to the problem, albeit not yet daring to name its source. A 1954 article declared:

> A large part of the blame falls on our top cinema officials. In planning film production they have not taken account of the interests and the

individual artistic bent of the director. And how is it possible to disregard the creative inspirations of the artist?[99]

AFTER STALIN

Despite rapid progress in demolishing at least the visible trappings of the 'cult of personality' during the mid 1950s, the ideological underpinning of thirty years was to prove more durable.[100] Cinema in particular had become a client profession and the post-Stalin director, deprived of his *raison d'être*, faced an anxious future, however 'free' it might prove. What the profession needed was a forum which Stalin had steadfastly, and perhaps shrewdly, refused to permit – namely a union equivalent to those of the writers, theatre workers, musicians and visual artists.[101] Although each of these unions had a different history – the theatre workers' union dated back to pre-Revolutionary times – they had all come to play a similar regulatory function within Stalinist culture, which was defined by the Writers' Union as formed in 1934.[102] This had the task of promulgating Socialist Realism as the official and only aesthetic of Soviet writing, with the inevitable result that much of its activity appeared restrictive and bureaucratic. The other unions largely followed suit, ensuring that their members accepted the Party's 'guidance' and that those unwilling to do so were denied professional standing.

Despite this undeniably repressive function, the creative unions also at least theoretically protected the interests of their members and certainly provided a secure basis for professional artistic practice.[103] They controlled access to public communication, to foreign contacts and increasingly to the material necessities (as well as luxuries) of life. Why then did Stalin so strongly oppose a film-makers' union? Might this have helped to create a cinema culture less directly responsive to his will and desire? Was it the fear that even a subservient film-makers' union might mediate his rule of 'divide and conquer' and imperil his close, almost personal, relations with key film-makers – in fact 'institutionalise' them? Did he *want* film directors to feel superior to other artists?

To some extent these fears (if such they were) proved well founded when a cinema union did finally emerge. It was not until 1957, with Khrushchev's express approval, that the first steps were taken towards forming a film-makers' union. The prime movers were Mikhail Romm, who had emerged from the toils of Stalinist cinema as a 'convert' and courageous proponent of greater artistic and individual freedom, and Ivan Pyriev, once a member of Eisenstein's Prolketkult theatre group and later his bitter opponent. However, it was neither of these older, compromised figures who became First Secretary, but a young director, Lev Kulidzhanov, whose *The House Where I Live* [Dom v kotorom ya zhivu, co-dir. Yakov Segal, 1957] chimed with the conciliatory themes of the 'Thaw' period.

The new Union of Cinematographers faced its first real test in the aftermath of the Manège affair in December 1962 and the formation of an Ideological Control Commission.[104] Two of the union's members, Romm and Marlen Khutsiev, were singled out for censure by Khrushchev. Romm, now revered by a generation of younger film-makers whom he had taught at VGIK, had made a speech denouncing the instigators of the 'cosmopolitanism' campaign of 1949 directed against leading Jews.[105] Khutsiev, a younger director who had launched Vasili Shukshin as a new kind of popular hero by starring him in *Two Fedors* [Dva Fedora, 1959], was engaged in an ambitious film about youth attitudes, *The Ilyich Gate* [Zastava Ilyicha], (eventually released as *I Am Twenty* [Mne dvadtsat' let] in 1965), part of which Khrushchev saw and disliked.[106] Attempts were made to suspend the Union when it refused to condemn these two but, despite a 'punishment' which required the members to pay their dues at factories and sent some to do 'voluntary' work on state farms, the Union stood its ground and in December 1965 proudly held its long-delayed 'Founding Congress' at which Kuleshov delivered the main speech.[107]

Many of the most challenging films made by its members in the period of the Soviet 'New Wave' between 1959 and 1966 remained little known outside professional circles. Post-completion censorship, once relatively rare but used increasingly from the mid 1960s, kept them from wide domestic circulation and denied them the foreign promotion which had created the reputation of Soviet cinema's founders. Indeed not until the Union of Cinematographers pioneered the era of glasnost in mid 1986 with its 'unshelving' initiative were many of the fruits of the early 1960s able to be appreciated.[108] The director had, however briefly, found a post-Stalin role, less as a reformer or an avatar of a new phase of 'socialism' than as a traditionally superfluous artist: hence the profusion of existential, 'spiritual' and stylistically eclectic films from this period – a veritable recapitulation of the rich cinema of the NEP, once this is seen without the narrowing perspective of Soviet canonisation.[109]

POSTSCRIPT: BEYOND THE HYPHEN

No other chapter in the relatively short history of cinema offers such a sharply defined case of canonisation as an absolute arbiter of reputation. We can now begin to look back at the trajectory of Soviet cinema, but we are still far from being able to disentangle value judgements about its artistic achievements from the ideological structures – Western as much as Soviet – which created and maintained its canon. As Mikhail Yampolsky noted in a 1990 article on the revision of Soviet cinema history, there is still a powerful Manichaean tendency to distinguish the 'good' from the 'bad', despite the evidence that these are intimately connected.[110] He took as an example two of Ermler's films, *Katka's Reinette Apples* [Kat'ka – bumazhnyi ranet, 1926] and *Peasants*: one from the 'good' and the other from the 'bad' period of this semi-canonic director. As in so many similar cases, he is able to show a continuity between the underlying schemas of the films (which both revolve around a pregnant woman, but take opposed attitudes towards fertility, nature and society). To deny this continuity is to falsify the transitive progression from early Soviet to Stalinist society, but it is also to falsify, or simply ignore, the continuity of Ermler's career as a film-maker.

Can we speak of the integrity of 'broken' careers such as those of Ermler, Dovzhenko, Pudovkin, Vertov, Room and even Chiaureli? Superficially, it is easier to come to terms with those who suffered, were criticised and in many cases silenced. Therefore a director like Room – despite being severely castigated for his sexually explicit *Bed and Sofa* [Tret'ya Meshchanskaya (literally *Third Meschchanskaya Street*), 1927], being dismissed from *Once One Summer* [Odnazhdy letom] in 1934 and suffering the total suppression of *A Severe Young Man* – was never perceived as a martyr and consequently achieved neither a fully validated Soviet 'career' nor an accredited Western 'crippled creative biography'.[111] Despite the consistency and quality of his individual films, made under immensely difficult and compromising conditions, he still awaits posthumous recognition – a casualty of the 'canonic Cold War' that ignored so many Soviet film-makers for so long.[112]

Another such casualty who was among the first to be rehabilitated is Boris Barnet, long dismissed as a gadfly or epigone of the Kuleshov school, but now increasingly recognised as a major film-maker, who survived over thirty years from the 1930s to the 1960s – including having a number of films banned – precisely by avoiding canonic status.[113] It was Barnet who deftly noted the gap between the canonised 'Soviet director' and the director *per se* in an exchange recalled by Otar Ioseliani, at that time a rising young member of the 'Thaw' generation:

> [Barnet] asked me: 'Who are you?' I said: 'A director' (this was when I was making *April* [Aprel'] in 1962). 'Soviet', he corrected, 'you must always say "Soviet-director". It is a very special profession.' 'In what way?' I asked. 'Because if you ever manage to become honest, which would surprise me, you can remove the word "Soviet". Now I am a "Soviet-director", although I only became one recently.'[114]

Deprived now of all the familiar institutions which for so long controlled the Soviet canon, it remains to be seen how many 'hyphenates' will eventually be admitted into an expanded Russian canon.

For such a process to happen, however, there will need to be some 'institutional' solution to the major problem of textual availability. Preparations for the conference on which this book is based revealed that *no* complete copy of any film directed by Alexandrov was available from a

Figure 34 Boris Barnet filming *The Wrestler and the Clown* (1957).

Western European source for screening. Currently, no film directed by Abram Room or by Mikhail Romm is in British distribution; and until recently no film of Barnet's was available.[115] What might be termed 'butter' in this context will have to come before 'can(n)on' revision. Equally important is the need to recognise two ironies of the canonic process noted by Jan Gorak:

> the irony by which the most significant critics of the canon also function as its defenders; and . . . the tendency throughout their history for canons to survive not by the fiat of authoritarian dogma but by a combination of narrative suggestiveness and ineradicable cultural need.[116]

In the case of 'classic' Soviet cinema, it remains to be seen whether scholars can survive *their* new freedoms and overcome the inertia of 'narrative suggestiveness' while recharting the Soviet labyrinth.[117]

Chapter 11

Documentary film – a Soviet source for Soviet historians

Valeriya Selunskaya and Maria Zezina

Film documents are a comparatively recent non-traditional source for the study of the past. Although cinema is approaching its centenary, historians are only now taking the first steps towards assimilating it.[1] At the same time the introduction of documentary films into scholarly circulation and into the practice of teaching history can enrich historical knowledge with information that cannot be obtained from any other kind of source.

Knowledge of history is broadened through the study of film. In this process, understanding comes to embrace not only the rational but also the emotional. Newsreels and documentary films open up the opportunity for our contemporaries to come face to face with an epoch half a century old. But, with the discovery of previously inaccessible archive films taken out of circulation under the authoritarian régime, the newsreels of the 1920s and 1930s have gained their civil rights and speak in a new language. They are an essential aid to historians in filling in the 'blank spots' of Soviet history, in defining the historical reality of the period of the personality cult, and in liberating them from conformist ideological and mythological conceptions in the reading of the past.

Film theorists rightly feel that 'no spiritual product, other than the spoken language, has ever been a document of mass thought and experience like cinema'.[2] Content analysis of documentary and newsreel films of the 1920s and 1930s allows the historian to create a socio-psychological profile of the audience and to understand better the spiritual climate of society. It enables us to clarify the essential characteristics of the ideological deformation of documentary cinema by the Stalin régime in order to manipulate public opinion. In addition, not even the most detailed description of a historical figure can replace the living human form preserved on film. The faces of people, their dress, their behaviour, their surroundings, all that we see on the screen creates a unique image of the time, of that spirit of the epoch that no other historical source can convey.

This essay is an attempt to provide a survey and interpretation of the newsreels of the 1920s and 1930s and of the documentary films compiled from them, from the point of view of the historian.[3] The Faculty of History of Moscow University has acquired a certain experience in working with film documents. In the middle of the 1970s a thematic catalogue of films on the history of Soviet society was compiled and recommendations for their use were devised.[4] What spectrum of film documents of the 1920s and 1930s does the historian now have to hand? How was the filming organised? What material and staff resources were at the disposal of documentary film producers? For answers we must turn to the history of the newsreels.

In the 1920s the material and technical possibilities for Soviet cinema were extremely limited. Documentary filming of the most important events in the life of the country was only fragmentary. There were no regular film newsreels, with the exception of Dziga Vertov's *Kino-Pravda* [Cine-Truth] from 1922 to 1925. The establishment of Soviet documentary cinema in these years took place with the minimum of interference from the state. As noted in an official document of the mid 1920s, 'up to now the Party has not managed to approach the question of the appropriate use of cinema in real earnest and to take control of it.'[5]

The achievements of Soviet documentarists in the 1920s are justifiably linked with the names of Lev Kuleshov, Dziga Vertov, Esfir Shub and others. But the works of these masters cannot be compared with the generally low professional level of the newsreel makers, who did not systematically prepare their shooting sequences until the 1930s. In the works of the masters themselves, a poetic interpretation of reality was characteristic, as shown in Vertov's films, *Forward, Soviet!* [Shagai, Sovet!, 1927], *The Eleventh Year* [Odinnadtsatyi, 1928], Ilya Kopalin's *Moscow* [Moskva, 1927], Mikhail Kaufman's *Springtime* [Vesnoi, 1929] and Viktor Turin's *Turksib* [1929]. In 1930 the first Soviet sound films were shot and amongst them were documentary films like Iosif Poselsky's *Thirteen Days: The Case of the Industrial Party* [Trinadtsat' dnei: delo Prompartii] and Vertov's *The Donbass Symphony* [Simfoniya o Donbasse; also known as *Enthusiasm* (Entuziazm), 1930].

At the beginning of the 1930s the All-Union Newsreel 'Factory' [Soyuzkinokhronika], which was to become the Central Studio of Documentary Films [TsSDF] in 1944, began to function. It had more than twenty sections across the country and its output amounted to 17 per cent of all film production. It regularly issued five newsreels: *Union Film Newsreel* [Soyuzkinozhurnal], *For the Socialist Countryside* [Za sotsialisticheskuyu derevnyu], *In Defence of the USSR* [Na strazhe SSSR], *Pioneer Life* [Pioneriya] and *News of Science and Technology* [Novosti nauki i tekhniki]. The sections of Soyuzkinokhronika provided information for the newsreels and also for the editorial correspondents who from the beginning of the first Five-Year Plan worked on the large construction sites. In 1932 a cinema train was organised. It was a kind of mobile film factory headed by the well-known director Alexander Medvedkin and it produced seventy-two films in one year.[6]

In the 1930s simplistic pragmatism and operational reporting replaced the earlier poetic interpretation of reality by the recognised masters of documentary cinema. This turning point in documentary film coincided with radical political and socio-economic changes in the life of Soviet society at the time.

At the end of the 1920s there was an ideological 'restructuring' [perestroika] of documentary cinema. On 7 December 1929, the USSR Council of People's Commissars [Sovnarkom] passed a decree 'On Strengthening the Production and Exhibition of Political-Educational Films' and the leadership of Sovkino 'turned the wheel of Soviet cinema' towards mass agitation and propaganda films.[7] Cinema was set purely utilitarian tasks: to provide up-to-date and accessible information on questions of politics and production. Debates developed in the press about documentarism in cinema. The insistence on reflecting life as it was was criticised as wrong and anti-Marxist.[8]

From the beginning of the 1930s the struggle for control of cinema production and distribution became fiercer. Glavrepertkom, the State Repertoire Committee, which had carried out these functions since 1923, began regularly to publish repertoire guides which listed films that had been passed for exhibition.[9] Glavrepertkom's instructions directed the local repertoire committees to keep track of the appearance on screen of productions from previous years and to warn of 'contradictions between the pictures and current reality'.[10]

Among the documentary films and newsreels which were removed from the screen in 1931 were all the film newsreels released before 1929 and the majority of films released before 1926. Among the banned films were relatively recent ones such as *May Day in Moscow* [1oe. maya v Moskve, 1930], *A Chronicle of 1929* [Khronika 1929] and *In Memory of Felix Dzerzhinsky* [Pamyati F. Dzerzhinskogo, 1927]. It is obvious that in these cases the motives for the ban were political. The banned films were not preserved in the archives, and they were probably blacklisted as a result of the defeat of the 'Right deviation' in the Party and exclusion of Bukharin, Rykov and Tomsky from political activity. It is well known that Bukharin spoke at the funeral of Dzerzhinsky. Rykov as Chairman of Sovnarkom must have been on the tribune of the Lenin Mausoleum during the May Day celebrations. As they were forced out of the political arena, they had also to disappear from the screen.

Regrettably, this kind of 'purging' of history became normal practice in the following years. It included not only bans on individual films, but also the direct falsification of film and photographic documents. Objectionable political figures were erased from group photographs by retouching and were excised from newsreels. A collection of photographs of this kind is kept at the Museum of the Revolution in Moscow.

The historian working with newsreel documents of the 1920s and 1930s must bear in mind that documentary films were aimed at the audience of that time, people who were not familiar with television and for whom radio was only just becoming a part of life, so that the significance for them of cinema as a source of information was enormous. However, in general the documentary cinema and newsreels did not reach the audience very effectively because of weaknesses in the distribution system. The situation was particularly deplorable in the rural areas where two-thirds of the population lived. Films only reached the villages after a considerable delay and in poor condition following urban distribution. In the 1920s cinema was generally a rarity for the village dweller. In the 1930s the vast majority of projectors in the countryside were for silent films as the villages were supplied with equipment discarded by the urban cinemas, so that the village audience was forced to watch old films, only 20–30 per cent of which were in good technical condition. The newsreel specifically aimed at the rural audience, *For the Socialist Countryside*, reached the villages a year late.[11]

In these conditions it is understandable that documentaries were unable to compete with feature films in audience popularity. All this undoubtedly restricted their impact on public consciousness. But how fully and truthfully did the documentary and newsreel films reflect reality? To what extent are they valuable as a historical source? The answers to these questions are quite fundamental.

Film has brought to us many important events of the history of the 1920s and 1930s: Party Congresses, speeches of the leaders of the Party and state, Congresses of Soviets, political trials, meetings, parades and sporting rallies, the organisation of the first collective farms, expeditions to the Arctic and meetings with the men who conquered it, the arrival of foreign visitors and the opening of the Moscow metro, the construction of hydroelectric power stations and other enterprises in the first Five-Year Plan and so on. Of course the cameramen were not detached chroniclers and in the very selection of subjects for shooting one can see a definite political direction. As stated in the decision of the First All-Union Cinema Production Conference: 'Newsreels must sharply and clearly reflect the process of development of socialist construction in the USSR.'[12] However, there is no direct surviving film evidence of many important events of pre-war Soviet history. This particularly relates to tragic episodes such as the elimination of the kulaks, the famine of 1932–3 and the mass repressions. Therefore, when we look at a film document we must, in the words of Auguste Rodin, see the whole truth and not only that which strikes the eye. Information about the past is conveyed not only by what has been fixed on film but also by what has *not* been a subject for filming, not only by the film documents that did reach the audience but also by those that were banned, confiscated, destroyed or sent to the 'special' repository [*spetskhran*].

In working with newsreels and the documentaries compiled from them, it is important for the historian to take account of the authorial position of the director and cameraman. The possibility that the author's interpretation of documentary material might conform to a personal perspective was clearly expressed by Dziga Vertov:

> I am the Cine-Eye.
>
> I take the strongest and most agile hands from one man, the fastest and best proportioned from another, the most handsome and expressive head from a third and through montage I create a new, perfect man . . .[13]

Esfir Shub's films *The Fall of the Romanov Dynasty* [Padenie dinastii Romanovykh, 1927] and *The Great Way* [Velikii put', 1927] represent an interesting example of her own interpretation of historical newsreel. The pre-Revolutionary shots depicting the Tsar's family are transformed in Shub's film into sharply critical material. If we compare the original shots with Shub's film we clearly see the role of the author as historian making sense of and interpreting a historical document.

Of particular interest for the historian are the documentary films of the Communist Party Congresses,[14] which retain the atmosphere of the time, communicating both the mood of the auditorium and the manner of speaking of the Party leaders. Until the Fifteenth Congress in 1927 these films were only fragmentary. But shots have survived showing a general view of the auditorium and the presidium of the Eighth Congress in 1919 and of the speeches given at later Congresses by Lenin, Trotsky, Zinoviev, Kamenev, Bukharin, Radek and other leaders. From Congress to Congress the length of the film record grows, as the catalogues of the film archive at Krasnogorsk demonstrate. We can see the ceremonial column of delegates to the Thirteenth Congress in 1924 crossing the Kremlin grounds to the Congress Hall. A band plays, and at the head of the column are Kalinin, Stalin, Bukharin, Kamenev and Zinoviev. The film record has preserved some episodes of this Congress including its opening, the greetings of the workers' delegates and of the Comintern, and the Pioneers' parade on Red Square in honour of the Congress. This film material is a clear illustration of the moral and psychological climate in which the Party lived. The Congress met only a few months after Lenin's death. During the Congress itself Stalin, with the help of Kamenev and Zinoviev, managed to prevent the publication of Lenin's testament, 'A Letter to the Congress', and to retain the key post of Party General Secretary. The struggle went on behind the scenes, hidden from the eyes of the majority of delegates who did not suspect what a high price the country would subsequently have to pay for their credulity and their inattention to Lenin's warnings.

The newsreel portrays the festive mood of the delegates. The leaders walk in a column together with rank-and-file Party members, the band thunders and young Leninists march in a celebratory parade by the walls of the Kremlin where their fathers had gathered before. There is no reason to doubt the genuineness of the smiles of the participants at the Congress. The country was gradually recovering after the devastation of war, industry was being re-established and the famine had been overcome. The power struggle had not yet divided the ranks of the leaders, who had been Lenin's comrades. Of course the newsreel shots of the Thirteenth Congress do not convey to us the whole truth of what took place, but those details and visual traits of the time which they do contain are not conveyed by other sources.

Newsreels of the 1920s and 1930s enable us to follow dynamically the political sympathies, the socio-psychological climate in broad Party circles and in the leading echelons of the Party and state against the background of the growth of the leadership cult and of the dictatorial régime. It is interesting to compare the film records of the Thirteenth, Fifteenth and Seventeenth Congresses of the Party which each reflect definite qualitative transitions in this process. In 1924 Stalin was preoccupied with consolidating his political authority after the content of the 'Letter to the Congress', in which Lenin had proposed removing Stalin from the post of General Secretary, had become known. In the shots of the funeral procession, he is the most prominent leader alongside Lenin's coffin. Trotsky, his main political rival, did not come to the funeral as he was misinformed of the time, a circumstance which benefited Stalin. In his speeches and articles in 1924, Stalin emphasised his loyalty to Leninism. In 1927 Stalin was presented as a self-confident political leader, the central attacking figure in the struggle against the opposition, eradicating dissidence under the banner of the defence of Leninism.

The Fifteenth Congress took place shortly after the celebration of the first decade of Soviet power in 1927. During the celebration, Trotsky's supporters tried to organise a demonstration in opposition to the official one. This demonstration was quickly dispersed and was not filmed, but amongst the newsreel shots indirect evidence has been preserved that the authorities were preparing for some possible undesirable incident. This is seen in the entry into Moscow and billeting in the Kremlin of a cavalry corps which, according to the intertitles, had come to take part in the anniversary celebrations. Trotsky's supporters suffered a defeat. The Fifteenth Congress confirmed the victory of the Stalinist majority and expelled from the Party about a hundred active members of the opposition. It was this that gave Stalin the confidence for his continuing struggle for sole power.

In 1929 newsreel shots illustrated the celebration of Stalin's fiftieth birthday, which was the moment when he ascended the pedestal of the cult. The November 1929 Plenum of the Party Central Committee had only recently taken place and had sanctioned the turn in the Party's political strategy and in the life of the country away from Lenin's New Economic Policy (NEP) towards forced industrialisation and collectivisation, towards the administrative-command system of government.

In 1934 Stalin's confidence and the strength of his régime of personal power were growing. This watershed was particularly clearly illustrated in the newsreel shots of the Seventeenth Party Congress in Stalin's unhurried, confident, firm speech, his rare gestures directed at the public, the long pauses filled with continuous applause during which the leader poured water into a glass and drank slowly. The general atmosphere of unorchestrated enthusiasm, of almost fanatical loyalty to his name, and the belief in him as the true inheritor of Lenin's work are of interest. But the film has preserved another side of Stalin, seen during the interval in the work of the Seventeenth Congress, when the votes were being counted in the secret ballot for elections to the Party Central Committee. It is well known that on the eve of the Congress the idea was secretly crystallising of the need to remove Stalin as General Secretary and to replace him by Sergei Kirov, leader of the Leningrad Communists and 'favourite' of the Party in those days. Stalin knew about this and for this reason he waited tensely for the results of the voting. Against the background of the general merriment of the relaxed delegates of the 'Congress of Victors' the tense, preoccupied face of Stalin stands out in sharp contrast.

These shots were cleverly used by V. Lopatin in his documentary film *Stalin and Others* [Stalin i drugie, 1989] made from newsreels of the 1930s. The shot was held as a still and the audience heard the commentary, which did not assert anything but forced them to reflect: 'What is Stalin thinking about? Why is his expression so guarded and concentrated? What is he waiting for?' This is evidently the author's discovery, uncovering a new semantic facet of the film shot, bringing it to the viewers' attention and forcing them to evaluate afresh the objective information of the film document.

The spontaneous enthusiasm of the Party delegates greeting Stalin grew from Congress to Congress. In the middle of the 1930s Stalin was already accepted by the majority of the population as the true heir to Lenin's work, the leader of a great country which was achieving a breakthrough to a bright future. Film has been preserved showing the inaugural meeting in the Bolshoi Theatre to mark the opening of the Moscow metro in 1935. This film shows 'the contact of the leader with the people'. It shows Stalin's speech and the reaction of his audience of metro builders to it. It is well known that he was a bad orator who spoke slowly with a strong accent, and these characteristics are evident in the sound recording. But his every word was received in the hall as a revelation, the hall literally exploded with laughter and with thunderous applause at his crude jokes. The young happy faces with shining eyes avidly absorbed Stalin's every gesture. The impression was as if it was not they, the shockworkers, who were the chief heroes of the celebration, but the stocky man on the stage in the white parade tunic, whose will shaped people's entire lives. Narrative sources from that time show that the relationship between Stalin and the people was by no means as one-sided as is shown by the film, which reflects rather the collective display of emotions. It is now clear that these strips of newsreel film combine together, as it were, the document and the myth, created under the direct influence of the aesthetic mythology of the Stalin era.

We fully endorse the view of Leonid Kozlov that, when we are working with the cinema record of the Stalin period, it is necessary to distinguish the layers of aesthetic mythology in the cultural–historical sense (as myth is one of the forms of culture) from the dominant ideological impress which in the final analysis governed aesthetics.[15]

The deliberate propagation of Stalin's personality linked all the successes of the country with his name and all the failures with 'enemy intrigues', and this shaped the cult's stereotypes in public consciousness. The figure of Lenin was slowly squeezed into a secondary position in the cinema mythology of the 1930s. In this context Dziga Vertov's romantic journalistic film essay *Three Songs of Lenin* [Tri pesni o Lenine, 1934] sounds almost non-conformist.

Thus the historian working with newsreel materials of the 1920s and 1930s has to take account of the fact that those who created the film document were adherents of particular aesthetic tendencies and that the ideology born of Stalinism satisfied them. Historians rightly consider that in every concrete historical situation it is absolutely essential to know how contemporaries perceived a particular film document and how our contemporaries perceive it today. Do they see in it reality or a myth about this reality? There is a danger of aberration when a person or society in its overwhelming majority sincerely takes the myth for reality.

This is how the Stalinist deformations in Soviet society were seen at that time and it is reflected in the documentary film of the period. It is remarkable that the record of the visits to the Soviet Union of Bernard Shaw, Henri Barbusse and Lion Feuchtwanger, combined with their written reports of their impressions and meetings with Stalin, permit us to conclude that even these writers, with their wisdom of experience and their knowledge of the real state of affairs, succumbed to a considerable extent to the ideological influence of Stalinist propaganda.

Documentary films and newsreels can be used as a source for the study of the possibilities of ideological influence on the everyday consciousness of citizens and in this connection it is useful to turn to the subjects most often dealt with in the films of the period. Almost all the important political trials of those years and the mass meetings in support of them were filmed, beginning with the trial of the Socialist Revolutionaries in 1922. These materials were used in the newsreels and in films such as *The Trial of the*

Right SRs [Protsess pravykh eserov], *The Trial of the Industrial Party* [Protsess prompartii], *The Plot of the Interventionists* [Zagovor interventov], *The Interventionists' Internationale* [International interventov], *The Interventionists' Bloc* [Blok interventov], *The Trial Proceeds* [Sud idet] and *The Judgement of the Court Is the Judgement of the People* [Prigovor suda – prigovor naroda]. Amongst other frequent subjects for the newsreels were the funerals for the victims of the kulak terror, and the trials of saboteurs and wreckers. These subjects could not fail to move the audience. That is how the idea of the exacerbation of the class struggle was implanted in the public consciousness, together with increased vigilance and the prevalence of class interests over common human values. By no means all the material used in the newsreels was genuine. *Pioneer Life*, for instance, was criticised for substituting staged scenes for newsreel materials.[16] It is now difficult to distinguish genuine newsreels from dramatisations but the very fact that the practice existed compels us to be highly critical of any subjects where substitution was possible. In a number of cases the boundary between genuine events and dramatic re-creation was a very relative one. It is well known, for instance, that the political show trials of the 1930s took place according to a previously determined scenario, which had been rehearsed several times. It is possible that the filming took place during these rehearsals and the episodes which were most successful from the point of view of the general objective were used in the films. This is confirmed by the psychological condition of the defendants, whose behaviour and manner of speech have come down to us through the film record. These people who were accused of the most heinous crimes seem to be relatively calm and not one of them attempts to reject the absurd accusations. The present-day observer, knowing the truth, cannot of course help sensing how difficult it was for the accused to cover this internal tension with an external mask of 'calm': for instance, the hand of one of the accused in the trial of the Industrial Party shakes as he pours a glass of water when he comes to the rostrum, and the clinking of the glass seems to convey the beating of a human heart.

There are preserved in the archives newsreels of meetings of Leningrad engineering and technical workers demanding severe punishment for the members of the Industrial Party, and also of a meeting of Leningrad workers in response to an article in *Pravda* on the struggle against counter-revolution and of a Moscow meeting against the Industrial Party. A series of meetings were organised round the trials of the Mensheviks in 1931, the trials of the Trotskyite–Zinovievite Centre in 1937 and the Right-Trotskyite Centre in 1938. The films of these convincingly demonstrate that such mass expressions of public indignation were not at all spontaneous. The meetings were well organised, well provided with accommodation and with film groups and the speeches were prepared in advance. This kind of subject was frequently used in the newsreels. The previously orchestrated meeting as a form of expression of political moods was an important instrument of influence on public opinion. People who in the consciousness of their contemporaries had been comrades of Lenin and who had only recently occupied leading positions in the Party and the state were accused of terrible and fantastic crimes. Could people really believe that Old Bolsheviks who had gone through tsarist prisons and exile, who had participated in the October Revolution and organised the victory in the Civil War, were spies and traitors? Alone with himself the individual could be overwhelmed by his doubts, but participation in mass action left no room for reflection. The collective was indignant and demanded severe punishment for the traitors, the elemental character of the meetings carried away all the participants and their individuality was dissolved. If we look at the faces of the participants in these meetings, they are all identical, there are no doubters, no one is indifferent, people are stern, their attention rapt, they are gripped by common emotions. The collective resolutions of these meetings made everybody, even the silent, into accomplices in the severe punishment of the imaginary 'enemies of the people'.

A completely contrasting atmosphere is conveyed by the film record of mass festivals. Very great significance was attached to the organisation of the filming of this kind of event – May Day, the anniversaries of the Revolution, sports parades or the ceremonial opening of the gigantic projects of the Five-Year Plans. A group of ten directors and forty cameramen were assigned to the filming of May Day in 1935, for instance, so that the film would be ready by that same evening. A sports parade on 30 June 1935 was filmed by thirty-six cameramen and a group of directors led by V. Iosilevich. The film shot at this sports parade, *Happy Youth* [Schastlivaya yunost'], was made in record time and shown to the delegates at the Seventh Congress of the Comintern which took place in July and August of the same year in Moscow. We can imagine how this film was received by the leaders of the international Communist movement who had travelled to the first country in the world where socialism had been victorious. One of the issues considered at the Congress was a report by Dmitri Manuilsky on the victory of socialism in the USSR and the film *Happy Youth* was a vivid illustration of his report. On the screen were shown orderly lines of young men and women in sports clothes, strong young bodies in synchronised movement fused into a single powerful organism. Happy young faces, flowers, music and the power of the human columns created an image of the triumphant young land of the Soviets. 'One felt that a huge human brain, a great human heart, was directing and uniting the hundreds of thousands of people in the square and our whole country into the new invincible force of the Communist future of the world', wrote one critic of this film.[17]

What was significant was that the film was not seen as a commentary on a real event – the sports parade in Red Square on 30 June 1935 – instead, it formed an image of the country and the age. There was nothing superfluous or accidental in the film, nothing that did not work towards the central idea. In this respect it is interesting to compare *Happy Youth* with the film *The Fifteenth Year* [Pyatnadtsatyi], directed by Iosif Poselsky and devoted to the celebration of May Day in Moscow in 1932. The name itself is neutral; it is simply the fifteenth May Day under Soviet power. The events of the festival are shown in chronological order: early morning, the empty, dark street; by 6 a.m. it begins to get light; the camera records every hour: now the first pedestrian appears and a group of people hurrying to the demonstration. The parade and demonstration in this film do not acquire a symbolic significance: they are real events of the holiday. The camera takes close-ups of the faces of Red Army soldiers and it is evident they are not specially selected by the cameramen, but simply the first ones they came across. Although the film was noted as one of the best at the Conference of Documentary Film-Makers, the director was criticised for the absence of any pronounced bias. 'The powerful impact of the million-strong demonstration has faded in the film', wrote the newspaper *Kino* [Cinema] 'its chief characteristic as a demonstration of the builders of socialism who have achieved the Five-Year Plan is not made evident.'[18] This critic demanded from the documentary film-maker not an illustration of *external* events, but the revelation of their *inner* meaning.

This orientation above all towards the 'inner meaning' of events fundamentally limits the value of the film documents of the 1930s as a historical source. The films are often evidence not of the actual course of events but of how these events *ought* to have been in the view of contemporaries. For instance in Mikhail Slutsky's film about the Dnieper Dam, *In the Name of Lenin* [Imeni Lenina, 1932], the emphasis is put on the joyful moment of starting up the power station and all the difficulties of construction are left outside the picture. In a film about the Solovki prison camp (made on the orders of OGPU, the secret police, themselves) everything is subordinated to the central idea of the successful re-education of the prisoners in the course of their collective labour. The life of the prisoners is portrayed in such a way that the film could not be released for public viewing. It appeared as if the prisoners in the camp were kept in better conditions than those in which the majority of Soviet citizens lived. In spite of obvious falsification, the film brings us unique shots of camp life. These are used to brilliant effect in Marina Goldovskaya's historical documentary film *Solovki Power* [Vlast' solovetskaya, 1988], recently shown successfully in the USSR and abroad. Letters from the camp and reminiscences of former inmates combine with the falsified film record to convey a double strand of information about what existed in reality and about how the truth was distorted in favour of a falsely understood 'inner meaning'.

In contrast to the OGPU film about Solovki, Alexander Lemberg's *The White Sea Construction Project Reports* [Belomorstroi raportuyet, 1933] was released and recommended for showing anywhere without restriction. The film tells of the labour of prisoners on the construction of the canal from the Baltic to the White Sea. This was a time when news from the islands of the Gulag Archipelago, although fragmentary and distorted, did still reach the mass audience. A large group of writers went on an expedition to the construction sites and as a result a book was published about the White Sea Canal. Stalin also visited the construction sites and this episode was filmed. The theme of the re-education of criminals through labour for the good of the country was so popular that, apart from the books and documentary film about the White Sea Canal, a feature film was also made – Yevgeni Chervyakov's *The Prisoners* [Zaklyuchennye, 1936] from a screenplay by Nikolai Pogodin. Subsequently the Gulag became a closed book. So the shots of the Solovki camp and of the White Sea Canal construction remain the only film evidence of their kind.

Of course the historical process is a complex one and so it would be wrong to reduce the history of Soviet society, even in as contradictory a period as the 1920s and 1930s, merely to the deformations, the mistakes, the miscalculations and the repressions. The documentary film record convincingly demonstrates this. However, in the conditions of perestroika, when the active process of renewing our thinking, of liberating it from conformism and dogmatic stereotypes, is going on, historians must use all the sources of reliable information that are now available in order to contribute to this progressive movement. Today we can express our recognition of the documentary film-makers of the 1920s and 1930s, acknowledging that, to a significant extent, they did not completely submit to that ideological processing, and did not totally accept the embellished ideology, but created a film record which in the years of the personality cult and the period of stagnation was firmly locked up in the 'special repository'. Luckily not only 'books do not burn': films do not either, although time does spoil them: nevertheless they still convey to us invaluable information about the life and activity of past generations.

We have the impression that present-day film critics, and often cinema historians as well, are inclined to censure excessively the vast majority of films of record from the distant 1920s and 1930s, both for their technical imperfections and for their tendentiousness, for their voluntary or involuntary perversion of historical reality. At the same time we are witnessing a real boom in non-played cinema and a widespread concentration by film journalists on historical problems on the basis of those very same film documents that have come down to us from the 1920s and 1930s and that may help in the difficult task of perestroika.

The first wave of attention to the banned newsreels was noticeable at the time of the so-called 'Thaw' in the 1950s. The attention of documentary film-makers at that time was mainly concentrated on those blocks of forgotten or 'arrested' newsreel film of the 1920s and 1930s in the special repositories, which made it possible to reinstate the role of the first leader of the Soviet state in the political life of the country and to rescue from oblivion the names and images of the posthumously rehabilitated victims of Stalin's Terror and to launch an assault on the most scandalous deformations associated with Stalinism. In the 1960s on the Moscow city cinema circuit documentary compilations circulated like the three-part film *The Living Lenin* [Zhivoi Lenin, 1969] made from newsreels shot during his lifetime; and *Lenin – Documents, Facts and Reminiscences* [Lenin – dokumenty, fakty i vospominaniya, 1969], a collective film portrait in six parts; and *One Day of Immortality* [Odin den' iz bessmertiya, 1967] about Lenin's arrival at the Second Comintern Congress in August 1920, *inter alia*.

Among the series of documentary films of the 1960s designed to re-establish the historical memory of the people about their past heroes, the compilation film *Heroes Never Die* [Geroi ne umirayut, 1963] deserves particular attention. It is a film in four parts about the life and deeds of the illustrious Soviet marshals and army commanders Tukhachevsky, Yakir, Blücher, Yegorov and Uborevich.

At the end of the 1960s when the last traces of the illusory Khrushchev 'Thaw' were disappearing, Alexander Novogrudsky and Solomon Zenin made a striking documentary film, *The Field Shirt and the Tail-coat* [Gimnasterka i frak, 1968], about the tragic fate of Fyodor Raskolnikov, the People's Commissar and Soviet diplomat. It was a film which was also to meet a sad fate. The process of renewal of Soviet documentary cinema was interrupted and there began a covert revival of Stalinism.

The first wave of perestroika documentaries to emerge from the apathy of stagnation resembled a 'cavalry charge' against the practices of the period of stagnation, against the system of conformism in the spiritual life of Soviet society, against the 'official engagement' of the film-makers.

Surveying and interpreting the documentaries of the 1920s and 1930s from the position of the contemporary historian actively participating in the process of perestroika, we cannot ignore the documentary films of the end of the 1980s and the beginning of the 1990s, created on the basis of the newsreels of the past, which in the new historical conditions spoke afresh.

The best-known historical documentary films made in the perestroika years on the basis of the newsreels of the 1920s and 1930s, were I. Belyayev's *The Trial* [Protsess, 1988], the above-mentioned *Solovki Power* and *Stalin and Others*, K. Smirnov's *The Coup* [Perevorot, 1989], A. Ivankin's *Revolution Square* [Ploshchad' revolyutsii, 1987] and R. Shurman's *The Stalin Syndrome* [Stalinskii sindrom, 1990]. For the centenary of Bukharin's birth Yevgeni Andrikanis made the documentary–publicistic film *Nikolai Bukharin*.

Of course not all the films mentioned or not mentioned can be positively evaluated. In many ways they represent a reconnaissance. The depth of the artistic interpretation of the newsreels of the 1920s and 1930s varies considerably. There are cases of neglect of the principles of using the film document as a historical source. Historians consider that the very concept of 'documentary film' needs to be strictly defined and isolated from the general run of films which are brought together under the concept of 'non-played films'. Viewers of a documentary film or the historical researcher working on it must be certain that they see in the shot a genuine film document, a genuine fact, a genuine event which can be dated and located, a real person who can be named. Another question is how far the event, fact or person reflected in the camera lens is typical of its time, how far it has been distorted by the cameraman and how it has been treated by the scriptwriter and director. Deviation from documentarism into journalism transforms the genre and lowers the objective value of the film document as a source of historical information.

It is well known that there is no consensus amongst film specialists on the question of the authenticity of the film document as a source of historical information: the debate has gone on since the mid 1920s. For historians working with newsreels and using them to make documentary films, there is no hesitation: the possibility of firm dating of the material is the necessary condition for a competent reading of the documentary shot and its historically based comprehension. Many of the recent films based on the newsreels of the 1920s and 1930s are subject to criticism beause they infringe this approach. For instance, the film *Nikolai Bukharin* was much criticised by historians: in it there was a failure to date various facts and documents in the biography of the hero of the film and exaggeration of the significance of some facts to the detriment of others. As a result the documentary film portrait of a multifaceted and talented person becomes one-dimensional: the viewer sees only the politician and his failure, his tragic fate.

The historian working on contemporary film journalism and on documentary films based on the newsreels of the 1920s and 1930s has to take account of the critical self-evaluation of specialists in this area and also of the leading figures in the discussions about the contemporary problems of historical documentary films. When he characterised the model of the 'documentary film of the perestroika period', V. Kuzin, the director of the Leningrad Studio of Documentary Films, noted that in his view it is based on three foundations: first, a strict orientation towards journalism in which political pathos dominates over art; second, 'a superficial and often igno-rant analysis of history', an unwillingness and inability to 'relate the past to the future'; and third, the rejection of any kind of moral norms, of elemen-tary ethics in working with their heroes.[19] Pessimistic stereotypes have replaced optimistic ones. The historian who is working with contemporary film journalism must take account of these ambiguities and contradictions in the process of assimilating the old films of record in the new conditions.

Analysts of Soviet film are obliged to admit not only the peculiar 'greed to discover new material' by contemporary documentary film-makers, but also the fact that unfortunately this all too often literally becomes a barbaric carelessness in the handling of the material, in making sense of it, and in treating it cinematically. Leonid Kozlov has clearly formulated this idea.[20] Other competent specialists on film documentaries have also concurred with him. 'Look how greedily and how . . . incompetently the newsreels are used today', states Kuzin, already quoted above, 'a minute part of the film-archival collections has been put into circulation – only the very top, the most straightforward, and the most politically engaged part. Essentially we have not moved closer to their analysis.'[21] Specialists confirm that under conditions of glasnost there has been a noticeable trend towards the extensive use of material that was previously banned, towards a purely formal change of emphasis, towards the formation of new myths to replace the old. The task of uncovering the possibilities of inner meaning in every newly discovered film shot is being rather weakly tackled in the practice of historical film journalism, but even here there are undoubtedly some models of craftsmanship.

The use of film documents by historians in research and teaching is fraught not only with source problems, but also technical ones. In the press the question of the establishment of an Information Centre has been raised. Annotated catalogues of the newsreel films in the archive repositories are needed, containing information about their use in historical documentary films and about the latter's circulation. Without such catalogues or codified information stored on computer, the search for the necessary film documents will be difficult. The time has come to establish a regular exchange of experience between the specialists who work in this field as historians, cinema historians and film-makers.

Chapter 12

The ghost that does return: exorcising Stalin

Anna Lawton

In the early 1960s Yevgeni Yevtushenko wrote a poem that went like this:

> We bore him out of the mausoleum.
> But how, out of Stalin, shall we bear Stalin's heirs!

> While the heirs of Stalin walk this earth,
> Stalin,
> I fancy, still lurks in the mausoleum.[1]

Yevtushenko was prophetic: the ghost of Stalin did indeed come back, and flourished throughout the 1970s and early 1980s under the guise of 'respectable' bureaucracy. Adapting to the times, the new bureaucrats, without dismantling the Gulag, replaced terror with subtler forms of repression – psychiatric asylum, character assassination, exile to the West. But from the mid 1980s with the onset of glasnost, the lurking ghost was unmasked and soon became the target for a lynch-mob of journalists, historians, novelists, artists and, of course, film-makers. Has it been exorcised yet? Many think it has not.

The film-makers' search for the historical causes of today's problems has paralleled and often anticipated the same process in the political sphere. As is often the case in the Soviet Union, cinema ran ahead of events. Soon after the Twenty-Seventh Party Congress in 1986, while politicians and economists were more involved in discussion than in action, documentarists from all over the country set out to fill in the 'blank spots' in the history books. One year later they were able to show an impressive array of films investigating the dark areas of recent history and revealing current problems, often providing a cause and effect link.[2]

A documentary that was given star billing when it made its appearance in February 1988 was *More Light* [Bol'she sveta], directed by Marina Babak. Made to celebrate the seventieth anniversary of the October Revolution, the film is a survey of seven decades of Soviet history, revised according to Gorbachev's vision – reaffirmation of Lenin's legacy, denunciation of Stalinism and Brezhnevism, rehabilitation of Bukharin and his economic policies, and praise of Khrushchev's honesty. Conspicuous by its absence is

the image of Gorbachev himself, as well as those of Andropov and Cher-
nenko. Their names are not even mentioned, and the film ends with a
celebration of folkish glasnost – rock music, popular diplomacy and peace
movements. The film's narrator is the stage and screen actor Mikhail
Ulyanov, a personal friend of Gorbachev, who played a major role in real
life at the 1988 Party Conference as a vocal sustainer of the General
Secretary's programme. Ulyanov starts the programme with a clear statement of intent: 'Everyone is sick of the silence. We are going to try to talk
about the past with more honesty, more light.' For all its good intentions,
however, *More Light* failed to satisfy demanding audiences. Yuri Afanasiev, the outspoken Rector of the Historical Archives Institute, criticised the
film for placing the blame on leaders only, exonerating society. The result,
he said, is 'a film that lies', because all those failures 'cannot be the fault of
only some people'.[3]

More Light is emblematic of the early phase of glasnost, when the
denunciation of some leaders and events was meant to improve the system,
not to shake its foundations. In reality, it opened a Pandora's box that could
not be resealed. The process of revelation got out of hand, acquiring a life
of its own. At first Stalin was flatly exposed as a demonic figure responsible for all past and present evils; then the responsibility was partly shifted
to the people who, whether passively or blindly, accepted and perpetuated
the injustices of the system; and finally the inquiry went on to point a finger
at the very principles of Marxism–Leninism. Today, as the Communist
Party has lost its pre-eminent leading position, old myths are debunked one
after another. Even Lenin is being stripped of his sacred halo, and the
historical continuities between Lenin and Stalin have been pointed out in
the press and in films.[4]

In keeping with the necrophiliac mood of Yevtushenko's poem, there
have been proposals to remove Lenin's body from his mausoleum and inter
him next to Stalin, where he belongs. The most provocative call came from
Mark Zakharov, the progressive director of the Komsomol Theatre, who
had staged plays featuring Lenin in a less than official light. Zakharov
appeared on the late-night television show *Vzglyad* [Opinion, 21 April
1989] and remarked: 'No matter how much we hate a person, no matter
how much we love him, we do not have the right to deprive a person of
burial.' Zakharov maintained that the embalmed corpse had turned Lenin
into a tourist attraction.[5] The idea was immediately denounced as blas-
phemous by some members of the Central Committee, but in the popular
imagination it gave birth to the latest joke on the subject: in tune with the
era of the joint venture, the government should sell the corpse to an
American entrepreneur for a fairground show.

'There are no more taboos for "the man with the movie camera". . . a
body of information that was unthinkable before has now reached the
viewer', noted a Soviet journalist as early as 1988.[6] At that time lack of

censorship was already a common practice but not a legal reality. It acquired legal force when the Law on the Press took effect on 1 August 1990. Nevertheless, the documentarists were already pushing the limits of the permissible. In the summer of 1988 an explosive documentary was shown on national television – *Risk-2*, directed by Dmitri Barshchevsky and Natalya Violina. The film equated Stalin with Hitler and Mao Tse-tung, and denounced their common criminal behaviour. The renowned film director and actor, Rolan Bykov, who played a prominent role in the restructuring of the film industry, said: 'Documentary film made such a jump ahead that it will take five to ten years for feature films to catch up with it.'[7] One is tempted to share Bykov's enthusiasm for the remarkable achievements in the documentary genre. Besides the boldness of the themes, the documentary was also an experimental ground for one of the most innovative film artists of the new era, Alexander Sokurov. But we should not demean what has been accomplished in the area of feature film in struggling to exorcise Stalin's ghost.

Some critical allusions to Stalin, veiled and guarded at first, appeared in feature films before perestroika, such as Nikolai Gubenko's *The Orphans* [Podranki, 1977] and Bykov's *Scarecrow* [Chuchelo, 1984]. The real turning point was Tengiz Abuladze's film *Repentance* [Pokayanie, 1987], which marked the beginning of openness and brought the vampire out of its bunker for all to see. Afterwards, with the opening of the archives, images of Stalin and his entourage flooded the cinemas. As a rudimentary classification, the Stalin films of the years 1985 to 1991 can be divided into three categories: first, Stalinism as a backdrop; second, Stalin implied in a symbolic character; and third, Stalin appearing as himself.

STALINISM AS A BACKDROP

In this first category the first swallow was Alexei Gherman's *My Friend Ivan Lapshin* [Moi drug Ivan Lapshin, 1983–5]. The film was at once exciting and disturbing and it offered a glimpse of a previously proscribed historical period. But the portrait of that period was very personal and left many viewers uncertain about the director's intentions. What was his point of view? Why did he choose an NKVD (secret police) officer as the hero? What was he really saying about the Stalinist years, apart from the fact that life was hard and drab in the provinces? The confusion was reinforced by the subjective camera and the postmodernist montage, virtually new in Soviet cinema.

It was too early for the general audience to believe what they were seeing on the big screen, in the open. Even more shocking was the television run of the film. Later it became obvious that Gherman's hero, Ivan Lapshin, was presented as a victim of the system – a true believer in Communist ideals, doomed to perish, strangled by the machine that he had helped to build. His fate was similar to that of many others, such as Sergei Kirov, the Leningrad Party chief whose portrait opens the retrospective segment of the film and casts a mournful shadow over the whole narrative. The year 1934, when Kirov was assassinated, was the last moment before the beginning of the Great Terror, a moment when it was still possible to nurture the illusion of a future, perfect world. Gherman intended to pay a tribute to a generation that believed in the Stalinist myth and perished with it. He said in an interview:

> The story I am telling is about the real life of these people, their faith, their melancholy, the fact that they go straight ahead toward communism without understanding that the road is long and dangerous. Maybe these people included my father and my mother.[8]

In the course of the film Stalin is alluded to only indirectly, through slogans and citations, but a portrait showing the generalissimo grinning under his moustache appears at the very end as a counterpoint to the portrait of Kirov. Embellished with red flags and ribbons, it is pinned to the steel chest of a tram headed for the land of Utopia. Given the context, this was already an ironical representation of the leader, meant to raise doubts rather than affirm beliefs. It was also clear by the narrative structure linking past and present that the consequences of Stalinism were to be seen as pervasive in contemporary society. The lurking ghost, the film implied, was still romping around in Ivan Lapshin's home town, fifty years later.

Subsequent films continued the debunking of the Stalin myth, some by oblique allusions, some with tragic realism, some through devastating parodies. But none reached the level of cinematic sophistication displayed by Gherman. His film, to this day, remains the best product of the Soviet New Wave.[9]

In the film, *Mirror for the Hero* [Zerkalo dlya geroya, 1988], directed by Vladimir Khotinenko, Stalin is left entirely off-screen. But, by following the lives of ordinary people, their trials and simple joys under the régime, the illusory atmosphere of the time is conveyed. Cleverly the film links past and present by means of a fantastic device. The hero, as if by magic, finds himself back in his native town – and back in time, in the year 1948, when he existed only in his mother's womb. He meets his pregnant mother who addresses him politely, like a stranger. He is able to observe the life of his parents shaped by collective songs, marching tunes and radio propaganda, and is tortured by the impossibility of warning them about the future, or changing the course of events in any way. Finally, he witnesses the arrest of his father, which enables him to develop a more compassionate relationship with the old man once he comes back into the present time.

In *The Cold Summer of '53* [Kholodnoe leto pyatdesyat' tret'ego, 1988], directed by Alexander Proshkin, the action is more closely linked with the crimes of Stalinism, and focuses on a specific episode in a small village. In the aftermath of Stalin's death a general amnesty opened the gates of the concentration camps, freeing political prisoners and criminals alike. The story highlights the heroism of two political exiles who singlehandedly defend the villagers against a gang of criminals. Echoes of *The Magnificent Seven* [USA, 1960], and in turn *The Seven Samurai* [Japan, 1954], are easily evoked, and the fast pace, dynamic editing, emotional camerawork and harrowing musical track – so atypical for a Soviet film – cast a dramatic episode of national history into the mould of the adventurous Western. The genre was certainly responsible for the popular success of this film but the subject matter and its implications provided it with substance.[10] The larger picture of official criminality is implied. Labour camps and mock trials are directly discussed. There is no explicit reference to the present but there is a projection of the perpetuation of the Big Lie into the future, when at the end of the film the son of one of the political exiles is reluctant to accept the truth about his father and prefers to ignore the tragedy that befell his family, afraid to lose 'respectability'.

A more recent film, *Zero City* [Gorod Zero, 1989], directed by Karen Shakhnazarov, is set in our days and only shows flashes in the retro style. But those, together with the grotesque exhibition of Russian history at the local historical museum, are enough to justify the nightmarish predicament of the hero. The unfortunate protagonist is lost in a world that does not make sense, a world without a beginning and without an end, pointlessly spinning on itself, while old patterns are repeated, building on the existing layers of absurdity. Stalin in a white uniform, surrounded by the symbols of his empire, is now a wax mannequin in the museum, but his ghost still lives on in the soul of the town's prosecutor, nostalgic for the law and order of the good old days. This, however, is not the most ominous manifestation of the ghost's survival. More disturbing is the fact that Stalin left behind him a trail of the living dead – the town's entire population is a community of puppets with dead souls. They support perestroika and hail the latest trend of openness for the simple reason that this gives them the freedom to inaugurate the first rock-and-roll club in town.

While *Zero City* relies on black humour and surrealism, another recent film, *Our Armoured Train* [Nash bronepoezd, 1988], directed by Mikhail Ptashuk, is a psychological drama. It is the tragic story of a former camp commandant, haunted by the memories of the past. His ex-colleagues have either adapted to the new times, or live in isolation, full of nostalgia and spite. But he cannot do either: he is still convinced that he has been an 'honest man', that he has performed a good and necessary job, and he expects society to acknowledge his service to the country. Instead, society rejects him – not necessarily because of his values, but because of the defiant and embarrassing way he upholds them. His 'style' is simply no longer in fashion. Finally he has no other way out but suicide. His nostalgic friends, however, endure, like dormant viruses in society's body. This has been called a film about 'corpse poison' – a poison whose 'terrible action' continues long after the corpse has been buried. Significantly, one of the main characters says: 'We are now retired, but tomorrow, if the enemies of the people or the cosmopolitans reappear, we'll be ready . . . Our armoured train is on the side track, waiting. We are this armoured train.'[11] This speech is so full of pathos that even those viewers who are inclined to dismiss it as the fantasy of a deranged mind are somewhat enticed by the image it conjures up – a phantom train bursting out of a cloud of steam in all its patriotic splendour. But often the dialogue is too long and pedantic, and the film is only saved by superb acting. There are notable performances from Mikhail Ulyanov and Alexei Petrenko and the two lesser-known actors who complete the quartet, Vladimir Gostyukhin and A. Filippenko.[12]

STALIN IMPLIED IN A SYMBOLIC CHARACTER

The first and foremost film in this category is *Repentance*, which is the most meticulous illustration of the motif of the recurring ghost. It is, in fact, a realised metaphor for the endurance of the Stalinist legacy. The corpse of the tyrant Varlam keeps reappearing in various ways and on various levels of reality – from the macabre farce of being dug out and exposed in a garden to the supernatural impersonation of a vampire lying in his coffin, from an apparition as the devil in the underground to the subtle mutation into the realistic character of his son Abel.

The film has a circular structure. It begins and ends at the same place and at the same time – at the moment when the heroine of the story, Keti Barateli, learns about the death of the despot who had destroyed her family. What constitutes the body of the story between the prologue and the epilogue takes place in Keti's mind and includes her repeated attempts to exhume Varlam's body, her trial, and her memories of childhood. It also includes her perception of Varlam's descendants – his son and heir to power, Abel (played by the same actor, Avtondil Makharadze, in a masterful performance), and his rebellious grandson, Tornike. The narrative structure is further complicated by the fact that this long dream sequence includes in turn other dreams (rather, nightmares) by different characters, so that the viewer is faced with a construction *en abîme* (a dream within a dream within a dream . . .).[13] All this reflects the effect of a 'tragic phantasmagoria', as Abuladze himself put it. The director's intent, however, was not to lead the viewer away from reality. On the contrary, the 'phantasmagoria' was supposed to reveal the truth about an epoch which, through its official mendacity, institutionalised hypocrisy, delusions of grandeur, secret trials and absurd executions, now appears to be more 'phantasmagoric' than any fiction.[14] The complex form of the film is also designed to deprive the viewer of an easy solution. In fact, the 'repentance'

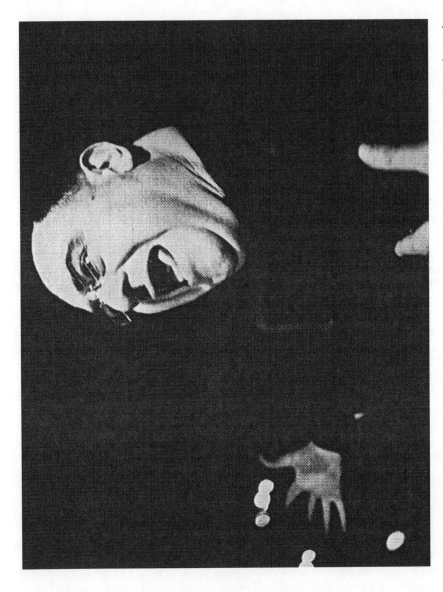

Figure 35 Avtandil Makharadze as the dictator Varlam in Tengiz Abuladze's *Repentance* (1984, released 1987).

Figure 36 Remembering the missing and/or dead millions in *Repentance*.

implied in the title is purely speculative. The film does not end with the exorcism of the ghost. Rather, it offers the audience an open ending.

Repentance became an instant sensation in Moscow intellectual circles and at international festivals. But what was a merit for the critics looked like a flaw to young Soviet audiences. The magazine *Sovetskii ekran* [Soviet Screen] was flooded with letters protesting about Abuladze's 'difficult form', which was perceived by many as another cover-up. A group of Moscow students asked:

> Who is Varlam Aravidze? A composite image of all tyrants from Nero to our day? But then he is lacking concrete social roots . . . What gave birth to Varlam? We do not find an answer to this question in the film and therefore the tyrant comes across as an attribute of fate . . . This approach certainly does not respond to the present demand for historical truth.

Another reader offered a suggestion as to what was needed:

> Today we need investigative films, film analyses without allusions and symbols. We need the naked, unadorned truth, where Stalin is shown without the mask of a demi-god . . . The problem of the 'cult of personality' is so big that it cannot be resolved through the language of Aesop.[15]

A monster similar to Varlam is the protagonist of the film *To Kill the Dragon* [Ubit' drakona, 1988], directed by Mark Zakharov. Based on a play by Yevgeni Schwartz, which was written in the early 1960s and promptly shelved, and starring celebrities such as Oleg Yankovsky and Yevgeni Leonov, the film was full of promise when it came out. However, it fell flat on its face aesthetically, despite the coproduction deal with West Germany that provided state-of-the-art technology and high-quality film stock. It is worth discussing, however, for its thematic similarities to *Repentance*. The core of this tale, set in a Gothic town, is the confrontation between Lancelot and the dragon, a symbol of tyranny and dictatorship. The monster appears in many forms: as the dragon itself, as an innocent-looking young man in a white suit, as a bloodthirsty samurai, and as an officer in a Nazi-like uniform. As expected, Lancelot wins the duel, fighting against all odds. But, as soon as he leaves town, heading for his next deed, the local *Bürgermeister* picks up the dragon's legacy and turns into the next tyrant. The power of the dragon to resurrect himself is suggested by an ominous metaphor. As the last sequence unfolds, Lancelot crosses an idyllic green prairie and leaves behind a group of children frolicking after a dragon kite.

The most recent film in this category, *The Servant* [Sluga, 1989], by Vadim Abdrashitov and Alexander Mindadze, stands on a higher artistic level, even though it does not reach the summit of the best films made by this famous pair.[16] It also features a central character symbolising Stalinist power who leaves behind a trail smelling of sulphur. The story is based on the Mephistopheles theme. A high-ranking, all-powerful bureaucrat possesses an uncanny ability to subjugate human beings to his will. His driver falls under the spell and, while acquiring talent and riches, he loses his soul. The Master eventually comes back after an absence of twenty years to exact his price, which in this case is the life of one of his old enemies. The Servant complies without a specific order, just by sensing the overpowering will of the demonic creature. The murderer is arrested in the end, but the Master is not. He remains in society and keeps corrupting the younger generation, literally making people dance to his own tune. And the scenario remains open to many more returns of the ghost.

STALIN APPEARING AS HIMSELF

In the films mentioned above Stalin appears in documentary clips, in portraits and on billboards. But in this category he is presented as himself and he plays a more or less prominent role within the narrative. These films appeared at a relatively late stage: all those discussed below were released in or after 1989.

In the film *It* [Ono, 1989], directed by Sergei Ovcharov, Stalin is one of the protagonists of Soviet history. The film is based on the nineteenth-century satirical tale, *The History of a Town* by Mikhail Saltykov-Shchedrin. The film's commentary follows the literary text to the letter, but characters and events are manipulated to accommodate contemporary history, with even a projection into the twenty-first century. Up to the fatal year 1917 the tone is farcical, the action sheer buffoonery. Then the slapstick gradually fades into the grotesque and laughter becomes uneasy and finally sinister. The character of Lenin fades into that of Stalin, then Beria (here there are already cinematic quotations from *Repentance*), and then Khrushchev. This line of continuity is masterfully established by the actor Rolan Bykov, who plays all four roles.

This is perhaps the first instance on film where the roots of Stalinism are directly linked to the figure of Lenin. With the progression of the fatal chain, the mood becomes more and more pessimistic. Next comes a hybrid character loosely associated with Brezhnev, whose mental and moral disarray is reflected in his dismembered body. His head is seen placed on a desk all by itself, emitting an incoherent slur, regularly sent to the repair shop for a quick fix. Finally, the 'nice guy' takes over. Good-looking, neatly dressed, well-intentioned, tolerant, he is a liberal and a democrat. But his laissez-faire policy is ineffectual. Soon things get out of control, as crime and violence cause social and political chaos. The leader, his handsome features hardened into a stone mask, turns into the enforcer of law and order who, in leading the country into the next century, leaves it a wasteland, ecologically devastated and populated by a dejected humanity – a surrealist new world.

A complex representation of Stalin is given in the film *Prishvin's Paper Eyes* [Bumazhnye glaza Prishvina, 1989], directed by Valeri Ogorodnikov. The film is a manifold text that once more links past and present by looking back to the Stalin period. The central character, Pavel Prishvin, is a television director/actor of the Gorbachev generation. He is engaged in shooting a film set in 1949, in which he plays a KGB captain. At the same time Prishvin is involved in researching for a television news unit which had been established in that year. Why the intriguing title? It seems to refer to a suggestion from one television viewer in those early years: the fact that the announcers often lower their eyes to read the text is annoying – better glue paper eyes on their eyelids and then let them read to their heart's content.[17] In Ogorodnikov's film this metaphor introduces the theme of double vision, or of mystification of reality, and the film's complex structure reinforces the central idea. Prishvin's vision of the world shifts from one narrative context to another – the film he is shooting, the world of the old news reporters he is interviewing, the newsreel footage he weaves into the film, his nightmarish fantasies and the contemporary reality that bears the marks of those days – leaving it to the viewer to fill the logical gaps between episodes.

Stalin pertains to all these narrative layers, and his representation varies according to Prishvin's perception, constantly shifting between levels (the story revolves around a love triangle and a personal vendetta). In the documentary footage, Stalin appears in person, and so do Hitler and Mussolini. By phantasmagorical montage the historical footage is given a surrealist twist: the three personalities merge into one single representation of totalitarianism. Mussolini delivers Stalin's speeches, and thousands of Nazi youths salute the generalissimo who waves benevolently at the crowd. To add to the film's surrealism, segments from classic feature films are inserted into the newsreels. Images of Stalin on the mausoleum are juxtaposed with the 'Odessa Steps' sequence from Eisenstein's *The Battleship Potemkin* [Bronenosets Potemkin, 1926], suggesting by analogical montage Stalin's responsibility for the massacre of the people. The phantasmagoria then stoops to the level of kitsch in the representation of Prishvin's nightmares. Here an actor gives a parodic impersonation of Stalin. Moreover, grotesque effigies of the dictator – his head blown up to gigantic proportions – haunt Prishvin's subconscious, suggesting his helplessness in coping with the legacy of the tyrant.

The hypnotising effect Stalin had on the people and, at the same time, the people's responsibility for having contributed to the creation of a monster, are emphasised in the film. Images of an adoring crowd parading in front of the leader, their eyes transfixed on the figure of their political idol, recur in the newsreel footage employed. The consequences of the 'cult of personality' are hinted at in the closing sequences. A lorry drags a huge statue of Stalin along a street by its feet. The street is empty, but strange figures appear on the balconies and at the windows. These are people crucified on broomsticks, stuck into the sleeves of their coats. The image refers to one specific episode of Prishvin's film within the film, but in the general context it is emblematic of a self-crucifixion that resides in the individual, inherited from the ideology of dictatorship. And, finally, Stalin's effigy disappears from sight. The huge statue is carried away by a helicopter, flying over the city of Leningrad. It is an obvious quotation from Federico Fellini's *La dolce vita* [Italy, 1959] – the flying Christ over the roofs of Rome. But all similarities end right there: the substance of this scene is peculiarly Soviet.[18] As Stalin fades out, nothing is left, not even Prishvin with his sincere but hopeless attempt at exorcising the demon. The screen is filled with emptiness, with the blinding, snowy whiteness of the northern Russian landscape. Is it time frozen before the return of the ghost?

Stalin makes cameo appearances in *Black Rose Stands for Sorrow, Red Rose Stands for Love* [Chernaya roza – emblema pechali, krasnaya roza – emblema lyubvi, 1989], directed by Sergei Solovyov, and in Vasili Pichul's *Dark Nights in Sochi* [V gorode Sochi temnye nochi, 1989]. In *Black Rose* he is part of the dream fantasies of one of the characters, in *Dark Nights* a character on a movie set. But these two films have more in common than flashes of the dictator: they have been produced and distributed by their authors, independently of the state system. They are among the first few ventures into real economic perestroika – a very constructive form of exorcism of the ghost.[19]

Another successful independent producer, Yuri Kara, has given Stalin a big role in his latest film, *Belshazzar's Feast* [Piry Baltazara, 1989], which is rather appropriately subtitled *A Night with Stalin* [Noch' so Stalinym]. Like other films by Kara, this is based on the writings of Fazil Iskander – in this case a chapter from the novel *Sandro of Chegem* [Sandro iz Chegema], published in 1973 – and is meant to be a popular thriller with box-office potential. The story supposedly relies on eye-witness accounts: the Sandro of the title, a member of an Abkhazian music and dance ensemble, is hired to entertain Stalin's entourage during a banquet. Kara has said that he wanted to convey the atmosphere of a 'feast in plague time', echoing Pushkin.[20] The plague, however, remains off-screen. Stalin appears in a private setting, as opposed to his more usual representation in his official capacities. Kara wanted to focus on the dictator at home, although the 'home' here is fit for royalty.

The feast takes place in a Kremlin hall with marble columns and gilded trim. The banquet table is sumptuously decorated with crystal and flowers. Stalin sits in the middle, flanked by his colleagues – Beria, Voroshilov, Kalinin – and a few other intimates. There are even a couple of women. The atmosphere is cordial and relaxed. Stalin smokes his pipe and pets a little furry creature on his lap. At first sight it looks like a cat. But we soon realise that it is not. Rather, it is some sort of hairy piglet (maybe a baby boar), like the ones that lie on the table, roasted and spiced, for the feasters' delight. This is just one of the 'surreal' elements Kara employs to convey both Iskander's black humour and the hallucinatory atmosphere of the epoch. The banquet is seen through a grey filter that distances the action from the viewer and gives both characters and objects a ghost-like tinge. These are clearly spectres from the past, insidiously coming back into our time and space. And they are even more frightening for looking so harmless, even 'human' in their 'homey' image.

Kara cast Alexei Petrenko, an actor with great dramatic skills, in the role of Stalin, because he did not want to portray the dictator in his traditional two-dimensional image, but to endow the character with psychological depth and complexity. Like the writer Anatoli Rybakov in his novel *Children of the Arbat* [Deti Arbata, 1988], Kara wanted to project the soul of a man who clearly understood mass psychology and turned it to his own advantage. As Iskander has pointed out, Stalin, like the archetypal Anti-Christ of Russian literature – the Grand Inquisitor – understood the desire of the masses 'to see in their leader the manifestation of the un-Holy Trinity: miracle, mystery and authority'.[21]

This desire is still alive today among what one hopes is a minority. There is no way to measure the real number of nostalgic Stalinists, but there is a way to measure the intensity of their feelings.

A documentary entitled *Stalin Is with Us?* [Stalin s nami?, 1989], directed by Tofik Shakhverdiev, focuses on a group of staunch followers, including a public prosecutor from Kharkov, a foreman from a factory in Tbilisi, a taxidriver also from Tbilisi, and a Moscow schoolmistress. The film presents their conversations and monologues without commentary. A few fragments are offered here in that same spirit.[22]

THE SCHOOLMISTRESS. My family is this one man, for whom I live ... Every year I go to the places connected with his life, to see those houses that he might have seen, to walk the streets he might have walked. This is a thread that ties me to the man who is now gone. He is my happiness. I love Stalin.

THE TAXIDRIVER. He will live in my heart for ever ... If tomorrow they put me against a wall to be shot, I will still shout 'Long live Stalin!' like those innocent prisoners did in 1937.

THE FACTORY FOREMAN. If the masses followed Stalin, and respected and loved him, it means that he was right in his great task.

The foreman also comments on the present situation in a typically Stalinist idiom:

The enemies of perestroika are those who disfigure Stalinist reality.

> Those who let the minds of our youth be governed by Western pornography, by the Western way of life, by Western ideology. Because Western ideology is attractive. This is the danger!

The taxidriver has only one thing to say about perestroika:

> Stalin uttered the word perestroika only once in his entire life. And the people, without flinching, obeyed! That was it! And now, take the newspapers: Perestroika! ... the magazines: Perestroika! ... Perestroika! ... Perestroika! ... Well, it means that the people don't get the message.[23]

Another indicator of people's feelings towards the 'Father of the peoples' is the mail received by newspapers and journals. Many readers feel like the protagonists of the film. But they are outnumbered by those who call Stalin a 'bloody tsar of socialism', and a 'dictator, executioner and murderer' who can only live on 'in the hearts of toadies and today's Berias'.[24]

For all the controversy raging around the ghost of the generalissimo, a sensation was created in Moscow in 1990 by a film that deliberately ignores him. The film, *We Cannot Live Like This* [Tak zhit' nel'zya], directed by Stanislav Govorukhin, skips one link in the chain and focuses directly on Lenin. The reader might think that Soviet audiences, having seen a whole array of documentaries throwing light on the possible dark spots of their political and social life, would have become desensitised. But the Muscovites who saw this film were shocked and deeply moved. And so was I. This is mainly due to Govorukhin's talent and his deep participation in the suffering he has portrayed. So heartrending is the director's despair over the devastation of the land that I felt the film was not for foreign eyes. It is too private, too intimate, like a family tragedy.

The film develops a main theme: crime. At first it is a social plague: we see interviews with criminals and policemen, and gory images of the victims. Then, gradually, the scope of the investigation broadens to show that the root of all crimes is the Big Crime that the country's leaders have perpetrated against the people: 'genocide, mass killing, man-made famine, the destruction of the economy and of culture'. The commentary is as direct as the visual representation and leaves no doubts: 'The régime's most atrocious crime is the creation of a new human type ... It should be borne in mind that seventy years of faulty genetic evolution cannot be corrected in a five-year period.'[25] Jump cuts to monuments and portraits of Lenin occur at strategic points throughout the film to bring across the message, at times in ironical counterpoint, at times with tragic pathos.

After its premiere at Dom kino, the headquarters of the Union of Filmmakers in Moscow, on 4 May 1990 the film was shown to the representatives of the Congresses of People's Deputies of the USSR and of the Russian Federation, and to the members of the Moscow City Council. In early June it opened at the Rossiya cinema in central Moscow. Govorukhin, interviewed by the newspaper *Sovetskaya kultura* [Soviet Culture], said that he tried to find the clearest form and the simplest words for his film, so that it would be understood by all the people. But he added that he conceived the film primarily as 'a letter to the Supreme Soviet'. 'I wanted to explain something to our government', he said. 'I tried to put together a number of mosaic pieces and present a comprehensive picture of our life.' And what was the reaction? Among the delegates to the Congress of the Russian Federation, the film generated a polarisation. Govorukhin commented: 'The leftists went more to the left, the rightists went more to the right, and the centre (which decides everything) moved slightly to the left. This is very significant: it means that we have achieved our goal.'

Criticism, of course, poured in from the right wing, which denounced the film as an inflammatory call to violence. The director dismissed the uproar: 'We cannot re-educate the staunch dogmatists who brought the country to this deplorable state. And we do not need to. We need only to vote them out.'[26]

So, as Stalin fades out, Lenin fades in. This may be the beginning of a new trend. Govorukhin's film will be remembered for its awesome honesty and compassion. But, as has already happened with Stalin, the commercialisation of the theme is inevitable in a market economy. And, in the end, it may serve a good purpose. The trivialisation of the demon may turn out to be more effective than any exorcism.

Chapter 13

Stalin is with us: Soviet documentary mythologies of the 1980s

Svetlana Boym

The subtitle of Semyon Aranovich's film *I Served in Stalin's Bodyguard* [Ya sluzhil v okhrane Stalina, 1989] is 'an experiment in documentary mythology'. At first glance, this sounds like an oxymoron, but only if one perceives the historical and mythological consciousnesses as opposed to each other, and conceives of a documentary as a 'factual' representation devoid of myth and mystification. In the Russian tradition, perhaps to a larger degree than in Western European traditions, the two seem to be inseparable, and the task of reconstructing or reinventing history has always been something of a mythological experiment. The two documentaries I shall be discussing in this chapter – *Stalin Is with Us?* [Stalin s nami?, 1989], directed by Tofik Shakhverdiev, and *I Served in Stalin's Bodyguard* – allow us to analyse the Soviet mythologisation of history, the phenomenon of Stalinist nostalgia, and the double bind of aesthetics and politics in Soviet culture. They explore the nature of Stalin's charisma and his uncanny photogenic spell which has haunted the cinema of perestroika. There is an anecdote circulating in Moscow film circles that the primal scene of glasnost cinema is 'a nude girl smoking marijuana, sitting in front of a portrait of Stalin'. Stalin's cinematic repertoire includes the tragic and the farcical, the sublime and the ridiculous, the terrifying and the banal, fiction and documentary. Stalin is a mythical fetish of the new Soviet cinema.

Unlike most of the Soviet documentaries, *Stalin Is with Us?* and *I Served in Stalin's Bodyguard* do not have an omniscient voice-over that provides a unifying narration and a central point of view. Thus, in their very form, these films question the authorial structure of communication and establish a more open-minded dialogue with the viewer. The two films do not engage in open denunciations of Stalinism, which by now have acquired a familiar, almost official ring. Rather, they portray convinced and unshaken Stalinists who cherish their dethroned idol and sing optimistic and nostalgically old-fashioned songs about the 'Great Leader of the people'. These films exemplify an unconventional revision of history that forces us to re-examine the relationships between myth and history in the Soviet context.

The concept of 'myth' has become prominent in recent Soviet criticism. It has significantly evolved from its former negative definition, whereby (as in the newspaper heading 'Myths and Reality') 'myth' seems to designate the opposite of reality and truth, and is synonymous with 'mystification'. 'Myth' has begun to signify a recurrent cultural narrative that exists in many versions but rarely changes its fundamental paradigm. Roland Barthes, developing the ideas of the Russian Formalist Roman Jakobson and the French anthropologist Claude Lévi-Strauss, defines 'myth' as a cultural phenomenon and not as a universal archetype.[1] In his view, myth is an anonymous depoliticised discourse that circulates in society and is perceived as an expression of common sense, as something 'natural' and self-evident. Myth masks its historicity in a disguise of naturalness which hinders critical investigation. Interestingly, in Barthes's view, this description characterises only 'the bourgeois cultural myth', the myth of the right, while the myth of the left is weak, because it is openly ideological and therefore more conscious of its own historicity, more explicitly politicised. Barthes's main example is the Soviet Stalin myth and the personality cult. The distinction between the 'depoliticised' and the political cultural myth is problematic, as is the definition of right and left. In fact, what we have in the Soviet case is something much more heterogeneous and impure: old myths in new trappings, new ideology building up on old beliefs and prejudices. Rather than insisting on the rupture between Russian and Soviet cultural myths that is currently prevalent among the Soviet intelligentsia, I will emphasise their paradoxical continuity. The cult of personality, for instance, is an immemorial Russian myth. It is the Russian version of the ancient Roman cult of emperors, which then developed into a particular cult of the Russian tsar, the 'little father of the people' (*batyushka*, like Ivan the Terrible), who saves his people from imminent apocalypse and disorder. The apocalyptic structure, as Nina Tumarkin argues in her book on the cult of Lenin, is fundamental to Marxist thinking, which is predicated on the 'end of the old world and the construction of the paradise on earth'.[2] This kind of thinking is conditioned by a binary opposition between Order – the rule of the great Orthodox tsar (or later the Communist leader) – and Chaos, Anarchy, the end of the world. There is no grey area in between.

As far as the concept of 'history' is concerned, it is not accidental that in Russian the word for history and story is the same [*istoriya*], while in English the two reveal their kinship, but also their historical evolution in different directions: one towards the constitution of historical science in the nineteenth century, and the other towards fiction. In Russia the intellectual divisions of labour, and the separation between historian and writer, between specialist and intellectual, between philosopher and politician, were not realised to the same extent as in other European countries. The writing of history was always perceived as too important to be relegated to a narrow professional function. Thus, from the late eighteenth right through the nineteenth centuries – the period when modern historiography and historical science were developing in the West – the writer and the poet in Russia were competing with the historian.[3] One thinks of the work of Karamzin,[4] or even of a dual text of history and fiction like Pushkin's *The History of Pugachev* and *The Captain's Daughter*. In the Soviet period the very status of documentary becomes problematic. A lot of archival documentary material which is now becoming available is, in fact, staged and camouflaged. It is more like the 'docu-drama' on American television and must be treated with caution. According to Aranovich, the visual representation of the 'Great October Socialist Revolution' must begin with mythification, since practically no filming was done during the events themselves. Instead, some footage from February 1917 has been used to illustrate the October uprising, and a lot of staged reconstruction was shot later. The 'documentary' representation of the participants and main protagonists of the Revolution varied greatly, according to the ideological whims of the time. In the Brezhnev period images of the Revolution were fixed and turned into cultural icons which were on display in all the Museums of the Revolution and were visited by Soviet schoolchildren on obligatory tours. In a somewhat similar manner, the supposed documentary footage of the Battle of Berlin and, specifically, of the capture of the Reichstag, was in fact restaged later because the cameraman had missed the historical event itself. In other words, the representation of history in the Soviet period was always to a large extent mythical or, at best, a mixture of mythical and factual.

Aranovich self-consciously acknowledges this in his film, and indeed places it in the foreground. The film is precisely about the difficulty of drawing the boundaries between documentary and myth in the Soviet context. *I Served in Stalin's Bodyguard* does not offer any explicit comment on the narrative of Rybin, the bodyguard. It allows the viewer to get used to this frightfully enticing story-teller with his wrinkled face and piercing eyes. Rybin's face is shot mostly in close-up, looking almost straight into the camera, so that it becomes uncannily unclear whether *we* are listening to *him* or *he* is inspecting *us* with his well-trained eyes. When asked why he chose not to comment on Rybin's story, Aranovich somewhat coyly remarked that he had promised that to Rybin. One thinks of Claude Lanzmann, who also promised the former Nazis he interviewed that he would not put them into his film, but he later admitted that he did not feel ethically constrained to keep that promise. Most of the viewers of his film congratulate him on this decision.

Moreover, Aranovich's poetic montage often does not contradict Rybin, but rather appears to illustrate his words in an almost childishly naïve manner, as if reinforcing them. Thus Rybin tells us about Stalin's love for borshch, porridge and dried fruit, his affection for the common people, and his extraordinary knowledge of *solfeggio*. The viewer is forced into the uncomfortable position of actually experiencing Stalin's personal charisma, while hearing Rybin's account portraying the Great Leader as a folkloric hero, modest but stern, strict but fair, tough but loving. But then Stalin's smiling, familiar face and his characteristic gesture of pointing at the crowd, as if in benevolent paternal reproach, recurs again and again in slow motion. This cinematic repetition is enacted as an ironic refrain throughout the film, it reduces the figure of Stalin to grotesque absurdity. Stalin is deprived of his aura. He appears like a marionette, no longer in charge of the terrifying spectacle, whose strings are pulled by another director. This kind of cinematic disempowerment is very subtly achieved throughout the film. The reduction to absurdity succeeds, more effectively than a direct political invective, in killing the aura of the Great Leader of the people.

Rybin's story allows the director to juxtapose three spheres of life, three spheres of Rybin's 'competence': politics, art and education. His biography is indeed quite picturesque – he guarded Stalin's dacha, then commanded the guard of the Bolshoi Theatre in Moscow, and currently teaches classes in accordion and patriotism in the capital. In the Bolshoi Theatre Stalin stages an operatic war, in which some of the characters become distinguished Voroshilov shooters. The theatre is mined, so that Hitler, if he occupies Moscow, will never be able to make his victory speech from the stage of the Bolshoi, the site of Russian national pride. It is as if Stalin and Hitler are embroiled in a secret aesthetic war as to who can stage history better (be it victory or defeat), to determine which of them is the most impressive choreographer. The sequences from 1930s performances that we see on the screen are wonderful examples of high Stalinist kitsch in the operatic field. Artistic authority is as important for Stalin and Rybin as is political authority: the old Russian quarrel between the poet and the tsar, who compete for cultural authority and the love of the nation, ends here in favour of the Communist leader. He is the leader in politics as well as art: as Rybin tells us, Stalin sang *solfeggio* better than any singer in the Bolshoi Theatre, and he was everybody's best art critic as well. Again in this Stalin could have competed with Hitler: if Hitler was an artist and an architect, Stalin distinguished himself as a singer and a philologist. Rybin, the mini-dictator, also has to excel in the arts: he teaches the accordion and writes Socialist Realist poetry for children. Thus his ambition is not only political but artistic as well, and this gives us an unexpected angle on the proverbial cult of the poet in Russian culture. Even the prosecutors of Stalin's time wrote poetry, often while prosecuting poets. Milan Kundera wrote that revolution and terror were accomplished by a collaboration between the hangman and the poet.[5] Thus aesthetics and politics in a totalitarian state are closely intertwined, and follow the same series of mythological patterns.

Rybin is also a teacher. He follows the 'method of distinguished pedagogues' and initiates his accordion classes with lessons in marching. Military discipline and the enticing rhythms of the march help to develop musical sensibility. Rybin tries carefully to orchestrate the scene, telling his pupils exactly how they should look and with what kind of expression they should recite his poetry. However, the way the scene is filmed contradicts Rybin's design. The children are fearfully obedient, giving answers to Rybin's questions that seem to have been learnt by heart. The camera glides over the children's faces, catching the mischievous expression of a younger boy, his funny and undisciplined gestures seeming to counteract the calm and authorial voice of Rybin.

The notable conflicts between documentary and mythical, personal and impersonal, between the powerful, larger-than-life monumental icons and a certain human singularity and fallibility are central to the film. Stalin, in Rybin's account, is not monumental: he is human, but human in the superlative – to paraphrase Mayakovsky's words about Lenin, 'the most human of all humans'.[6] Rybin himself is a man of stereotypes: he speaks in what in Soviet high schools are called the 'permanent epithets' of political jargon. Interestingly, Aranovich remarked that he had had an idea for a documentary a long time before, and had had a character in mind, but he had not been able to find a suitable candidate for the role. Thus the initial impulse for Aranovich's film is both mythological and documentary: Rybin himself is at once a mythical image of a devoted Stalinist bodyguard and a unique character whose minute gestures and passing facial expressions are commemorated in the cinematic close-up. He is a great story-teller, a man of details, and this gives his tale a charming specificity, a 'human touch'. The second part of the film opens with an uncanny hesitation as to who is the main protagonist. He uses two different names – Alexei Rybin and Leonid Lebedev. Of these Lebedev is his official pseudonym, the name of the man from Stalin's guard, which he used in contact with 'well-wishers'. Yet the two names, that of the guard and that of the person, appear to be interchangeable. As the protagonist remarks, even his wife calls him Lyona and not Alyosha. Thus the distinction between the private person and the public persona is difficult to trace.

Rybin's story is the story of the gradual elimination of any possibility of human error. The little clouds of dust in the Bolshoi Theatre that irritated 'the Great Leader of the people' caused a major problem in Rybin's work as commandant of the Theatre Guard. What is to be done to guard against the accidental dust? How can one obtain total control and order? There are several episodes in Rybin's account – the story of a young girl, an informant crying on the staircase of the Bolshoi, a drunken sailor boasting about placing a bomb in the Kremlin, Nemirovich-Danchenko apologising in front of Stalin for a shot in a play which never occurred – all those ordinary accidents, those absurdities of daily life, reveal different degrees of 'human error' that have to be controlled from above, explained or punished. One recalls the episode in Andrey Tarkovsky's *Mirror* [Zerkalo, 1974] of the accident of the hero's mother Masha with her printing press that could have cost her her freedom, with Stalin's portrait in the background.

Milan Kundera ironically calls this human element construed in a totalitarian society a 'blemish'. In *The Book of Laughter and Forgetting* it is what we can call the 'poetics of blemish' that constitute in fact the major field of resistance to totalitarianism. *The Book of Laughter and Forgetting* opens with a description of a historical photograph taken in 1948 showing the Czechoslovak Communist leaders Gottwald and Clementis, with the latter solicitously offering the former his fur hat.[7] Four years later Clementis was charged with treason, hanged and 'airbrushed from history' and from all historical documentation. At this moment a documentary photograph turns into an icon, a perfect representation of totalitarian kitsch, an image of Communist brotherhood. The only thing that remained of Clementis was his fur hat on Gottwald's head, a 'blemish' that spoils a perfect iconography of the new historical picture. 'Blemish' is a seemingly insignificant detail that hinders any attempt at seamless representation and embarrasses Stalinist grand style, or the age of 'unblemished idyll', in Kundera's words. The hat of the erased and purged Czech leader functions as a trace that triggers one's memory beyond the official commonplaces. The blemishes point at the erasures both in private and in the collective memory linking personal and political lives together. Kundera manipulates an already manipulated official photograph: he turns an icon into a narrative, injects history into an iconic and mythical image, offering a new map of reading that foregrounds blemishes on the surfaces of a seemingly seamless idyll. At the same time, Kundera's 'poetics of blemish' strives within the romantic revolutionary idyll it attempts to undermine, enacting an uncomfortable double bind between the kitschman and the critic of kitsch. The same principle operates in the documentary *I Served in Stalin's Bodyguard*. Rybin's story attempts to erase the 'blemishes', but they continue to reappear in the flow of details and are subtly foregrounded by the film. For the film-maker it is precisely those details, non-codifiable human elements, imperfections, that are of extreme importance. The film foregrounds seams and erasures, exposes the blackspots and scars of forgotten history, but also, like Kundera's novel, it depends upon the iconic idyllic image of the totalitarian epoch that must be familiar to the Soviet audience, especially of the older generation.

Stalin Is with Us? is identified by its subtitle as an 'artistic–publicistic' film, which, curiously, is translated into English as 'feature-cum-documentary'. The subtitle 'artistic–publicistic' points to another dilemma faced by many Soviet cinematogaphers today – the double bind between politics and aesthetics. Soviet critics constantly voice their concern that in the Gorbachev era art has turned into journalism. According to this view, the veiled, so-called 'Aesopian language' characteristic of Soviet letters before glasnost could actually nurture artistic production. In direction, as an artistic device *par excellence*, it forces both writer and reader to think metaphorically, to read and write between the lines. Shakhverdiev's film is an interesting experiment in this respect, not merely because the film juxtaposes art and civic journalism, documentation and forceful authorial montage. What is even more important in this conjunction is that the film explores the aestheticisation of politics – in the carefully orchestrated Stalinist marches and songs, as well as the militarisation of art, especially in the scenes of the chorus of Red Army veterans.

'Stalin used the word *perestroika* in 1941 and we got things restructured [*perestroilis'*]. We are for perestroika and for Stalin,' says one of Shakhverdiev's protagonists, a Tbilisi cab-driver and a veteran Stalinist. Thus, the word *perestoika* is not new in the Soviet political lexicon: it has a history of its own, a history that has to be reconsidered and rewritten in order to understand the present. Interestingly, the initial title proposed by Shakhverdiev was in the affirmative: simply *Stalin Is with Us*. The question mark was a creative addition by the Vice-President of the State Cinema Company [Goskino], who told the film-maker that, without the question mark, the film would not be released, because it undermined the achievements of glasnost.[8] Of course, ten or even five years earlier, a film like *Stalin Is with Us?* would not have been made at all, and yet there is something uncanny about this authorial ambiguity prescribed by the new boss, ambiguity in the spirit of glasnost. The story of the change in the title of the film exemplifies the paradoxes of censorship in the period of perestroika. Moreover, according to Shakhverdiev, this incident only proves that the answer to the gently imposed question is in the affirmative, and that Stalin is still with us.

The title of the film is in fact proposed by its protagonists, the members of the Stalinist club in the scene where they nostalgically sing the patriotic songs of their youth. Among their suggestions are: 'Stalin Is with Us?', 'With Stalin in Our Hearts' and 'For Us His Name Is Sacred'. Not surprisingly, their wildest imagination offers them only fixed sentences, clichés, permanent epithets which they learned at school and have seen many times written in red and gold on city streets and public buildings. Thus, the very title of the film is a palimpsest that reveals many cultural clichés and 'reconstructions': from 'Lenin Is with Us' it has turned into 'Stalin Is with Us' – words pronounced by Stalinists – then been reframed by the director, and then called into question by Goskino.

Nevertheless there is a major difference in approach between Shakhverdiev and Aranovich. Aranovich avoids any verbal commentary on Rybin and does not incorporate into the film any alternative point of view. In Shakhverdiev's film one character, the prisoner Chekal, who ironically wears a tattoo of Stalin on his chest, tells us a parable of a visceral link between Stalinism and socialism:

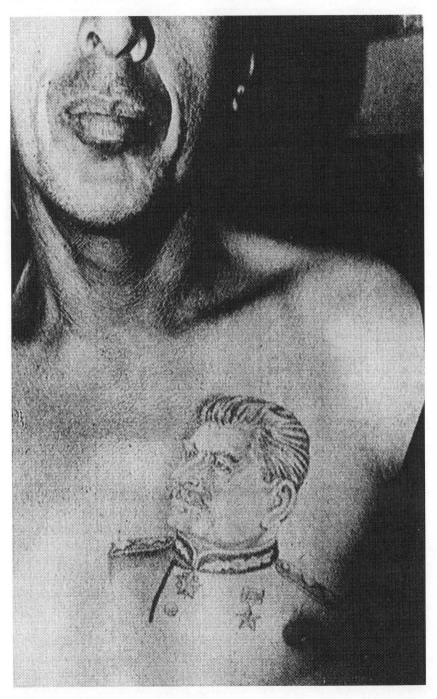

Figure 37 An indelible and affirmative answer to the question posed by Tofik Shakhverdiev's *Stalin Is with Us?* (1989).

All our life is on rations. Not a step to the left or to the right ... We march in lines. We live modestly but joyfully. In a word, this is social-ism, Stalin's kind of socialism. In prison we have true socialism in miniature ...

These powerful words of the prisoner are intercut with the images of prison marching and flocks of sheep in the mountains. Stalinism is with us as long as a certain kind of socialism persists. The documentary turns into an explicit allegory. Moreover, the whole film has an allegorical framing: the scenes of a hypnosis session during which the hypnotist practises his art on the young men and women of today. And, as in the time of the show trials, they confess. At the end, a young Komsomol girl is shown a piece of white paper, and she says with great conviction that it is black; then, looking at black, she claims that it is white. Of course the audience present at the session and we, the film viewers, know the real colour of the paper – or do we? Stalinism as mass hypnosis: the viewer is struck by the allegory. Unfortunately, the old cultural myths are not dis-pelled as easily and quickly as hypnosis in the show. In fact there is hardly anyone within the culture who has the privilege of an absolutely clear vision. Perhaps the final scene in the film, the hypnosis scene, was a bit heavy-handed, particularly for a film that is not at all black and white. Its strength is precisely in documenting the shades of grey, presenting a series of striking human portraits of Stalin's true believers that make us experience Stalin's charisma and question the foundations of common faith.

The Stalinists, who are presented in Shakhverdiev's film without direc-torial voice-over, appear human, all too human. One such is the school-teacher Kornienkova, whom we see in a cosy domestic environment, feeding birds. She quietly tells the story of her lifetime love for one person only – the one with 'little devils in his eyes'. Her love for Stalin is very personal and almost mystical. It reminds one of female mystic recollections of Christ. The camera forces us to look at Stalin's monument through her loving eyes. One of the most amazing scenes is the one in the park, where Kornienkova affectionately brushes away dry autumnal leaves from Sta-lin's buried monument. We see a close-up of Stalin's face, with his blind stone eyes, framed by the leaves on the ground.

For those who keep the cult of Stalin alive, their only alternative to Stalin's order and discipline is, in Shakhverdiev's words, 'uncertainty, chaos, haze, horror of horrors'.[9] It seems that the end of Stalinism is perceived as some kind of new apocalypse, an inescapable theme in Rus-sian cultural mythology. The Christian, and later the Marxist–Leninist–Stalinist, binary structure of paradise on earth, as opposed to apocalypse, or 'He who is not with us is against us', is still in place. It puts blindfolds on people and does not allow them to confront complex issues of freedom, choice and human existence in the broad sense, with all its everyday blemishes and imperfections, ordinary chores and minor epiphanies.[10]

The film gives us a rare insight into the phenomenon of historical nostalgia. Stalin's epoch is not construed as a historical past, but rather as a mythical time which can be evoked and recreated through old rituals that provide an emotional bondage between the people and their leader. 'Tyranny is terrible. Tyranny is wonderful. It depends on how you look at it,' says Shakhverdiev.[11] For these ageing Stalinists, the era from the 1930s to the 1950s is the time of their youth, of splendid marches on Red Square, an aesthetic embodiment of Order and Patriotism. What they lament is the loss of a totalitarian worldview that helped to keep all the nuts and bolts in place, of the larger than life ideological and aesthetic system that offered a clear 'road to life'. 'Before, there were songs about the Leader,' says one of the old Stalinists, 'now nobody writes songs about the leaders.' This is a nostalgia for totalitarian aesthetics, for the Grand Style, for a joyful Socialist Realist march together with thousands of other athletic citizens of the new world. We remember Kundera's reflection on kitsch from *The Unbearable Lightness of Being*, where kitsch is defined as a universal dictatorship of the heart that creates the collective Revolutionary idyll. The heroine of the novel, Sabina, leaves Communist Czechoslovakia not for political but for aesthetic reasons – she declares that she is tired of kitsch. The paradox of kitsch cannot be unveiled by mere distancing from it: then one is in danger of turning into an unselfconscious and self-righteous practitioner of kitschy idealism. The paradox of kitsch is not merely reified and ironically erased as another kind of aesthetic blemish, rather it is presented as an important kind of aesthetic and life experience that has to be re-enacted by readers and viewers in order to be revised later.

Nostalgia means a longing for the home, a desire for a place from which one has been dislocated. But it is always a home that no longer exists, that perhaps never existed, the place that one believes one once inhabited, but that – like a Utopia – is nowhere to be found. Nostalgia is in many ways hostile to history, although both are motivated by a backward glance towards the past. While history, at least in the traditional nineteenth-century conception, attempts to discover origins, recover the past, and construct the chronology of events, nostalgia decries the impossibility of that recovery and continuously forces us to retrace the non-linear operations of desire, the desire that bites its own tail. Yet people often experience history as personal nostalgia. History and nostalgia often stimulate one another. One often tries to overcome nostalgia by writing history but ends up merely by historicising one's own nostalgia. It is nostalgia that perpetuates cultural myths and helps to sustain cultural identity.

What is characteristic of *I Served in Stalin's Bodyguard*, and to a lesser degree of *Stalin Is with Us?*, is that they are not iconoclastic: rather they find unconventional cinematic means for staging totalitarian nostalgia.

These two films do not denounce Stalinists and bury the old monuments, but rather show the monument as an almost elegiac ruin cherished by an old Stalinist and schoolteacher. Iconoclasm is often only mythification in reverse. The new documentaries give the viewer a larger degree of freedom to fill the gaps and to remember what Rybin calls 'all the things that should not be spoken about' – the Stalinist repressions, the purges and the slanders. These films do in fact document the very process of the mythologising of Soviet history but what they demonstrate above all else is that the old myths – however 'restructured' they might be – are still very much with us.

Today, in the early 1990s, these two outstanding films made in 1989 have themselves turned into nostalgic objects, reminders of the early cultural euphoria of glasnost. In the former Soviet Union of the 1990s Stalin, Lenin, Gorbachev and Yeltsin dolls are sold on the streets as 'totalitarian antiques', alongside the pictures of Russian birch trees, Easter eggs, pink pussy-cats, samovars and Young Octobrist banners. Soviet critics have started using the prefix 'post-' almost as often as their Western colleagues, speaking about 'post-totalitarianism', 'post-glasnost' and 'post-modernism'. Nevertheless, the events of the August 1991 coup, especially the rhetoric of Order and Apocalypse used by the coup organisers, have demonstrated that those who believe in the rapid succession of 'post-' prefixes tend to underestimate the vitality of old Russian cultural myths and of all kinds of nostalgias for the former Soviet Union. One of these is a nostalgia for monumental culture, and that is becoming more pronounced as urban monuments to the Revolutionaries, KGB agents and Party leaders are being pulled down, while more and more subversive *matryoshka* dolls appear on the market. The well-known pioneers of 'Sots Art', Vitali Komar and Alex Melamid, are planning, in collaboration with other Russian artists, to turn the former Lenin Museum on Red Square into a post-totalitarian exhibit in which all the monuments will be displayed caught in their moment of dismantlement: Lenin with ropes around his neck, Dzerzhinsky with his boots cut off, and so on. One could certainly put among them the gigantic head of Stalin covered with autumnal leaves that was worshipped by the schoolteacher Kornienkova in *Stalin Is with Us?* The Lenin Museum will turn from an official Soviet exhibit into a new museum of Soviet official culture. Visitors to this extraordinary exhibit, like the active audience of the documentaries, will have to trace their own paths between myth and history, nostalgia and outrage, affection and horror, tying up ropes on Lenin's and Stalin's necks, or else remembering the gilded curls of the baby leader on the Young Octobrist badges of their childhood.

Chapter 14

Unshelving Stalin: after the period of stagnation

Julian Graffy

I

In the first years of the Gorbachev period, Soviet artists seemed pre-occupied with historical subjects, both in their artistic works and in their public statements. There seems to have been a consensus, shared with the Soviet population as a whole, that no fundamental reform of the crisis-ridden Soviet present could be effected without a clearer understanding of the past, and of the threads which connect them. Much of this analysis had, indeed, already been done, and was (in the case of writers for example) either awaiting its moment in desk drawers or published and translated abroad, where it had helped to deepen the Western public's understanding of the Soviet experience. In both their sense of themselves as 'citizens as well as poets' and in getting their works published abroad, Soviet writers were consciously siting themselves in a tradition that went back far further than the Revolution. An added impulse for the artists was a widely held sense that the task of analysis was not being performed by historians, members of perhaps the most ideologised discipline in Soviet scholarship.[1]

Though pride of place in this historical reclamation should probably go to writers, the contribution of the Soviet cinema has also been fundamental. The picture of Soviet history offered by the Soviet cinema during the last five years is made up of a number of different strands using very different approaches. Some of the most important recently seen films on historical subjects were made long ago but 'shelved' by the intervention of the censors. Of these, some, such as Alexei Gherman's *My Friend Ivan Lapshin* [Moi drug Ivan Lapshin, 1985] and *Trial on the Road* [also known as *Roadcheck*, Proverka na dorogakh, 1971] finally reached the screen just before the Fifth Congress of the Union of Cinematographers in May 1986 and the institution of the famous 'Conflict Commission'. The Conflict Commission played its part in the release of Tengiz Abuladze's *Repentance* [Pokayanie] premiered in Tbilisi in October 1986. A second, much larger group finally reached the screen through the direct intervention of the

Conflict Commission. From the list of 159 films which the Commission had looked at and discussed by August 1988,[2] some are on directly historical subjects: Irakli Kvirikadze's *The Swimmer* [Plovets, 1981], Alexander Askoldov's *The Commissar* [Komissar, 1967], the episodes *Homeland of Electricity* [Rodina elektrichestva] by Larisa Shepitko and *Angel* [Angel] by Andrei Smirnov in *The Beginning of an Unknown Century* [Nachalo nevedomogo veka, 1967] and Andrey Tarkovsky's *Mirror* [Zerkalo, 1974].

At the same time as the release of these shelved films, a number of new films on historical subjects began to appear. In general the first of these to cause a stir were documentaries, which can treat their subject matter more directly and are usually quicker and cheaper to set up than feature films. The most famous of these is perhaps Marina Goldovskaya's *Solovki Power* [Vlast' solovetskaya, 1988], but something of the number and range of these works (both in subject and approach) has been indicated by other contributions to this volume. These documentaries have differed in the degree of authorial commentary, and in the extent to which modern footage is interspersed with material from archives. Use of archival newsreel is a striking feature of some of them: Igor Belyayev's *The Trial* [Protsess, 1988], for example, includes footage of Vyshinsky in 1938. The incorporation of historical newsreel footage makes it possible to demythologise the politicians of the period, by reducing them from the monumentality of statues and larger-than-life posters. After the initial shock, their hitherto tabooed and therefore invisible opponents are also revealed to be ordinary human beings with a succession of contradictory human traits.[3]

Connected to the use of newsreel is the use of the more overtly propagandistic 'documentaries' of that period. *Solovki Power* includes scenes from the film *Solovki*, made on the orders of the secret police, the OGPU, in 1927–8. Goldovskaya and her team first conceived their film as a 'commentary film on the 1920s film'.[4] Scenes from a commissioned propaganda film are also included in a recent feature film, Yevgeni Tsymbal's *Defence Counsel Sedov* [Zashchitnik Sedov, 1988], which follows its climactic scene of the unnamed chief prosecutor's vituperative speech with Mikoyan using exactly the same rhetoric in a speech at the Bolshoi Theatre on 20 December 1937 at the celebration of the twentieth anniversary of the VChK-OGPU-NKVD (the successive names by which the security organs were known) and recorded at the time in a film called *The Glorious Twenty Years*.[5]

The final and increasingly the most visible group of films providing us with versions of or allusions to Soviet history, consists of feature films made during the Gorbachev period. Twenty-five years of cinematic readings of Soviet history have reached the viewer in the last five years. Films made during a period of heavy and overt censorship (and self-censorship) jostle for the viewer's attention with films made when the censorship has been almost totally relaxed and when it has become fashionable to give an angry or mocking picture of the Soviet past. In current feature production an enormous range of approaches is once again evident, from the sobriety of films like *Defence Counsel Sedov* to a number of overtly commercial films using set pieces of Soviet history. For example, the plot of Sergei Solovyov's *Black Rose Stands for Sadness, Red Rose Stands for Love* [Chernaya roza – emblema pechali, krasnaya roza – emblema lyubvi, 1989] is described in *Sovetskii fil'm* [Soviet Film 1990, no. 1] as follows:

> A beautiful woman expecting a baby, her lover who is married to an ambassador's daughter, a crazy dissident, Joseph Stalin and a 15-year-old millionaire who is both a nobleman and a member of the Young Communist League – these are the characters of the film its director defines as 'marasmic comedy'.

The sheer number of current films which refer to Stalin has been revealed in Anna Lawton's contribution to this volume.[6] But concern with history is not limited to Stalin himself. Some indication of the current popularity of the subject is provided by the monthly *Sovetskii fil'm* 'billboard' of new releases, which has recently announced N. Adomenaite and B. Gorlov's *Coma* [Koma, 1989] ('An intelligent young girl has to pass through the hell of the Gulag in the early 1950s'); S. Mamilov's *Little Golden Cloud* [Nochevala tuchka zolotaya, 1989] ('The Stalinist deportation of Caucasian peoples in 1944 shown through the eyes of children'); A. Aivazyan's *Privy Counsellor* [Tainyi sovetnik, 1988] ('Fantasy on the theme "Stalin Today" '); Valeri Ogorodnikov's *Prishvin's Paper Eyes* [Bumazhnye glaza Prishvina, 1989] ('Studying the archives of the Stalin era for his new film, a TV director discovers the secret of a crime'); U. Ibragimov's *Pursuit* [Presledovanie, 1989] ('Was the forced collectivisation in Central Asia not one of the causes of the Basmach movement? The film offers an answer to this question through the genre of the Eastern'); Mikhail Ptashuk's *Our Armoured Train* [Nash bronepoezd, 1988] ('A butcher, a former guard in a Stalin labour camp and his victim meet again in 1966'); K. Kamalova's *The Savage* [Dikar', 1988] ('A young champion of justice during Stalin's time slaps the face of a corrupt official and thus signs his own death sentence').

More films on historical subject matter are on their way: Yevgeni Tsymbal has just completed *The Tale of the Unextinguished Moon* [Povest' nepogashennoi luny, 1990], based on Boris Pilnyak's story of the death of the Commissar for War, Frunze; in a recent interview Alexei Gherman talked of a project on the Doctors' Plot, and of Americans being interested in coproduction if Stalin could be played by an American – to which he appends his own fears of being misunderstood in Russia 'if Stalin appears with the features of Jack Nicholson'.[7]

Another manifestation of the same concerns, as noted by François Niney,

Figure 38 'A "sign" of the epoch': 'our Soviet Pinkerton's' leather coat in Alexei Gherman's *My Friend Ivan Lapshin* (1985).

is the fashion for films set in orphanages, borstals, prisons and other places of incarceration.[8] The allegorical approach has long been used in Soviet cinema to address questions of history, the state and the individual, Vadim Abdrashitov's *Plyumbum* [1986] and *The Servant* [Sluga, 1988] being recent examples of the genre. If we consider films taking this approach, the range presently addressing themselves to historical subjects (and the range of motivations) will be seen to be very large indeed.

Immediately apparent too to anyone attempting to provide an overview of recent developments in Soviet cinema is the similarity of the situation in cinema to that of the other arts, and in particular to literature. In literature too the last five years have seen the simultaneous publication of works written long ago but banned or published only abroad, often because of their unacceptable readings of Soviet history; and new works – as in the cinema, by now predominating over the old – many of which address themselves to the revelation and interpretation of the 'blank spots' of Soviet history. Sometimes the links between the two are very close: it is literary originals that are brought to the screen. *My Friend Ivan Lapshin* is a reinterpretation of stories by Gherman's father, the writer Yuri Gherman;

Shepitko's *Homeland of Electricity* is from Platonov; Smirnov's *Angel* from Olesha. *The Commissar* is based on Vasili Grossman's story 'In the Town of Berdichev' [V gorode Berdicheve]. One of the most powerful scenes in *Repentance*, in which women queue at a window to find out whether they can send parcels to their imprisoned husbands and sons, parallels the setting of Akhmatova's poem 'Requiem' [Rekviem, 1940, unpublished in the USSR until 1987]. Among recent films, Yuri Kara's *Belshazzar's Feast, or a Night with Stalin* [Piry Baltazara, ili noch' so Stalinym, 1989] is from a chapter of Fazil Iskander's novel *Sandro of Chegem* [Sandro iz Chegema]; *Little Golden Cloud* from the novel by Anatoli Pristavkin; there are scenes from a staging of Mikhail Shatrov's play *The Dictatorship of Conscience* [Diktatura sovesti, 1986] in Belyayev's documentary *The Trial*. In these cases film-makers are using literary texts that were themselves sensations in the literary press in recent years.[9]

II

The answer to the question why films were banned would seem to be very simple: they treated key episodes of Soviet history in the wrong way. *Repentance* looked at a town in the grip of a manic dictator and included notorious episodes from Soviet history: in addition to the queue mentioned above there are prisoners confessing to participation in ludicrous plots (in this case digging a tunnel from Bombay to London) and prisoners carving their names on logs that are to be sent down river in the hope of alerting someone to the fact that they are still alive. Gherman's *Trial on the Road* gave the 'wrong' picture of the character and fate of a Soviet soldier who had been in German imprisonment, his *Twenty Days without War* [Dvadt-sat' dnei bez voiny, 1976, release delayed for a year] portrayed life in wartime evacuation in a similarly unacceptable way. *Angel* showed too violent a picture of the Civil War, *The Commissar* one that was too philosemitic.[10]

Stalin, the Second World War, the Civil War are all heavily mythologised 'set themes' of Soviet history and art, and this required that they be treated in a certain mythological way, yet the list of shelved films shows very clearly that it was not just films on historical subjects that were banned, and that the explanation that 'certain films got banned because they approached sensitive subjects in the wrong way' is inadequate. The censors through whose hands all cinematic production had to pass were interested in the minutest details of how 'reality' was represented, since any of these details could be construed as ideologically significant. Concentration on famous cases can give only a partial picture since watchfulness was ubiquitous.

One of the resolutions of the Fifth Congress was to encourage improve-ments in the quality of the cinema press,[11] and one of the manifestations of this improvement has been a series of pieces shedding light on the bannings, using documentary evidence to re-examine the 'blank spots' of cinema history just as the blank spots of literary history have been illuminated in literary journals. These range from individual case histories to attempts at an overview and the establishment of the aesthetics and ethics in the name of which the bannings were effected.

Writing in the journal *Iskusstvo kino* [The Art of Cinema] in January 1989,[12] Yelena Stishova traced the history of *The Commissar*, using the 'Case of the Film *The Commissar*', which consists of 'two weighty tomes' and is deposited in the archives of TsGALI [Tsentral'nyi Gosudarstvennyi Arkhiv Literatury i Iskusstva, Central State Archive of Literature and Art] in Moscow. Final sentence was passed on the film on 29 December 1967 by the then head of the State Cinema Committee [Goskino] A. V. Romanov in the words: 'Askoldov's diploma film is quite unacceptable for our screen.'[13] From the records of the early studio discussions of the screenplay it is obvious that such a treatment of the Civil War was immediately perceived as dangerous. A. Turkov is quoted as saying:

> I feel doubtful about the scene where Yemelin [a deserter] gets shot. I can imagine that it is historically authentic, that that is the way things were. But the trouble is that it arouses a chain reaction of associations about the sources of certain phenomena in the life of Soviet society. I'm just afraid of such a turn of events in this screenplay.

As Stishova comments, the screenplay exposed the ambiguities of Soviet morality which wanted to present the Revolution as romantic and bloodless:

> We want to unite that which cannot be united. On the one hand we hold on tightly to the punitive sword of the proletariat which is merciless to the enemies of the Revolution, on the other hand we are humanists, the tear of a child is a barrier which we cannot cross.[14]

The response to the screenplay by the State Cinema Committee was an immediate expression of concern that the film would be 'deheroicised' [*degeroicheskii*]. As work on the film progressed and as, simultaneously, the Brezhnev period established its aesthetic requirements, responses from Goskino became more extreme. A letter of 2 August 1966 under the title 'O nedostatkakh stsenariya *Komissar*' [On the shortcomings of the screenplay *The Commissar*] suggested: 'Above all we are alarmed by the fact that the humanitarian essence of the proletarian revolution is distorted ... A second shortcoming, closely connected with the first, is the extreme poverty of the intellectual world of the main heroine of the film.'[15] By late 1967, after the film had been shot, the conclusions of the Goskino editorial board made the first reference to Askoldov's 'secret plot'. At the final discussions of the film on 29 December 1967 it was found to be 'at odds with our understanding of proletarian internationalism and humanism in general'.[16]

Just as we have, therefore, a detailed history of the shelving of *The Commissar*, so too, through a number of interviews, Alexei Gherman has told us the reasons why and the methods by which his films were delayed, hindered and shelved.[17] On *Trial on the Road* he recalls: 'They responded to the film inimically at Goskino. The editor dealing with us shouted: "How could you have done this? Who gave you permission?" '[18] A Goskino document on the film dated 1 November 1971 states:

> 'The film . . . suffers from extreme conceptual failings . . . [it] distorts the image of a heroic time and the image of the Soviet people who rose up in the occupied territories in mortal battle with the German fascist occupiers. The film's main subject, the subject of the heroic battle with the occupiers, fades into the background . . .

Another, dated 28 March 1972, adds: 'The film does not develop the theme of the partisan struggle, it deheroicises this great popular movement . . .'[19] Goskino delayed *Twenty Days without War* and called it 'the shame of Lenfilm', because 'the people it depicts could only have lost the war'.[20] The recurrence of words like 'distort the image', 'deheroicise' gives us a clue to the process that was at work. What concerned Goskino was the overall picture, the 'official version', the myth of how things had been, and this picture covered every possible detail. As Gherman has recalled, he was also told that there were too many puddles in *Twenty Days without War*.[21]

There are other examples, in films with a contemporary setting, of censorial attention to detail. Kira Muratova was told that the characters in her film *The Long Farewell* [Dolgie provody, 1971] did not dance in the right way, and that she had produced 'not Socialist Realism but bourgeois realism'.[22] This mention of Socialist Realism leads closer to an understanding of the process that was at work. In a recent analysis of Stalinist thematics, François Niney has isolated five themes, five myths of Socialist Realism that had to be reflected in the art of the time:

1. The radiant future.
2. The guiding genius, father of the peoples, master of the arts and sciences.
3. The plots of the enemies of the people, traitors and saboteurs.
4. The prowess of the heroes of labour.
5. The victories of production.

In contemporary films, these myths are being deconstructed, the second in a number of recent films, the third in, for example, *Defence Counsel Sedov*.[23]

This attempt at an overview of the myths and the censorship they provoked has also been a feature of recent Soviet film writing. The September 1989 issue of the monthly *Sovetskii fil'm* examined, under the title 'Stalin-Superstar', different aspects of the art and the cult. Of crucial importance are a succession of articles by the film historian Valeri Fomin that have appeared in the last two years in *Iskusstvo kino* and *Sovetskii ekran* [Soviet Screen][24] as part of a project by VNIIK [the All-Union Research Institute for the History of Cinema] to produce, under the title 'Lessons of Stagnation', a history of the cinema of the Brezhnev period. What Fomin's studies prove, if proof were needed, is that the case histories mentioned above are only the visible peaks of an iceberg of intervention and reshaping. The articles are based upon a mass of documentary material and show that, for example, a scene was cut from Konchalovsky's *Asya's Happiness* [Istoriya Asi Klyachinoi, kotoraya lyubila, da ne vyshla zamuzh, 1967] because in it a boy was asked if he knew who Stalin was;[25] and that in Osepyan's *Ivan's Launch* [Ivanov kater, 1972] the amount of drinking was cut down.[26] Andrey Tarkovsky was told that in the episode of the Spanish children arriving in the USSR in his *Mirror* 'there should be a more elevated and optimistic' mood. Even after the director made changes to the scene, he was told: 'It has not proved possible to weaken the sad and tragic tonality of the episode as a whole. Such a one-sided treatment of the Spanish children in the USSR is incorrect in essence.'[27] Nikita Mikhalkov was told that there was too much gaiety in his *Kinfolk* [Rodnya, 1981] and that the number of jokes should be cut.[28] On the other hand Andrei Smirnov was instructed to add a little gaiety to his *Autumn* [Osen', 1973]. The film-makers duly reported that they had:

> introduced a scene of a walk in the woods to counter the impression that there was too much gloomy weather throughout the film.
> In consequence the film is 48.3 metres longer. We ask permission for a new length for the film of 2509.4 metres.[29]

These are examples of the process in microcosm. At the other end of the scale a film could be stopped at the screenplay stage because the entire subject was considered inappropriate. Thus Vasil Bykov's own screenplay of his story 'Sotnikov' was not allowed to go forward,[30] nor, in 1964, was Alov and Naumov's *The Law* [Zakon], which concerned the attempt by an investigator to look again at the case of innocent people who had been repressed. This film thus had something in common with *Defence Counsel Sedov*, made twenty-four years later, and indeed Naumov is finally making *The Law* in 1990.[31]

Another example of attention to the grand scale on the part of the censors is the gradual removal during the first years of the Brezhnev era of any cinematic reference to the Stalin cult, so that eventually Dymshits, of the screenplay editorial board of Goskino, could say of a screenplay submitted to him: 'This film should not be a film about the epoch of the cult of personality because there was no such epoch.'[32]

Figures 39 and 40 The Great Terror re-enacted: the crazed and haunted faces of Skripko and the State Prosecutor in Yevgeni Tsymbal's *Defence Counsel Sedov* (1988).

As Fomin notes, the sentences passed on films and screenplays regularly included the phrase 'on thematic grounds', but what reading these many case histories reveals is that all themes had to be treated in a manner that Goskino could approve, they had to be lacquered and mythologised according to the aesthetic of Socialist Realism.

Thus an examination of the treatment of historical subject matter in the recent Soviet cinema can benefit from attention not only to actual film production, but also to the remarkable new writing about cinema: the case histories of the tribulations of particular films and directors, the attempts at an overview, not to mention such impressive analyses of individual films as Yuri Karabchievsky's recent assessment of *Repentance* and Oleg Kovalov's consideration of *My Friend Ivan Lapshin*, two studies which brilliantly illuminate the aesthetic shortcomings of Abuladze's film and the triumphant capture of the underside of an epoch by Gherman.[33]

III

Two of the most successful films at capturing the mood of the Stalinist 1930s in recent years have been Gherman's *My Friend Ivan Lapshin* and Tsymbal's *Defence Counsel Sedov*.[34] The screenplay for *Lapshin* was written in 1969, work on the film was delayed until 1979, and the film was finally released in 1985. *Sedov* was made in 1988. They thus date from two very different periods of Soviet cinema history, though both reached the screen during the Gorbachev period. What unites them is their shared aesthetic of sober marginality. Neither of them attempts to portray Stalin or other leading figures directly. We can list the various ways in which the films take a similar approach, as well as noting certain significant differences.

1. Both titles include the name of their main protagonist, on whose experiences the films concentrate.

2. Both these heroes are connected through their jobs with the functioning of Soviet law. Lapshin is head of the local criminal police [*ugolovnyi rozysk*]; Sedov is a lawyer, a defence counsel [*zashchitnik*].

3. Both films eschew the use of colour. *Lapshin* is made almost entirely in black and white with a succession of filters, colour being used for the framing scenes set in the present and very occasionally and briefly in the body of the film. *Sedov* is shot entirely in black and white.[35]

4. Both films use a large number of close-ups of faces.

5. Both films are set 'in the town of N.' Alexei Gherman has replaced the Leningrad setting of his father's stories with the fictional town of 'Unchansk'. *Sedov* is set in 'Ensk'.[36]

6. Both films make use of portraits of political and military leaders framed on walls and posters. At the beginning of *Lapshin* there is a portrait

of Kirov on the wall of the flat. Then we see a poster of Voroshilov on the same wall. Later there will be other portraits of Voroshilov and Budyonny. At the end of the film, one of the many bands who have been providing the film's martial music makes its way though the town seated on the back of a tram. At the front of the tram is a portrait of Stalin, who is thus seen for the first time in the film. The logic of the appearance of these portraits, from Kirov to Stalin, thus mirrors the darkening of the film's political analysis.

The use of portraits is also a feature of *Sedov*. There is a picture of Yezhov in the prison. Here, though, portraits of Stalin are glimpsed throughout the film, culminating in a slow revelation of the full-length portrait hanging over the chief prosecutor's desk, preparing for the appearance of the leaders themselves in the film's archival coda.

7. The slogans and banners of the time are also much in evidence. The sign over the prison in *Sedov* reads 'Criminality is eradicated by work, upbringing and rational education.' In *Lapshin* we hear the phrase 'He who does not work does not eat'. The social experiment of the young pioneers with a fox and a cockerel in the same cage is presided over by a poster with the slogan from Michurin: 'We should not wait for favours from nature, our task is to take them from her ourselves.'[37] Lapshin and others continually repeat 'We'll clear the land, plant an orchard – and still have time to take a walk in that orchard', as they cross the bleak snowy expanses of the town. Other 'signs' of the epoch that feature in these films include the triumphal arch that is being constructed in *Lapshin*, and the leather coat worn by Lapshin. When he falls noisily from Adashova's window, a woman out walking sees the coat, recognises it as the kind notoriously favoured by the security police and backs away apologetically muttering 'Never mind! Never mind!' [*Nichego! Nichego*!]. The same leather coats are worn by the men who come for Sedov at the end of the other film and are 'read' in the same way by Sedov's colleagues (and by the audience). In *Lapshin* there is irony at the expense of the empty slogans of the period in the scene of Lapshin, Khanin and Adashova eating in her room. Adashova cannot remember whether 12,000 or 12 million bottles of Abrau-Derso champagne are to be produced in 1941. The message on the piece of paper that had wrapped the meat and turns up in the soup is read by Khanin and turns out to be 'Let us rejoice!' ['Raduemsya!'], a microcosmic allusion to the gap between the mendacious rhetoric of official discourse and the real conditions of people's lives.

8. Both films have an acute ear for the language and terminology of the period. All the phraseology of the show trials is on display in *Sedov*. There are allusions to 'fascist hirelings' [*fashistskie naimity*], to 'double-dyed enemies of the people' [*materye vragi naroda*] and 'hangers-on of Yagoda' [*posledyshi Yagody*], to plots and to wrecking. Soviet phraseology has utterly permeated the lexis of the characters. Protesting their innocence, they speak of 'revolutionary conscience', of being a 'crystalline party-

member', of being 'Soviet people'. A powerful rebuke is to say to someone 'You are not a Soviet person' [*Vy ne sovetskii chelovek*]. The film's rhetorical peak is reached in the stream of invective unleashed by the chief prosecutor, a figure based on Andrei Vyshinsky.[38] The subsequent archival film of Mikoyan's speech shows that this rhetoric is not exaggerated. In *Lapshin* people are endlessly addressed as 'comrade' [*tovarishch*] and 'boss' [*nachal'nik*], Lapshin himself being 'comrade boss'.

9. Both films also make use of the art of the time. In *Sedov* the march 'Moskva maiskaya' (Moscow in May) is heard on the train, and later, in Ensk, Sedov goes to see Grigori Alexandrov's 1936 film *The Circus* [Tsirk] starring Lyubov Orlova, one of the most successful Soviet films of the period.[39] The film ends with the extract from the propaganda film *The Glorious Twenty Years* discussed above.

Lapshin is full of artistic reference points, from the amateur agit-sketches on Mussolini's Abyssinian invasion at the birthday party at the start to the posters for a forthcoming production at the local theatre by a travelling Leningrad company of a play called *Glory* [Slava] at the end. The play that the actors in the film are rehearsing is Nikolai Pogodin's *Aristocrats* [Aristokraty] of 1934, set on the Baltic–White Sea Canal.[40] The disparity between the character played by Adashova in the play and the real-life prostitute Katka Napoleon, who will end the film on the canal, is just one of the ways in which this film undercuts the art of the period. Another, noted by Herbert Eagle, is the allusion to *The Battleship Potemkin* when an old woman with a pram is hustled out of the way before the assault on Solovyov's lair.[41] There is only martial music on the soundtrack – the town is said to boast a band for every citizen.[42] As one of the characters says: 'I like marches; they remind me of the youth of our country.' Sitting at table, the actors strike up Eisler's 'Arise, proletarian, for your cause', the march of the German Communists.

Of particular interest in this context is the figure of the journalist Khanin, a failed writer reduced to extolling the exploits of Soviet airmen and gold miners. This character has been compared by Gherman himself to Stenich[43] and by the critic Oleg Kovalov to Mayakovsky and others:

Khanin is a grandiose embodiment of the bankruptcy of the Weltanschauung [*zhizneustroenie*] of the 'left' intelligentsia of the 1920s, and plastically he is made to resemble several of them: Mayakovsky, Ilf, Fogel ... But gradually his Lef uniform is replaced by a rubberised raincoat and the 'gangster's' hat of a hero from boulevard cinema: this is a clear sign of the devaluation of social ideals, a tragi-comic variant on the relationship between man and social ideal.[44]

It is interesting in the context of comparisons with Mayakovsky that Khanin announces that he 'rejects the rumours about Mayakovsky's suicide', and that he is reduced to finding excitement by hanging around with Lapshin and joining his men at work.[45]

Thus the art and the artists of the period come under scrutiny in *Lapshin* and ironic attention is drawn to the contrast between the art and the reality. Gherman also uses allusions to classical writers to underline his points. When the actors are first glimpsed at work, the play they are rehearsing is Pushkin's *A Feast in Plague Time*. The lines being declaimed read as follows:

> [There is ecstasy in battle,]
> And on the edge of the gloomy abyss,
> And in the furious ocean,
> Among the threatening waves and stormy darkness,
> And in the Arabian hurricane,
> And in the breath of Plague.[46]

On Adashova's wall there is a poster for a production of Alexander Ostrovsky's play *Guilty without Guilt* [Bez viny vinovatye, 1884].

The film also seems to have a developed Chekhovian sub-text. At the leaving scene by the river, Adashova makes an ironical reference to 'Chekhovian young ladies' [*Chekhovskie baryshni*]. But she herself seems to be closely modelled on Chekhov's Nina Zarechnaya in *The Seagull*, a poor provincial actress (as she admits to Lapshin at the actors' table), in love with a failed writer but spurned by him. There are other allusions to Chekhov. Okoshkin's 'Au revoir. Reservoir. Samovar' refrain recalls the 'meaningless' refrains of Chebutykin in *Three Sisters*. The arrivals and departures in a provincial town mirror the structure of Chekhov's four major plays. There is even an ironic reference to leaving for Moscow at the end. And the sequence of unrequited loves recited by Adashova also has its parallels in the Chekhov plays, in particular *Uncle Vanya*. Khanin, with his failed writing and his failed suicide, can also be seen in a Chekhovian context. This reading in Chekhovian terms underlines both the superficiality of the art of the period in which the film is set and the doomed, constrained lives of the characters in the film.[47]

10. The spatial organisation of the films is similar. Both begin inside, in an interior representative of order, comfort and safety, and move from that interior to an exterior that is bleak and dangerous. *Lapshin* starts in the hero's flat and moves into the barren expanses of the town and the dilapidated house in which Solovyov's gang are holed up. In *Sedov*, the hero moves from his own flat to an unknown town.

In addition both films employ the device of starting with people sitting at a meal table, and having the peace of that mealtime disturbed. At the beginning of *Sedov* the hero and his wife are eating dinner: the bell rings; the wife is terrified. 'Olya', says Sedov, 'it's ten o'clock. *They* come either late at night or just before dawn.' Though it is indeed not *them*, the arrival of the three women utterly disrupts the order of Sedov's life and sets in motion the train of events that will end by including him in the horror that already affects them. The irruption motif will be repeated when the women come into Sedov's quarters on the train. The youngest woman leaves Sedov a photograph of her sons which draws him further into compassionate involvement. In the film's final use of the motif, Sedov's wife's apprehensions are justified. This time, three men in leather coats come into Sedov's office and utter the chilling words: 'We've come for you' [*My za vami*].

Lapshin starts with the celebrations of the hero's fortieth birthday but this scene darkens when one of the guests mentions that he is married to a priest's daughter and therefore not allowed to be a member of the Party. Two later table scenes are similarly darkened. In the scene at the table of the actors, their drunken tailor has to be ejected, and Lapshin is asked whether he has ever killed a man. In the scene in Adashova's room the owners of the flat come in for their kettle and an irritated Adashova asks Lapshin to have them arrested. The cosiness of these interiors is also ironically contrasted with the scenes inside Solovyov's lair at the end of the film. A connected profanation of the interior occurs when the guest Khanin tries to shoot himself in Lapshin's bathroom.[48]

11. This move from inside to outside echoes in microcosm the marginality of the films' settings. Gherman has moved *Lapshin* from the original Leningrad to the marginal town of Unchansk. In *Sedov*, the hero moves from Moscow to Ensk. The smallness of these towns is stressed, and links these works to earlier sagas of provincial life in Russian literature, and to such 'Chekhovian' films as Boris Barnet's *Outskirts* [Okraina, 1933]. In *Sedov*, Skripko explains his concern about the case by saying 'It's a small town', in which everyone knows each other. Both film-makers use an analysis of life on the margin to capture the essence of the time.

In one sense, however, directness in *Sedov* can be contrasted with indirectness in *Lapshin*. *Sedov*, a short film lasting only forty-five minutes, concentrates on a single case in the life of its hero, the condemnation of four agronomists to death on charges of sabotage. The film is based on a story by Ilya Zverev.[49] The story itself is dedicated to and based on the life of Vladimir Rossels, a pre-Revolutionary lawyer who remained in Russia after the Revolution because he wanted to help create a society governed by law.[50] In an early exchange between Sedov and a colleague there is a reference to another famous lawyer, Anatoly Fyodorovich Koni.[51] Since it was made in 1988, *Sedov* is able to be quite explicit about the chain of responsibility for Soviet legality. Sedov encounters in turn his own boss at the legal bureau; the 'referent', the assistant to the Chief Prosecutor; Skripko, the secretary of the court at Ensk; Korenev, assistant to the president of the local court, Ryabokon, who is 'ill', and 'will not be needing his chair again'; Kopyonkin, the warder on duty at the local prison;

Matyukhin, the prison governor, a young Communist; and finally the Chief Prosecutor himself. Repeatedly these characters are shown to be capable of kindness on a human level (there is much concentration on filming their faces), but on an official level they are cogs in the Stalinist wheel. After the crazed speech of the prosecutor comes the *Glorious Twenty Years* film and the faces of the real-life protagonists in this drama. The film is also explicit in references to the code of laws ('Article 58! You must be mad!' says Sedov's wife when he seems likely to take on the case), and to such trials as that of the 'Industrial Party'.[52]

Sedov concerns itself with a political case [*spetsdelo*] in 1937. Gherman has purposely moved his film from the 1937 of the original to 1935, and made Lapshin a *criminal* investigator, not directly involved in political cases. He is on the trail of a gang of thugs, 'our Soviet Pinkerton'.[53] In this his aim seems to be, as he has stated, 'to make a film about the time'. The ambiguity of this epoch has been brilliantly described by Lidiya Ginzburg:

> People are wrong to imagine the calamitous epochs of the past as totally taken up by calamity. They also consist of a great deal else – the sort of things which life in general consists of, although against a particular background. The 1930s is not just hard work and fear, it is also a mass of talented people with a will to carry things out . . .
>
> The terrible background never left your consciousness. The people who went to the ballet and went visiting, played poker and relaxed in their dachas were precisely those to whom the morning would bring news of the loss of those close to them, who themselves, turning cold with every evening ring of the doorbell, waited for their dear guests . . . As long as they were all right they turned aside, distracted themselves: if they're offering you something, take it . . .[54]

It is not difficult to apply these words to *My Friend Ivan Lapshin*. Instead of the ballet, the characters in the film go to the theatre; instead of poker, they play chess. Writing directly about *Lapshin*, Oleg Kovalov says:

> They say that in the 1930s people did not know about the law being broken. So tell me, what did Lapshin, and other grown-up aunties and uncles 'not know'? . . . having doubts is arduous, it is easier joining the work collective and the general opinion . . .
>
> Lapshin seems to be unconsciously oppressed . . . he senses the *bogging down* of reality, the murk creeping up, the instability of ordinary daily life, the difference between words and deeds – the feverish succession of slogans . . .
>
> Lapshin's heroism is a paradoxical form of cowardice, the ostrich position. So as not to see, not to sense the lack of wellbeing in modern life, he hides from it in illusions, diving into danger, into vulgar clashes

with criminal elements, a pitiful surrogate of his earlier noble struggle.[55]

It is for this reason that Kovalov detects in the film the symbolic ubiquitousness of illness. From the very first scene in which Okoshkin is taking his temperature to the boy in the invalid carriage at the end, everyone seems to have some kind of illness, in marked contrast to official cults of health and physical fitness (Lapshin is glimpsed exercising with weights) and the talk of 'improving' nature. The use of this metaphor in the film is in Kovalov's words, 'startlingly literal'. Lapshin's epilepsy is viewed by Kovalov as 'the embodiment of the *sick health* of artificial heartiness'.[56] It is notable in this context that Lapshin considers his epilepsy a source of shame; and that in 1984 the censors cut from the film a scene of another epileptic attack in Solovyov's hut.[57]

The scene of the arrest in the overcrowded house on the outskirts has been frequently praised as a *tour de force* of film-making. In its combination of horror, violence, hysteria and farce, the scene contains, to quote Kovalov, 'a physiologically sensible concentration of the imagistic essence of the 1930s . . .'[58]

As has been suggested in this and other contributions to this volume, the Stalinist theme has recently been extremely fashionable in Soviet cinema. It is in the nature of fashions that they pass almost as quickly as they spring up, and there is already evidence that the gaze of the mass of Soviet filmmakers is now directed at a more recent period. But the Stalinist period continues to stimulate such remarkable work as Vitali Kanevsky's *Freeze. Die. Resuscitate* [Zamri. Umri. Voskresni, 1990]. Kanevsky's film is also set on the periphery of history, in a settlement in Eastern Siberia, near the town of Suchan, in 1947. The squalor of the settlement, the mud, puddles, dilapidated housing, drunkenness, violence and threats are all marvellously evoked, and are reminiscent of the squalid outskirts of *Lapshin*. Here, too, is a concentration on ordinary lives, and a sly portrayal of how the plangent rhetoric of Soviet law is actually experienced. The Stalin years have been crucial to the formation of what the former Soviet Union is today (Stalin held power for longer than any other Soviet ruler), and their hold on the allegiance of a substantial section of the ex-Soviet population is still so great that they will continue to stimulate the imagination of those who were once Soviet artists. The lesson of recent cinema is that the 'aesthetic of marginality' can reveal the tenor of those times with a devastating directness.

Notes

Throughout these endnotes the abbreviation *FF* is used to denote: R. Taylor and I. Christie (eds), *The Film Factory. Russian and Soviet Cinema in Documents, 1896–1939* (London and Cambridge, MA, 1988).

1 STALINISM – THE HISTORICAL DEBATE

1 R. W. Davies, *Soviet History in the Gorbachev Revolution* (London, 1989); A. Nove, *Glasnost' in Action* (Boston, MA, 1989); W. Laqueur, *Stalin. The Glasnost Revelations* (London, 1990); also D. W. Spring 'Re-making History: Soviet Perspectives on the Past', in: D. W. Spring (ed.), *The Impact of Gorbachev* (London, 1991), pp. 68–91.

2 Discussion in: *Russian Review*, vol. 45 (1986), no. 4, pp. 357–414 and vol. 46 (1987), no. 4, pp. 379–433; V. Andrle, 'Demons and Devil's Advocates: Problems in Historical Writing on the Stalin Era', in N. Lampert and G. Rittersporn (eds), *Stalinism: Its Nature and Aftermath. Essays in Honour of Moshe Lewin* (London, 1991), pp. 25–47; J. Keep in *Times Literary Supplement* (hereafter *TLS*), 5 October 1990, pp. 1057–8; R. Conquest in *TLS*, 20 September 1991, pp. 3–5.

3 'Ultimately only a Soviet historian can write the history of Stalinism because he feels the spirit of the people, that atmosphere, those informal relations between people which a foreigner cannot understand in the same way' (Interview, as quoted by J. Barber in *TLS* review of Medvedev, 17 November 1989, p. 1258).

4 B. Oreshin and A. Rubtsov, 'Stalinizm: ideologiya i soznanie' [Stalinism, Ideology and Consciousness], in Kh. Kobo (ed.), *Osmyslit' kul't Stalina* [Making Sense of the Stalin Cult] (Moscow, 1989), p. 590.

5 Nove, p. 15.

6 V. V. Tsaplin, 'Statistika zhertv stalinizma v 30–e gody' [The Statistics for the Victims of Stalinism in the 1930s], *Voprosy istorii* [Problems of History], 1990, no. 4, pp. 175–81.

7 R. Medvedev, 'Stalinizm: sushchnost', genezis, evolyutsiya' [Stalinism: Essence, Genesis, Evolution], *Voprosy istorii*, 1990, no. 3, pp. 5–6.

8 O. Latsis, 'Perelom' [The Break], *Znamya* [The Banner], 1988, no. 7, pp. 124–78, and 'Stalin protiv Lenina' [Stalin contra Lenin], in: Kobo, pp. 215–46. Cf. S. L. Cohen, *Bukharin and the Bolshevik Revolution* (London, 1974).

9 G. Gill, *The Origins of the Stalinist Political System* (Cambridge, 1990), particularly pp. 307–27.

10 S. Fitzpatrick, *The Russian Revolution 1917–1932* (Oxford, 1982), pp. 117, 167.

11 B. G. Mogilnitskii, 'Al'ternativnost' v istorii sovetskogo obshchestva' [Alternativism in the History of Soviet Society], *Voprosy istorii*, 1989, no.11, pp. 3–15.

12 R. Conquest, p. 5, quoting *Pravda*.

13 I. Klyamkin, 'Kakaya ulitsa vedet k khramu' [Which Street Leads to the Temple], *Novyi mir* [New World], 1987, no. 11, pp. 150–88.

14 M. Heller and A. Nekrich, *Utopia in Power* (London, 1986).

15 A. Tsipko, 'Istoki stalinizma' [The Origins of Stalinism], *Nauka i zhizn'* [Science and Life], 1988, nos 11 and 12; 1989, nos 1 and 2; also: Spring 1989, pp.77–9.

16 L. Sedov, 'I zhrets i zhnets. K voprosu o kornyakh kul'ta Vozhdya' [Both Priest and Reaper. On the Question of the Roots of the Cult of the Leader], in Kobo, pp. 430–1.

17 R. Stites, *Revolutionary Dreams: Utopian Visions and Experimental Life in the Russian Revolution*, (Oxford, 1990), p. 4.

18 See for instance G. Gill, *Stalinism* (London, 1990). On the war and post-war periods, see J. Barber and M. Harrison, *The Soviet Home Front, 1941–1945* (London, 1991); and T. Dunmore, *Soviet Politics, 1945–53* (London, 1984).

19 Andrle in Lampert and Rittersporn, p. 40. Oreshin and Rubtsov also emphasise, in the context of the 1920s and 1930s, 'the string of "micro-fluctuations" which transformed a distinctively unbalanced system into something essentially different' in Kobo, pp. 601ff.

20 R. Medvedev, *Let History Judge* (2nd edn, London, 1990); D. Volkogonov, *Triumf i tragediya. I. V. Stalin; Politicheskii portret* (4 vols, Moscow, 1989), translated by H. Shukman as *Stalin. Triumph and Tragedy* (London, 1991). John Barber, review in *TLS*, 17 November 1989, p. 1258.

21 R. C. Tucker, *Stalin in Power: the Revolution from Above 1928–41* (New York and London, 1990). For criticism on this point see: M. Perrie, 'The Tsar, the Emperor, the Leader: Ivan the Terrible, Peter the Great and Anatolii Rybakov's Stalin', in: Lampert and Rittersporn, pp. 77–100. See also Chapter 8 of the present volume.

22 V. Andrle, in Lampert and Rittersporn, p. 34.

23 Oreshin and Rubtsov in Kobo, p. 548.

24 S. Fitzpatrick, 'New Perspectives on Stalinism' and 'Afterword: Revisionism Revisited', *Russian Review*, vol. 45, 1986, no. 4, pp. 357–73, 409–14.

25 Andrle in Lampert and Rittersporn, pp. 29–34; Oreshin and Rubtsov in Kobo, pp. 546–608, particularly 548–9.

26 M. Lewin, *The Making of the Soviet System* (London, 1985), particularly pp.3–45, 286–314.

27 For instance R. Conquest, 'Revisionizing Stalin's Russia', *Russian Review*, vol. 46 (1987), no. 4, p. 389, where he expresses his irritation at the over-simplification of his views.

28 Fitzpatrick, 'New Perspectives', pp. 357–74.

29 A. Getty, *The Origins of the Great Purges* (Cambridge, 1985).

30 Oreshin and Rubtsov in Kobo, pp. 579–80.

31 V. Andrle, *Workers in Stalin's Russia: Industry and Social Change in a Planned Economy* (London, 1988), pp. 202, 207.

32 S. Cohen, 'Stalin's Terror as Social History', *Russian Review*, vol. 45, 1986, no. 4, pp. 375–84, especially 383–4.

33 Kobo, pp. 579–80.

34 R. W. Thurston, 'Fear and Belief in the USSR's Great Terror: Responses to Arrest' and the reply by R. Conquest in *Slavic Review*, vol. 45, 1986, pp. 213–44; R. W. Thurston, 'The Soviet Family during the Great Terror', *Soviet Studies*, vol. 43, 1991, pp. 553–74.

35 Most recently, see S. Wheatcroft in *Soviet Studies*, vol. 42, 1990, no. 2, pp. 355–68; V. N. Zemskov, 'Zaklyuchennye, spetsposelentsy, ssylnoposelentsy, ssylnye, vyslannye. Statistiko-geograficheskii ocherk' [Prisoners, Special Settlers, Exiled Settlers, Exiles and Deportees: A Statistical–Geographical Survey], *Istoriya SSSR* [The History of the USSR], vol. 43, 1991, no. 5, pp.151–65; R. Conquest, 'Excess Deaths and Camp Numbers: Some Comments', *Istoriya SSSR*, vol. 43, 1991, no. 5, pp. 949–52.

36 Dunmore, pp. 126–45, 156.

2 *ONWARDS AND UPWARDS!*: THE ORIGINS OF THE LENIN CULT IN SOVIET CINEMA

1 The following collections of documents deserve attention: A. M. Gak (ed.), *Samoe vazhnoe iz vsekh iskusstv. Lenin o kino* [The Most Important of All the Arts. Lenin on Cinema] (2nd edn, Moscow, 1973); A. M. Gak and N. A. Glagoleva (eds), *Lunacharskii o kino* [Lunacharsky on Cinema] (Moscow, 1965); *Partiya o kino* [The Party on Cinema], produced by VNIIK [the All-Union Research Institute for the History of Cinema] under the rubric 'for staff use only' (3 vols, Moscow, 1980). The most serious monograph on the subject is V. Listov, *Lenin i kinematograf* [Lenin and Cinema] (Moscow, 1986).

2 Martemyan N. Ryutin (1890–1939) was the only leading Communist to organise an opposition to Stalin after 1930. He had held posts in Irkutsk, Daghestan and elsewhere and supported the Right Opposition. He was arrested in November 1930 but was soon released. In March 1932 he drew up the opposition 'Ryutin Platform'. He was arrested once more and shot in 1937. (Eds)

  Ryutin was the first chairman of Soyuzkino from February to November 1930. This little-known fact is confirmed by issues of the *Informatsionnyi byulleten' Soyuzkino* [Soyuzkino Information Bulletin] for the period, which are missing from the central archives but have been deposited in provincial archive collections. See the Chuvashkino papers in the Central State Archive of the Chuvash ASSR, 483/1/75. In assessing his appointment as 'the very modest position of chairman of the board of the unified film industry', recent Soviet biographers of Ryutin demonstrate their complete ignorance of the subject. See A. Vaksberg, 'Prochitav, peredai drugomu!' [When You've Read It, Pass It On!], *Yunost'* [Youth], 1988, no. 11 (November), p. 23.

3 Boris Shumyatsky is almost the only exception to the rule. He is the subject of R. Taylor, 'Boris Shumyatsky and Soviet Cinema in the 1930s: Ideology as Mass Entertainment', *Historical Journal of Film, Radio and Television*, vol. 6, no. 1, 1986, pp. 43–64; reprinted with minor alterations in: R. Taylor and I. Christie (eds), *Inside the Film Factory. New Approaches to Russian and Soviet Cinema* (London and New York, 1991), pp. 193–216.

4 The career of Semyon Dukelsky – who was later head of Soviet cinema for a short time – in the Cheka can be traced from *ChK na Ukraine* [The Cheka in the Ukraine] (Part 1, Kharkov, 1923; reprinted in the USA, 1989) and the reminiscences of Mikhail Romm in his book *Ustnye rasskazy* [Oral Tales] (Moscow, 1989).

5 Gak, p. 129. This decision was taken at the session of the Maly [Little] Sovnarkom (effectively Lenin's inner cabinet) on 16 May 1921. See also Gak, p. 190.

6 From the 'Explanatory Note' sent by Voyevodin to Sovnarkom on 20 February 1922; ibid., p. 86.
7 Letter from Voyevodin to Lenin, 10 June 1921; ibid., p. 35.
8 The VFKO materials connected with Voyevodin were first published in *Leninskii sbornik XXXVI* [Lenin Collection XXXVI] (Moscow, 1959); and partly in *Iskusstvo kino* [The Art of Cinema], 1960, no. 2. They are published more fully in Gak.
9 The Goskino papers in the Central State Archive of Literature and Art (hereafter TsGALI) *fond* 989 and the Glavpolitprosvet papers in the Central State Archive of the RSFSR (hereafter TsGA RSFSR) *fond* 2313.
10 TsGA RSFSR, 2313/6/302, p. 13. The film *Andrei Gudok* remained solely in negative form because there was no positive stock and was released only in October 1923. The history of the 'Auto-Cine-Base' is examined in detail in Listov, pp. 92–7.
11 TsGA RSFSR, 2313/6/302, p. 11.
12 The so-called 'export fund' of films included 130 feature films. See: Gak, pp. 75, 77; TsGA RSFSR, 2313/6/302, p. 12.
13 In Voyevodin's archive there is a dossier on a number of German film firms and documents confirming discussions that had taken place between their representatives and the Chairman of the Cinema Section in Germany, Gorky's wife, Maria Andreyeva; Central State Archive of the National Economy (hereafter TsGANKh) 160/1/374, pp. 1–3, 5. See also Voyevodin's letter of 19 September 1921 to the Deputy People's Commissar for Enlightenment, Litkens, in Gak, p. 77.
14 In 1905 Lenin wrote his seminal article 'Party Organisation and Party Literature', a rejection of the notion of 'art for art's sake' and a statement of the case for a utilitarian role for art in the socialist movement and in socialist society. This later served as an important part of the justification for the doctrine of Socialist Realism. (Eds)
15 See *Zritel'* [The Spectator], no. 1, 15 January 1922, p. 13.
16 Voyevodin's original contribution to the subject cannot be in doubt. In the 1950s one authoritative scholar wrote somewhat hesitantly: 'Nonetheless, it seems to me that the "mise-en-scène" of living historical figures has taken on central importance only with Stalin. Films about Lenin were not made until after his death, except by accident, whereas since the war Stalin has appeared on screen not just in newsreels but in historical films as well' (A. Bazin, 'Le mythe de Staline dans le cinéma soviétique', first published in *Esprit*, July–August 1950, reprinted with an appendix in: A. Bazin, *Qu'est-ce que le cinéma?* (Paris, 1958), pp. 75–89; translated into English by Georgia Gurrieri with an introduction by Dudley Andrew as 'The Stalin Myth in Soviet Cinema', *Film Criticism*, vol. 3, no. 1 (Fall 1978), pp. 17–26, and first published in Russian translation as 'Mif Stalina v sovetskom kino' [The Stalin Myth in Soviet Cinema], *Kinovedcheskie zapiski* [Scholarly Film Notes], 1988, no. 1, pp. 155–69). This quotation comes from p. 18 of the English translation.
17 There is confirmation of this in Voyevodin's papers. See, for instance, the unpublished memoir, 'Kak ya rabotal nad stsenariem *Vladimir Il'ich Lenin*' [How I Worked on the Script for *Vladimir Ilyich Lenin*], TsGANKh, 160/1/285.
18 It is remarkable that, among Soviet scholars who have been preoccupied with the content of the 'sacral' image of Lenin, the existence of this film has aroused no interest at all and was in fact regarded as semi-legendary. The circumstances surrounding the making of the film have been established by Kevin Brownlow

and are recounted in his book, *Behind the Mask of Innocence* (New York, 1990 and London, 1991), pp. 371–4. I should like to use this opportunity to express my heartfelt gratitude to Brownlow for drawing my attention to these materials in November 1990.

19 One of these games was Krasin's invitation to the sculptress Clare Sheridan, Winston Churchill's first cousin, to visit Moscow. She described the experience vividly in her diary of the journey, *Mayfair in Moscow* (New York, 1921). Of particular interest is her conversation with Lenin on the problems of art while she was working on a bust of him.

20 E. Drabkina, 'Arkhivazhneishee delo' [The Most Important Matter], in Gak, p. 143.

21 See I. Smirnov, 'Dragotsennye stroki' [Precious Lines], *Iskusstvo kino*, 1960, no. 2 (February), pp. 15–17; N. Zaitsev, *Pravda i poeziya leninskogo obraza* [The Veracity and Poetry of Lenin's Image] (Leningrad, 1967), pp. 12–13; G. Dolidze, *V. I. Lenin i voprosy kino* [Lenin and the Problems of Cinema] (Tbilisi, 1980), pp. 167–70.

22 See my 'Kinorabota osoboi vazhnosti' [A Film Work of Particular Importance], which includes the text of the script and a number of materials that have been used for the present article, in *Sovetskoe kino 20–kh godov* [Soviet Cinema in the 1920s] (Moscow, forthcoming).

23 The story-teller's prologue in the Russian tradition of orally transmitted folk-lore does not have anything to do with the plot of the fairy tale, but serves to put the audience in the right frame of mind for the tale. (Eds)

24 E. V. Pomerantseva, *Russkaya ustnaya proza* [Russian Oral Prose] (Moscow, 1985), p. 51. The reference here is to the final title in the second version of the script: 'Working hard here/In the Kremlin.'

25 The script reviewer (Krupskaya?) made a note in the margin: 'This won't do.' Almost a third of the episodes in the script that Voyevodin had submitted were rejected because they did not correspond to the facts or treated historical events too freely. Many of them were accompanied by the reviewer's remarks 'Impossible', 'This won't do', or by question marks. See TsGANKh, 160/1/17, pp. 11–19. See also n. 40.

26 D. S. Likhachev, *Chelovek v literature Drevnei Rusi* [Man in the Literature of Medieval Russia] (Moscow, 1970), pp. 77–9.

27 From reminiscences of Lenin read out at the celebration evening for Lenin's fiftieth birthday on 23 April 1920; TsGANKh, 160/1/17, pp. 27–9; published in *Proletarskaya revolyutsiya* [Proletarian Revolution], 1922, no. 6. There is an almost complete collection of Voyevodin's memoir material about Lenin in TsGANKh, 160/1/16. It is interesting that Voyevodin's visual impressions cited here almost exactly coincide in detail with the image left in the memory of another memoirist who, unlike Voyevodin, felt no sympathy for Lenin when he saw him for the first time in April 1917: 'I saw Lenin standing on the platform, a bald man with a large pumpkin-shaped head, who felt at ease on a platform and was responding to various questions and accusations that rained down on him from the audience' (N. Evreinov, 'Vospominaniya. 1916–1920' [Memoirs 1916–20], Central State Archive of the October Revolution (TsGAOR), 5881/2/328, p. 22; Russian Historical Archive Abroad, no. 7866).

28 From speeches delivered at an evening meeting of Old Bolsheviks on 7 February 1924, dedicated to Lenin's memory; TsGANKh, 160/1/17, pp. 53–4. Other memoirists have also noted this remarkable characteristic of Lenin's political tactics with admiration. See, for instance, M. Gorienko, 'V noch' na 1918-i' [On the Eve of 1918], *Ogonek* [The Torch], 1957, no. 1, p. 3.

29 *Ekran* [the Screen], no. 9, 22–24 November 1921, p. 10.

30 The mesmeric effect, associated with supreme power, that Lenin exerted on those around him has also been noted by his Western biographers; see L. Fischer, *Zhizn' Lenina* [Lenin's Life] (New York and London, 1964), pp. 904–6. English version: *The Life of Lenin* (London, 1965), pp. 624–5.

31 TsGANKh, 160/1/17, reverse of p. 103.

32 Nikolay Valentinov (pen-name of N. V. Volsky), *Encounters with Lenin* (trans. P. Rosta and B. Pierce) (Oxford, 1968), pp. 45–6.

33 Istpart is the acronym for *Komissiya po sobiraniyu i izucheniyu materialov po istorii Oktyabr'skoi revolyutsii i istorii Kommunisticheskoi partii* [The Commission for the Collection and Study of Materials on the History of the October Revolution and the History of the Communist Party]. TsGANKh, 160/1/294, p. 274.

34 TsGANKh, 160/1/48. See Olminsky's article 'O t. Lenine' [On Comrade Lenin] in the newspaper *Sotsial-Demokrat* [Social-Democrat], 26 May 1917. For more details, see N. Tumarkin, *Lenin Lives! The Lenin Cult in Soviet Russia* (Cambridge, MA, and London, 1983), especially Chapter 3, 'Lenin in Bolshevik Myth, 1917–1922', pp. 64–111. For a list of these publications, see pp. 278–81. See also N. Tumarkin, 'The Myth of Lenin during the Civil War', in A. Gleason *et al.* (eds), *Bolshevik Culture: Experiment and Order in the Russian Revolution* (Bloomington, IN, 1985), pp. 77–92. In Voyevodin's archive there is a small collection of printed sources from the period that he probably used in the process of his work on the script.

35 Mikhail Ye. Koltsov (1898–1942) was a writer and journalist who frequently contributed to the Party newspaper *Pravda*.

36 M. Kol'tsov, *Oktyabr'* (Moscow, 1927), pp. 52–3. He is generally considered to be one of the foremost organisers of the Soviet film industry; see, for instance: V. S. Listov, 'Mikhail Kol'tsov i "Desyataya muza" ' [Mikhail Koltsov and the "Tenth Muse" '], *Kinovedcheskie zapiski*, no. 5 (Moscow, 1990), pp. 41–52.

37 'On P. I. Voyevodin's instructions as early as 1921 Comrade Svilova and I began work on selecting the negatives that showed V. I. Lenin in connection with my proposed script on V. I. Lenin' (G. Boltyanskii, *Lenin i Kino* [Lenin and Cinema] (Moscow, 1965), p. 76).

38 Quoted from the typewritten copy, which differs in insignificant ways from the version published in Gak, pp. 100–1; TsGANKh, 160/1/10, p. 1.

39 TsGANKh, 160/1/18, p. 3.

40 Listov, pp. 145–7.

41 ibid., p. 146.

42 TsGANKh, 160/1/41, p. 7.

43 ibid., p. 8.

44 M. Geller, 'Pervoe predosterezhenie – udar khlystom' [The First Warning – A Flick of the Whip], republished in *Voprosy filosofii* [Problems of Philosophy], 1990, no. 9.

45 TsGANKh, 160/1/10, p. 2.

46 ibid.

47 N. Lebedev, *Ocherk istorii kino SSSR. Nemoe kino, 1918–1934* [An Outline History of the Cinema of the USSR. Silent Cinema, 1918–1934] (2nd edn, Moscow, 1965), p. 127.

48 Grigori M. Boltyansky (1885–1953), who witnessed the event, found some difficulty in explaining why Lenin liked this film and could only suggest as a possible reason 'the really powerful class approach' of the director to the

production. See Boltyanskii, pp. 42–4. All kinds of genre characteristics put Lenin off films. It seems that the evolution of cinema from the *lubok* to the melodrama in the course of the first half of the 1910s had passed him by. The Ulyanov family correspondence serves to confirm this. In March 1914 in a letter to her mother-in-law Krupskaya expressed the 'family' verdict on a film that they had seen whose primary interest was political. 'We saw in the cinema here *The Beilis Affair*. (They've turned it into a melodrama.)' (V. I. Lenin, *Polnoe sobranie sochinenii* [Complete Collected Works], (55 vols, Moscow, 1971–5), vol. 55, p. 353).

49 We find this self-characterisation in Krupskaya's letters from emigration. In December 1913 in a letter to her mother-in-law she, expressing as always the 'family' view on matters of everyday life, interpreted it in the following way: 'The cinemas here are awfully ridiculous, they all show five-act melodramas . . . We all joke here that we have a party of "cinemists" (those who like to go to the cinema), "anticinemists" . . . and a party of "ambulists" [*progulisty*], whose aim is always to make off for a walk.' Lenin, in accordance with this jocular but, as always, political-sounding classification, was a decided anticinemist and a 'confirmed walkist' (Lenin, pp. 346–7). It should be noted that at the time public opinion in various countries was hotly debating the question of longer cinema performances in view of the greater length of films, which had been made possible by advances in cinema technology and an improvement in projection quality.

50 A. V. Lunacharskii, 'Beseda s V. I. Leninym o kino', republished in Gak, pp. 163–4; translated as 'Conversation with Lenin' in *FF*, pp. 56–7.

51 *FF*, p. 57. On 1 March 1922 Sovnarkom had enquired, 'Who in Narkompros is going to take charge of cinema: Voyevodin or someone else?' (Gak, p. 88).

52 TsGANKh, 160/1/17, p. 9.

53 In the course of correction the script was reduced to two reels.

54 TsGANKh, 160/1/160, p. 7. *Svobodnaya Rossiya* [Free Russia] was the news-reel issued under the auspices of the Provisional Government in 1917 and *Kino-nedelya* [Cine-Week], written and directed by Dziga Vertov, was the VFKO equivalent issued between June 1918 and December 1919. Yelizaveta I. Svilova (1900–76) was Vertov's wife and professional assistant.

55 ibid., p. 8.

56 ibid., p. 6.

57 See above, n. 37.

58 See Voyevodin's complaint to the Chief Engineer of the Regional Council about the unlawful alterations to the Goskino building (Maly Gnezdnikovsky, 7) undertaken by its new leaders in 1925 (Moscow City Architectural History Archive, Tverskaya section, file no. 202).

59 Another script by Voyevodin, 'Salavat Yulayev', which he submitted in turn to the studios in Moscow and Leningrad, also dates from 1925. It too remained unfilmed.

60 'Ivanych', 'O Krasnom Pinkertone' [About a Red Pinkerton], *Kino. Dvukhne-del'nik Obshchestva kinodeyatelei* [Cinema. Fortnightly of the Society of Film-makers], 1923, no. 5 (9), pp. 7–8. This article prefaced the publication of an extract from Nikolai Aseyev's script 'Chem eto konchitsya' [How It Will End], which Lev Kuleshov made into the film *The Extraordinary Adventures of Mr West in the Land of the Bolsheviks* [Neobychainye priklyucheniya mis-tera Vesta v strane bol'shevikov, 1924]. The style of the article and its familiar pathos lead one to 'suspect' that Voyevodin was the author and that he had decided to put his project forward in a new guise, in the spirit of Bukharin's

unadopted proposal for a 'red detective story'. On this genre, which arose in Soviet art in the first half of the 1920s, see my article, 'K istorii odnoi kinoutopii' [Towards a History of One Cinema Utopia], *Kinostsenarii* [Film Script], 1989, no. 5 (May), p. 157; see also *Kinovedcheskie zapiski*, no. 8, pp. 189–92.

61 TsGANKh, 160/1/294, pp. 274–6. Mikhail Olminsky (1863–1933) was already dead when this letter was written in 1939, which is why it was safe for Voyevodin to cite his name.

62 *Obrazy Lenina i Stalina v kino* [Images of Lenin and Stalin in Cinema] (Moscow, 1939), p. 3.

3   THE 1930s AND 1940s: CINEMA IN CONTEXT

1 This paper is based upon materials brought together by a group of scholars at VNIIK [the All-Union Research Institute for the History of Cinema] in Moscow, which we hope to publish in English under the title *The Film Process*. The most useful sources are *Za bol'shoe kinoiskusstvo* [For a Great Cinema Art] (Moscow, 1935); E. G. Lemberg, *Kinopromyshlennost' SSSR. Ekonomika sovetskoi kinematografii* [The Cinema Industry of the USSR. The Economics of Soviet Cinema] (Moscow, 1930); B. Z. Shumyatskii, *Kinematografiya millionov* [Cinema for the Millions] (Moscow 1935).

2 Arina Rodionovna was Pushkin's peasant nurse who conveyed to him the lore and language of the countryside. (Eds)

3 Eisenstein occupied a room in the flat belonging to his childhood friend Maxim Strauch in the street called Chistye Prudy in central Moscow before moving into his own flat in the Mosfilm complex at Potylikha on the outskirts of the city. (Eds)

4 Of course those people free from what Hitler called the 'chimera of so-called conscience' prospered more in Soviet society as the emerging Party-state carried out 'negative selection'.

5 ZIF was the publishing house 'Zemlya i fabrika' [Land and Factory] which from 1922 to 1930 specialised in publishing literature in translation aimed at workers and peasants. (Eds)

6 The 'GTO complex' was a physical training programme. The Russian initials GTO derive from 'Gotov k trude i oborone SSSR' [Ready for Labour and the Defence of the USSR]. (Eds)

7 *Yozh* [The Hedgehog] and *Chizh* [The Siskin] were popular and innovative children's magazines published in Leningrad. *Yozh* was published between 1928 and 1935 and was edited among others by Samuil Marshak and included stories such as those of Marshak and Kornei Chukovsky which have since become classics of Russian children's literature. (Eds)

8 I have asked myself why Andrei Platonov was such a 'blank spot' for me, such a 'discovery', when Russian poetry of the 'Silver Age', the works of Mikhail Bulgakov and even the names of pre-Revolutionary philosophers were little more than adjuncts to what I already knew. Then I realised that Platonov – at least nominally – belonged to that Soviet 'proletarian' branch of literature. This was enough for him to be dismissed *a priori*.

9 This is reminiscent of Eisenstein's dismissal of such 'petty-bourgeois' culture in 1922 with the term 'heliotrope auntie'. See S. M. Eisenstein, *Selected Works. Vol. 1: Writings, 1922–34* (London and Bloomington, IN, 1988), p. 32. (Eds)

10 Compare this with the similar appropriation of Goethe and Schiller by Nazi culture.

11 The rationing system for food and clothes dated from the Civil War period and continued as a method of patronage for the *nomenklatura* until the collapse of Soviet power in 1991. (Eds)

12 On the architecture and symbolism of this Exhibition see V. Papernyi, *Kul'tura 'dva'* [Culture 'Two'] (Ann Arbor, MI, 1985). (Eds)

13 The reference here is to the method of prefabricated building construction used for the façades of the large public buildings of the Stalin era, of which the 'wedding-cake' architecture of high-rise edifices like Moscow State University is one instance. (Eds)

14 Translation by Alan Bodger. Kozma Prutkov was a pseudonym created in the 1850s by a collective of satirical poets including A. M. and V. M. Zhemchuzhnik and Count A. K. Tolstoi. They wrote the biography of the fictitious Kozma Prutkov, 'romantic poet and well-intentioned bureaucrat'. Medyn is a village not far from Moscow. (Eds)

15 B. Brecht, *Die Dreigroschenprozeß. Grosse kommentierte Berliner und Frankfurter Ausgabe* [The *Threepenny Opera* Trial. The Great Annotated Berlin and Frankfurt Edition], vol. 21 (Frankfurt am Main, 1992), pp. 472–3. (Eds)

16 From an anonymous report written in 1927, in the uncatalogued Sovkino files held at the Central State Archive of the October Revolution [TsGAOR].

17 ibid. In fact a model of this sort was achieved in the Third Reich. Although there was total 'indoctrination' under firm Nazi Party control, only a small number of films were overtly 'ideological', given Goebbels's view that 'Propaganda becomes ineffective the moment we become aware of it'. Production was orientated basically towards entertainment as in the old UFA of the Weimar period: the old economic structure still functioned. The monopolisation of the German film industry required a full ten years and was only achieved in 1943, but by then it was already too late.

18 The decline from seventy-four films in 1932 to twenty-nine in 1933 was not accidental. It was a result of Party criticisms. (MT)

See A. I. Rubailo, *Partiinoe rukovodstvo razvitiem kinoiskusstva (1928–1937gg.)* [Party Leadership in the Development of Cinema, 1928–37] (Moscow, 1976). There is a table showing film production from 1918 to 1941 in *FF*, p. 424. (Eds)

19 These films were Semyon Timoshenko's *To Live* [Zhit', 1933]; Vladimir Vainshtok's *The Glory of Peace* [Slava mira, 1932]; the Georgian film about a German kolkhoz settlement in the Caucasus, *The Red Flag* [Rote Fahne, alternative title: *Shakir*, 1932]; Lev Kuleshov's *Gorizont* [1933]; *Heil, Moscow!* [Heil, Moskau!, 1932]; Yuri Zhelyabuzhsky's *Prosperity* [Prosperiti, 1933]. (MT)

Some of these films are discussed in R. Taylor and K. R. M. Short, 'Soviet Cinema and the International Menace, 1928–1939', *Historical Journal of Film, Radio and Television*, vol. 6, no. 2, October 1986, pp. 131–59. (Eds)

20 These figures are not just for one year but for the whole time that the film was in distribution.

21 It was the Cheka under Felix Dzerzhinsky that had taken on the task of rooting out child homelessness, which was the subject of this film.

22 Elsewhere we have come across a reminder that *The Path to Life* achieved a record profit figure for a Soviet film: around 15 million roubles for the end of 1931 and 1932. Apparently included in this figure are the expenses of the cinema network, which the studio did not include in its own accounts.

23 Cf. Chapter 5.

24 See above, Chapter 2, n. 16.

25 Unfortunately we do not yet have the statistical details for *Chapayev*.

26 This direct link with the American mass cinema is obvious from the history of the adventure film *The Thirteen* [Trinadtsat', 1937], scripted by Iosif Prut and directed by Mikhail Romm, which Stalin personally ordered to be modelled on John Ford's *The Lost Patrol* [USA, 1934]. Unfortunately the statistics for this film have also not yet been traced.

27 Translated in *FF*, pp. 334–5.

28 ibid., p. 335.

29 ibid.

30 Hermann Kosterlitz emigrated in 1936 to Hollywood and took the name Henry Koster. (Eds)

31 Vodka had been a monopoly even under the tsars. Stalin drew the analogy with cinema at the Fifteenth Party Congress in 1927. See R. Taylor, *The Politics of the Soviet Cinema, 1917–1929* (Cambridge, 1979), p. 105. (Eds)

32 In the course of our researches we have elaborated a system of contexts – domestic political, international political, cultural, cinematic – against which background the film process develops. These contain certain contradictory factors which caused this destabilisation at the end of the 1930s.

33 In accounting for this box-office success we should not overlook the audience's interest in the portrayal of a legendary figure and the quasi-authentic manner in which Boris Shchukin achieved it. This remarkable actor offered a humane, even worldly, version of Lenin.

34 Something similar may also be observed at that time in German cinema: Veit Harlan's *The Great King* [Der grosse König, 1942] and his *Jew Süss* [Jud Süss, 1940] were overtly ideological films and had high distribution figures that demonstrate the level of the 'indoctrination' of society. Nonetheless, in box-office terms, the absolute champion in the Third Reich was Rolf Hansen's melodrama *The Great Love* [Die grosse Liebe, 1942], a musical starring Zarah Leander that was the product of market supply.

35 This refers to a theme of Vasili Grossman's novel of the 1941–5 war, *Zhizn' i sud'ba* [Life and Fate]. It was completed in 1960, first published abroad (in Lausanne in 1980) and then in Russia in successive issues of the journal *Oktyabr'* [October] from 1988, no. 3 (March).

36 Cf. n. 34 above.

37 The basic corpus of everyday distribution right through to the 1950s remained, of course, the films of the 1930s. There is a list of the Nazi films released in the USSR after the war in the booklet prepared by Maya Turovskaya and others for the retrospective held during the 1989 Moscow Film Festival, *Kino totalitarnoi epokhi 1933–45 / Filme der totalitären Epoche, 1933–45* [Films of the Totalitarian Epoch, 1933–45] (Moscow, 1989), pp. 45–6. (Eds)

4 SOVIET CINEMA IN THE AGE OF STALIN

1 The section on the censorship apparatus is from my book *Cinema and Soviet Society, 1917–1953* (Cambridge, 1992).

2 *FF*, p. 423.

3 *Repertuarnyi ukazatel'. Deistvitel'nyi ukazatel' kinokartin* [The Repertoire Guide. A Current Guide to Films] (Moscow, 1943).

4 *Repertuarnyi ukazatel'* (Moscow, 1936).

5 *Iskusstvo kino* [The Art of Cinema], 1936, no. 11 (November), pp. 36–40.

6 K. Clark, *The Soviet Novel: History as Ritual* (Chicago, 1981).

7 All of the following data are taken from: *Sovetskie khudozhestvennye fil'my*.

Annotirovannyi katalog [Soviet Feature Films. An Annotated Catalogue] (4 vols, Moscow, 1960–8).

8 On these films see: K. R. M. Short and R. Taylor, 'Soviet Cinema and the International Menace, 1928–1939', *Historical Journal of Film, Radio and Television*, 1986, vol. 6, no. 2, pp. 131–59.

9 A. Dubrovskii, *Iskusstvo kino*, 1938, no. 1 (January), p. 23.

10 *Sovetskoe kino* [Soviet Cinema], 1933, no. 5/6 (May/June), p. 1.

11 N. Otten, 'Snova ob "emotsional'nom" stsenarii' [On the 'Emotional Scenario' Once Again], *Iskusstvo kino*, 1937, no. 5 (May), p. 30.

12 B. Z. Shumyatskii, 'Tvorcheskie voprosy templana' [Creative Questions of the Thematic Plan], *Sovetskoe kino*, 1933, no. 12 (December), p. 3.

13 'Partiya proveryaet svoi ryady' [The Party is Examining Its Own Ranks], editorial in *Sovetskoe kino*, 1933, no. 10 (October), p. 3.

14 K. Yukov, 'Doklad po soveshchanii kinodramaturgov' [Report to the Conference of Film Dramatists], *Sovetskoe kino*, 1934, no. 8/9 (August/September), p. 10.

15 'Partiya proveryaet . . .'.

16 A. I. Rubailo, *Partiinoe rukovodstvo razvitiem kinoiskusstva 1928–1937gg.* [Party Leadership of the Development of Cinema, 1928–37] (Moscow, 1976), pp. 130–7. Information concerning censorship organisations comes from this book.

17 G. Ermolaev, 'Chto tormozit razvitie sovetskogo kino' [What Is Holding Up the Development of Soviet Cinema], *Pravda*, 9 January 1938, p. 4; translated in *FF*, p. 386.

18 E. Sinko, *Egy regeny regenye. Moszkvai Naplojegzetek, 1935–1937* [*The Novel of a Novel. Moscow Diary, 1935–1937*] (Budapest, 1985), p. 523. On Balázs see also J. Zsuffa, *Béla Balázs: The Man and the Artist* (Berkeley, CA, 1987).

19 ibid., p. 290.

20 Shumyatskii, p. 124.

21 A few examples must suffice. Among the victims were: Boris Babitsky, director of Mezhrabpom and then Mosfilm; Margarita Barskaya, actress, scenarist and director; Yevgeniya Gorkushka-Shirshova, actress; Alexander Kurbas, actor and director; Vladimir Nilsen, scenarist; Adrian Piotrovsky, critic and scenarist; Yelena Sokolovskaya, director of Mosfilm; and Boris Shumyatsky; see: *Sovetskii ekran* [Soviet Screen], 1989, no. 1, p. 23.

22 A. Latyshev, 'Stalin i kino', in: Yu. P. Senokosov (ed.), *Surovaya drama naroda* [The Severe Drama of the People] (Moscow, 1989), pp. 494–5.

23 On the cult of the Party membership card see, for instance, Z. Vas, 'A kelet-Europai barati kapcsolatok' [Fraternal Contacts in Eastern Europe], *Latohatar* [Horizon], June 1989, p. 64.

24 I. A. Pyr'ev, *Izbrannye proizvedeniya* [Selected Works] (Moscow, 1978), vol. 1, pp. 74–84.

25 J. Leyda, *Kino: A History of the Russian and Soviet Film* (London and New York, 1960), p. 348.

26 The story first appeared in *Izvestiya* [The News]. It was reprinted in *Iskusstvo kino*, 1937, no. 10, pp. 15–16; translated in *FF*, pp. 383–5.

27 On Dovzhenko see V. Kepley, *In the Service of the State: The Cinema of A. Dovzhenko* (Madison, WI, 1986).

28 ibid., p. 494. Zhelyabov was a nineteenth-century revolutionary; Shakhov was the character based on Kirov.

29 *Repertuarnyi ukazatel'* (Moscow, 1936). It should be remembered that the country lacked projectors capable of showing sound films and that there was therefore already a shortage of silent films at the time.

30 *Ezhegodnik* [Yearbook], 1938, pp. 299–300.
31 *Kino* [Cinema], 24 March 1937, pp. 1–2; 11 April 1937, p. 1.

5 RED STARS, POSITIVE HEROES AND PERSONALITY CULTS

1 The conference papers not included in the present volume were gathered together in June 1991 in a special issue of the Historical Journal of Film, Radio and Television, vol. 11, no. 2, entitled 'Russian and Soviet Cinema: Continuity and Change' and edited by Richard Taylor and Derek Spring.

2 This was originally written before the attempted coup in August 1991, which did of course bring the entire edifice crumbling down upon their heads.

3 *Trinadtsatyi s''ezd RKP(b), 23–31 maya 1924 goda. Stenographicheskii otchet* [Thirteenth Party Congress of the RCP(b), 23–31 May 1924. Stenographic Report] (Moscow, 1924), p. 132.

4 N. S. Khrushchev, *The 'Secret' Speech* (Nottingham, 1976), p. 72. Khrushchev also mentions the role of film in the promotion of the personality cult (pp. 57, 71).

5 The editors of Stalin's *Collected Works* were, at the time of the dictator's death, compiling the fourteenth volume. For 1940 they were unable to find anything written by Stalin other than three sets of notes on three separate film scripts. See A. Latyshev, 'Vzyat' eto delo v svoi ruki' [Take This Matter into Our Own Hands], *Sovetskii ekran* [Sovit Screen], 1988, no. 22, p. 14.

6 There will now, of course, be a third such key transition, from Soviet to post-Soviet cinema.

7 Yakov A. Protazanov (1881–1945) was a prolific film director, whose films included *The Queen of Spades* [Pikovaya Dama, 1916], *Father Sergius* [Otets Sergii 1918], *Aelita* [1924], *The Three Millions Trial* [Protsess o trekh million-akh,1926], *The Forty-First* [Sorok pervyi, 1927], *The Feast of St Jorgen* [Prazdnik svyatovo Iorgena, 1929], *Tommy* [Tommi, 1931], *The Girl with No Dowry* [Bespridannitsa, 1937], *Salavat Yulayev* [1941] and *Nasreddin in Bukhara* [Nazreddin v Bukhare, 1943]. See also the contributions by Ian Christie and Denise Youngblood in R. Taylor and I. Christie (eds), *Inside the Film Factory: New Approaches to Russian and Soviet Cinema* (London and New York, 1991), pp. 80–123; and I. Christie and J. Graffy (eds), *Yakov Protazanov: A Career in Russian Cinema* (London, 1992).

8 Yuri A. Zhelyabuzhsky (1888–1955) began his cinema career in 1915 and directed, *inter alia*, *The Cigarette Girl from Mosselprom* [Papirosnitsa iz Mosselproma, 1924], *The Station Master* [Kollezhskii registrator, 1925], *Prosperity* [Prosperiti, 1933] and two films about peat extraction [1938–9]. Towards the end of his life he made several films about the life and work of Russian artists, including Ilya Repin [1946], Vasili Surikov [1947], Ivan Kramskoy [1951], Viktor Vasnetsov [1952] and Valentin Serov [1953].

9 Konstantin V. Eggert (1883–1955) directed *The Bear's Wedding* [Medvezhya svad'ba, 1926], *The Alien Woman* [Chuzhaya, 1927], *The Ice House* [Ledyanoi dom, 1928] and *The Lame Gentleman* [Khromoi barin, 1929]. He was also a major shareholder in the Mezhrabpom studio, which produced his films.

10. Formalism began as an aesthetic movement concerned primarily, as the name suggests, with the exploration of suitable new forms for Revolutionary artistic activity. From the late 1920s onwards it was increasingly used as a pejorative term to attack those who, so the allegation went, were interested in form rather than content and were therefore not fulfilling their Revolutionary duty as

artists. By the middle of the 1930s the term had become little more than an insult – but one with potentially fatal consequences.

11 See for example E. Lemberg, *Kinopromyshlennost' SSSR* [The Cinema Industry of the USSR] (Moscow, 1930), p. 71.

12 See the essay on 'Futurism' in L. D. Trotsky, *Literature and Revolution* (Ann Arbor, MI, 1960), p. 137.

13 In 1925 the Antaeus cinema in Moscow offered an eight-piece orchestra in the auditorium and a trio in the foyer; the Ars, on Tverskaya, offered a symphony orchestra with thirty-six players in the auditorium and a seven-piece band in the foyer; the Belgium, on the other hand, provided only a piano in the auditorium, but an orchestra in the foyer, while the Great Silent [Velikii nemoi] had a piano in the auditorium and a Romanian four-piece orchestra in the foyer (*Teatral'naya Moskva. Teatr – muzyka – kino: Putevoditel'* [Theatrical Moscow. Theatre – Music – Cinema: A Guide] (Moscow, 1926), pp.187–203). I am indebted to Rashit Yangirov for drawing this source to my attention. Mikhail Boitler, a cinema owner who wrote a book on the subject of 'cultured cinemas', argued that, 'The foyer must not be a place where people wait idly for the show, a place that reminds the patron of a railway platform' (M. Boitler, *Kul'turnyi kino-teatr* [The Cultured Cinema Theatre] (Moscow, 1930), p. 4).

14 In 1927 99% of cinemas in the Russian Federation were run by representative organs of the state or Soviet society: 40% of 'commercial' cinemas belonged to trade unions, 35% to Narkompros and its local organs, 21% to other state and social organisations, 3% to Sovkino (the centralised state cinema organisation) and only 1% to private individuals such as Boitler.

15 G. M. Boltyanskii (ed.), *Lenin i kino* [Lenin and Cinema] (Moscow/Leningrad, 1925), pp. 16–19; translated in *FF*, pp. 56–7.

16 See, for instance, the Party Conference resolution translated in *FF*, pp. 208–15.

17 See above, n. 13. In his introduction Boitler remarked, 'The cinema theatre must help not only to raise the general cultural level of the patron but to instil more cultured habits into his everyday life' (Boitler, p. 4).

18 *Zhizn' iskusstva* [Life of Art], 24 January 1928; translated in *FF*, pp. 195–7.

19 Thematic plans had originated in Sovkino in the mid 1920s but became a weapon of political control in the 1930s. On the introduction and function of Party cells see A. I. Rubailo, *Partiinoe rukovodstvo razvitiem kinoiskusstva (1928–1937gg.)* [Party Leadership in the Development of Cinema, 1928–37] (Moscow, 1976).

20 British documentary film-makers in the Second World War complained bitterly that their films were given only non-theatrical distribution, where, in the official view, they could do no harm. See, for instance, A. Aldgate and J. Richards, *Britain Can Take It: The British Cinema in the Second World War* (Oxford, 1986), p. 8; and P. Rotha, *Rotha on the Film* (London, 1958), p. 229.

21 V. Sutyrin, 'Ot intelligentskikh illyuzii k real'noi deistvitel'nosti', *Proletarskoe kino* [Proletarian Cinema], no. 5/6 (May/June) 1931, pp. 14–24.

22 Quoted in *FF*, p. 259.

23 Extracts from the conference proceedings are translated in *FF*, pp. 348–55.

24 On Shumyatsky see R. Taylor, 'Ideology as Mass Entertainment: Boris Shumyatsky and Soviet Cinema in the 1930s', in Taylor and Christie, *Inside the Film Factory*, pp. 193–216.

25 *A. Khokhlova* (Moscow, 1926). Eisenstein's article 'Kak ni stranno – o Khokhlovoi' (pp. 5–9) is translated as 'However Odd – Khokhlova!' in S. M. Eisenstein,

Selected Works. Vol. 1: Writings, 1922–34 (ed. and trans. R. Taylor) (London and Bloomington, IN, 1988), pp. 71–3.

26 Igor V. Ilyinsky (1901–87) also acted with the Meyerhold Theatre. His films from the 1920s included *Aelita* and *The Cigarette Girl from Mosselprom* [both 1924], *Miss Mend* and *The Three Millions Trial* [both 1926], *The Kiss of Mary Pickford* [Potselui Meri Pickford, 1927], *The Doll with Millions* [Kukla s millionami, 1928], *The Feast of St Jorgen* [1930]. The pamphlets were by the poet Vadim Shershenevich (1927) and the film director Sergei Yutkevich (1929).

27 Nina Lee, in an interview with the author, 1985.

28 Details in *Sovetskie khudozhestvennye fil'my. Annotirovannyi katalog* [Soviet Feature Films. An Annotated Catalogue], vol. 1 (Moscow, 1961), pp. 219, 242.

29 The notion of 'Pickfordisation' lay at the heart of the Lef group's objections to the depiction of Lenin in Eisenstein's *October* [Oktyabr', 1927] and their promotion of the 'fixing of fact'. See *FF*, pp. 184–7, 225–32; and *Screen Reader 1: Cinema / Ideology / Politics* (London, 1977), pp. 290–332.

30 Interview with Medvedkin in Taylor and Christie, *Inside the Film Factory*, p. 169.

31 On *Aelita* see I. Christie, 'Down to Earth: *Aelita* Relocated', in ibid., pp. 80–102.

32 See Yu. Tsivian (ed.), *Silent Witnesses. Russian Films 1908–19* (Pordenone and London, 1989).

33 S. Eisenstein, V. Pudovkin and G. Alexandrov, 'Zayavka' [Statement], *Zhizn' iskusstva*, 5 August 1929, pp. 4–5; translated in *FF*, pp. 234–5.

34 B. Z. Shumyatskii, *Kinematografiya millionov* [A Cinema for the Millions] (Moscow, 1935), p. 148, cited in Taylor and Christie, *Inside the Film Factory*, p. 212.

35 *Kinoslovar'* [Cinema Dictionary], vol. 1 (Moscow, 1966), col. 129.

36 S. Nikolaevich, 'Poslednii seans, ili Sud'ba beloi zhenshchiny v SSSR' [The Last Show, or the Fate of a White Woman in the USSR], *Ogonek* [The Torch], 1992, no. 4, p. 22.

37 ibid., p. 24.

38 ibid., p. 23.

39 See p. 108.

40 *Kinoslovar'*, vol. 2 (Moscow, 1970), col. 892.

41 His unfinished writings of that period are gathered together in English in S. M. Eisenstein, *Selected Works. Vol. 2: Towards a Theory of Montage* (ed. and trans. M. Glenny, co-ed. R. Taylor) (London, 1991).

42 See p. 44.

43 See Chapter 2.

44 N. Tumarkin, *Lenin Lives! The Lenin Cult in Soviet Russia* (Cambridge, MA, 1983), pp. 248–51.

45 To use the analogy deployed so effectively by Katerina Clark in her *The Soviet Novel. History as Ritual* (2nd edn, Chicago, 1985), pp. 16–17.

46 There is an analysis of this film by Natasha Nusinova in *Iskusstvo kino* [The Art of Cinema], 1991, no. 12 (December), pp. 162–4.

47 See Chapter 7.

48 A. Dovzhenko, 'Uchitel'' i drug khudozhnika', *Iskusstvo kino*, 1937, no. 10 (October), pp. 15–16; translated in *FF*, pp. 383–5.

49 See Chapter 8.

6 FORBIDDEN FILMS OF THE 1930s

1 See the translations in *FF*, pp. 56–7.
2 *Kino* [Cinema], 17 January 1928.
3 B. S. Ol'khovyi (ed.), *Puti kino. Pervoe vsesoyuznoe partiinoe soveshchanie po kinomatografii* [The Paths of Cinema. The First All-Union Party Conference on Cinema] (Moscow, 1929), p. 430. The resolutions of the conference are translated in *FF*, pp. 208–15.
4 Ol'khovyi, p. 228.
5 ibid.
6 *Kino*, 15 May 1928.
7 'Davno pora!', *Kino*, 15 May 1928.
8 V. S. Listov (ed.), *Sovetskoe kino (1917–1978). Resheniya partii i pravitel'stva o kino. Sbornik dokumentov. Tom 1: 1917–1936* [Soviet Cinema, 1917–78. Party and Government Resolutions on Cinema. A Collection of Documents. Vol. 1: 1917–36] (Moscow, 1979), pp. 92–4.
9 On Shumyatsky, see R. Taylor, 'Ideology as Mass Entertainment: Boris Shumyatsky and Soviet Cinema in the 1930s', in R. Taylor and I. Christie (eds), *Inside the Film Factory. New Approaches to Russian and Soviet Cinema* (London and New York, 1991), pp. 193–216.
10 TsGALI, 2496/2/13 pp. 140–1.
11 Translated in *FF*, p. 325.
12 Listov, pp. 132–3.
13 'Grubaya skhema vmesto istoricheskoi praydy', *Pravda*, 13 February 1936.
14 Decision of the Ukrainfilm Trust on the banning of the film *A Severe Young Man*, 10 June 1936. See *Kino*, 28 July 1936.
15 D. Mar'yan, *V otryve ot deistvitel'nosti* [Out of Touch with Reality]. See *Kino*, 24 March 1937.
16 This point is borne out in B. Eisenschitz, 'A Fickle Man, or Portrait of Boris Barnet as a Soviet Director', in Taylor and Christie, *Inside the Film Factory*, pp. 151–64.

7 'WE WERE BORN TO TURN A FAIRY TALE INTO REALITY': GRIGORI ALEXANDROV'S *THE RADIANT PATH*

I want to thank Artyom Demenok, Marina and Anatoli Maximov and all the employees of the Central Cinema Museum in Moscow for their assistance with the research for this paper.

1 M. Turovskaya, 'I. A. Pyr'ev i ego muzykal'nye komedii. K probleme zhanra' [I. A. Pyriev and His Musical Comedies. On the Problem of Genre], *Kino-vedcheskie zapiski* [Scholarly Film Notes], no. 1, Moscow, 1988, pp. 111–46. The article is subtitled 'Stat'ya snyataya s polki' [An Article Taken Off the Shelf].
2 Stakhanovism was the movement named after the Ukrainian miner Alexei Stakhanov who in 1935 set a productivity record by devising a more efficient system of labour. Workers throughout the country followed him, introducing the spirit of competition and an incentive payment scheme into Soviet industry. The labour élite, *Stakhanovtsy*, enjoyed high official esteem and an exceptionally high standard of living and, for this and other reasons, tended to be unpopular with rank-and-file workers.
3 R. Dyer, 'Entertainment and Utopia', in R. Altman (ed.), *Genre: The Musical*

(London, 1981), pp. 187–8.
4 R. Altman, 'The American Film Musical: Paradigmatic Structure and Mediatory Function', in ibid.
5 TsGALI, 2450/2/1295.
6 Dyer, pp. 187–8.
7 Turovskaya, p. 132.
8 B. Bettelheim, *The Uses of Enchantment* (Harmondsworth, 1978).
9 TsGALI, 2450/2/1295.
10 Bettelheim.
11 TsGALI, 2450/2/1295.
12 Bettelheim, pp. 10–11.
13 ibid.
14 The highest honorary title awarded to actors and actresses in the Soviet Union.
15 One is reminded of a similar tribute paid to Gracie Fields, who was recorded by a cinema newsreel as the star guest at the gala opening of a new factory, thus indicating the breaking down of the distinction between big screen and real life.
16 G. V. Aleksandrov, *Epokha i kino* [The Epoch and Cinema] (Moscow, 1976), pp. 222–3.

8   THE ARTIST AND THE SHADOW OF IVAN

1 An aphorism of Eisenstein which he frequently repeated, according to various sources.
2 From Eisenstein's letter to Esfir Shub, February 1946, in E. I. Shub, *Zhizn' moya – kinematograf* [Cinema, My Life] (Moscow, 1972), p. 383.
3 See M. Seton, *Sergei M. Eisenstein* (London, 1978), pp. 447–8; R. Yurenev, 'Ya byl svetil'nikom' [I Was a Lamp], in *Eizenshtein v vospominaniyakh sovremennikov* [Eisenstein in the Reminiscences of Contemporaries] (Moscow, 1974), p. 278. Dom kino had been the meeting place for Soviet film-makers from the 1920s onwards and is now the headquarters of the Union of Cinematographers.
4 The decree of the USSR Council of People's Commissars, 'On the Award of Stalin Prizes for Distinguished Works in the Field of Art and Literature for 1943–4', signed by Stalin, was published on 26 January 1946. The Stalin Prize, First Class, for *Ivan the Terrible* was awarded to Eisenstein, Nikolai Cherkasov, Serafima Birman, Andrei Moskvin, Eduard Tisse and Sergei Prokofiev.
5 S. M. Eizenshtein, *Izbrannye proizvedeniya v shesti tomakh* [Selected Works in Six Volumes], vol. 1 (Moscow, 1964), p. 539. Further references to this edition will be in the style: *IP 1*, p. 539. English translation in H. Marshall (trans.), *Immoral Memories. An Autobiography by S. M. Eisenstein* (Boston, MA, and London, 1985), p. 261.
6 *IP 1*, p. 465; Marshall, p. 196.
7 *IP 1*, pp. 465, 468; Marshall, pp. 196, 198. The original order is slightly different from that cited here, and there is a mistranslation in Marshall.
8 Andrei A. Zhdanov (1896–1948), First Secretary of the Leningrad Party following the assassination of Kirov and a Secretary to the Party Central Committee, oversaw ideological and cultural affairs from 1944 until his death.
9 Vsevolod Emilevich Meyerhold (1874–1940) was the innovative theatre director whom Eisenstein once described as his 'spiritual father'. After the closure of his theatre in 1938, Meyerhold was given protection by Konstantin Stani-

slavsky until the latter's death in August. Meyerhold was arrested in June 1939 and shot in February 1940. (Eds)

10 *IP 1*, p. 527; Marshall, pp. 250–1.

11 TsGALI, 1923/2/1164.

12 ibid.

13 The dark irony of this situation consisted in the fact that the play on the shameful 'Beilis case' had been written by Lev Sheinin, a popular writer who also worked for the USSR State Prosecutor's Office on particularly important cases and who had flourished during the show trials of 1936–8. But he had to turn to Andrei Vyshinsky, the State Prosecutor and protagonist in these trials, for his 'blessing' for the film version, because in 1940 Vyshinsky was Deputy Chairman of the USSR Council of People's Commissars and was responsible for the arts, among other things. Vyshinsky's approval proved insufficient: the matter was resolved at a higher level. Production of the film was deemed inappropriate, possibly because of Stalin's 'friendship' with Hitler at the time, but very probably because the film inevitably showed the *prestige of the empire* in a scandalous light. Sheinin's play was not performed in a single theatre. See also p. 140.

14 TsGALI, 1923/2/1165.

15 TsGALI, 1923/1/529. This note on the conversation with Zhdanov was made on a copy of the letter from Eisenstein and Sheinin, dated 31 December 1940, about the film *The Prestige of the Empire* [Prestizh imperii] in which the main theme of the film was defined as that of a duel between the people and autocracy on the eve of the First World War.

16 For a description of this discussion (somewhat embellished) see R. Yurenev, *Sergei Eizenshtein. Zamysli. Fil'my. Metod* [Sergei Eisenstein. Projects. Films. Method], Part 1 (Moscow, 1988), p. 210.

17 The preconditions and motives for the 'Ivan cult', which developed in 1940–1, are examined in detail in the serious and interesting study by B. Uhlenbruch, 'The Annexation of History: Eisenstein and the Ivan Grozny Cult of the 1940s', in H. Günther (ed.), *The Culture of the Stalin Period* (London, 1990), pp. 266–87.

18 On the personal political situation of Stalin in 1940 – after real or suspected opposition within the country had been extirpated, after the change in foreign policy culminating in the pact with Hitler and the consequent 'adjustment' of the USSR's western frontiers, and after the long-awaited murder of Trotsky – on the situation of a leader who has achieved 'supreme power', see the article: M. Gefter, 'Stalin umer vchera ...' [Stalin Died Yesterday ...] in Yu. N. Afanas'ev (ed.), *Inogo ne dano* [There Is No Alternative] (Moscow, 1988), pp. 321–2; and Yu. N. Afanas'ev, *Iz tekh i etikh let* [From Those and These Years] (Moscow, 1991), pp. 261–3. The distinguished addressee of his then still welcome telegrams, 'Herr Adolf Hitler', once remarked: 'Stalin is in his own way a genius of a fellow: he is well aware of his antecedents.' See H. Picker, *Hitlers Tischgespräche im Führerhauptquartier, 1941–2* [Hitler's Table Talk in the Führer's HQ, 1941–2] (Stuttgart, 1963) p. 468.

19 Letter from Boris Pasternak to Olga Freidenberg, 4 February 1941, published in *Novyi mir* [New World], 1988, no. 6 (June), p. 218.

20 It was only later, at the end of 1941, when work on the script was coming to an end, that Eisenstein resolved to invite the well-known prose-writer and dramatist, Leonid Leonov, to collaborate in working out the dialogues. Because of the evacuation Leonov was unable to do this and Vladimir Lugovskoy, the author of the verse texts for the film, became Eisenstein's collaborator on the dialogues.

21 See S. Khentova, *Shostakovich. Zhizn' i tvorchestvo* [Shostakovich. Life and Work], vol. 1 (Leningrad, 1985), p. 519. It should be noted that this proposal was made to Shostakovich by Samuil Samosud, acting with Stalin's personal blessing. At that time Samosud was the director-in-chief of the Bolshoi Theatre and it was on his initiative that Eisenstein had been invited to produce Wagner's *Die Walküre*.

22 *IP 1*, pp. 85, 249.

23 In Eisenstein's writings relating to his work on this film there are frequent references to the epithet 'poet of the state idea' applied by the Russian historian K. D. Kavelin (1818–85) to Ivan IV.

24 On the inadequacy of real historical evidence about Ivan the Terrible see, for instance, the article by V. Listov, 'Ten' dokumenta na kinoekrane' [The Shadow of the Document on the Cinema Screen], in *Iz proshlogo v budushchee: proverka na dorogakh* [From the Past into the Future: Trials on the Road] (Moscow, 1990), pp. 38–9.

25 It is characteristic that Eisenstein himself linked the etymology of the sobriquet 'Terrible' [*Groznyi*] with the conventional metaphor of 'thunderstorm' [*groza*] (see, for instance, *IP 5*, p. 277). 'A thunderstorm approaches' is how the principal musical theme denoting the Tsar is indicated in the script (*IP 6*, p. 202). Viewed from this angle the generally accepted translations – 'Ivan the Terrible', 'Iwan der Schreckliche', etc. – do not completely convey the meaning of the Russian popular nickname of Ivan IV. The published English translation, adapted to correspond to the final version of the film, omits the separate Prologue with its title 'A Thunderstorm Approaches', S. Eisenstein, *Ivan the Terrible* (London, 1970), p. 25.

26 See A. S. Pushkin, *Boris Godunov*, Scene 7, 'Night. Garden. Fountain'.

27 *Iskusstvo kino* [The Art of Cinema], 1973, no. 1 (January), p. 86.

28 'Moskva vo vremeni' [Moscow in Time], *IP 1*, pp. 154–8.

29 TsGALI, 1923/2/833.

30 On the social experience of generations of the Russian intelligentsia, see the essays by Lidia Ginzburg, 'Pokolenie na perevorote' [Generation at the Cataclysm] and 'I zaodno s pravoporyadkom' [At One with Law and Order], in the book *Lidiya Ginzburg. Chelovek za pis'mennom stolom* [Lidia Ginzburg. A Person at the Writing Desk] (Leningrad, 1989), pp. 294–319.

31 We can in any case confirm that there was no foundation for the report that, after finishing *Ivan the Terrible*, Eisenstein was intending to make a film trilogy about Stalin. *Today's Cinema* (London), 21 August 1945; Seton, p. 447.

32 *Izvestiya*, 30 April 1941.

33 'Neskol'ko slov', *IP 1*, p. 197.

34 Cf. *IP 6*, pp. 378–83ff.

35 See *Iskusstvo kino*, 1959, no. 3 (March), pp. 111–30.

36 In English in the original.

37 It was Jay Leyda who first pointed out that Eisenstein's analysis of Boris Godunov's monologue anticipated *Ivan the Terrible*. J. Leyda, *Kino. A History of the Russian and Soviet Film* (London, 1960), p. 383.

38 V. V. Ivanov, *Ocherki po istorii semiotiki v SSSR* [Essays on the History of Semiotics in the USSR] (Moscow, 1976), pp. 99–100.

39 In English and French in the original; TsGALI, 1923/2/1168.

40 From Eisentein's diary entries published in *Voprosy kinodramaturgii 4* [Problems of Cinema Dramaturgy 4] (Moscow, 1962), p. 384.

41 Not that long ago I propounded the hypothesis that Eisenstein's psychological model for the treatment of Ivan was the living, and to him tragic, figure of his

teacher Meyerhold (see above, n.9). See L. Kozlov, 'Gipoteza o nevyska-zannom posvyashchenii' [A Hypothesis about an Unspoken Dedication], *Voprosy kinoiskusstva 12* [Problems of Cinema Art 12] (Moscow, 1970, pp. 109–33.

42 *IP 1*, p. 196.

43 Ivan G. Bolshakov (1902–80) was head of the Soviet film industry from June 1939 and, from March 1946, the first Minister of Cinematography.

44 TsGALI, 1923/1/652.

45 TsGALI, 1923/2/1166.

46 TsGALI, 1923/2/1058. Nikolai Erdman (1902–70), the dramatist, who found himself on active service in the army in 1941, recalled, 'At the front I saw German leaflets with Meyerhold's portrait, depicting him as the man princi-pally responsible for the demise of Russian culture and calling for reprisals against him.' From the declaration made by Erdman on 4 September 1955 to the Military Procurator investigating the rehabilitation of Meyerhold see *Nikolai Erdman. P'esy. Intermedii. Pis'ma. Dokumenty. Vospominaniya sovremennikov* [Nikolai Erdman. Plays. Interludes. Letters. Documents. Reminiscences of Contemporaries] (Moscow, 1990), p. 298.

47 TsGALI, 1923/2/1168.

48 *IP 1*, p. 193.

49 *IP 3*, pp. 330–1.

50 In 1945 Eisenstein introduced this preface into the text of *Nonindifferent Nature*, with the exception of a few lines: 'They say that classical antiquity had temples dedicated to an "unknown deity". It is to that same "unknown deity" that mankind's current sacrificial struggle is dedicated, to the dimly perceived ideal of the New Democracy of the Future, which, we are promised, will triumph on Earth.' See TsGALI, 1923/2/365. This passage is not included in the translation by Herbert Marshall (Cambridge, 1987).

51 M. Gefter, 'Sud'ba Khrushcheva' [Khrushchev's Fate], *Oktyabr'* [October], 1989, no. 1 (January), p. 156.

52 Gefter, 'Stalin umer vchera . . .', p. 305.

53 We can find a direct expression of this spiritual uplift in the work from that time of poets such as Anna Akhmatova and Alexander Tvardovsky, in the plays of Leonid Leonov such as *The Invasion* [Nashestvie], in the diaries and letters of V. I. Vernadsky. Cf. Vasili Grossman's novel *Life and Fate* [Zhizn' i sud'ba], the prose work by Olga Bergholz *Daily Stars* [Dnevnye zvezdy], the memoirs of Ilya Ehrenburg, Daniil Granin, David Samoilov and Andrei Sakharov.

54 A note by Boris Pasternak dated 11 February 1956, *Novyi mir*, 1988, no. 6 (June), p. 219.

55 *IP 1*, p. 468.

56 This text is reproduced from a photocopy preserved in the personal archive of Ivan Bolshakov. I must express my profound gratitude to the late D. S. Pisar-evsky, who familiarised me with the materials in Bolshakov's personal archive.

57 A number of events are symptomatic of the reactivation of the cult of Ivan the Terrible at this particular time. On 17 September 1943 in the Hall of Columns of the House of Unions in Moscow there was a public lecture by Professor Robert Yu. Vipper, a well-known historian who had published an apologia for Ivan IV as early as the 1920s. *Pravda* reported this lecture on 19 September in a special note, underlining the fact that it disproved the 'idea that Ivan the Terrible was a needlessly cruel tyrant'. On 30 September *Pravda* reported that Professor Vipper had been 'elected' a Full Member of the USSR Academy of Sciences.

58 Cf. the analysis of the conception and graphic structure of *Ivan the Terrible* in a recent article by V. Tsukerman [Zuckerman], 'Dvoinaya "myshelovka", ili Samoubiistvo fil'mom' [A Double 'Mousetrap', or Suicide by Film], *Iskusstvo kino*], 1991, no. 9 (September), pp. 93–102.

59 N. K. Cherkasov, *Zapiski sovetsogo aktera* (Moscow, 1953), p. 164. Not included in the English translation, *Notes of a Soviet Actor* (Moscow, n.d.). (Eds)

60 Eisenstein's clear statement of this intention is reproduced in the memoir by Iosif Yuzovsky in *Eizenshtein v vospominaniyakh sovremennikov* (Moscow, 1974), p.402.

61 *IP 1*, p. 197.

62 TsGALI, 1923/2/1171.

63 TsGALI, 1923/1/657.

64 TsGALI, 1923/2/1165.

65 Mikhail Yu. Bleiman (1904–73) was a prolific scriptwriter. His works include *My Homeland* [Moya rodina, 1933], mentioned in this volume by Ekaterina Khokhlova, and Friedrich Ermler's *A Great Citizen* [Velikii grazhdanin, 1937].

66 M. Bleiman, *O kino – svidetel'skie pokazaniya* [On Cinema – Eye-Witness Evidence] (Moscow, 1973), pp. 424–5.

67 From an interview granted by Mikhail Kuznetsov to Naum Kleiman and Leonid Kozlov in 1967; the tape-recording is held in the Eisenstein Museum Collection.

68 See L. Kozlov, ' "Ivan groznyi" – muzykal'no-tematicheskoe stroenie' [*Ivan the Terrible* – A Musical-Thematic Structure], *Voprosy kinoiskusstva*, no. 10 (Moscow, 1967), pp. 245.

The 'Burning Fiery Furnace' [*Peshchnoe deistvo*] was one of the biblical scenes acted out in the cathedral churches of old Muscovy. It took place on 17 December and enacted the casting of the three youths, Shadrach, Meshach and Abednego, into the 'burning fiery furnace' by Nebuchadnezzar and their miraculous preservation which caused Nebuchadnezzar's conversion. Cf. Daniel 3: 13–30. (Eds)

69 Tsukerman.

70 Eisenstein's words are reproduced in the reminiscences of I. I. Yuzovsky in *Eizenshtein v vospominaniyakh sovremennikov*, p. 405.

71 E. Levin, 'Istoricheskaya tragediya kak zhanr i kak sud'ba' [Historical Tragedy as Genre and Fate], *Iskusstvo kino*, 1991, no. 9 (September), pp. 93–102.

72 The story of Pavlenko's review was told me by S. S. Ginzburg in 1965. The galley proofs of the review have been preserved in his personal archive. Vishnevsky's review appeared in *Pravda* on 28 January 1945.

73 *IP 1*, p. 85.

74 'Mister Linkol'n Mistera Forda' [Mr Ford's Mr Lincoln], *IP 5*, p. 272.

75 ibid., p. 283.

76 Recounted to Naum Kleiman and the author in 1962. 'Old man' [*starik*] was the affectionate term used of Eisenstein by his friends and pupils. (Eds)

77 TsGALI, 1923/2/124.

78 Nikolai P. Khmelyov (1901–45), Moscow Art Theatre actor who began his screen career with an agit-film appearance in 1919. (Eds)

79 From the interview with Kuznetsov; see above, n. 67.

80 M. Romm, *Besedy o kino* [Conversations on Cinema] (Moscow, 1965), p. 91. Mikhail I. Romm (1901–71) was a director and scriptwriter whose films included the last Soviet silent feature *Boule de Suif* [Pyshka, 1934], *Lenin in*

October [Lenin v oktyabre, 1937], *Lenin in 1918* [Lenin v 1918g., 1939] and *Ordinary Fascism* [Obyknovennyi fashizm, 1966]. He was also known for his witty and somewhat vicious anecdotes. (Eds)

81 From Bolshakov's memoirs, preserved in the archive of D. S. Pisarevsky.

82 Romm, p. 92.

83 Anna A. Akhmatova (1889–1966), the poet and author of the epic cycles *Poem without a Hero* and *Requiem*, and Mikhail M. Zoshchenko (1895–1958), the writer of humorous short stories, were singled out for criticism by Zhdanov in his Leningrad speech on 21 September 1946, which signalled the onset of the post-war clampdown on the Soviet arts. (Eds)

84 *Kul'tura i zhizn'* [Culture and Life], 4 September 1946.

85 *Kul'tura i zhizn'*, 20 October 1946. The drafts of this letter, one of which is addressed to Zhdanov, are in TsGALI, 1923/1/664. The published version is taken from *Kul'tura i zhizn'*, 20 October 1946. Bernd Uhlenbruch (pp. 280–1) has interpreted this letter – and, on a wider basis, Eisenstein's behaviour at that time – by precisely identifying in Eisenstein's self-criticism a 'rhetorical masquerade' behind which there is not the slightest sign of the tortured reflexes that can be detected in his statements in 1937 about the 'mistakes' of *Bezhin Meadow*.

86 TsGALI, 1923/1/657.

87 The most complete version was published in *Moskovskie novosti* [Moscow News], 7 August 1988, pp. 8–9.

88 Since January 1937, shortly before the débâcle over *Bezhin Meadow*, Eisenstein had been Professor of Direction at VGIK [the All-Union State Institute of Cinematography (as it was called from 1934 to 1991)], the principal school for Soviet film-makers. (Eds)

89 Interview by Bleiman with the author in 1971.

90 Eisenstein's lecture of 19 March 1947; text preserved at VGIK.

91 'I remember when Eisenstein and Cherkasov came out of their conversation with Stalin and Zhdanov. I phoned him up and asked, "How did it go?" He said, "We'll hardly change a thing. It was an interesting meeting. I'll tell you some time . . ." ' (from the interview with Kuznetsov).

There was one other response by Eisenstein to a question on the reworking of the film: 'What re-shooting? . . . Don't you realise that I'd die at the first shot? . . .' (Yurenev, 'Ya byl svetil'nikom', p. 283).

92 I. I. Yuzovskii in *Eizenshtein v vospominaniyakh . . .*, pp. 412–13.

93 Cited in Ivanov, p. 103.

94 TsGALI, 1923/2/1178. Eisenstein often used the Latin word *opus* in the sense of his whole life's work, rather than an individual work. Cf. the French *oeuvre* and *ouvrage*. (Eds)

95 See L. Kozlov, 'Eizenshtein i problema sintetichnosti kinoiskusstva' [Eisenstein and the Problem of Synthesism in Cinema Art], *Voprosy kinoiskusstva*, no. 7 (Moscow, 1963), p. 105. After writing that article I discovered in Eisenstein's notes for 1947 (TsGALI, 1923/2/1178) this same parallel in a somewhat different version, 'childishly naïve (an idiot) – Vl[adimir] And[reyevich]. A baby in a pram.'

96 Ivan A. Pyriev (1901–68) had a reputation for making films that closely reflected the Party line, e.g. *The Conveyor-Belt of Death* [Konveier smerti, 1933], *The Party Card* [Partiinyi bilet, 1936] and the kolkhoz musical comedy *Tractor-Drivers* [Traktoristy, 1939]. (Eds)

9 SOVIET FILMS OF THE 'COLD WAR'

1 *'Zapechatlennoe vremya'* – literally 'imprinted time' was the title chosen by Andrey Tarkovsky for his book, published in English as *Sculpting in Time. Reflections on the Cinema* (trans. K. Hunter-Blair) (London, 1986).
2 From Alexander Pushkin's poem 'Poet i tolpa' [The Poet and the Crowd] written in 1828. (Eds)
3 These figures come from our recent archival researches, which we hope to publish in English as *The Film Process*.
4 See above, Chapter 3, n. 37.
5 Some of the events depicted certainly did take place, but in the films there is a direct equation between the former ally and Nazism, even a suggestion that the former has 'learnt' something from the latter.
6 The term employed by Turovskaya here is 'golubaya rol' ' [literally 'blue role'], which is used ironically to mean 'idealised role'. (Eds)
7 Pavel P. Kadochnikov (b. 1915), Vladimir V. Druzhinikov (b. 1922) and Rostislav Ya. Plyatt (b. 1908) were all leading film actors of the post-war period. Maxim M. Strauch (1900–74), a close friend of Eisenstein, began his career in silent cinema and was one of the first people to play Lenin on stage and screen, as in Yutkevich's *The Man with a Gun* [Chelovek s ruzh'em, 1938]. (Eds)
8 *Semnadtsat' mgnovenii vesny*, directed by Tatyana Lioznova, was a popular television series about the activities of Soviet intelligence services during the Second World War. It was first shown on Soviet television in the late 1970s and was based on the novel of the same title by Iyuliyan Semyonov. (Eds)
9 See Kozlov's arguments, in the previous chapter.
10 Nikolai A. Kryuchkov (b. 1911), Boris F. Andreyev (1915–82), Pyotr M. Aleinikov (1914–65) and Nikolai I. Bogolyubov (1899–1980) were all leading Soviet film actors. Boris P. Chirkov (1901–82) played the principal role in the Maxim trilogy. (Eds)
11 For Plyatt and Strauch, see above, n. 7. Erast P. Garin (1902–80) had acted with the Meyerhold Theatre. Alexander N. Vertinsky (1889–1957) was a popular singer as well as an actor: he emigrated in 1919 but returned to the USSR in 1943 and played a number of leading screen roles. (Eds)
12 Cf. K. S. Stanislavsky, *An Actor Prepares* (London, 1936). (Eds)
13 Mikhail E. Chiaureli (1894–1974) was the Georgian-born director of several key films of the Stalin period: *The Great Dawn* [Velikoe zarevo, 1938], *The Vow* [Klyatva, 1946], *The Fall of Berlin* [Padenie Berlina, 1949]. All three films were awarded the Stalin Prize. See also A. Bernshtein, 'V roli Stalina' [In the Role of Stalin], *Ogonek* [The Torch], 1988, no. 2, pp. 18–19. (Eds)
14 Vladlen [after Vladimir Lenin] S. Davydov (b. 1924) made his screen début in *Meeting on the Elbe*.
15 Stalin's order no. 270 of 16 August 1941 stated that soldiers surrendering to the enemy, even when surrounded, should be considered deserters who were to be shot on the spot and whose families were to be arrested as traitors and deprived of state support. See D. Volkogonov, *Triumf i tragediya. Politicheskii portret I. V. Stalina* [Triumph and Tragedy. A Political Portrait of J. V. Stalin] (Moscow, 1989), vol. 2, part 2, pp. 204–5. (Eds)
16 This refers to the 'social command' [*sotsial'nyi zakaz*] which, from the early 1930s onwards, meant that the artist was supposed to fulfil the 'commands' of society as interpreted by the Party.

10   CANONS AND CAREERS: THE DIRECTOR IN SOVIET CINEMA

1 H. Kenner, 'The Making of the Modernist Canon', in R. von Hallberg (ed.), *Canons* (Chicago and London, 1984), p. 373.

2 In an interview with the author, Moscow, 1989.

3 See the articles, mainly from *Critical Inquiry*, collected in von Hallberg; also, for an overview and extensive bibliography, J. Gorak, *The Making of the Modern Canon* (London and Atlantic Highlands, NJ, 1991).

4 See, for instance, B. M. Metzger, *The Canon of the New Testament: Its Origins, Development and Significance* (Oxford, 1987); J. Barr, *Holy Scripture: Canon, Authority, Criticism* (Philadelphia, PA, 1983).

5 I. Christie and M. Coad, 'Between Institutions: Interview with Raul Ruiz', *Afterimage* (London), no. 10 (Autumn 1981), p. 104; reprinted in J. Burton (ed.), *Cinema and Social Change in Latin America* (Austin, TX, 1986), p. 183.

6 Soviet 'friendship' organisations and sympathetic distributors were supplied with free or heavily subsidised prints of 'canonic' works, while other films were expensive and often impossible to obtain through Goskino (although inter-archive 'exchanges' placed important extra-canonic holdings in archives such as the Cinémathèque Royale de Belgique and the Pacific Film Archive, Berkeley, CA, during the 1960s and 1970s). The Lenin quotation is in *FF*, p. 57.

7 The 'removal' of Stalin began soon after Khrushchev's speech to the Twentieth CPSU Congress in 1956, by means of withdrawing some films *in toto*, truncating others and ingeniously 'tricking' some by means of cartooning and matte process. One such revision is described in detail by A. Seskonse, 'Reediting History: *Lenin in October*, 1937–83', *Sight and Sound*, vol. 53, no. 1 (Winter 1983–4), pp. 56–8. Another is apparent in Kozintsev and Trauberg's *The Vyborg Side* [Vyborgskaya storona, 1938] from the frame stills reproduced in *Trilogiya o Maksime* [The Maxim Trilogy] (Moscow, 1981), p. 274, when this is compared with the still of the same scene reproduced in *FF*, p. 370. See Plates 30–3.

8 F. Kermode, 'Institutional Control of Interpretation', *Salmagundi*, no. 43 (Winter 1979), pp. 72–86.

9 F. Ermash, foreword to *Sovetskoe kino/Soviet Cinema* (Moscow, 1979), a bilingual illustrated book 'prepared in collaboration with the USSR State Cinema Committee', p. 13. (Note: Vertov's commemorative edition of his newsreel *Leninskaya kinopravda* [Leninist Cine-Truth] is entertainingly mistranslated in the English text.)

10 Kermode, p. 81. On Western perceptions of Kozintsev and Trauberg's canonic position, see I. Christie, 'Feks za granitsei. Kul'turno-politicheskie aspekty vospriyatiya sovetskogo kino za rubezhom' [FEKS Abroad: The Cultural Politics of Soviet Cinema's Reception Abroad], *Kinovedcheskie zapiski* [Scholarly Film Notes] (Moscow), no. 7, 1990, pp. 172–5.

11 V. Baskakov, *Soviet Cinema (A Brief Essay)* (Moscow, n.d.). This twenty-two-page essay, published in English translation, was probably intended to mark the 1968 jubilee of Soviet cinema. Its author, then a deputy chairman of Goskino, was later ousted in a power struggle and became first director of the All-Union Research Institute for the History of Cinema, [VNIIK], in 1972.

12 P. Wollen, *Signs and Meaning in the Cinema* (London, 1969), p. 46.

13 Yu. Vorontsov and I. Rachuk, *Fenomen sovetskogo kinematografa* (Moscow,

1980); translated as *The Phenomenon of the Soviet Cinema* (Moscow, 1980), p. 49.

14 ibid., pp. 50–1.

15 Most obviously in the cults of Vertov, Paradzhanov and Tarkovsky, which developed during the 1970s and 1980s, encouraged by reports of the hardships these film-makers had suffered.

16 H. Bloom, 'Criticism, Canon-Formation, and Prophecy: The Sorrows of Facticity', *Raritan* (New Brunswick, NJ), no. 3 (Winter 1984), pp. 1–20.

17 S. Eisenstein, 'Through Theatre to Cinema', in J. Leyda (ed.), *Film Form*, (New York, 1949), p. 3.

18 J. Brooks, 'Situating Cinema: Movies in their Cultural Contexts, 1900–30' (unpublished paper communicated to the conference 'Russian and Soviet Cinema: Continuity and Change'). The published version of the paper, 'Russian Cinema and Public Discourse, 1900–1930' is in *Historical Journal of Film, Radio and Television*, vol. 11, no. 2 (June 1991), pp. 141–8.

19 On reconceptualising early Soviet cinema, see especially the Introduction to *FF*; also V. Kepley, 'The Origins of Soviet Cinema: A Study in Industry Development', in R. Taylor and I. Christie (eds), *Inside the Film Factory. New Approaches to Russian and Soviet Cinema* (London and New York, 1991), pp. 60–79.

20 On the Rus studio, see J. Leyda, *Kino. A History of the Russian and Soviet Film* (London, 1960), p. 147; I. Christie, 'Protazanov: A Timely Case for Treatment', in I. Christie and J. Graffy (eds), *Protazanov and the Continuity of Russian Cinema* (London, 1993), pp. 8–22. On the Kuleshov workshop and Gardin's involvement, see M. Yampolsky, 'Kuleshov's Experiments and the New Anthropology of the Actor', in Taylor and Christie, pp. 31–50.

21 Yu. Tsivian, 'Eisenstein and Russian Symbolist Culture: An Unknown Script of *October*', in I. Christie and R. Taylor (eds), *Eisenstein Rediscovered* (London and New York, 1993), pp. 79–109.

22 'How does one become a director or cameraman, or even actor in Russia? Chiefly through the State School of Cinematography in Moscow' (Bryher [W. Ellerman], *Film Problems of Soviet Russia* (Territet, Switzerland, 1929), p.15).

23 Mikhail Romm was the course director at VGIK [the All-Union State Film Industry] for Andrey Tarkovsky and many of the leading directors who emerged in the 1960s; Leonid Trauberg played a similar role at the Higher Courses school, encouraging such film-makers as Gleb Panfilov and Sergei Mikaelyan.

24 Yuli Raizman, for instance, supported and protected the partnership of Vadim Abdrashitov and Alexander Mindadze during the 1970s and 1980s in the unit he headed at Mosfilm Studio.

25 On early Soviet theatre in relation to cinema, see M. Gordon, 'Russian Eccentric Theatre: The Rhythm of America on the Early Soviet Stage', in N. Van Norman Baer (ed.) *Theatre in Revolution* (London, 1991), pp. 114–27. Wollen (p. 46) suggests (in a passage omitted from the extract quoted above) that Eisenstein 'was at his strongest when he was working within the theatrical tradition which exerted such influence on him in the 1920s'.

26 The 1923 'Resolution on Questions of Propaganda, the Press and Agitation' stated that 'no one literary direction, school or group can or should speak in the name of the Party', quoted in C. V. James, *Soviet Socialist Realism* (London, 1973), p. 62.

27 A. Lunacharsky, 'Cinema – the Greatest of the Arts', translated in *FF*, p. 155.

28 See V. Kepley, Jr, 'The Workers International Relief and the Cinema of the Left 1921–35', *Cinema Journal*, vol. 23, no. 1 (Autumn 1983), pp. 7–23; also Christie and Graffy, pp. 49–50.

29 Cited in D. Youngblood, *Soviet Cinema in the Silent Era, 1918–1935* (Ann Arbor, MI, 1985; reprinted Austin, TX, 1991), p. 83.

30 Seton notes that 'as originally planned, the film *Potemkin* was one of eight episodes in a panoramic picture entitled *1905*. It was authorised by the Central Committee of the Communist Party on the 19th of March 1925, as one of a series of films commemorating the 1905 Revolution.' See M. Seton, *(Sergei M. Eisenstein. A Biography* (London, 1952), p. 74.

31 Baskakov, p. 4.

32 Youngblood indicates 'The Five' as a common term by 1929 (p. 199).

33 V. Kepley, Jr, '*Intolerance* and the Soviets: A Historical Investigation', in Taylor and Christie, pp. 51–9. Baskakov (p. 5) approvingly quotes the view that 'Eisenstein . . . looked upon Griffith as his distant teacher'.

34 In Ben Jonson's plays, a 'humour' is 'the embodiment in one of the characters of some dominating individual passion or propensity' (M. Drabble (ed.), *Oxford Companion to English Literature* (5th edn, Oxford, 1985), p. 483).

35 'To the Party Conference on Cinema from a Group of Film Directors', *FF*, p. 206.

36 ibid.

37 ibid., p. 207.

38 Percy Bysshe Shelley proclaimed artists 'the unacknowledged legislators'; *In the Service of the State* is the evocative title of V. Kepley Jr's book on Dovzhenko: see below, n.76.

39 I. Montagu, *With Eisenstein in Hollywood* (Berlin, GDR, 1968), p. 143; see also H. Marshall, *Masters of the Soviet Cinema. Crippled Creative Biographies* (London, 1983), pp. 199–200.

40 For example Griffith's *America* [USA, 1924]; Gance's *Napoléon* [France, 1927].

41 See R. Taylor, *Film Propaganda. Soviet Russia and Nazi Germany* (London, 1979), on Goebbels's admiration for especially Eisenstein's *Potemkin* (pp. 158–9).

42 Leyda, *Kino*, p. 269.

43 ibid.

44 Lev Kuleshov, 'Chto nado delat'?' [What Do We Have to Do?], *Kino i kult'ura*, [Cinema and Culture], 1930, no. 11/12 (November/December), pp. 8–15 (translated by R. Taylor).

45 I. Sokolov, 'The Legend of "Left" Cinema', *FF*, p. 289.

46 ibid., p. 290.

47 Most documents relevant to Eisenstein's Mexican venture, including Stalin's notorious telegram, are translated in H. M. Geduld and R. Gottesman (eds), *Sergei Eisenstein and Upton Sinclair: The Making and Unmaking of 'Que Viva Mexico!'* (London and Bloomington, IN, 1970).

48 R. Taylor, 'Ideology as Mass Entertainment: Boris Shumyatsky and Soviet Cinema in the 1930s', in Taylor and Christie, pp. 193–216.

49 I. Christie, 'Making Sense of Early Soviet Sound', in Taylor and Christie, pp. 176–92.

50 ibid., pp. 183–4.

51 L. Kuleshov, 'Fifty Years in Films', *Selected Works* (English-language edition) (Moscow, 1987), pp. 234–40.

52 On the privileges claimed by 'shock brigades', see H. Kuromiya, *Stalin's*

Industrial Revolution. Politics and Workers, 1928–1932 (Cambridge, 1988), pp. 115–35, 237.

53 According to Leonid Trauberg, in an interview with the author and R. Taylor, Moscow 1983. This phase of 'incentivisation' has proved difficult to document from other sources.

54 D. Vertov, 'My Illness' (1935), *FF*, p. 357.

55 Attempts to enforce labour discipline by means of a 'work book' system were first considered in 1930–1, then dropped in face of widespread opposition, before being imposed in December 1938. See D. Filtzer, *Soviet Workers and Stalinist Industrialisation* (London, 1986), pp. 111 and 233.

56 Yuri Norstein, in a filmed interview transmitted on Channel Four, 1991.

57 Leyda, *Kino*, p. 319.

58 M. Bourke-White, *Shooting the Russian War* (New York, 1944), p. 158.

59 ibid.

60 Kuleshov, 'Fifty Years in Films', p. 247.

61 ibid., p. 249.

62 Letter from Samuel Beckett to Eisenstein, dated 2 March 1936; reproduced in J. Leyda (ed.), *Eisenstein 2. A Premature Celebration of Eisenstein's Centenary* (Calcutta, 1985), p. 59. Telegram from Erich von Stroheim to Eisenstein requesting 'work for me private or government', apparently sent soon before Christmas 1936, presumably soon before Stroheim left America for France, to appear in Renoir's *La Grande Illusion*.

63 The original negatives of both *Potemkin* and *October* were apparently sold to Germany for hard currency, while *The Old and the New* was withdrawn in 1931 and cannibalised for a documentary on kolkhozes (information from Naum Kleiman). Other mass withdrawals took place during the Cultural Revolution.

64 Eisenstein, *Immoral Memories*, pp. 204–5.

65 Albert Gendelstein (1906–81) made only two other features before turning to popular science documentaries, a traditional haven for experimentally inclined Soviet film-makers. No other information is currently available on Dubson. Both of these films were included in Naum Kleiman's pioneering 'Unknown Soviet Cinema' programme, first shown at the Moscow Film Centre in 1987.

66 G. Ermolaev, 'What is Holding Up the Development of Soviet Cinema?', *Pravda*, 9 January 1938; *FF*, p. 387.

67 Yu. Tsivian has remarked that Romanov censorship had forbidden any representation of the imperial family. Stalin soon moved from encouraging the portrayal of Lenin and himself to offering tsarist parallels in films about Peter the Great and Ivan the Terrible.

68 Ermolaev catalogues GUK's repeated failure to meet its targets, moving from forty-three films completed out of 120 planned in 1935 to an actual output of twenty-four films in 1937. He is especially scornful of Shumyatsky's claim to need 'only 40–50 "proven masters"' to meet his plan requirements.

69 A. Dovzhenko, *Za bol'shoe kinoiskusstvo* [For a Great Cinema Art] (Moscow, 1935), p. 65.

70 M. Yampolsky, 'Censure ou la triomphe de la vie: le fonctionnement de la censure en URSS de 1930 à 1950' [Censorship or the Triumph of Life: the Operation of Censorship in the USSR from 1930 to 1950], *Les écrans de la liberté: URSS, 50 ans de cinéma retrouvé* [Screens of Liberty: USSR. Fifty Years of Rediscovered Cinema] (Paris, 1989), p. 27.

71 See, for instance, O. Brik, 'From Pictures to Textile Prints', *Lef*, no 2, 1924: 'the artistic culture of the future is being created in factories and plants, not in attic studios'; and A. Rodchenko, 'Against the Synthetic Portrait, For the Snapshot', *Novyi lef*, no. 4, 1928: 'Art has no place in modern life. It will continue to exist as long as there is a mania for the romantic ... Every modern cultured man must wage war against art, as against opium.' Both in J. E. Bowlt (ed.), *Russian Art of the Avant-Garde: Theory and Criticism 1902–1934* (New York, 1976), pp. 249, 253.

72 Yampolsky, p. 28.

73 B. Shumyatsky, 'The Film *Bezhin Meadow*', *Pravda*, 19 March 1937; *FF*, p. 380.

74 Trauberg's speech to the 1935 Conference noted that 'the principal admirers of our style, and sometimes also of the stylisation of our films, have been the snobs and gourmands of the West' (*FF*, p. 351). In the following year, A. Fedorov-Davydov condemned Vertov's *The Man With the Movie Camera* [Chelovek s kinoapparatom] because it 'received the greatest recognition abroad by the aesthetes belonging to European avant-garde cinema' (quoted by V. Petrić, *Constructivism in Film* (Cambridge, 1987), p. 66).

75 Shumyatsky, ibid.

76 Stalin apparently first 'suggested' a 'Ukrainian *Chapayev*' when he met Dovzhenko in 1935, presumably during the cinema conference. See V. Kepley, *In The Service of the State. The Cinema of Alexander Dovzhenko* (Madison, WI, and London, 1986), p. 121.

77 A. Dovzhenko, 'The Artist's Teacher and Friend', *Iskusstvo kino* [The Art of Cinema], no. 10, 1937; *FF*, p. 384.

78 Leonid Trauberg explained in an interview how, when he and Kozintsev were preparing *Plain People* [Prostye lyudi] in 1945, they received the expected call inquiring about Stalin's role. Despite arranging that the head of the evacuated factory reports his success to Stalin by telephone, the film was banned until 1954.

79 A. Bazin, 'Le mythe de Staline', first published in *Esprit*, July–August 1950; reprinted in *Qu'est-ce que le cinéma*, vol. 1 (Paris, 1958), pp. 75–89; translated by G. Gurrieri as 'The Stalin Myth in Soviet Cinema', *Film Criticism*, vol. 3, no. 1 (Fall 1978), pp. 17–26. The Stalin sequence is now missing from *Plain People*, from Vertov's *Lullaby* [Kolybel'naya, 1937] and, as noted above, from *Lenin in October* and *The Vyborg Side*. Films in which Stalin was really the central character, like *The Vow* and *The Fall of Berlin* [Padenie Berlina, 1949], were completely withdrawn until very recently.

80 Bazin, 'Le mythe de Staline', p. 85.

81 P. Burke, *The Fabrication of Louis XIV* (New Haven, CT, 1992).

82 B. Groys, *Gesamtkunstwerk Stalin* [Stalin – Total Work of Art] (Munich, 1988).

83 V. Sutyrin argued against directors continuing to be involved in scripting or editing in *Problemy sotsialisticheskoi rekonstruktsii sovetskoi kinopromyshlennosti* [Problems of Socialist Reconstruction of the Soviet Cinema Industry] (Moscow, 1932), cited by Youngblood, p. 203.

84 Leyda, *Kino*, p. 390.

85 A. Bernstein, 'Mikhail Gelovani: One-Role Actor', *Soviet Film*, no. 9, 1989, pp. 16–17.

86 J. Leyda (ed.), *Eisenstein: Two Films* (London, 1984), includes 'final scenes of an earlier version of the script' for *Alexander Nevsky*, pp. 144–8.

87 Seton's biography includes an outline and quotations from the original

scenario for *Ivan the Terrible*, Parts Two and Three (pp. 437–41).

88 See Chapter 8.

89 Transcript by Sergei Eisenstein and Nikolai Cherkasov, edited by R. Trofimov, published in *Moscow News*, no. 32, 1988, pp. 8–9.

90 ibid.

91 ibid.

92 Pasternak's account of the conversation was corroborated by Nadezhda Mandelstam and Anna Akhmatova; the fullest account of the episode is by O. Ivinskaya, *A Captive of Time: My Years with Pasternak* (London, 1978), pp. 64–70.

93 G. Kozintsev, *Glubokii ekran* [Deep Screen] (Moscow, 1971); this extract translated by J. Gambrell (ed.) in A. Konchalovsky and A. Lipkov, *The Inner Circle* (New York, 1992), p. 28.

94 Neither Hitler nor Mussolini allowed himself to be portrayed by actors in German or Italian films, although both appeared – together with Roosevelt and Churchill – in Soviet films.

95 A magnificent print of *The Fall of Berlin* from the Cinémathèque de Toulouse was screened at the Ciné-Mémoire festival in Paris in October 1991 and at the London Film Festival in 1992. Ivinskaya (p. 70) recalls Mandelstam asking Pasternak: 'Why is Stalin so afraid of genius? It's like a superstition with him. He thinks we might put a spell on him, like shamans.'

96 Leyda, *Kino*, p. 399.

97 I. Bolshakov in *Sovetskoe iskusstvo* [Soviet Art], 20 March 1951.

98 I. Pyriev in *Literaturnaya gazeta* [Literary Gazette], 2 September 1952.

99 *Literaturnaya gazeta*, 1 July 1954.

100 Khrushchev's 'secret speech' to the Twentieth Congress of the CPSU in 1956 contained a number of references to Stalin's use of cinema for self-glorification and self-delusion.

101 There had been pre-Revolutionary artists' unions (one of which mutated into the Soviet Theatre Workers' Union); and a number of polemical groups flourished in the arts world during the Cultural Revolution. The ideological warfare of that period was abruptly suppressed in April 1932 with a Central Committee Resolution on 'The Reorganisation of Literary and Artistic Organisations' which abolished all pressure groups and proclaimed the need for 'a single union of Soviet writers', followed by an undertaking that 'a similar change with regard to other art forms be carried out' (*FF*, p. 325). Following the first Writers' Union Congress in 1934, other 'creative unions' soon followed – except for cinema.

102 The First Congress of Soviet Writers proclaimed 'Socialist Realism' as the *only* method for Soviet writers, defining it as 'a true and historically concrete artistic depiction of reality . . . combined with the task of educating the workers in the spirit of Communism'.

103 Pasternak told Stalin during their 1934 exchange that 'the writers' organisation haven't bothered with cases like [Mandelstam's arrest] since 1927' (Ivinskaya, p. 69).

104 Khrushchev's visit to a painting exhibition at the Manège, the former tsarist riding school near the Kremlin, provoked an angry reaction to the small number of Modernist works included and the threat, 'Gentlemen, we are declaring war on you!' An Ideological Commission was established by the Central Committee later in December. See P. Johnson and L. Labedz (eds), *Khrushchev and the Arts* (Cambridge, MA, 1965), pp. 101–5.

105 Romm's speech, on the theme 'Traditions and Innovations', was given to a

meeting of theatre and cinema workers in autumn 1962. It called for internationalism and innovation in the face of continuing Stalinist inertia (text translated in Johnson and Labedz, pp. 95–101).

106 Khrushchev's bitter attack on *The Ilyich Gate* came in the course of a major speech given at the second meeting of creative artists and Party leaders, 8 March 1963, 'Lofty Ideology and Artistic Craftsmanship are the Great Forces of Soviet Literature and Art'; translated in Johnson and Labedz, pp. 152–5.

107 Information on the aftermath of the Union's resistance kindly provided to the author by Andrei Smirnov, former Acting First Secretary of the Union of Cinematographers.

108 For an account of 'unshelving', see I. Christie, 'The Cinema', in J. Graffy and G. Hosking (eds), *Culture and the Media in the USSR Today* (London, 1989), pp. 43–77.

109 Sergo Paradzhanov's films evoked mystical and ethnic Armenian–Georgian themes, while Tarkovsky pursued an increasingly spiritual path after his début with *The Childhood of Ivan* [Ivanovo detstvo, 1962]. Elem Klimov's films of the 1960s show the influence of West European Modernism, and Larisa Shepitko continued the 'poetic' vein of Dovzhenko's early work.

110 M. Yampolsky, 'Mythologies', *Cahiers du cinéma*, 'Spécial URSS', supplement to no. 427 (January 1990), pp. 49–51.

111 Youngblood, p. 202; J. Heil, '*A Strict Youth*, an Oneiric Film: Restoration of the Cultural Memory, and Beyond' (unpublished paper, 1989–90). The subtitle of H. Marshall, *Masters of the Soviet Cinema*, is 'Crippled Creative Biographies', from a 1972 speech by Sergei Yutkevich.

112 Room's *Bed and Sofa* has never been in UK distribution, although it may have been shown at the National Film Theatre; while *A Severe Young Man* has not been seen in the UK.

113 On Barnet's exclusion from the canon, see I. Christie, 'Barnet tel qu'en lui-même? ou L'exception et la règle', in F. Albera and R. Cosandey (eds), *Boris Barnet. Ecrits, Documents, Etudes, Filmographie*, (Locarno, 1985), pp. 74–85; also B. Eisenschitz, 'A Fickle Man, or Portrait of Boris Barnet as a Soviet Director', Taylor and Christie, pp. 151–64.

114 Quoted by Eisenschitz, p. 163. This translation from the French omitted the hyphen present in Eisenschitz's original phrase 'metteur-en-scène-soviétique'.

115 Until the mid 1980s, when the British Film Institute started a new round of acquisitions on the basis of research by the author and Richard Taylor, only the 'first canon' of pre-World War Two Soviet cinema was in UK distribution. A solitary nitrate print of Alexandrov's *Volga-Volga* [1938] from the National Film Archive – presumably dating from its pre-war or wartime importation – was found on projection at the Imperial War Museum in 1990 to lack its last reel. Video publication of Soviet films is beginning to resolve the longstanding problem of textual availability, but many video copies are based on inferior and 'corrupt' prints, while the video 'repertoire' also remains limited by canonic constraint.

116 Gorak, p. 7.

117 Thanks are due to Julian Graffy and to Richard Taylor for generous help, as in the past, with translations, sources and advice; also to participants at the 1990 Conference, especially Maya Turovskaya and Katya Khokhlova, for information and confirmation when the first version of this paper was given at the Imperial War Museum Conference in July 1990.

11   DOCUMENTARY FILM – A SOVIET SOURCE FOR SOVIET HISTORIANS

1 Questions relating to the use of newsreels and documentary films in historical research are reviewed in the following works: V. Listov, *Sovetskoe dokumental'noe kino 1917–1919gg. kak istochnik istoricheskogo issledovaniya (ot Oktyabrya do natsionalizatsii kinematografii)* [Soviet Documentary Cinema 1917–1919 as a Source for Historical Research (from October 1917 to the Nationalisation of the Cinema)] (Moscow, 1968); V. Listov, *Istoriya smotrit v ob"ektiv* [History Looks into the Lens] (Moscow, 1974); M. Magidov, *Zrimaya pamyat' istorii* [The Visual Memory of History] (Moscow, 1974); V. Kote, *Arkhivy kinofotodokumentov. Doklad na VII mezhdunarodnom kongresse arkhivistov* [Documentary Film Archives. A Paper Read at the Seventh International Congress of Archivists] (Moscow, 1972); W. Levy (ed.), *The Second Australian History and Film Conference Papers 1984* (North Ryde, 1985); 'Istoriya na ekrane: dokument i mif (Beseda za kruglym stolom)' [History on the Screen: Document and Myth (A Round-Table Discussion)], *Iskusstvo kino* [The Art of Cinema], 1991, no. 1 (January).

2 B. Balash [i.e. Balázs], *Kino. Stanovlenie, sushchnost' novogo iskusstva* [Cinema. The Establishment and Essence of a New Art] (Moscow, 1968), p. 311.

3 Feature films are not covered by this essay although they are undoubtedly an important historical source, as is shown in particular by the interesting analysis of the film *Bed and Sofa* [also known as *Third Meshchanskaya Street* (Tret'ya Meshchanskaya), 1927] in the article by Denise Youngblood, 'The Fiction Film as a Source for Soviet Social History: the *Third Meshchanskaia Street* Affair', *Film and History*, vol. 19, no. 3 (September 1989), pp. 50–60.

4 *Tematicheskii katalog fil'mov po istorii SSSR (1917–73)* [A Thematic Catalogue of Films on the History of the USSR (1917–73)] (Moscow, 1975).

5 *KPSS v rezolyutsiyakh i resheniyakh s"ezdov, konferentsii i plenumov TsK* [The CPSU in the Resolutions and Decisions of Congresses, Conferences and Plenums of the Central Committee], Part 2 (7th edn, Moscow, 1954), p. 74.

6 See the interview with Medvedkin in R. Taylor and I. Christie (eds), *Inside the Film Factory. New Approaches to Russian and Soviet Cinema* (London and New York, 1991), pp. 165–75.

7 G. Zosimov, 'Obzor kinokhroniki za 1932 g.' [A Survey of 1932 Newsreels], *Iskusstvo kino*, 1933, no. 8 (August), p. 39.

8 See for more detail *Literatura i iskusstvo* [Literature and Art], 1931, nos 9–10; *Kino* [Cinema], 21 January, 6 March and 6 April 1932.

9 *Repertuarnyi ukazatel'. Kinorepertuar* [The Repertoire Guide. The Film Repertoire] (Moscow, 1931, 1934 and 1936). The guide for 1931, in contrast to later issues, included a list of banned films as well as those passed.

10 ibid., 1934, p. 125.

11 *Kino*, 18 July 1932.

12 *Kino*, 6 January 1932.

13 *Lef*, 1923, no. 3, p. 140; translated in *FF*, p. 93.

14 The newsreels of the Communist Party Congresses are preserved in the Central State Archive of Cinema and Photographic Documents [TsGAKFD] at Krasnogorsk. But a significant part of these newsreels, including those showing the personnel of the Party leadership, are kept in the Central Party Archive of the Central Committee's Institute of Marxism–Leninism.

15 *Iskusstvo kino*, 1991, no. 1 (January), p. 26.

16 *Iskusstvo kino*, 1933, no. 8 (August), p. 39.

17 *Kino*, 5 August 1935.
18 *Kino*, 18 June 1932.
19 *Iskusstvo kino*, 1990, no. 2 (February), p. 10.
20 *Iskusstvo kino*, 1991, no. 1 (January), p. 24.
21 *Iskusstvo kino*, 1990, no. 2 (February), p. 9.

12   THE GHOST THAT DOES RETURN: EXORCISING STALIN

1 P. Blake and M. Hayward (eds), *Half-Way to the Moon* (New York, 1965), pp.179–80.
2 S. Muratov, 'Neizvestnoe kino' [Unknown Cinema], *Iskusstvo kino* [The Art of Cinema], 1989, no. 3 (March), pp. 22–39; V. Kondrat'ev, 'Ochen' nadeyus'' [I Very Much Hope], *Iskusstvo kino*, 1989, no. 1 (January), pp. 52–5; F. Barringer, 'Soviet Documentaries That Face Up to Reality', *New York Times*, 29 March 1989, p. C17; K. Rosenberg, 'Glasnost at the Movies', *Washington Post*, 26 March 1989, p. G1; A. Lawton, 'Rewriting History: A New Trend in the Documentary Film', *The Soviet Observer*, 29 September 1988, p. 6; A. Lawton, 'Searching for New Values', *The Soviet Observer*, 25 April 1989, p. 6.
3 D. Remnick, 'Glasnost: The Movie', *Washington Post*, 8 February 1988, p. B10.
4 B. Nelan, 'Chipping Away at an Icon', *Time*, 14 August 1989, pp. 34–5; A. Lawton, 'Happy Glasnost', *The World and I*, December 1989, pp. 30–43.
5 E. B. Fein, 'Bury Lenin? Russian Die-Hards Aghast', *New York Times*, 28 April 1989, p. A10. In 1986 Zakharov staged *The Dictatorship of Conscience* [Diktatura sovesti] by Mikhail Shatrov, in which Lenin and his ideology were put on trial but eventually acquitted. Shatrov managed to acquire for himself the monopoly on the theme of Lenin that had earlier belonged to Nikolai Pogodin, the classic playwright of the Stalin era. Shatrov was able to write non-standard plays on this theme even in the pre-glasnost period: among them *Blue Steeds on Red Grass* [Sinie koni na krasnoi trave, staged in 1985] and *The Peace of Brest-Litovsk* [Brestskii mir, staged in 1988].
6 Ya. Varshavskii, 'Kto protiv?' [Who Is Against?], *Sovetskaya kul'tura* [Soviet Culture], 19 July 1988, p. 5.
7 L. Bortvina, 'Neschastnaya lyubov'' [Unhappy Love], *Sovetskaya Rossiya* [Soviet Russia], 22 July 1988, p. 3.
8 *Catalog of the 30th International San Francisco Film Festival*, April 1987, p. 37. The director's father was the writer Yuri Gherman, and the film is based on one of his stories.
9 In 1987 twelve Soviet critics thought it was the best Soviet film of all time (*Nedelya* [The Week], 1987, no. 44, p. 18). See the evaluation chart, pp. 73–7, appended to I. Christie, 'The Cinema', in J. Graffy and G. Hosking (eds), *Culture and the Media in the USSR Today* (London, 1989 and New York, 1990), pp. 43–75.
10 *Cold Summer* won the popular contest of the journal *Sovetskii ekran* [Soviet Screen] for the year 1988 and *Little Vera* [Malenkaya Vera] came second (*Sovetskii ekran*. 1989, no. 8, pp. 4–7).
11 *Novye fil'my* [New Films], 1989, no. 9, pp. 6–7.
12 Among the numerous other films using the 1930s as a background are: *Tomorrow There Was War* [Zavtra byla voina, 1988, dir. Yuri Kara]; *The Ascent of Fujiyama* [Voskhozhdenie na Fudziyamu, 1988, dir. Bolotbek Shamshiev]; *The Kerosene Seller's Wife* [Zhena kerosinchika, 1989, dir. Alexander

Kaidanovsky]; *Defence Counsel Sedov* [Zashchitnik Sedov, 1989, dir. Yevgeni Tsymbal]; *From the Life of Fyodor Kuskin* [Iz zhizni Fedora Kuz'kina, 1988, dir. Stanislav Rostotsky]; and *The Swimmer* [Plovets, released 1988, dir. Irakli Kvirikadze].

13 See N. Zorkaya, 'Dorogoi, kotoraya vedet k Khramu' [By the Road That Leads to the Temple], *Iskusstvo kino*, 1987, no. 5 (May), pp. 33–53.

14 See the interview by Alla Gerber, 'Dve vstrechi s Tengizom Abuladze' [Two Meetings with Tengiz Abuladze], *Sovetskii fil'm* [Soviet Film], 1987, no. 7, pp. 11 and 14.

15 T. Khlopyankina, 'Pod zvuki nabatnogo kolokola' [At the Sound of the Alarm Bell], *Sovetskii ekran*, 1987, no. 15, pp. 4–5.

16 The director Vadim Abdrashitov and the scriptwriter Alexander Mindadze have been collaborating for more than a decade and their co-signature has always been a guarantee of aesthetic achievement and moral commitment. See A. Lawton, 'Toward a New Openness in Soviet Cinema, 1976–1987', in D. J. Goulding (ed.), *Post New Wave Cinema in the Soviet Union and Eastern Europe* (Bloomington, IN, 1989), pp. 1–50.

17 See V. Mikhalkovich, 'Sumbur vmesto kino' [Confusion instead of Cinema], *Sovetskii ekran*, 1990, no. 6, p. 10.

18 L. Anninskii, 'Po ischeznovenii Stalina' [On Stalin's Disappearance], *Sovetskii ekran*, 1990, no. 4, pp. 12–13.

19 *Dark Nights* was produced by the co-operative Podarok [Gift], headed by Vasili Pichul, who directed *Little Vera* in 1988. Other members are the scriptwriter Maria Khmelik, the cameraman Yefim Reznivov, the editor Yelena Zabolotskaya and the manager Mark Levin. The film was financed by a 500,000–rouble loan from the Bank for Social Innovation [Zhilsotsbank], guaranteed by a distribution deal with the Italian broadcasting organisation, RAI. Podarok rented space and facilities at the Gorky Studios in Moscow and received technical assistance in production and post-production from the Italian producer, Silvia D'Amico. *Black Rose* was originally produced at Mosfilm by the Krug [Circle] production unit. Subsequently Krug bought the rights to the film and organised its own publicity and distribution. The official distribution channels responded by blocking its circulation in a number of cities and regions. See A. Lawton, 'Hands Off Distribution', *Variety*, 27 June 1990, p. 9; and A. Lawton, 'Soviet Cinema Four Years Later', *Wide Angle*, forthcoming.

20 Pushkin translated as a drama in verse *A Feast in Plague Time* [Pir vo vremya chumy], an extract from the tragedy *The City of the Plague* by John Wilson (1789–1854). In Pushkin's case the plague referred to in the title was the cholera epidemic of 1830 which forced him to stay in the countryside.

21 T. Kononova, 'Pir Valtazara' [Belshazzar's Feast], *Sovetskii ekran*, 1990, no. 1, p. 9.

22 For further analysis see Svetlana Boym's chapter below.

23 L. Karpinskii, 'Stalin v nas?' [Stalin within Us?], *Sovetskii ekran*, 1989, no.18, pp. 4–5.

24 A. Yerokhin, 'Razve delo tol'ko v Staline?' [Is it Really Only a Matter of Stalin?], *Sovetskii ekran*, 1989, no. 3, p. 14.

25 Quotations taken from V. Merezhko, 'The Govorukhin Effect', *Moscow News*, 10–17 June 1990, p. 14. See also A. Lawton, 'Soviet Documentary Pleads: This Is No Way to Live', *The World and I*, November 1990.

26 'Ot glasnosti k pravde' [From Glasnost to Truth], *Sovetskoe kino* [Soviet Cinema], 2 June 1990, p. 11.

13   STALIN IS WITH US: SOVIET DOCUMENTARY MYTHOLOGIES OF THE 1980s

1 R. Barthes, *Mythologies* (trans. R. Howard) (New York, 1979).
2 N. Tumarkin, *Lenin Lives! The Lenin Cult in Soviet Russia* (Cambridge, MA, 1983). Interestingly, we encounter elements of this apocalyptic rhetoric in the speeches of the members of the Emergency Committee of the CPSU that organised the attempted military coup in August 1991. The enemy is presented abstractly but the threat of chaos and unruliness is real, and the rule of order, rather than the rule of law, is invoked. What they failed to provide was the leader of the people and the saviour, who is a crucial hero in this apocalyptic structure.
3 See G. S. Morson (ed.), *Literature and History: Theoretical Problems and Russian Case Studies* (Stanford, CA, 1986). I am also indebted to Andrew Wachtell who is completing his book on the fiction of history in the Russian tradition. During the Imperial War Museum Conference I learned of the recent work done by Soviet film scholars, especially L. Kozlov and V. Listov, *Iz proshlogo v budushchee. Proverki na dorogakh* [From the Past into the Future: Trials on the Road] (Moscow, 1990).
4 Nikolai M. Karamzin (1766–1826) was a Russian historian, poet and journalist. His magnum opus was the unfinished twelve-volume *History of the Russian State* [Istoriya gosudarstva rossiiskogo], published between 1816 and 1829, which was, in effect, an apologia for Russian autocracy. (Eds)
5 M. Kundera, *The Book of Laughter and Forgetting* (trans. M. Heim) (Harmondsworth, 1986), pp. 65–8.
6 Mayakovsky's description of Lenin comes in the opening lines of his long poem 'Vladimir Ilyich Lenin', written shortly after Lenin's death in 1924. (Eds)
7 Kundera, p. 3.
8 The man in question was Oleg Uralov, who was also the Deputy Director of the 'Videofilm' Production Group: T. Shakhverdiev, 'Stalin s nami?', *Sovetskii fil'm*, 1989, no. 9, p. 7; translated as: 'Stalin Is with Us?', *Soviet Film*, 1989, no. 9, p. 7. Andrei Ya. Vyshinsky (1883–1954) was chief State Prosecutor at the show trials of 1936–8. (Eds)
9 ibid.
10 In 1990 investigations into Stalinism were superseded by investigations into Leninism. One of the first films reflecting this change is Stanislav Govorukhin's 'artistic–publicistic' film *We Cannot Live Like This* [Tak zhit' nel'zya, 1990]. At the centre of the film is a forceful analogy between petty, seemingly disparate individual crimes and the global Crime committed by the Soviet government. Like many other Soviet documentaries, this film uses many explicit allegories. The Russian Revolution, bringing the destruction of churches, is the source of all evil, and the image of Lenin's monument recurring at various crucial moments in the film is the visual embodiment of it. For polemical reasons, perhaps, Stalin is not even mentioned in the film. However, unlike *I Served in Stalin's Bodyguard*, the film uses an authoritative narrative that offers the viewer a shocking, courageous, but also overwhelmingly authoritarian vision that is in fact strikingly representative of the same cultural tradition that it denounces.
11 Shakhverdiev, p. 7.

14 UNSHELVING STALIN: AFTER THE PERIOD OF STAGNATION

1 On the treatment of Soviet history in the Soviet periodical press of recent years, see J. Graffy, 'The Literary Press', in J. Graffy and G. Hosking (eds), *Culture and the Media in the USSR Today* (London, 1989), pp.107–58, but especially pp. 113–14, 127–30, 148–51. On the shortcomings of historians, see especially p. 141, n. 29.

2 'Spisok fil'mov, kotorye obsuzhdalis' Konfliktnoi komissiei i sekretariatom Soyuza kinematografistov do nachala avgusta 1988 goda' [List of the Films Discussed by the Conflict Commission and the Secretariat of the Union of Cinematographers up to the Beginning of August 1988], *Kinostsenarii* [Film Scripts], 1988, no. 4. Speaking in London in December 1990, the film director Andrei Smirnov, who had been acting head of the Union, put the number at 'about 250'.

3 A number of new historical documentaries are discussed by a 'round table' of scholars in 'Istoriya na ekrane: dokument i mif' [History on Screen: Document and Myth], *Iskusstvo kino* [The Art of Cinema], 1991, no. 1 (January), pp. 23–34.

4 N. Izyumova, 'Ston' [Groan], *Moskovskie novosti* [Moscow News], 1988, no. 43, p. 16. The Russian title of the film, *Vlast' solovetskaya*, plays on the words *sovetskaya vlast'* [Soviet power]. New arrivals at the island camp were greeted with the words, 'There's no Soviet power here, it's Solovki power' [Zdes' vlast' ne sovetskaya – zdes' vlast' solovetskaya] (Izyumova).

5 There had already been unobtrusive use of archival footage in this film, in scenes on a train and at a skating rink, as well as an extract from one of the great box-office successes of the period, Grigori Alexandrov's *The Circus* [Tsirk, 1936]. This material was found at the Central State Archive of Cinema and Photographic Documents [TsGAKFD] at Krasnogorsk. It was not held in the *spetskhran*, the secret collection, apparently because the title led people to believe that it celebrated the 'glorious twentieth anniversary' of the Revolution. The speech for the occasion was to be made by Stalin, but he failed to turn up. There are different versions as to how the speech came to be made by Mikoyan: one says that Stalin phoned and ordered Mikoyan to do it, another that the others present 'chose' him (conversation with the director, Pesaro, 7 June 1989). Mikoyan had to improvise: speaking in a strong Armenian accent, he remembered all the clichés about Trotskyite–Bukharinite plots and the infection of cattle familiar from other speeches of the time. Among those sitting at the Presidium are Zhdanov, Voroshilov and Khrushchev. In the middle, in uniform, is Yezhov. Next to him, also in uniform, is one of his deputies, Mikhail Frinovsky, former head of the frontier forces of the NKVD, who participated in the purge of Tukhachevsky and the officer class. He, his wife and son would be arrested and shot in 1938. Yezhov would soon suffer the same fate.

6 See above, Chapter 12.

7 A. Guerman, 'Les temps sont durs pour l'inspiration' [Times Are Hard for Inspiration], interview in *Cahiers du cinéma*, 'Spécial URSS' supplement to no. 427, January 1990, p. 68.

8 F. Niney, 'L'avenir radié' [The Future Erased], *Cahiers du cinéma*, ibid., p. 16.

9 The liberalisation of Soviet literature in the years after 1986 began with the publication of a number of works by both Soviet and émigré writers which, though written long ago, had either been published only abroad or remained

unpublished. The suppression of these works was very often caused by their unacceptable approach to events from Soviet history. The sudden publication in the literary journals of a large number of these banned works, including those mentioned here, provoked a wide-ranging debate about Soviet literature and a fundamental reassessment of the literary pantheon. See n.1 above.

10 In interviews Askoldov recalls how he was summoned by the head of the State Cinema Committee [Goskino], A. V. Romanov, and asked 'to think about changing that Jewish family into one of some other nationality'. See, for example, '"Nuzhno byt' muzhestvennym i delat' svoe delo ..." Press-konferentsiya Aleksandra Askol'dova v San Frantsisko' ['You Have to Be Courageous and Do What You Have to Do ...' Alexander Askoldov's Press Conference in San Francisco], *Russkaya mysl'* [Russian Thought], Paris, no. 3727, 3 June 1988, p. 12. He also suffered the accusation that 'You're trying to avenge your parents with your *Commissar*': 'Put' k *Komissaru*' [The Path to *The Commissar*], *Nedelya* [The Week], 1989, no. 49, p. 21. Askoldov's parents were arrested in 1937.

11 *Iskusstvo kino*, 1986, no. 10 (October), p. 124.

12 E. Stishova, 'Strasti po *Komissaru*' [The Passion according to *The Commissar*], *Iskusstvo kino*, 1989, no. 1 (January), pp. 110–21. Details of the case of *The Commissar* are taken from this article.

13 ibid., p. 110.

14 ibid., p. 112.

15 ibid., p. 114.

16 ibid., p. 118.

17 The most substantial of these happen to have appeared in the non-cinematic press: A. Lipkov, 'Proverka ... na dorogakh' [Trial on the Road], *Novyi mir* [New World], 1987, no. 2 (February), pp. 202–25, and A. Gherman, 'Kino proizrastaet iz poezii' [Cinema Grows out of Poetry], *Voprosy literatury* [Problems of Literature], 1986, no. 12 (December), pp. 124–56. See also A. Gherman, 'Sovremennost' – eto my s vami' [The Contemporary World is You and Me], *Sovetskaya kul'tura* [Soviet Culture], 14 January 1986, p. 5; I. Shul'zhenko, 'A u menya vopros ... k Alekseyu Germanu' [I Have a Question for ... Alexei Gherman], *Yunost'* [Youth], 1986, no. 8 (August), pp. 100–2; A. Gherman, 'Razrushenie mifov' [The Destruction of Myths], *Teatr* [The Theatre], 1987, no. 10 (October), pp. 153–67; A. Lipkov, 'Pervye uroki' [First Lessons] *Rodnik* [The Spring], Riga, 1988, no. 3 (March), pp. 49–51; A. Gherman, 'I Greet Everything that Happens in this Country with Joy and Anxiety', *Soviet Literature*, 1988, no. 11 (November), pp. 117–24; A. Gherman, 'Pogovorim ob otstavke' [Let's Talk about Retirement], *Sovetskaya kul'tura*, 10 January 1989, p. 4; A. Gherman, 'Ne bud' my takimi ...' [If We Weren't Like This], *Iskusstvo kino*, 1989, no. 6 (June), pp. 26–9; A. Gherman, 'I Am Not Lying', *The Louisiana Conference on Literature and Perestroika, 2–4 March 1988* (Esbjerg, 1989), pp. 51–7; A. Gherman, 'Po *Gamburgskomu schetu*' [According to *The Hamburg Reckoning*], *Ogonek* [The Torch], 1989, no. 41, pp. 17–19; A. Guerman, 'Les temps sont durs ...', p. 68.

18 Lipkov, 'Proverka ...', p. 206.

19 ibid., pp. 206, 207. The same word had been used in the accusations levelled against *The Commissar*. *My Friend Ivan Lapshin* was also accused by a Brezhnevite minister of being 'Khrushchevian': Guerman, 'Les temps sont durs ...', p. 67.

20 Lipkov, 'Proverka ...', p. 216.

21 Guerman, 'Les temps sont durs ...', p. 67.

22 'Eto nesotsialisticheskii, meshchanskii realizm' [It's Not Socialist Realism, It's Bourgeois Realism], *Iskusstvo kino*, 1987, no. 9 (September), p. 64.
23 Niney, p. 16. The same deconstruction process has already happened in Eastern European cinema, notably of points four and five in Andrzej Wajda's *Man of Marble* [Czlowek z marmuru, Poland, 1976] and of point two in Márta Mészáros's *Diary for My Children* [Napló gyermekeimnek, Hungary, 1982].
24 V. Fomin, ' "Nikakoi epokhi kul'ta lichnosti ne bylo . . .", ili Kak kino izbavlyali ot kramol'noi temy' ['There Was No Epoch of the Personality Cult . . .', or How Cinema Was Saved from a Seditious Theme], *Iskusstvo kino*, 1989, no. 1 (January), pp. 96–109; V. Fomin, 'Ot cheloveka k "chelovecheskomu faktoru" ' [From Man to the 'Human Factor'], *Iskusstvo kino*, 1989, no. 4 (April), pp. 78–87; V. Fomin, 'Vse nerazreshennoe – zapreshcheno' [Everything That Is Not Allowed Is Forbidden], *Iskusstvo kino*, 1989, no. 5 (May), pp. 101–18; V. Fomin, ' "Ubrat' flag Sovetskogo Soyuza . . ." ' ['Take Away the Flag of the Soviet Union'], *Sovetskii ekran* [Soviet Screen], 1989, no. 10 (October), pp. 24–7; V. Fomin, ' "Na bratskikh mogilakh ne stavyat krestov . . ." *Sovetskoe kino* 1965–1985 godov. Neosushchestvlennoe' ['They Don't Place Crosses on Their Brothers' Graves.' Soviet Cinema, 1965–85. Unrealised Work], *Iskusstvo kino*, 1990, no. 1 (January), pp. 100–10; no. 2 (February), pp. 102–8; no. 3 (March), pp. 92–9.
25 Fomin, ' "Ubrat' flag . . ." ', p. 24.
26 ibid., pp. 24–5; Fomin, 'Vse nerazreshennoe . . .', p. 109.
27 Fomin, 'Vse nerazreshennoe . . .', p. 110.
28 ibid., p. 114.
29 ibid., pp. 110–11.
30 Fomin, ' "Na bratskikh mogilakh . . ." ', pp. 108–9, ' "Ubrat' flag . . ." ', p. 26.
31 Fomin, ' "Nikakoi . . ." ', pp. 100–3; for the current work on the film see, for example, the interview with Valeri Naumov in *Sovetskii fil'm* [Soviet Film], 1990, no.1 (January), pp. 25–7.
32 Fomin, ' "Nikakoi . . ." ', p. 108.
33 Yu. Karabchievskii, 'V poiskakh utrachennogo vremeni' [In Search of Lost Time], *Iskusstvo kino*, 1989, no. 4 (April), pp. 33–44 (on *Repentance*, pp. 37–41); O. Kovalov, 'Byl' pro to, kak lisa petukha s"ela' [The Tale of How the Fox Ate the Cockerel], *Iskusstvo kino* 1989, no. 6 (June), pp. 4–25.

   Bemoaning *Repentance*'s arbitrary and unsystematic use of symbolism, Karabchievskii writes: '*Repentance* is not just an unsuccessful film, but a deliberate evasion of concrete questions, of a direct conversation on matters of substance, an intentional and pretentious surrogate, the latest in an endless line of surrogates.' (p. 38). He continues, on the film's famous 'complexity' (p. 39):

> More complex is more comprehensible for them [audiences]. And also, one might add, more accessible, more easily accomplished than everything direct, simple and precise. And in addition – less dangerous, in all senses of that word. It is far easier to operate through arbitrary symbols, having initially established that your language and method will be that of metaphor, than to raise real events to the level of metaphor.

34 Gherman has said of *Lapshin*: 'the main thing for us was not the detective intrigue, not the love story, but the time itself. That's what we made the film about' (Lipkov, 'Proverka . . .', p. 219).
35 *Sedov* was shot on film stock used for aerial photography to heighten the sense

of period. The technical division at Mosfilm consequently refused to pass the film until it had won a prize at the Mannheim Festival (conversation with the director, Urbino, 4 June 1989).

36 The name 'Ensk' comes from the original story by Ilya Zverev. By sticking to it, Tsymbal also makes a covert allusion to his own birthplace, Eisk, on the Sea of Azov.

37 Ivan V. Michurin (1855–1935) was a horticulturalist, the founder in the USSR of the scientific selection of crops. Lenin showed a particular interest in Michurin's work, and over the years the Soviet government supported his work and rewarded him with honours. Both the Stalin and Khrushchev periods saw massive but disastrous campaigns for 'remaking' nature.

38 In his recent study, *The Prosecutor and the Prey. Vyshinsky and the 1930s Moscow Show Trials* (London, 1990), Arkady Vaksberg pays particular attention to Vyshinsky's propensity for abusive language, including animal metaphors, and its influence on the lexis of others. See especially pp. 81–3, 107–8 and 120.

39 Sedov's visit to *The Circus* can superficially be seen as a moment of lightness in the film. Even here, however, the other face of the 1930s is not far away. In September 1937, just before Sedov watched the film, its cameraman, Vladimir S. Nilsen (real name Alper, b. 1906 in St Petersburg), who also shot Alexandrov's earlier success, the musical comedy *The Happy Guys* [Veselye rebyata, also known as *Jolly Fellows*, 1934], had been arrested on charges of spying and 'malevolent enmity'. He was shot on 27 January 1942. See A. Bernshtein, 'Vozvrashchenie iz nebytiya' [Return from Nonexistence], *Sovetskaya kul'tura*, 18 April 1989, p. 6. Almost exactly the same extract from *The Circus* was recently used by Andrei Konchalovsky in his film about Stalin's projectionist, *The Inner Circle* [USA, 1991].

40 On *Aristocrats* see, for example, H. B. Segal, *Twentieth-Century Russian Drama. From Gorky to the Present* (New York, 1979), pp. 266–71. While the White Sea Canal was being constructed, it was visited by a delegation of 120 writers in August 1933. Thirty-four of them contributed to the notoriously propagandistic *The White Sea Canal. Being an Account of the Construction of the New Canal between the White Sea and the Baltic Sea* (edited by Maxim Gorky and others) (English edn, London, 1935).

41 H. Eagle, 'Soviet Cinema Today: On the Semantic Potential of a Discredited Canon', in 'Perestroika and Soviet Culture', special issue of *Michigan Quarterly Review*, vol. 28, 1989, no. 4, p. 747.

42 The film's music is only the music of the town's bands: there is no 'background music'. As Gherman has said, 'I don't value music in cinema too highly . . .' (Lipkov, 'Proverka . . .', p. 222).

43 In his interview in *Sovetskaya kul'tura*, 14 January 1986, p. 5, Gherman suggests that Adashova is to some extent based upon his own mother, and that some features of his father appear in both Lapshin and Khanin. 'But Khanin is absolutely not my father. There was a translator called Stenich. He's the one who is portrayed here.' Valentin O. Stenich-Smetanich was born in 1898. As a young poet he came to the attention of Blok, who described him in his 1918 essay 'Russkie dendi' [Russian Dandies] (A. Blok, *Sobranie sochinenii v vos'mi tomakh* [Collected Works in Eight Volumes] (Moscow, 1960–5), vol. 6, pp. 53–7. During the Soviet period, Stenich was a leading translator and a member of the Union of Writers. He was arrested by the NKVD on 16 November 1937 and shot on 21 September 1938. See 'Pis'mo O. N. Gil'debrandt-Arbeninoi Yu. I. Yurkunu 13.02.1946' [Letter from O. N. Gildebrandt-

Arbenina to Yu. I. Yurkun of 13 February 1946], published by G.A. Morev in G.A. Morev (ed.), *Mikhail Kuzmin i russkaya kul'tura XX veka* [Mikhail Kuzmin and Twentieth-Century Russian Culture] (Leningrad, 1990), p. 244; and *Daugava*, Riga, 1988, no. 3, p. 116.

44 Kovalov, p. 21.

45 During the last years of his life, through his friendship with Osip and Lily Brik, Mayakovsky spent much of his time in the company of members of the security police, notably Yakov Agranov, head of the secret political section and later first deputy to Yagoda. See, for example, the assessment in Yu. Karabchievskii, *Voskresen'e Mayakovskogo* [Mayakovsky's Resurrection] (Munich, 1985), p. 192:

> Here we have a contemporary man, a poet and writer, who for many years had almost daily meetings with employees of the secret police. His friends from the GPU come to visit him at his dacha and teach him how to shoot. There are verses about it ...

46 A. S. Pushkin, *Polnoe sobranie sochinenii v desyati tomakh* [Collected Works in Ten Volumes] (Moscow, 1962–5), vol. 5, p. 419. The theme of *A Feast in Plague Time*, which Pushkin adapted from the English writer John Wilson, is wild abandon in the face of death. The quoted passage continues: 'All, all that threatens disaster holds inexpressible delight for the heart of man. Therefore, praise to you, O Plague ...'

47 In this context it is interesting to note Gherman's remarks to Alexander Lipkov:

> In *Lapshin* as written by my father I felt a Chekhovian intonation. That is why we moved the location from Leningrad to a small town: the smaller the town, the smaller the boss, the sadder and more accurate – this was our feeling – the story would be.
>
> (Lipkov, 'Proverka ...', p. 221)

Gherman makes another reference to Chekhov in a later interview, recalling his long-term plans to film Chekhov's story 'Ward Six' (Gherman, 'I Greet Everything ...', p. 119).

48 The theme of profanation is echoed in the ubiquitousness of threats of violence and death in the film. In an argument between Okoshkin and the old housekeeper Patrikeyevna, for example, she threatens to report him to Kalinin. This threat of denunciation, a commonplace of 1930s Russia, is met by another, when Okoshkin counters that he will have her sent to the labour camp of Solovki. Evidence that such threats were widespread at the time is provided by comparison with the first chapter of Mikhail Bulgakov's novel *The Master and Margarita*. Ivan Bezdomny responds to Woland's mention of Kant's proofs of the existence of God by insisting that 'For proving such things they should take that Kant and give him three years on Solovki.' Analogically in *Defence Council Sedov*, Sedov 'profanes' the interiors of Korenev and Kopyonkin by threatening to report them to the Chief Prosecutor.

49 Ilya Zverev was born in the Ukraine in March 1926. His work began to appear in print in 1947. The story 'Defence Council Sedov' was written in late 1962 and early 1963 and included in a collection of his work called *Vse dni, vklyuchaya voskresen'e* [Every Day, Including Sunday], published by the *Sovetskii pisatel'* publishing house in Moscow in 1964. The book appeared in the shops in early October in an edition of 30,000. But on 14 October 1964 Khrushchev was removed from power and Leonid Brezhnev was appointed

First Secretary of the Communist Party.

In late November 1964 the writer Yuri Gherman (upon whose stories his son Alexei was to base his film *My Friend Ivan Lapshin*) lavishly praised Zverev, and in particular the 'magnificent story "Defence Council Sedov" ' in a review entitled ' "Novatsii" i pravda zhizni' ['Innovations' and the Truth of Life] in *Komsomol'skaya pravda* [Young Communist League Truth], 28 November 1964. This in turn provoked a mockingly hostile response from the critic Yuri Barabash under the title 'Chto takoe khorosho i chto takoe plokho' [What Is Good and What Is Bad] in *Literaturnaya gazeta* [Literary Gazette], 10 December 1964. Zverev then endured a wave of criticism at meetings of writers. He was by now ill with a serious kidney disease and he died in December 1966. 'Defence Council Sedov' is only now to be republished.

Most of the dialogue in the film, with its heavily Soviet lexis, is taken directly from the story. The Chief Prosecutor's name is not given in either story or film, but in the story there are two mentions of Vyshinsky and discussions of his speeches. Certain background episodes such as Sedov's film-going have been added by Tsymbal, as, of course, has the archival material of Mikoyan's speech at the end. The story ends with the suggestion that a week after the Chief Prosecutor's speech a 'Japanese spy' was discovered in Ensk. The four agronomists were freed, and Sedov was not arrested – fear of his own possible arrest is an ever-present motif in the story: 'And Sedov was not arrested. That is not then ... He was arrested many years later, in 1952 ...' (Zverev, *Vse dni ...*, p. 272).

50 Vladimir L. Rossels (1878–1966) was one of the most famous lawyers in Moscow before the Revolution, with a reputation for winning hopeless cases. He continued his work as a lawyer after the Revolution.

51 Anatoli F. Koni (1844–1927) was a leading Russian lawyer and, in the Soviet period, a professor at Petrograd University and a number of other institutions. He was famous for his rhetoric and for his insistence on the application of the law. On Koni, see, for example, V. I. Smolyarchuk, *A. F. Koni i ego okruzhenie* [A. F. Koni and His Circle] (Moscow, 1990).

52 Of Article 58 of the Criminal Code, Solzhenitsyn wrote:

> Paradoxically enough, every act of the all-penetrating, eternally wakeful *Organs* over a span of many years, was based solely on *one* article of the Criminal Code of 1926 ...
>
> Who among us has not experienced its all-encompassing embrace? In all truth, there is no step, thought, action or lack of action under heaven, which could not be punished by the heavy hand of Article 58.
>
> (A. Solzhenitsyn, *The Gulag Archipelago*, vol. 1 (London, 1974), p. 60)

The trial of the Industrial Party [Prompartiya] took place in November–December 1930, and was the second (after the trial of the Shakhty engineers of 1928) of the new large-scale show trials. The indictment alleged that the Industrial Party had over 2,000 members, though only eight of them were put on trial, accused of wrecking and of following the orders of the President of France and Lawrence of Arabia. All pleaded guilty. See, for example, M. Heller and A. Nekrich, *Utopia in Power. The History of the Soviet Union from 1917 to the Present* (London, 1986), pp. 228–9.

53 On this see R. Russell, 'Red Pinkertonism: An Aspect of Soviet Literature of the 1920s', *Slavonic and East European Review*, vol. 60, 1982, pp. 390–412.

54 L. Ginzburg, ' "I zaodno s pravoporyadkom ..." ' [And with Law and Order Too ...], in M. O. Chudakova (ed.), *Tynyanovskii sbornik. Tret'i Tynyanovskie*

chteniya [The Tynyanov Collection. The Third Tynyanov Readings] (Riga, 1988), p. 219.

55 Kovalov, pp. 13, 15.
56 ibid., pp. 16–17, 23.
57 ibid., p. 46. This attack, against the background of rousing march music, was clearly considered an inappropriate sign of weakness in a Soviet hero in the context of the aesthetic examined above in section II.
58 ibid., p. 24.

Index